THE BATTLE ATLAS
of the CIVIL WAR

THE BATTLE ATLAS
of the CIVIL WAR

By the Editors of Time-Life Books

BARNES
&NOBLE
B O O K S
NEW YORK

The Battle Atlas of the Civil War was originally published as *Echoes of Glory* by Time-Life Books in 1991.

Printed in U.S.A.

Published simultaneously in Canada.

TIME-LIFE is a trademark of Time Warner Inc. U.S.A.

This edition published by Barnes & Noble, Inc., by arrangement with Time Life Inc.

1996 Barnes & Noble Books

ISBN 0-7607-0409-0

Time-Life Books is a division of Time Life Inc.

TIME LIFE INC.

PRESIDENT and CEO: George Artandi

TIME-LIFE BOOKS

PRESIDENT: John D. Hall
PUBLISHER/MANAGING EDITOR: Neil Kagan

Vice President, Director of Finance: Christopher Hearing
Vice President, Book Production: Marjann Caldwell
Director of Operations: Eileen Bradley
Director of Photography and Research: John Conrad Weiser
Director of Editorial Administration: Barbara Levitt
Chief Librarian: Louise D. Forstall

ECHOES OF GLORY

Editor: Henry Woodhead
Administrator: Jane Edwin
Art Directors: Dale Pollekoff, Herbert H. Quarmby
Deputy Editors: Harris J. Andrews, Kirk E. Denkler

Editorial Staff for *Illustrated Atlas of the Civil War*
Writer: Maggie Debelius
Associate Editor/Research: Quentin Gaines Story
Senior Copy Coordinator: Anne Farr
Picture Coordinator: Gail V. Feinberg
Research Assistant/Maps: Jayne A. L. Dover
Production Manager: Prudence G. Harris
Quality Assurance Manager: James King

Special Contributors: Margery A. duMond, Stephen G. Hyslop, M. Linda Lee, Brian C. Pohanka, David S. Thomson (text); Anthony K. Pordes, Carolee B. Walker (copy); Adam Cornelius (maps); Anne K. DuVivier (art); Roy Nanovic (index).

Correspondents: Elisabeth Kraemer-Singh (Bonn), Christine Hinze (London), Christina Lieberman (New York), Maria Vincenza Alosi (Paris), Ann Natonson (Rome).

Consultant:
Col. John R. Elting, USA (Ret.), former associate professor at West Point, has written or edited some 20 books, including *Swords around a Throne, The Superstrategists,* and *American Army Life,* as well as *Battles for Scandinavia* in the Time-Life Books World War II series. He was chief consultant to the Time-Life series The Civil War.

Contents

INTRODUCTION 6

EASTERN THEATER 20

FIRST BULL RUN/FIRST MANASSAS 24

1862 VALLEY CAMPAIGN 34

PENINSULAR CAMPAIGN 44

SECOND BULL RUN CAMPAIGN 56

ANTIETAM CAMPAIGN 68

FREDERICKSBURG 86

CHANCELLORSVILLE 98

GETTYSBURG CAMPAIGN 110

WILDERNESS CAMPAIGN 134

1864 VALLEY CAMPAIGN 152

PETERSBURG TO APPOMATTOX 166

WESTERN THEATER 190

SHILOH 194

1862 KENTUCKY/TENNESSEE CAMPAIGN 206

MISSISSIPPI RIVER CAMPAIGN 216

CHATTANOOGA CAMPAIGN 232

ATLANTA CAMPAIGN 248

1864 TENNESSEE CAMPAIGN 270

SHERMAN'S MARCH 280

COASTAL WAR 286

ATLANTIC COAST 288

MOBILE BAY 298

FORT FISHER 300

FAR WEST 302

MISSOURI/ARKANSAS CAMPAIGN 304

NEW MEXICO CAMPAIGN 308

RED RIVER CAMPAIGN 310

ACKNOWLEDGMENTS 314

PICTURE CREDITS 314

BIBLIOGRAPHY 316

INDEX 317

The Trials of Command

The Civil War was less than four months old, but the soldiers of the 79th New York reckoned they had already seen enough fighting to last a lifetime. Like many of the Northern and Southern volunteers who answered the call to arms in April 1861, these New Yorkers had mustered around the nucleus of a pre-War militia unit, the Highland Guard, one of Manhattan's most colorful military organizations. Its 300 members sported full Scottish regalia, including rakish glengarry caps, kilts, and checkered stockings. When the Highlanders marched off to war on June 2, they mustered a full 10 companies, their ranks having been swelled by nearly 600 recruits eager to take part in the great battle most thought would bring a quick end to the fledgling Southern Confederacy.

That battle came near a Virginia stream called Bull Run on July 21, 1861. It was a brutal introduction to combat for the 79th New York and other hastily recruited volunteer regiments. The Highlanders lost 198 men killed, wounded, or missing, 11 of them officers. Colonel James Cameron, the regimental commander and brother of United States Secretary of War Simon Cameron, was among the slain. Swept away in the rout of Brigadier General Irvin McDowell's Federal forces, the survivors of the 79th New York straggled back to the safety of Washington. Surveying his chastened comrades, Private William Todd thought that " 'I want to go home' was pictured on every countenance."

After 17 officers signed a petition asking that the regiment be allowed to return to New York to "reorganize," Secretary of War Cameron indicated he would endorse the request. Lieutenant Colonel Samuel Elliott, now in charge, told his men to prepare for the trip. But instead of a furlough, on August 10 the Highlanders received a new colonel.

Isaac Ingalls Stevens stood only an inch over five feet; but the swarthy little colonel exhibited a stern determination that belied his diminutive stature. After graduating first in the class of 1839 at West Point, Stevens had served with distinction as a military engineer in the Mexican War before leaving the army to seek his fortune on the western frontier. He had led several surveying expeditions, fought Indians, and pursued a political career as the governor of the Washington Territory and territorial delegate to Congress. Hot-tempered, ambitious, and profane, Stevens had a penchant for controversy; his sympathy for proslavery Democrats at first made it difficult for him to obtain a command in the Federal forces. Stevens was "strong in his likes and dislikes," one associate recalled, "but the very best organizer and disciplinarian that I ever met." Major General George B. McClellan, who had assumed command of the army at Washington in the wake of the disaster at Bull Run, believed Stevens' skills could be put to good use in shaping up the battered 79th New York.

Isaac Stevens had no intention of allowing his homesick volunteers to take a holiday from the grim realities of war. For their part, the men in the ranks considered Stevens' appointment "a piece of high-handed interference on the part of the government"; in accordance with standard militia procedure, they had wanted to elect their new commander. All but 10 subordinate officers promptly resigned, dozens of enlisted men sought to drown their troubles in cheap whiskey, and on August 14, when Colonel Stevens ordered his unit to fall in and march to a new campsite, the troops refused to budge.

When word of the apparent mutiny reached McClellan, he dispatched Regular Army troops with artillery to surround the Highlanders' camp at Meridian Hill on the outskirts of Washington. As the regulars filed into line around the muttering New Yorkers, Stevens again called his men to attention. "You are soldiers, and your duty is to obey," he barked. "I am your colonel, and your obedience is due to me." If they refused to fall into line, they would be fired upon. The Highlanders grudgingly obliged, whereupon the ringleaders of the mutiny were called out of formation, put in irons, and led away to a military prison. Stevens told Lieutenant Colonel Elliott he had half an hour in which to resign or face a court-martial. Elliott resigned.

An order from McClellan was read, depriving the 79th New York of its colors. The flags would not be returned to the Highlanders until they "learned the first duty of soldiers—obedience—and have proven on the field of battle that they are not wanting in courage." An observer recalled when the colorbearers surrendered their banners, "a low cry like a protesting moan" rose from the assembled ranks. The cowed New Yorkers marched to their new encampment, cherishing a bitter hatred and a healthy respect for their commander.

At "Camp Hope," Colonel Stevens set about the task of transforming his malcontents into military men. There were predawn roll calls, constant drills, and an unrelenting insistence on Regular Army standards of dress and deportment. Men who refused to wash regularly were marched to the Potomac River under guard, stripped, and scrubbed with brooms. At the same time, Stevens made sure that good conduct was rewarded with promotion and leaves of absence. Most important, Stevens saw to it that after his unit performed well in a skirmish with Confederate forces near Lewinsville, Virginia, the precious regimental colors were returned. General McClellan made the presentation in person, telling the men they "had acquitted themselves as true soldiers."

So completely had Isaac Stevens won over the recalcitrant New Yorkers that when he was promoted to brigadier general the men of the 79th insisted on

Considered an officer of great promise, Isaac I. Stevens adroitly restored order to the mutinous 79th New York Highlanders after he was appointed their colonel in August 1861. Promoted to brigadier and later major general, he distinguished himself in the South Carolina coastal campaign and commanded a division at Second Bull Run.

being transferred to his new command. The noncommissioned officers and privates raised funds for an ornate sword, sash, and spurs, which they presented to Stevens with "a unanimous feeling of gratitude and respect for our colonel, our friend, and our counselor," who had rescued the regiment "from the vortex of anarchy."

At the height of the Battle of Chantilly, Virginia, on September 1, 1862, Isaac Stevens again took the flag of the 79th New York, this time to lead the embattled unit in a charge on Stonewall Jackson's Confederates. Stevens was shouting "Highlanders, my Highlanders, follow your general!" when he was killed instantly by a bullet through the head. The regiment's surivors later sent the ripped and bloodstained banner to Stevens' widow, along with a note that read, "His memory is engraven on the hearts of every one of his Highlanders."

One of Napoleon's military maxims was that "in war, moral considerations make up three-quarters of the game." In Isaac Stevens, the 79th New York had been fortunate to find a commander who possessed those qualities of leadership that infused a command—be it a company or an army—with the esprit de corps so necessary to success in war.

The quality of leadership was crucial to the outcome of the battles and campaigns detailed in this volume. From Bull Run to Appomattox Courthouse, the tactics and strategies that came to be symbolized on the battle maps of the War evolved in the minds of men whose abilities ranged from stellar to abysmal. Both armies possessed, in full measure, their share of excellent and poor leaders, and those in between. From the lieutenants to the generals, the men who led troops in the Civil War came in every variety: the brilliant and the dull-witted, the reckless and the cautious, the pious and the profane.

While the Civil War saw both armies take advantage of technological advances in weaponry and communications—the railroad and the telegraph —the art of generalship had changed little in a hundred years. Generals were expected not only to plan, to administer, to organize, to oversee; they were frequently called upon to lead their men in a literal sense. At times, as in the case of Stevens, they paid for it with their lives: 47 Federal and 77 Confederate generals were either killed or mortally wounded in the forefront of attack.

Heroics on the part of senior officers, however, were no guarantee of success on the battlefield. Virginia cavalryman Frank Myers judged his swashbuckling brigade commander, Brigadier General Thomas L. Rosser, to be "as brave a man as ever drew breath"; but, Myers noted, "he knows no more about putting a command into a fight than a schoolboy." At the Battle of Antietam, Federal Major General Edwin V. Sumner, commander of II Corps, personally led one of his divisions in an assault, but left the commanders of his remaining two divisions with only the vaguest idea of what they were supposed to do. The resulting attacks were disjointed and less than successful.

"No great mental powers are needed to maneuver a brigade of infantry," claimed Federal Brigadier General Francis Barlow. "The difficulty of the problem increases as the numbers increase, and therefore it happens that many a man can handle a brigade admirably, who can do nothing with a corps or even a division." Just as the regimental commander had to master the intricacies of battalion drill, so the brigade or division commander had to familiarize himself with the geometrical choreography involved in maneuvering larger bodies of troops. "School teaching is at best a laborious business," wrote John Gibbon, who was appointed to lead a brigade of Union infantry after serving 14 years in the Regular Army artillery. "But when the scholars number several thousand and the head teacher has as assistants but few who know even the ABC of the subject to be taught, the task becomes Herculean." Gibbon found his artillery experience of limited value in deploying four regiments of infantry. Like many of his volunteer officers, Gibbon often resorted to consulting the drill manual before giving his commands.

Perhaps the most common cause of mistakes on the battlefield was poor staff work. A general's staff was his military family, and could vary in number from six or eight officers for a brigade commander up to as many as two dozen or more for an army commander. Their duties were many, and often of an administrative nature. Depending upon the size of the organization, there were commissaries to oversee the distribution of food, quartermasters to deal with supply, a medical director to coordinate the ambulance trains and field hospitals, as well as adjutants who kept track of the daily troop strength through reports required of every regimental commander.

Once the battle was joined, a commander communicated with his officers in the field through his staff. Not only orderlies and aides-de-camp, but frequently administrative personnel were called upon to carry orders—written or oral— to implement the wishes of their superior. But in battles in which the fronts of the opposing armies often measured more than five miles, generals habitually found their overworked staffs inadequate for the task at hand. "Scarcely any of our generals had what they needed to keep a constant and close supervision on the execution of important orders," recalled the Confederate artillerist Porter Alexander. "An army is like a great machine, and putting it into battle it is not enough for its commander to merely issue the necessary orders. He should have a staff ample to supervise the execution of each step and to promptly report any difficulty or misunderstanding."

Despite the flaws found in Northern and Southern armies, one of the irrefutable facts of the Civil War was the superiority of Confederate military leadership during the first two years of the conflict. There were many reasons for the strength of the Southern officer corps. Jefferson Davis, the Confederate president, was an 1828 graduate of West Point, had served with distinction as colonel of Mississippi volunteers in the Mexican War, and had held the post of secretary of war in the administration of Franklin Pierce. Unlike Lincoln—whose only military experience had consisted of a three-month stint in the Illinois militia during the Black Hawk War—Davis rarely permitted politics to dictate his selection of military commanders.

"An army is like a great machine, and putting it into battle it is not enough for its commander to merely issue the necessary orders. He should have a staff ample to supervise the execution of each step."

COL. E. PORTER ALEXANDER
ARTILLERY COMMANDER
LONGSTREET'S CORPS
ARMY OF NORTHERN VIRGINIA

The Confederacy, in addition, possessed a wealth of homegrown military talent. Although a majority of West Pointers stood by the Union, many of the military academy's most distinguished alumni resigned from the Regular Army to cast their lot with the Confederacy. The prewar South had an established military tradition that made the pursuit of an army career far more attractive there than in the North. Schools such as the Virginia Military Institute and the South Carolina Military Academy provided the Confederacy with some two dozen generals and scores of talented regimental and staff officers. The Army of Northern Virginia alone counted 167 field-grade officers who had graduated from Southern military institutions. In the South, moreover, there was a sense of great urgency about choosing military leaders; the fledgling nation faced an immediate threat to its survival that made the recognition of military talent of vital importance.

The Federal army, conversely, was to some extent saddled with the existing military structure—a hierarchy founded upon seniority rather than ability. Federal Brigadier General Alpheus Williams referred to it as "the cursed policy of old fogyism." Those tough, dashing officers who had made names for themselves in earlier wars, and who aroused great expectations, had grown old and stiff in staff or garrison duties. Moreover, political patronage was a fact of life for the Lincoln administration, and the price for the cooperation of the Northern "war governors" was often the promotion of a political crony to a rank he was not qualified to hold.

Federal commanders often seemed to be working at cross-purposes rather than employing the cohesive strategy that Winfield Scott had envisioned. Even before the first battles were fought, Scott—the physically infirm but mentally acute septuagenarian who had served for 30 years as general-in-chief of the U.S. Army—determined that the War was likely to be a drawn-out and bloody affair. Victory would be attained only if the Union could make full use of its marked superiority in industry, transport, and manpower.

Scott proposed a naval blockade of Southern coastal ports, together with the seizure of the Mississippi River from the mouth of the Ohio to the Gulf of Mexico. Union occupation of these vital arteries of supply would slowly but inexorably strangle the Confederacy into submission.

Northern firebrands who cherished delusions of a quick and easy victory over the rebellious states scoffed at Scott's so-called Anaconda Plan, named for the huge South American snake that slowly crushes its prey to death. Scott would soon step aside so that younger men might take up the challenges of command. But his plan provided the framework for the successful coordination of Northern forces that ultimately vanquished the Southern Confederacy.

At the beginning of the War, however, coordination seemed an unattainable goal. In 1862, Stonewall Jackson was able to defeat four separate Federal contingents in the Shenandoah Valley despite odds that were four to one in his opponents' favor. Jackson's rapid marches and superior strategy played a part

Major Thomas Jonathan Jackson, later to be known as Stonewall *(above),* joined the faculty of the Virginia Military Institute in 1851 to teach science and artillery tactics—a career he was still pursuing six years later when this picture was taken. Although destined for greatness, Jackson as a teacher was a droning pedagogue and an object of ridicule known to his students as Fool Tom.

12

General Robert E. Lee, astride his gray mount Traveller, pauses under an oak tree with his senior officers to reconnoiter an enemy position. The artist took creative license with this painting by including several prominent generals who never served in Lee's Army of Northern Virginia.

in his triumph, but so did the utter lack of cooperation among the Union commanders. Indeed, many of the Union's officers appeared to be more interested in personal glory than in a shared victory. "Officers are more selfish, dishonest, and grasping in their struggle for notoriety than the miser for gold," Colonel John Beatty complained.

Repeated failures spurred Abraham Lincoln's frustrating quest for generals who would vigorously prosecute the War. When Major General Don Carlos Buell failed to exploit strategically his tactical victory at Perryville, Kentucky, in October 1862, Lincoln said he could not comprehend why the Northern forces seemed unable to "march as the enemy marches, live as he lives, and fight as he fights, unless we admit the inferiority of our troops and of our generals."

Ironically, the administration's penchant for allowing political expediency to override military necessity was itself a prime cause of Union failure on the battlefield. Until the last year of the War, politically influential but militarily inept commanders like Benjamin F. Butler, Nathaniel P. Banks, and Franz Sigel were entrusted with the command of armies in the field. It was a situation that fostered a cynical pessimism among many subordinate Federal officers.

David A. Russell, commander of a division in VI Corps, Army of the Potomac, concluded that the Union army had become "about as much a political machine as any other branch or department of our government." In a letter to his family, Captain William Lusk declared that "the whole batch of our political generals are objects of honest terror to every soldier in the Union army." Some officers were outspoken in their condemnation of what they considered the deplorable inefficiency of the authorities in Washington. "Was there ever such a government, such fools, such idiots?" Lieutenant Colonel Alexander Webb wrote his father after the Union defeat at Second Bull Run in August 1862. "I hate and despise them more intensely than I do the Rebels."

> *"The whole batch of our political generals are objects of honest terror to every soldier in the Union army."*
>
> CAPT. WILLIAM LUSK
> 79TH NEW YORK INFANTRY REGIMENT
> ARMY OF THE POTOMAC

Webb was no churlish malcontent. Educated at West Point, he became a general at 28, was twice wounded, and received the Congressional Medal of Honor for his gallantry at Gettysburg. His views were shared by many of the young officers who rose to prominence in the Federal service. Undoubtedly one aspect of Webb's frustration was that the force in which he served—the Army of the Potomac—was the best trained, armed, and equipped but least successful of the major Federal armies. It failed mainly because it suffered from a series of flawed commanders, but also because its principal foe, the Army of Northern Virginia, was led by the greatest of all Confederate generals: Robert E. Lee.

The most highly regarded officer of the U.S. Army to join the Confederacy, Lee embodied innate dignity, aristocratic reserve, and quiet determination that elicited almost instinctive respect from his subordinates. "The fear of incurring his displeasure at all times enforced implicit obedience," wrote Colonel

William Oates. Lee maintained a close and deferential working relationship with Jefferson Davis, and gained his support when he set about reorganizing his forces and reshuffling his army's command structure in the wake of the Seven Days' Battles in the summer of 1862.

There was more to Lee, however, than his dignified image and administrative skills. He was a consummate campaigner, a skilled tactician, and a daring strategist. He was willing to risk defeat to attain victory. "He never allowed his adversary quietly to mature and carry out his own plan of campaign," an artilleryman recalled. "Although conducting a defensive struggle, he was yet generally the attacking party." Lee's willingness to divide his forces in the face of a numerically superior foe, then to fall on his enemy's flank or rear, as he did in the Second Manassas campaign and at Chancellorsville, prompted the Confed-

Abraham Lincoln confers privately with General George B. McClellan inside the general's tent at Sharpsburg, Maryland, in early October 1862, following the Battle of Antietam. On the ground at lower left is a Confederate battle flag taken during the Maryland campaign. In early November, Lincoln relieved McClellan of command of the Army of the Potomac for his failure to pursue the Confederates.

erate cavalry officer William P. Roberts to call him "the greatest general the world has produced, Napoleon not excepted."

Lee's soldiers regarded him with a devotion that bordered on reverence. General Porter Alexander described the "wave of sentiment" that swept through the ranks at an 1864 review of the artillery of Longstreet's corps. "Each man seemed to feel the bond which held us all to Lee," Alexander wrote. "The effect was that of a military sacrament, in which we pledged anew our lives." When a Confederate chaplain asked one of Lee's aides, "Does it not make the General proud to see how these men love him?" the officer replied, "Not proud, it awes him."

The Virginia artillery officer Robert Stiles recognized the military strength inspired by the symbiotic connection between Lee and his army, an alliance "constant and permanent, undissolved and indissoluble." What was more, Stiles and his Confederate comrades recognized a difference between Lee and his counterparts in the Union camp. "We came to look with wonder, not unmixed with pity, upon the contrasted condition of the opposing Federal army, with generals jealous of and plotting against one another, and the government forever pulling down one and putting up another."

Lee's principal antagonist in the first two years of the War was Major General George Brinton McClellan, a man whose undenied organizational skills transformed the Army of the Potomac into a well-drilled military machine and whose youthful energy seemed to presage great deeds on the field of battle. The newspapers dubbed him the Young Napoleon, and the bond he forged with his men elicited a devotion not unlike that which the Army of Northern Virginia felt for Lee. While enforcing discipline, McClellan nonetheless was careful to maintain a rapport with the enlisted men. One officer thought "his bow and smile seemed to carry a little of personal good fellowship even to the humblest private soldier." The brigade commander Alexander Hays declared that the excitement McClellan generated as he rode along the lines of cheering troops "amounted to wildness."

Unlike Lee, however, McClellan proved consistently unable to make decisive use of his army's potential, nor was he able to maintain an amicable working relationship with the Lincoln administration. "The realities of war seemed to daze him," General Joshua Chamberlain recalled. "With all that marvelous magnetism which won the love and enthusiasm of his subordinates, he lacked the skill, or the will, to gain the sympathy of his superiors."

In fact, what General McClellan lacked most of all was that Napoleonic virtue that Confederate Robert E. Lee possessed in abundance: the willingness to take risks. "I feel that the salvation of the country demands the utmost prudence on my part," McClellan wrote. "I must not run the slightest risk of disaster." He believed "the one safe rule in war" was "to decide what is the very worst thing that can happen to you and prepare to meet it." The Union general professed to seek "bloodless victories," as he abhorred "the sickening sight of the battlefield, with its mangled corpses and poor suffering wounded."

McClellan's inability to take Richmond in the summer of 1862, after having brought his forces to within six miles of the Confederate capital, his yielding of the initiative to his opponents in the Seven Days' Battles, and most of all his failure to destroy Lee's army in the wake of the strategic Federal victory at Antietam ultimately cost the Young Napoleon his command. But in light of other generals' even more costly reverses—Ambrose Burnside's repulse at Fredericksburg and Joseph Hooker's defeat at Chancellorsville—McClellan's name continued to hold a certain magic for his old soldiers. "Give us back McClellan and we will fight again," one New Yorker wrote after the slaughter at Fredericksburg, "feeling certain that we shall not be led to certain death without accomplishing anything." As late as the summer of 1864, Captain Oliver Wendell Holmes, Jr., told his family, "There's no use in disguising that the feeling for McClellan has grown."

Even the most successful commander of the Army of the Potomac, Major General George G. Meade, fell prey to a McClellan-like inertia after the Union victory at Gettysburg. "It was a grand battle," Meade informed his wife, "and is in my judgment a most decided victory, though I did not annihilate or bag the Confederate army." Rather than risk a bloody repulse, Meade allowed Robert E. Lee's forces to complete their withdrawal across the Potomac River. When Lincoln expressed his displeasure at the lost opportunity, Meade reported that his troops were exhausted and needed "rest and reorganization." To Meade's way of thinking, "The proper policy for the Government would have been to be contented with driving Lee out of Maryland."

Most of the early Federal leaders in the War's Western theater shared McClellan's shortcomings. The army commanders Don Carlos Buell, Henry Halleck, and William S. Rosecrans all proved unwilling or unable to exploit a strategic advantage. It was perhaps fortunate for the Union cause that for a crucial year and a half the Confederacy's most important Western force—the Army of Tennessee—was entrusted to Braxton Bragg.

"This officer is in appearance the least prepossessing of the Confederate generals," wrote the British observer Arthur Fremantle. "He stoops, and has a sickly, cadaverous, haggard appearance." Bragg had a distinguished record as a battery commander in the Mexican War, where he had struck up a friendship with then-Colonel Jefferson Davis. He was hardworking and a good organizer; but he was also dour, irascible, and quirky.

Although he had once asserted that victory was "never complete until every enemy is killed, wounded, or captured," Bragg chose to abandon his invasion of Kentucky after a hard-fought battle with Buell's Army of the Ohio at Perryville. Three months later, on January 3, 1863, Bragg again withdrew, this time after being turned back by Rosecrans' troops at Stones River in Tennessee. In September 1863, Bragg failed to pursue Rosecrans' retreating forces from the battlefield of Chickamauga. Had he done so, Bragg might well have been

Ironically, Major General Braxton Bragg *(above)*, an officer generally despised by the rank and file of the Confederate army for his flawed leadership, once paid an eloquent tribute to the common soldier. "We have had to trust to the individuality and self-reliance of the private soldier," he wrote after the Battle of Stones River during the winter of 1862-1863. "Without the incentive which controls the officer; without the hope of reward, and actuated only by a sense of duty and of patriotism, he has, in this great contest, justly judged that the cause was his own and gone into it with a determination to conquer or die."

able to deal the North a severe setback by finishing off Rosecrans' army.

Unlike the courtly and tactful Lee, Bragg was unable to mollify his often quarrelsome subordinates, many of whom bore an ill-concealed contempt for their commander. When General Nathan Bedford Forrest took exception to one of Bragg's orders, the fiery cavalryman told his superior, "You have played the part of a damned scoundrel and are a coward; if you ever again try to interfere with me or cross my path it will be at the peril of your life." In October of 1863, a dozen of the Army of Tennessee's senior generals addressed a petition to President Davis requesting Bragg's replacement.

Bragg was just as unpopular with the men in the ranks. "He loved to crush the spirit of his men," declared the Tennessee private Sam Watkins. "Not a single soldier in the whole army ever loved or respected him." Bragg's humiliating defeat in the November 1863 Battle of Chattanooga finally brought about his transfer, but he left the army in a state one soldier described as a "sullen, dangerous demoralization."

Bragg's military demise coincided with the emergence of Ulysses S. Grant as the preeminent Federal leader. Grant's early victories at Forts Henry and Donelson had secured the Tennessee River for the Union, and he had demonstrated a remarkable capacity for tactical skill during the campaign that culminated in the surrender of the Confederate stronghold of Vicksburg, Mississippi. His defeat of Bragg at Chattanooga was one of the War's turning points.

Though singularly colorless by standards of martial bearing, the unostentatious general had the aggressive instinct so many Federal commanders lacked. "Grant is not a very fine looking general," a Federal colonel wrote, "but he has the appearance of a man of determination." Lieutenant Colonel Theodore Lyman told his wife that Grant "habitually wears an expression as if he had determined to drive his head through a brick wall, and was about to do it."

By early 1864, the Confederacy had lost more than 100,000 square miles of territory, had relinquished the transportation lifeline of the Mississippi River, and was slowly starving from the effects of the Federal naval blockade. Troop morale was eroding, and irreplaceable losses were crippling the offensive capabilities of Southern armies. Foreign recognition and military assistance for the Confederacy seemed a distant hope. The Anaconda was strangling its prey.

With his elevation to general-in-chief of all Federal forces, Grant embarked on a coordinated strategy to put an end to the Confederacy. Major General William T. Sherman, Grant's most talented and trusted subordinate, would use Chattanooga as base of operations for a three-army drive at the heart of the Confederacy: "to get into the enemy's country as far as you can, inflicting all the damage you can against their war resources."

In the campaign that culminated in the capture of Atlanta and the epic march to Savannah and the sea, Sherman gained the enmity of generations of Southerners but took the art of war a step closer to the modern age. He cut loose from his bases of supply, confiscated the produce and livestock of the

"Grant habitually wears an expression as if he had determined to drive his head through a brick wall, and was about to do it."

LT. COL. THEODORE LYMAN
AIDE-DE-CAMP, GEN. GEORGE MEADE
ARMY OF THE POTOMAC

civilian population, and burned what could not be consumed. "Since they have been doing so much to destroy us and our government, we have to destroy them," Sherman told an aide. "In war everything is right."

Sherman's opponent in the Atlanta campaign was in many respects a Confederate McClellan. Like McClellan, General Joseph E. Johnston was a talented organizer and a figure of respect for the men in the ranks. Johnston was "almost worshiped by his troops," one veteran stated. "I do not believe there was a soldier in his army but would gladly have died for him." As McClellan had relinquished the initiative to Lee by his retreat in the Seven Days' Battles, so Johnston chose to wage a skillfully executed but strategically counterproductive withdrawal before Sherman's forces. Like McClellan, Johnston proved unable to maintain a good working relationship with his president and was ulti-

Renowned Civil War photographer Mathew Brady took this photograph of Gen. Ulysses S. Grant *(leaning against tree at left)* at his headquarters at Cold Harbor, Virginia, in June 1864. The portrait was taken eight days after the costly Union failure at Cold Harbor, about which General Grant later wrote, "I regret this assault more than any one I ever ordered."

mately relieved of command—a move that outraged the soldiers in the Army of Tennessee as much as McClellan's removal had angered the troops in the Army of the Potomac. Just as McClellan's successor, Ambrose Burnside, had damaged morale by his futile and bloody assault at Fredericksburg, so two years later Johnston's successor, General John Bell Hood, squandered his troops in the costly battles around Atlanta. Heavy losses, inadequate supplies, and low morale finally contributed to the decisive defeat of Hood's forces in the Franklin-Nashville campaign.

When Grant came east in the spring of 1864, the war in Virginia entered its last and deadliest phase. Resolved not to repeat the failures of earlier commanders, Grant pushed Lee's army back on Richmond. Forced to go on the defensive, Lee's troops fought from the cover of earthen and log breastworks, and inflicted terrible losses on the more numerous Federals, who were frequently compelled to entrench in turn. While many Federal officers despaired at the casualty rates in battles such as the Wilderness, Spotsylvania, and Cold Harbor, Grant knew that a war of attrition would inevitably work to the North's advantage. By late summer of 1864, Lee was confined to the defenses of Richmond and Petersburg, and the stage was set for the final campaign that ended in Confederate surrender at Appomattox.

Not long after the War, Lee remarked to his son Custis that during the last desperate march of the Army of Northern Virginia from Petersburg to Appomattox, "Every move I made was at once checkmated by Grant." That Grant was able to achieve what so many Federal leaders had tried and failed to do was not merely a function of his dogged determination, of a cohesive strategy, or of superior Federal numbers. Plain military necessity had at last weeded out most of the incompetents in the Union high command. By 1865 a new generation of Federal brigade and division commanders had come to the fore, many of them in their midtwenties. Major General Ranald Slidell Mackenzie, whom Grant regarded as "the most promising young officer in the army," had not even graduated from West Point until the summer of 1862. Young generals like James Wilson, Wesley Merritt, Emory Upton, and Nelson Miles had climbed the chain of command through ability, not political influence. They had arrived on the battlefield in time to help Grant put an end to the Confederacy.

EASTERN THEATER

Of the dozen bloodiest battles of the Civil War, nine were fought within the roughly 20,000-square-mile area that constituted the Eastern theater of operations. Seven of the nine engagements took place on Virginia soil. The locus of this carnage was as much the result of symbolic as of strategic considerations. In a defiant gesture during the War's second month, the new Confederacy transferred its capital from Montgomery, Alabama, to Richmond, Virginia—only 100 miles from the seat of the Federal government at Washington, D.C. The brash act set the stage for four bitter years of combat that ebbed and flowed across the ravaged farmland of the Old Dominion, and north into Maryland and Pennsylvania.

While the Federal government professed to fight for the preservation of the Republic and sought to restore the seceded states to the Union by force of arms, the South viewed the struggle as a battle for survival. "The Confederate Government is waging this war solely for self-defense," President Jefferson Davis claimed, "it has no designs of conquest or any other purpose than to secure peace."

To a large extent, the geography of the Eastern theater favored the defensive posture chosen by the Confederate leaders. The Blue Ridge and Allegheny mountain ranges, running southwest to northeast, narrowed the frontage the Confederates had to defend. And although the Union navy asserted control of the Atlantic coast and Chesapeake Bay early in the War, the bay's principal tributaries—the Potomac, Rappahannock, York, and James rivers—were natural east-west barriers that blocked the movement of invading Federal armies.

From the outset of the War, Union troops seized sections of Virginia's railroad system, which they augmented with the construction of numerous branch lines. The efficient U.S. Military Railroads service was capable of transporting 800 tons of supplies a day to troops in the field. But despite the North's decided advantage in men and matériel, the Army of the Potomac—the principal Federal force in the Eastern theater—was unable to achieve a decisive victory on the battlefield in the first three years of fighting.

In the eight months that followed the Confederate victory at Bull Run on July 21, 1861, neither of the opposing commanders in the Eastern theater seemed disposed to risk another major engagement. George B. McClellan, commander of the Army of the Potomac, busied himself with organizational tasks. McClellan's opposite number, Confederate General Joseph E. Johnston, professed, "Our troops have always wished for the offensive." But it was General Johnston's withdrawal from Manassas—a scant 20 miles from Washington—that brought about active operations in the spring of 1862.

Rather than advance overland toward Johnston's new line on the Rappahannock, McClellan launched a massive amphibious expedition to the peninsula formed by the York and James rivers. The bold flanking maneuver forced the Confederates to rally to the defense of Richmond. But McClellan's ponderous advance up the peninsula stood in sharp contrast to the lightning maneuvers of Confederate commander Thomas J. "Stonewall" Jackson in the Shenandoah Valley. Jackson's victories in the Valley spurred the Union government's perennial fears for the safety of the city of Washington; 40,000 Federal troops earmarked for the advance on Richmond were held in reserve to protect the Northern capital.

In late June, the new commander of the Army of Northern Virginia, Robert E. Lee, launched a series of assaults that caused McClellan to abandon his position on the outskirts of Richmond. But Lee's success in the Seven Days' Battles was marred by lost opportunities that prevented the Confederates from smashing the Army of the Potomac. One Southern general complained, "the Confederate commanders knew no more about the topography of the country than they did about Central Africa."

Determined to improve his army's organization, Lee purged scores of incompetent, lackluster officers, replacing them with a hard-fighting cadre of dynamic, solid subordinates. In the Second Bull Run campaign of August 1862, Lee proved himself a master of the Napoleonic concept of *la manoeuvre sur les derrières*—the strategic envelopment of an opposing army's flank and rear. Using the Blue Ridge's easternmost range to screen his movements, Lee soundly thrashed the Yankees on the old battlefield of Bull Run.

Judging his foes "much weakened and demoralized," Lee crossed the Potomac into Maryland, carrying the war into Northern territory. On September 17, 1862, McClellan's Army of the Potomac squared off against Lee on the banks of Antietam Creek. The bloodiest day's fighting of the War was a tactical draw but caused Lee to abandon his invasion, a decision that denied the South hoped-for recognition from foreign powers and that paved the way for Abraham Lincoln's Emancipation Proclamation.

McClellan's reluctance to make decisive use of his superior numbers to pursue and engage the battered Army of Northern Virginia cost him his job. McClellan's successors in command of the Army of the Potomac, Ambrose Burnside and Joseph Hooker, followed Lincoln's mandate to assail Lee's forces. Both failed: Burnside in an unimaginative head-on assault at Fredericksburg on December 13, 1862, and Hooker in the cleverly conceived but poorly executed Chancellorsville campaign of May 1863. But while Lincoln's Eastern generals seemed incapable of vanquishing the Army of Northern Virginia, neither could Lee succeed in crippling Northern resolve to prosecute the War. In July 1863, a second invasion of the North was repulsed by Hooker's successor, General George Meade, at Gettysburg, Pennsylvania. It was the turning point of the war in the East.

In the spring of 1864, the principal Eastern armies seemed to be in a deadlock along the old line of the Rappahannock and its tributary, the Rapidan. But Lincoln had at last found a general determined to lead the Union to victory. Newly appointed as general-in-chief, Ulysses S. Grant launched a multifront offensive in the East and West, and personally took the field with Meade's Army of the Potomac. In a single month, Grant waged three pitched battles and half a dozen smaller engagements, relentlessly maneuvering around Lee's right flank, forcing the Army of Northern Virginia to withdraw to the fortifications of Richmond and Petersburg.

Confederate artillerist Edward Porter Alexander correctly recognized Grant's new strategy as "practically one of extermination—to reduce our numbers at all costs."

Grant indeed spent lives freely. In about 45 days of combat, he lost perhaps 68,000 men killed, wounded, and captured, while inflicting 42,000 casualties on the Confederates. As Grant well knew, his losses were replaceable, while Lee's were not. Although a bloody nine-month siege of Petersburg lay ahead, Northern victory appeared inevitable in the hard-fought Eastern theater.

"With the liberal supply of men and means which our superior resources ought to furnish, we will win in the long run," Meade wrote; "it is a question of tenacity and nerve, and it won't do to look behind, or to calculate the cost in blood and treasure." The resolution of Grant's grim war of attrition came at Appomattox on April 9, 1865, when the Army of Northern Virginia, the last hope of the Confederate cause, laid down its arms.

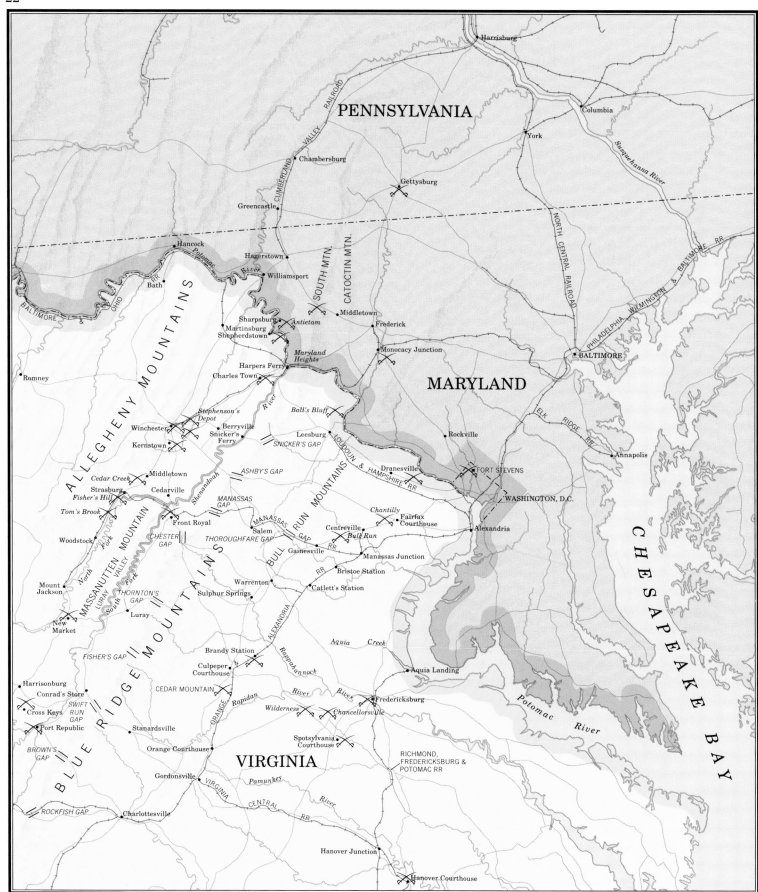

BATTLEFIELDS OF THE EASTERN THEATER

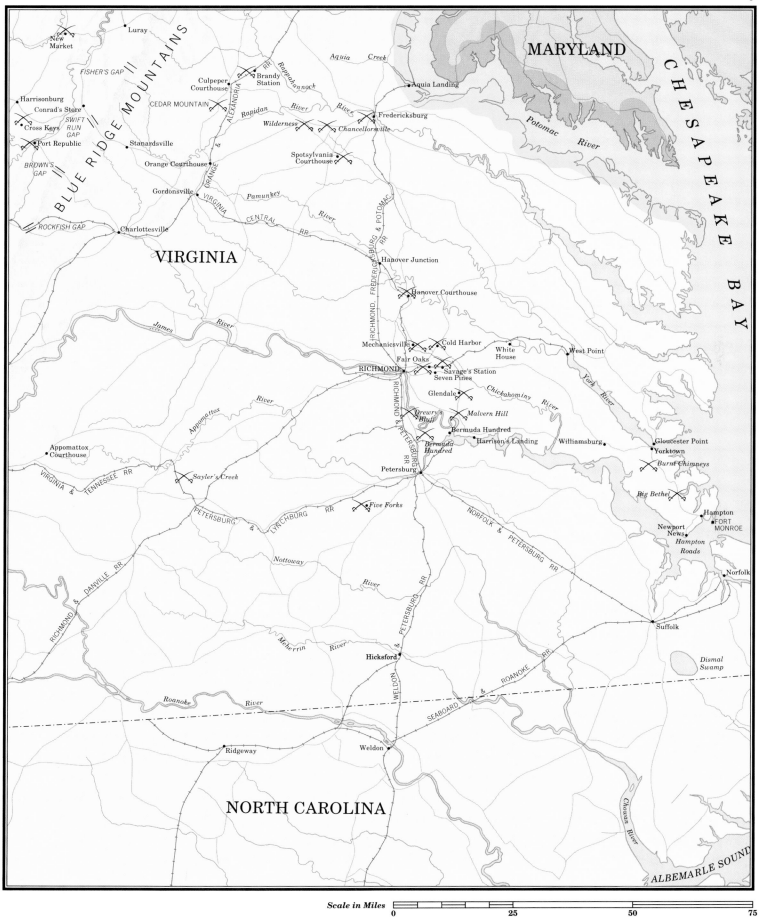

MARYLAND

CHESAPEAKE BAY

Luray

New
Market

FISHER'S GAP

Aquia Creek

Culpeper
Courthouse

Brandy
Station

Rappahannock

BLUE RIDGE MOUNTAINS

Harrisonburg

Conrad's Store

CEDAR MOUNTAIN

Rapidan River

River

Aquia Landing

Fredericksburg

Potomac River

*SWIFT
RUN
GAP*

Cross Keys

Wilderness

Chancellorsville

ALEXANDRIA

Port Republic

Stanardsville

Spotsylvania
Courthouse

*BROWN'S
GAP*

Orange Courthouse

ORANGE &

Gordonsville

Pamunkey

VIRGINIA

ROCKFISH GAP

Charlottesville

VIRGINIA CENTRAL RR

River

Hanover Junction

RICHMOND, FREDERICKSBURG & POTOMAC RR

James River

Hanover Courthouse

Mechanicsville

Cold Harbor

White
House

West Point

Fair Oaks

RICHMOND

Savage's Station

Seven Pines

York River

Glendale

Chickahominy River

Appomattox River

*Drewry's
Bluff*

Malvern Hill

Bermuda Hundred

Appomattox
Courthouse

RICHMOND & PETERSBURG RR

*Bermuda
Hundred*

Harrison's Landing

Williamsburg

Gloucester Point

Yorktown

Burnt Chimneys

VIRGINIA & TENNESSEE RR

Sayler's Creek

Petersburg

Big Bethel

PETERSBURG &

LYNCHBURG RR

Five Forks

NORFOLK & PETERSBURG RR

Hampton

FORT
MONROE

Newport
News

*Hampton
Roads*

RICHMOND & DANVILLE RR

Nottoway

PETERSBURG RR

Norfolk

River

Meherrin River

Suffolk

*Dismal
Swamp*

Hicksford

WELDON

SEABOARD & ROANOKE RR

Roanoke River

Ridgeway

Weldon

NORTH CAROLINA

Chowan River

ALBEMARLE SOUND

Scale in Miles

0   25   50   75

Through the spring of 1861, the Northern press and public angrily prodded President Abraham Lincoln and his government to launch the Union army into action. The presence of Confederate forces within a day's march of the nation's capital seemed intolerable, and pressure mounted for the Federals to attack, crush the Rebels, march on Richmond and end Secession with one blow. In early July the president, becoming impatient himself, ordered Brigadier General Irvin McDowell, his commander in the field, to go on the offensive.

McDowell was desperate. His army of about 35,000 men, forming around Wash-

GEN. IRVIN McDOWELL, UNION COMMANDER AT BULL RUN

ington, was by far the largest ever assembled in North America, but it was woefully ill-prepared for action—poorly trained, inadequately equipped, and led mostly by mossbacked old-timers and inexperienced amateurs. McDowell protested his unreadiness to Winfield Scott, the elderly and sage army chief. Scott pointed out that the enemy, too, lacked experience. "You are green, it is true," Scott observed, "but they are green also; you are all green alike."

Reluctantly, McDowell came up with a plan. He and his army would march westward from the Union camps around Washington, D.C., and clear the Confederates from their positions at Fairfax Courthouse and Centreville. From there, part of the Union force would move on the Confederate army thought to be camped behind a meandering stream called Bull Run, near the town of Manassas Junction. Another Federal column would attempt to outflank the Rebels, cut their main line of supply from Richmond, and force a withdrawal at least to the next natural line of defense, the Rappahannock River near Fredericksburg.

The main Confederate force, under Brigadier General Pierre Gustave Toutant Beauregard, was indeed near Manassas—a rail junction that afforded the Rebels excellent lines of communication. One track stretched south to Richmond, and another headed west into the Shenandoah Valley, connecting Beauregard's army with a smaller force commanded by General Joseph E. Johnston. In combination, the two Confederate armies totaled nearly as many men as the Federal army. When McDowell finally sent his brigades toward Bull Run on July 16, the stage was set for the first great battle of the War—a confused fight filled with miscalculations on both sides, and a surprisingly vicious one considering the inexperience of the two armies.

Briefly detraining during their dash to Bull Run, some of Johnston's troops from the Valley accept refreshments offered by local women at a stop on the Manassas Gap Railroad.

When McDowell's Federals started westward toward Fairfax Courthouse and Centreville on July 16 and 17, Confederate President Jefferson Davis and his chief military adviser, Robert E. Lee, were still desperately speeding reinforcements from all over the South through Richmond to Manassas. At the same time, other small units, including Theophilus Holmes' brigade from Aquia Creek and the Hampton Legion from Richmond, also headed for the contested ground. Then, as the Union attack loomed, Johnston in the Shenandoah Valley swiftly put his four brigades aboard trains for the 50-mile trip to join Beauregard's army.

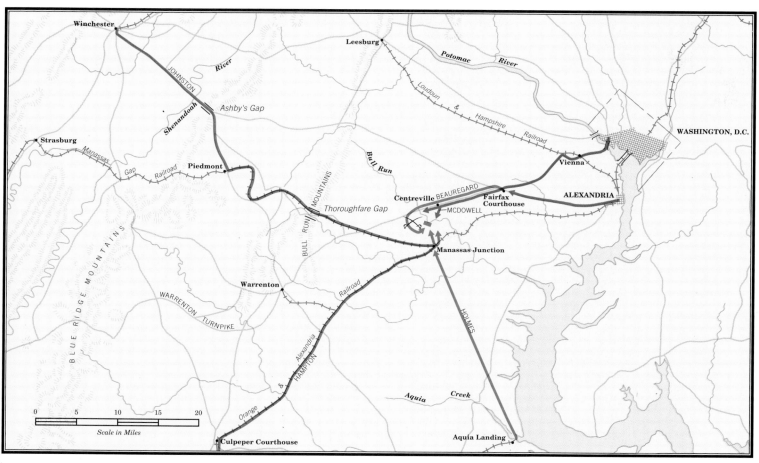

OPENING MOVEMENTS, JULY 21

Probing Federal attacks on Mitchell's and Blackburn's fords on July 18 ran into fierce opposition, and McDowell gave up any idea of a direct movement toward Manassas Junction. Instead, he decided on a wide flanking movement around the Confederate left. On the morning of July 21, the leading Union brigades of Colonels Ambrose Burnside and Andrew Porter *(blue)* splashed across Bull Run at Sudley Ford, well to the north of Beauregard's defensive positions. Heintzelman's division followed and reinforced Burnside and Porter while other Federal units moved down the Warrenton Turnpike to threaten the Stone Bridge, and still others feinted toward the main fords farther downstream. The Confederate brigades *(red)* were caught badly out of position, spread over a six-mile front with most troops on the right, where Beauregard was convinced the main Federal blow must fall. Only Nathan Evans' small two-regiment brigade moved at first to meet the dangerous Union thrust that threatened to turn the lightly held Rebel left.

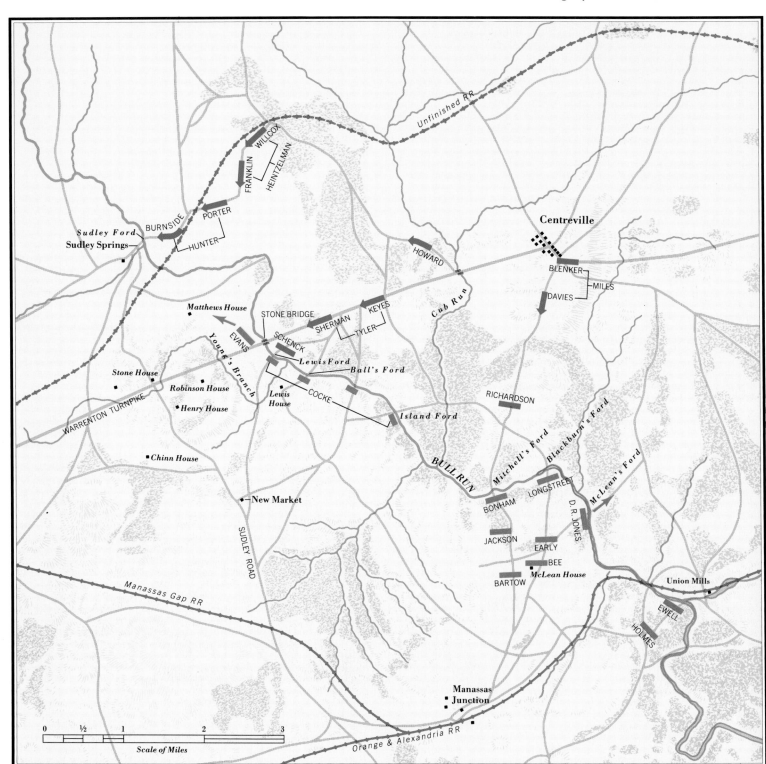

ORDER OF BATTLE

CONFEDERATE FORCES
JOHNSTON

ARMY OF THE POTOMAC
BEAUREGARD
21,800 MEN

FIRST BRIGADE BONHAM	**SECOND BRIGADE** EWELL	**THIRD BRIGADE** D. R. JONES	**FOURTH BRIGADE** LONGSTREET
FIFTH BRIGADE COCKE	**SIXTH BRIGADE** EARLY	**"SEVENTH BRIGADE"** EVANS	**"RESERVE BRIGADE"** HOLMES

ARMY OF THE SHENANDOAH
JOHNSTON
9,500 MEN

FIRST BRIGADE JACKSON	**SECOND BRIGADE** BARTOW	**THIRD BRIGADE** BEE	**FOURTH BRIGADE** KIRBY SMITH

ADDITIONAL FORCES
Several unbrigaded infantry, cavalry, and artillery units
including the Hampton Legion and Stuart's and Radford's Virginia cavalry regiments.

UNION ARMY
McDOWELL
35,700 MEN

FIRST DIVISION: TYLER *Brigades:* KEYES, SCHENCK, SHERMAN, RICHARDSON	**SECOND DIVISION: HUNTER** *Brigades:* PORTER, BURNSIDE	**THIRD DIVISION: HEINTZELMAN** *Brigades:* FRANKLIN, WILLCOX, HOWARD
FOURTH DIVISION: RUNYON EIGHT UNBRIGADED REGIMENTS	**FIFTH DIVISION: MILES** *Brigades:* BLENKER, DAVIES	

Beauregard doffs his cap to a regiment of boisterous Mississippi soldiers as they pass in ragged review, brandishing bowie knives. The Louisiana general's informal style of leadership kept the spirits of his men high; he often dropped in on their camps to mix with the rank and file.

The three fast-acting, resolute Confederate officers who wheeled their brigades to meet the main Federal attack are shown at right. Evans, a West Point graduate, was a gruff, heavy-drinking South Carolinian, known as Shanks for his skinny bowlegs. Bee, also a West Pointer, was known for his courage and independence. Bartow, who had energetically taught himself soldiering, was a lawyer in Savannah before the War. Both Bee and Bartow were mortally wounded at Bull Run.

COL. NATHAN G. EVANS

BRIG. GEN. BARNARD E. BEE

MATTHEWS HILL

Only minutes after Burnside's and Porter's brigades had crossed Sudley Ford and turned southward across rolling, partially wooded ground, Evans threw his brigade in their path on Matthews Hill. There Evans' small force, vastly outnumbered, held the Federals at bay until he was reinforced on his right, first by Bee's brigade, then by Bartow's. Together the three Confederate brigades fought furiously to hold off three times as many attacking Union troops and stalled McDowell's flanking movement for almost two hours. Finally, however, Federal pressure was too great. Porter's and Burnside's brigades threatened the left flank of the Confederate line, and Union brigades led by Colonels William Tecumseh Sherman and Erasmus D. Keyes that had crossed Bull Run just above the Stone Bridge were moving on the Confederates' rear. By 11:00 a.m., Evans, Bee, and Bartow were forced to withdraw their remaining troops back across Warrenton Turnpike and up the lower slope of Henry House Hill. But by then, Beauregard had realized the extent of the threat to his left flank and had begun to send more reinforcements in that direction. First to arrive was the so-called Hampton Legion, organized and led by the wealthy planter Colonel Wade Hampton. His small, 600-man unit was soon followed by the large brigade commanded by Thomas J. Jackson, who led his men smartly through the hot morning toward the slopes of Henry House Hill.

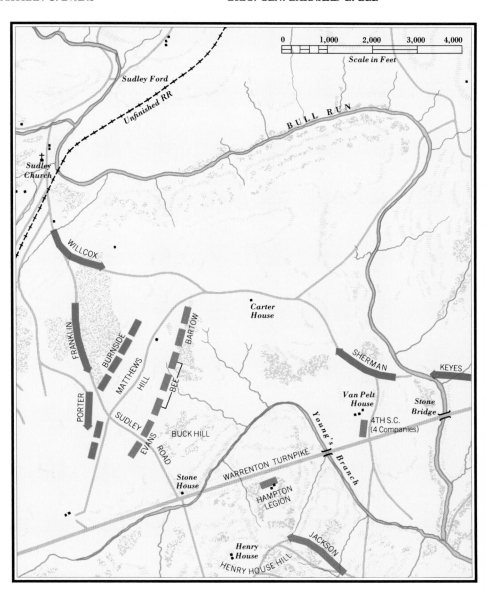

COL. FRANCIS S. BARTOW

In the opening phase of the battle, the regiments of Burnside's brigade—foreground in the painting below—advance past the Matthews farmhouse (also shown in the photo at right) toward the Confederate line *(background)*.

Disaster strikes the Federal batteries commanded by Ricketts and Griffin as the 33d Virginia charges their flank. Because the Virginians wore blue uniforms, the artillerymen held their fire and lost their guns as a result.

HENRY HOUSE HILL

By late morning, the Federals had clearly gained the upper hand. The leading brigades had shoved aside the badly mauled troops of Bee, Bartow, and Evans, and heavy Union reinforcements led by Sherman, Franklin, and others had advanced across the turnpike and were heading up Henry House Hill. With the Federal infantry came powerful artillery support—20 or more guns commanded by a pair of daring and able officers, Captains Charles Griffin and James B. Ricketts, who deployed their cannon near the crest of the hill and began pounding the Confederate line. But around 2:30 p.m., the momentum shifted. Disobeying the orders of Jackson—who had just earned his nickname by standing "like a stone wall"—Colonel Arthur Cummings boldly led his 33d Virginia against the Union batteries. This headlong attack by the Virginians overwhelmed the exposed artillery and routed a battalion of U.S. Marines and the 11th New York, which were supporting the Union guns.

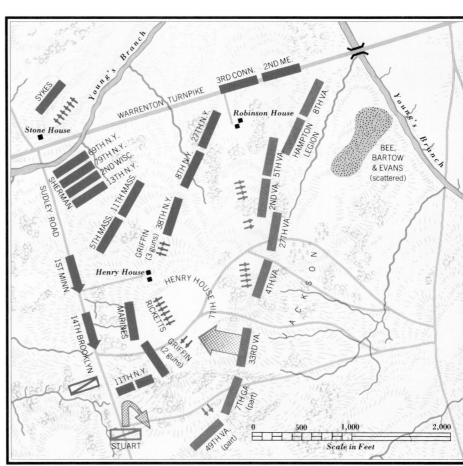

General Joseph E. Johnston *(foreground)*, arriving at the threat-ened Confederate left flank, helps reorganize the sagging defense by rallying a Georgia regiment while Colonel Bartow, waving a flag *(left)*, gallops through enemy fire to regroup his hard-hit brigade.

Trying to recapture the Union artillery, Vermont and Maine regiments of Colonel Oliver O. Howard's brigade charge up Henry House Hill. The New Englanders were soon flanked and routed by Edmund Kirby Smith's brigade, which rushed to reinforce Jackson.

Fleeing in panic from Bull Run in what became known as "the great skedaddle," Union troops and supply wagons race eastward along one of the roads leading to Centreville and Washington.

Trying to prevent a total rout, a sword-waving Colonel Louis Blenker orders his New York troops, stationed near Centreville, to fire on the Confederate cavalry that spearheaded the pursuit of the Federal forces.

FEDERAL RETREAT

Having shifted large reserves to Jackson's left, Beauregard sent fresh troops moving down Henry House Hill and the adjacent Bald Hill and Chinn Ridge. Kirby Smith's brigade, followed by Colonel Jubal A. Early's, slammed into Howard's weary men and routed them. Soon more Federal units, disorganized and disheartened, began to leave the field. Now Beauregard ordered a general attack that caved in the entire right wing of McDowell's army. The Federal soldiers threw away their guns and packs and fled, some by way of Sudley Ford, others by the shorter route across the Stone Bridge. "The retreat soon became a rout," McDowell later said, "and this soon degenerated still further into a panic." Beauregard ordered a pursuit; but his troops, too, were tired, and the Union army—less 3,000 killed, wounded, or captured—managed to straggle back into Washington over the next several days. The Confederates lost fewer men, however—perhaps 2,000—and gained a glorious victory that put an end to Northern expectations of a short war.

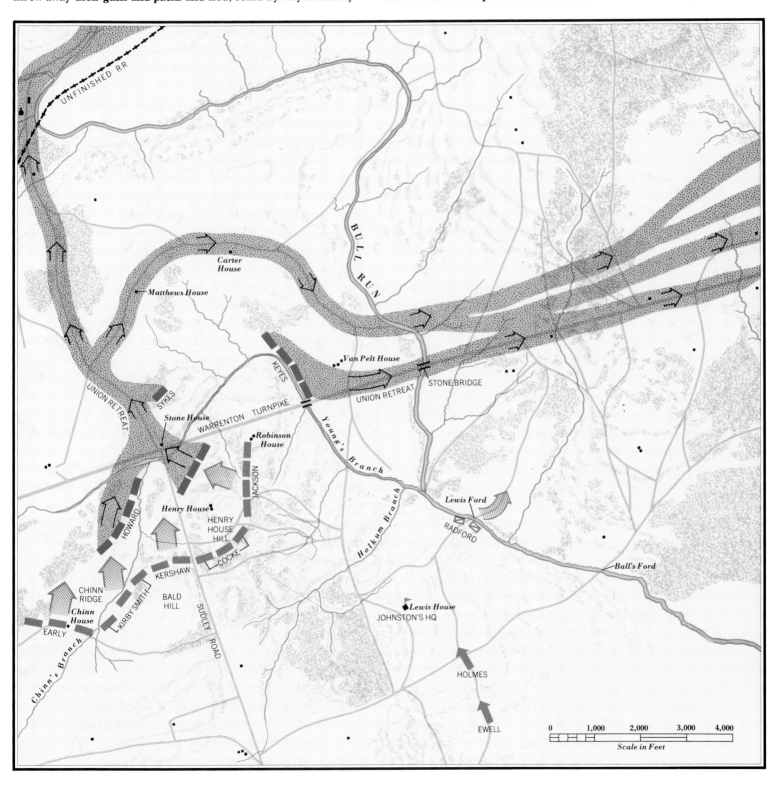

Already celebrated for his prowess at Bull Run, Stonewall Jackson took command of the Confederate force guarding the Shenandoah Valley in November of 1861. During the next six months he waged a dazzling war of movement, outthinking and defeating no fewer than three Federal commands sent to destroy his army, which at its largest numbered only 17,000 men. In a string of battles, he saved the grain-rich Shenandoah for the Confederacy. By posing a threat to Washington, he drew off thousands of Federal troops that would otherwise have strengthened George McClellan's march on Richmond, the main Union effort in the spring of 1862. The Valley campaign was a superb strategic diversion—and it instilled a lasting fear of the combative Jackson in the hearts of Federal commanders.

Jackson was successful in part because of his own daring and quickness—he sometimes marched his men 35 miles in a day— but he had other assets as well. One was his dashing cavalry commander and head scout, Turner Ashby, who kept Jackson informed of Federal movements. Another was Jedediah Hotchkiss, an expert cartographer who tirelessly mapped the Shenandoah Valley so that Jackson knew every wrinkle in its topography and the network of roads and passes that crisscrossed it. Especially important was the 45-mile-long Massanutten Mountain that bisected the central part of the Valley and that Jackson would use brilliantly to screen his movements and outmaneuver the enemy.

Jackson had a further advantage: his opponents. One was John C. Frémont, a daring explorer of the West before the War but inept as a general, who commanded a force camped west of the Valley in the Allegheny foothills. Jackson's chief adversary was Nathaniel P. Banks, a successful politician who had been governor of Massachusetts and Speaker of the U.S. House of Representatives. As a military leader, however, Banks proved amateurish, hesitant, and slow. Both Union generals had able subordinates who fought well and handed Jackson an unpleasant surprise or two. But Banks especially was an ideal foil whom Jackson would hoodwink repeatedly. When Banks began the main campaign by bringing his 38,000-man army across the Potomac in February 1862, Jackson—although outnumbered at that point by about eight to one—was ready to play a frustrating game of cat and mouse.

MAJ. GEN.
THOMAS J. "STONEWALL" JACKSON

Stonewall Jackson's campaign in the Shenandoah from December 1861 to June 1862 was marked by furious marching and countermarching up and down the length of the Valley. After a winter trek to Romney, Virginia, to forestall a threat to his western flank, Jackson returned to the central Valley, narrowly losing the first battle at Kernstown but spreading alarm among the Federals. He then took his army more than 100 miles to the southwest to drive back part of Frémont's army under General Robert Milroy near the town of McDowell. Back north by late May, he teamed up with Richard Ewell's division to crush Banks at Front Royal, then again at Winchester, subsequently pursuing some Federal units all the way to the Potomac River. This was followed by a double victory over both Frémont and Brigadier General James Shields in two days of fighting at Cross Keys and Port Republic that cleared the Valley of Yankees.

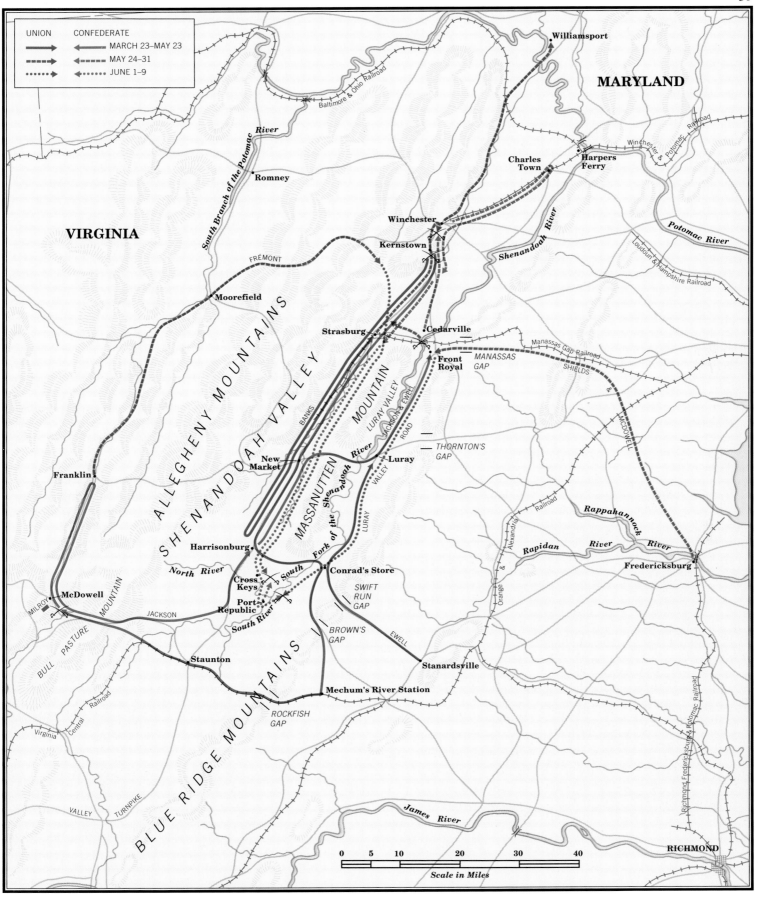

MARYLAND

VIRGINIA

UNION · CONFEDERATE

	MARCH 23–MAY 23
	MAY 24–31
	JUNE 1–9

Williamsport

Charles Town

Harpers Ferry

Romney

South Branch of the Potomac River

Winchester

Kernstown

FRÉMONT

Shenandoah River

Potomac River

Moorefield

Strasburg

Cedarville

Front Royal

MANASSAS GAP

Manassas Gap Railroad

SHIELDS

New Market

Luray

THORNTON'S GAP

MOUNTAIN

LURAY VALLEY

JACKSON & EWELL

ROAD

Franklin

Shenandoah River

MASSANUTTEN

Fork of the

LURAY VALLEY

MCDOWELL

Rappahannock

Railroad

Harrisonburg

North River

Conrad's Store

Cross Keys

South

SWIFT RUN GAP

Rapidan

River

River

Fredericksburg

McDowell

MILROY

JACKSON

Port Republic

South River

BROWN'S GAP

EWELL

Staunton

Stanardsville

BULL PASTURE MOUNTAIN

Mechum's River Station

Virginia Central Railroad

ROCKFISH GAP

BLUE RIDGE MOUNTAINS

James River

VALLEY TURNPIKE

ALLEGHENY MOUNTAINS

SHENANDOAH VALLEY

RICHMOND

Richmond, Fredericksburg & Potomac Railroad

Loudoun & Hampshire Railroad

Winchester & Potomac Railroad

Baltimore & Ohio Railroad

| 0 | 5 | 10 | 20 | 30 | 40 |

Scale in Miles

KERNSTOWN

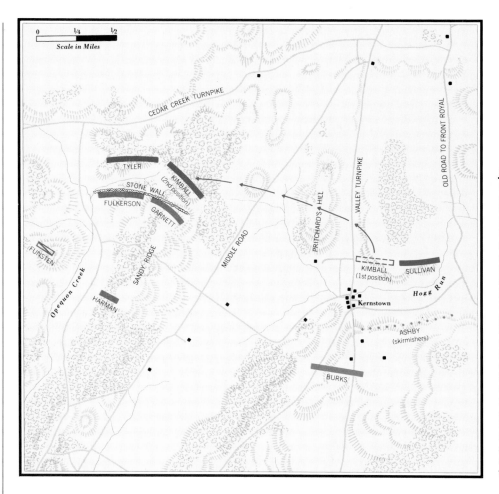

Jackson initiated the first battle of the campaign when, on March 21, his scouts reported that two of Banks' divisions had been ordered eastward across the Blue Ridge, leaving only Shields' 9,000-man Union division near Winchester. Although still sorely outnumbered, Jackson immediately put his 4,200 foot soldiers and horsemen on the Valley Turnpike heading northward from their camps around Mount Jackson. On the afternoon of March 23, finding Robert O. Tyler's Union brigade deployed on a ridge near Kernstown, he ordered Fulkerson's and Garnett's brigades to wheel left to flank the Federal position while Burks' brigade and Ashby's cavalry held the Federals on the right. Reaching the cover of a stone wall, Fulkerson's and Garnett's men fired on Tyler's troops. The Federals countered by shifting six regiments under Nathan Kimball to the left to support Tyler. In a fierce two-hour fight, the Federals beat back the Confederates. The battle was a minor defeat for Jackson, but it warned the Federals that they were facing a dangerously belligerent foe.

The stone wall used as cover by Jackson's men crosses Sandy Ridge in the photograph above. At right, the 84th Pennsylvania attacks the wall in a headlong charge late in the afternoon, forcing the Confederates to retreat. The cost to the Pennsylvanians was dear, their regiment losing one-third of its men.

Although footsore and weary from their long marches, Stonewall Jackson's troops nevertheless raise a cheer as they file past their commander, who sits his favorite mount, the small and unimpressive Little Sorrel.

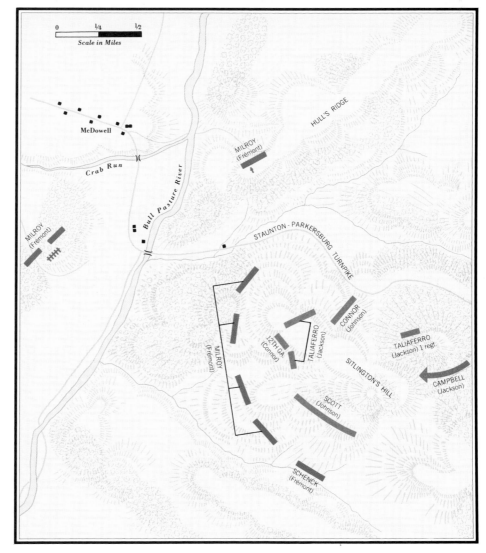

Jackson's army more than doubled in size on April 30 when Ewell's division crossed the Blue Ridge into the Valley. Deciding that Ewell and his 8,500 men could watch the slow-moving Banks, Jackson immediately set off across the Valley with his own brigades, joining en route the 2,800-man detachment under Johnson, already guarding the Allegheny passes. Jackson's object: to attack whatever part of Frémont's army he met and forestall any linkup of Frémont with Banks. Finding a Union force under Milroy near the hamlet of McDowell on May 8, Jackson deployed his troops in a wedge-shaped line atop steepsided Sitlington's Hill. Milroy's Federals repeatedly stormed the hill but were savagely beaten back. As night fell, the defeated Federals retreated across Bull Pasture River, freeing Jackson's little army to return to the Valley to deal with Banks.

FRONT ROYAL

After driving Colonel John Kenly's outnumbered Federals from Front Royal, Confederate cavalry swarm over some of Kenly's troops who made a stand outside town. In the background, other Federals retreat across a bridge spanning the South Fork of the Shenandoah.

Having returned from McDowell, Jackson soon resolved to deal with Banks' army, most of which was now around Strasburg. Jackson's first move was to march his brigades down the Valley Turnpike as though to attack Banks at Strasburg. He then abruptly turned his army eastward on the road that crossed the Massanutten to join Ewell, who was advancing along the eastern side of the mountain. The idea: to flank Banks by surprising Kenly's 1,100-man detachment at Front Royal. Sending Ashby's cavalry across the South Fork to cut off Kenly's retreat, Jackson and Ewell attacked on May 23 with Wheat's Louisiana and Johnson's Maryland regiments. The Rebel troops quickly drove Kenly's outnumbered garrison from Front Royal, but the Federals made a stand on a hill north of the town. When Kenly saw Confederate cavalry across the river racing toward the bridges—his only escape route—he ordered his men to dash for the spans. Most of the Union troops made it across, but Rebel cavalry caught up with them at Cedarville, and fewer than 200 of Kenly's men managed to get away.

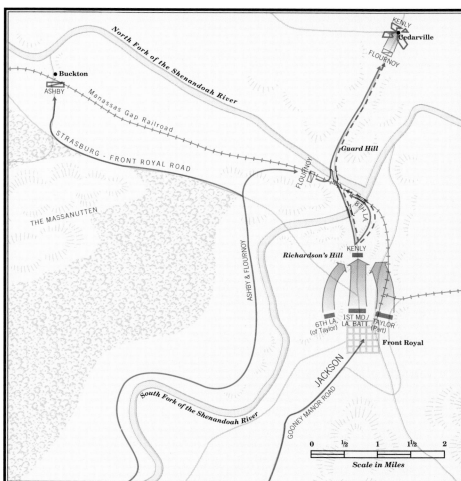

BRIG. GEN. TURNER ASHBY

On a height overlooking the Shenandoah Valley, Jackson *(left)* confers with two of his chief subordinates, the cranky and pugnacious Richard Ewell *(center)* and the rakishly bearded cavalry leader, Turner Ashby.

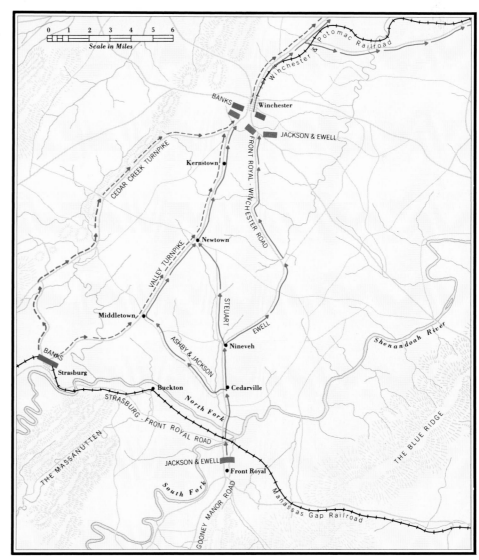

PURSUIT OF BANKS

Front Royal taken, Jackson hurried his troops along the roads to the north and west in an effort to cut off and annihilate the rest of Banks' army. He and Ashby headed for Middletown, the first village on Banks' line of retreat up the turnpike. Two regiments of Ewell's cavalry under George H. Steuart rode for the next hamlet of Newtown. Ewell himself marched for Cedarville and Nineveh, ready to follow Steuart or to head straight northward. Banks failed to realize how close he was to being cut off at Strasburg until hours after the Front Royal battle. He ordered a retreat only in midmorning on May 24. Still, his troops made such speed up the turnpike that Jackson and Ashby—slowed by hard-fighting companies of Maine and Vermont cavalry—managed to catch and destroy just the tail of the Federal army at Middletown. Realizing Banks had escaped, Jackson ordered a fast pursuit up the turnpike while Ewell moved his division along a parallel road. By dawn on May 25, the leading Confederate units were a few miles from Winchester, and Jackson was planning a full-scale attack.

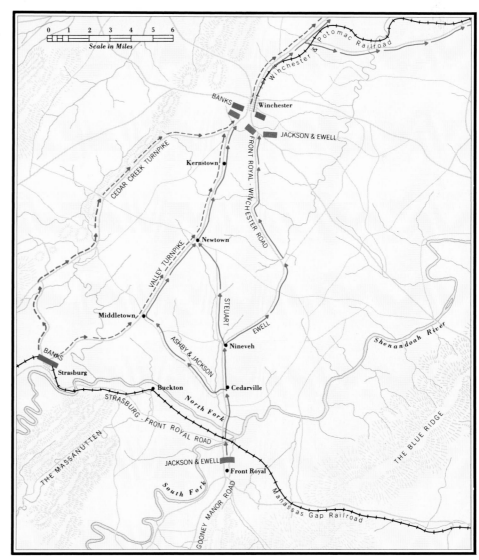

Almost as combative as Jackson, Richard Ewell nevertheless thought his superior was reckless. "I never saw one of Jackson's couriers approach," Ewell said, "without expecting an order to assault the North Pole."

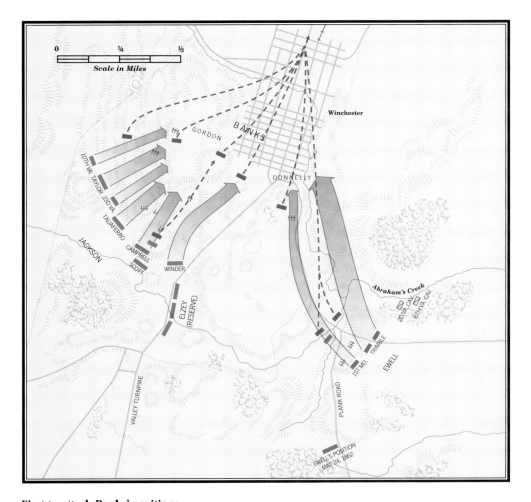

Accepting a hero's welcome from the people of Winchester, Jackson gallantly doffs his hat as he rides through the town after routing its Federal occupiers.

First to attack Banks' positions south of Winchester on May 25 was Jackson's old command, the Stonewall Brigade, now under Charles Winder. Storming up a hill against light opposition, Winder and his men found themselves pinned down by heavy Federal fire from a second hill. Jackson immediately sent in Taylor's Louisiana brigade on the far left, supported by Confederate artillery that bombarded the right side of the Federal line. Ewell attacked at the same time, outflanking the Federal left. Soon the entire Union line broke, the troops racing rearward through the streets of Winchester. Jackson's pursuit was slowed because Ashby's cavalry, chasing a distant Federal detachment, was out of reach. Still the Federals continued to retreat until they had covered the 35 miles to the Potomac and crossed into Maryland.

Although a timid leader, Major General Nathaniel Banks, according to one observer, was a "faultless-looking soldier" who loved military pomp and glitter.

CROSS KEYS & PORT REPUBLIC

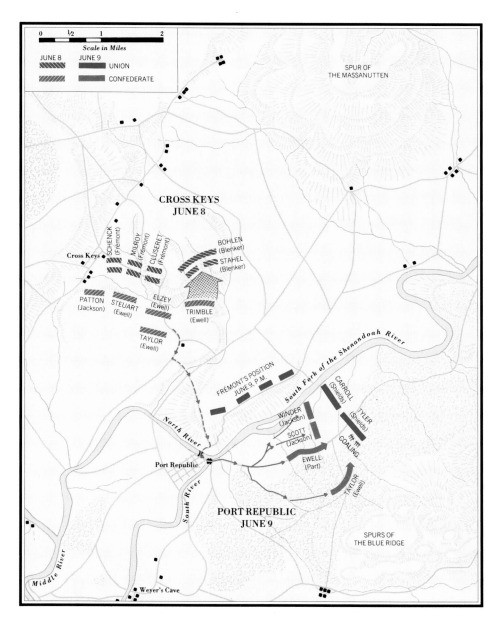

BRIG. GEN. JAMES SHIELDS

To prevent the Confederates from moving northward across the Potomac, and to trap Jackson in a pincers movement, President Lincoln ordered Frémont to march out of the Alleghenies and get to Jackson's rear while McDowell was to move part of his army south from Washington to Front Royal, with Shields' division in the lead. Jackson soon retreated southward to Strasburg, where Ewell hit Frémont's ill-equipped and ill-led forces, slowing that part of the pincers. By June 6, Jackson had reached Port Republic, well ahead of Shields, who was advancing up the Luray Valley east of the Massanutten. Jackson lashed out first at Frémont's force on June 8, deploying Ewell's four brigades and a fifth from Jackson's command, under Patton, just east of Cross Keys. Trimble's brigade easily repulsed and drove back a Federal division under Blenker, temporarily paralyzing Frémont. During the night, Jackson boldly shifted the bulk of his forces across the North River and on June 9 attacked Shields. The Confederates were raked by Federal artillery fire, but Taylor's brigade saved the day by capturing the Federal guns. Frémont, who had resumed his advance, was stymied when Jackson burned the North River Bridge. Retreating to Mount Jackson and Luray, the Federals left behind 1,018 casualties. Jackson, whose army suffered 615 casualties, remained in the Valley only until June 17, when Lee called him to Richmond for a new assignment.

MAJ. GEN. JOHN C. FRÉMONT

A bridge spans the North River replacing the one burned by Jackson on June 9.

Frémont's Federals deploy to attack Ewell's troops positioned on a distant wooded ridge line near Cross Keys.

PENINSULAR CAMPAIGN

To rebuild the Union army shattered at Bull Run, Lincoln, in late July 1861, called on a 35-year-old organizational wizard, Major General George B. McClellan. The new commander swiftly went about restoring order. The troops were drilled assiduously, camps tidied up, and equipment improved until the newly christened Army of the Potomac encamped around Washington radiated a new pride and confidence.

McClellan kept on organizing for eight months. During this time, except for a pair of minor forays, he made no move to attack the Confederates—now known as the Army of Northern Virginia—who had with-drawn from Manassas to positions along the Rappahannock River. Finally, Lincoln ordered his dilatory general to move.

The Young Napoleon, as the press called McClellan, came up with an elaborate plan. Instead of advancing overland to the south against Richmond, he took most of his now-huge army by ship to the Peninsula, the area between the York and James rivers. From there he moved westward, and two months later, his forwardmost units stood only six miles from Richmond. But there McClellan was assailed by ferocious Confederate counterattacks that rendered him even more cautious.

WILLIAM F. SMITH   WILLIAM B. FRANKLIN   SAMUEL P. HEINTZELMAN   ANDREW PORTER   IRVIN MCDOWELL

Landing from paddle-wheel transports at Fort Monroe on the tip of the Peninsula, Union troops assemble for the march toward the first Rebel stronghold at Yorktown in this watercolor by the Prince de Joinville, a French observer in McClellan's retinue.

McClellan *(center)*, hand thrust in his jacket, stands with the senior generals of his remade Union force, now called the Army of the Potomac. All except Buell, Blenker, and McDowell would serve on the Peninsula.

EORGE B. MCCLELLAN   GEORGE A. MCCALL   DON CARLOS BUELL   LOUIS BLENKER   SILAS CASEY   FITZ-JOHN PORTER

46

GEN. JOSEPH E. JOHNSTON

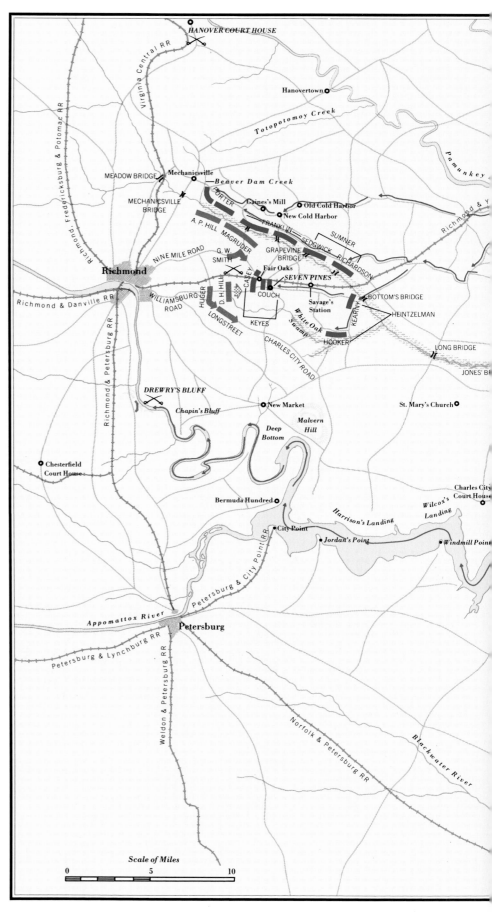

ADVANCE UP THE PENINSULA, APRIL-MAY 1862

As soon as the vanguard of his army
reached Fort Monroe in late March, McClellan started two divisions probing inland.
The Federal advance soon bogged down,
however, at the Warwick River and at a set
of earthworks guarding Yorktown. Both
were defended only by small Rebel units,
but the Confederates made such a show of
force that, instead of launching an assault,
McClellan hesitated and prepared to lay
siege. At length, after a clash at Burnt
Chimneys and a skirmish at Lee's Mill, the
Confederates, led by Joseph Johnston, retreated to Williamsburg, where in a
pitched battle they again delayed the Federal advance. Meanwhile, Johnston had ordered the main body of his army to move
southeastward from the Rappahannock and
throw a ring of defenses around Richmond. With the Confederates withdrawing,
McClellan sent most of his army marching
in pursuit and put the rest on ships that
carried them up the York River to the
ports of West Point and White House. By
the end of May, after two months of snail-
like progress, the Federals could see Richmond—and were soon hit by Johnston at
the Battle of Seven Pines. A Union naval
squadron, trying to reach Richmond up
the James River, also was stopped cold by
Confederate artillery at Drewry's Bluff.

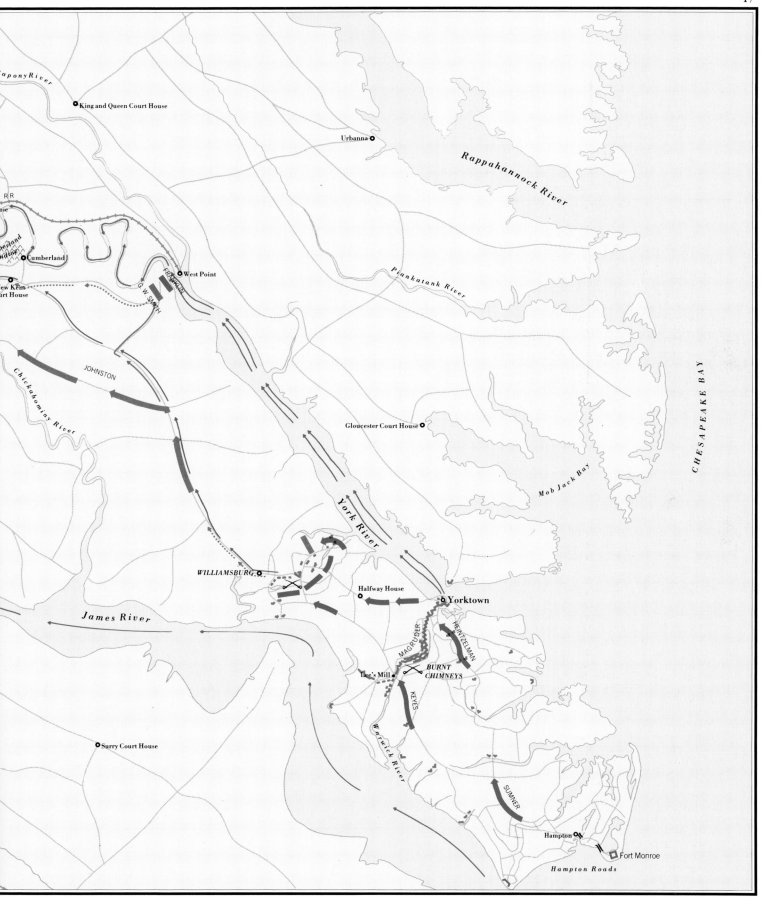

King and Queen Court House

Urbanna

Rappahannock River

apony River

R R

erland nding

Cumberland

New Kent rt House

G W SMITH

FRANKLIN

West Point

Piankatank River

JOHNSTON

Chickahominy River

Gloucester Court House

Mob Jack Bay

C H E S A P E A K E   B A Y

York River

WILLIAMSBURG

Halfway House

Yorktown

James River

MAGRUDER

HEINTZELMAN

Lee's Mill

*BURNT
CHIMNEYS*

KEYES

Warwick River

Surry Court House

SUMNER

Hampton

Fort Monroe

Hampton Roads

General Daniel Harvey Hill, one of the South's ablest commanders, led the main Confederate attack at Seven Pines, encouraging his men by riding through enemy fire while puffing a cigar.

CONFEDERATE ATTACK, MAY 31

The two-day battle called Seven Pines by the South, Fair Oaks by the Union, began at 1:00 p.m. when D. H. Hill's 8,500-man Rebel division attacked and routed the Federal division of Silas Casey. Hill's swift advance was stopped by a second Union line made up of Darius Couch's division and Philip Kearny's two brigades. Then, however, two Confederate regiments led by Colonel Micah Jenkins moved behind the Federals' flank and forced them to retreat down the Williamsburg Stage Road. In a virtually separate battle to the north, W. H. C. Whiting's Confederates made little headway against a Union line that was reinforced by the division of John Sedgwick.

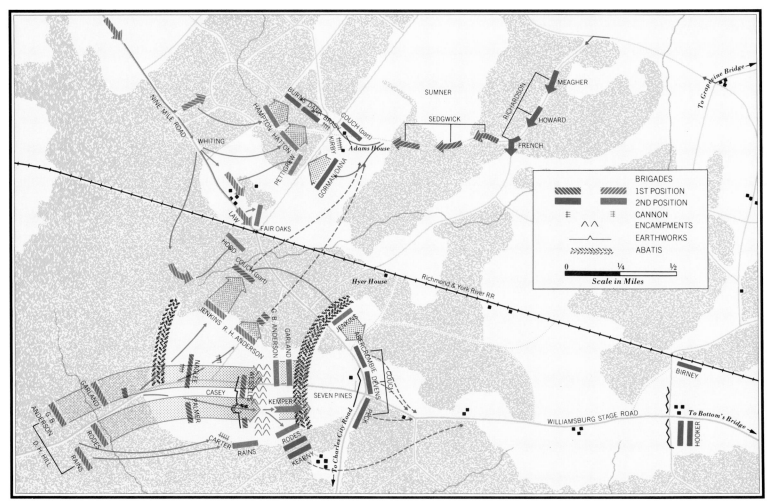

Troops of the 104th Pennsylvania, part of H. M. Naglee's brigade, bravely counterattack west of Seven Pines on the afternoon of May 31, trying to slow D. H. Hill's advancing Confederates *(right)*.

FEDERAL COUNTERATTACK, JUNE 1

Shortly after dawn, D. H. Hill sent two brigades along Williamsburg Road to relieve Micah Jenkins and block any counterattack westward. He then ordered three brigades northward toward the railroad in an attack that was violently repulsed by Israel Richardson's division. First pushing back William Mahone's troops, the Federals then exploited a gap between the brigades of George E. Pickett and Lewis A. Armistead, inflicting heavy casualties. At the same time, fresh Federal troops under General Joseph Hooker pushed back the Rebels on Williamsburg Road. Around 1:00 p.m., Hill ordered a general retreat and the battle sputtered to a conclusion.

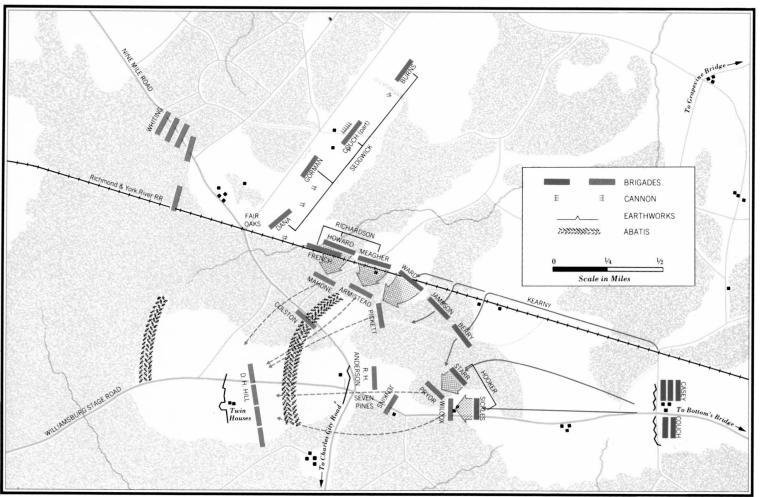

ORDER OF BATTLE

ARMY OF NORTHERN VIRGINIA
LEE
60,000 MEN

LONGSTREET'S DIVISION	D. H. HILL'S DIVISION	A. P. HILL'S DIVISION	HUGER'S DIVISION	HOLMES' "COMMAND"
KEMPER'S BRIGADE	RODES' BRIGADE	FIELD'S BRIGADE	MAHONE'S BRIGADE	RANSOM'S BRIGADE
R. H. ANDERSON'S BRIGADE	G. B. ANDERSON'S BRIGADE	GREGG'S BRIGADE	WRIGHT'S BRIGADE	DANIEL'S BRIGADE
PICKETT'S BRIGADE	GARLAND'S BRIGADE	J. R. ANDERSON'S BRIGADE	ARMISTEAD'S BRIGADE	WALKER'S BRIGADE
WILCOX'S BRIGADE	COLQUITT'S BRIGADE	BRANCH'S BRIGADE		WISE'S BRIGADE
PRYOR'S BRIGADE	RIPLEY'S BRIGADE	ARCHER'S BRIGADE		
FEATHERSTON'S BRIGADE		PENDER'S BRIGADE		

JACKSON'S "COMMAND"

WHITING'S DIVISION	JACKSON'S DIVISION	EWELL'S DIVISION
HOOD'S BRIGADE	WINDER'S BRIGADE	ELZEY'S BRIGADE
LAW'S BRIGADE	CUNNINGHAM'S BRIGADE	TRIMBLE'S BRIGADE
	FULKERSON'S BRIGADE	SEYMOUR'S BRIGADE
	LAWTON'S BRIGADE	

MAGRUDER'S "COMMAND"

D. R. JONES' DIVISION	McLAWS' DIVISION	MAGRUDER'S DIVISION
TOOMBS' BRIGADE	SEMMES' BRIGADE	COBB'S BRIGADE
G. T. ANDERSON'S BRIGADE	KERSHAW'S BRIGADE	BARKSDALE'S BRIGADE

CAVALRY
STUART
UNBRIGADED REGIMENTS

ARMY OF THE POTOMAC
McCLELLAN
100,000 MEN

II CORPS SUMNER

FIRST DIVISION: RICHARDSON
Brigades: CALDWELL, MEAGHER, FRENCH

SECOND DIVISION: SEDGWICK
Brigades: SULLY, BURNS, DANA

III CORPS HEINTZELMAN

SECOND DIVISION: HOOKER
Brigades: GROVER, SICKLES, CARR

THIRD DIVISION: KEARNY
Brigades: ROBINSON, BIRNEY, BERRY

IV CORPS KEYES

FIRST DIVISION: COUCH
Brigades: HOWE, ABERCROMBIE, PALMER

SECOND DIVISION: PECK
Brigades: NAGLEE, WESSELLS

V CORPS PORTER

FIRST DIVISION: MORELL
Brigades: MARTINDALE, GRIFFIN, BUTTERFIELD

SECOND DIVISION: SYKES
Brigades: BUCHANAN, LOVELL, WARREN

THIRD DIVISION: McCALL
Brigades: REYNOLDS, SEYMOUR, MEADE

VI CORPS FRANKLIN

FIRST DIVISION: SLOCUM
Brigades: TAYLOR, BARTLETT, NEWTON

SECOND DIVISION: SMITH
Brigades: HANCOCK, BROOKS, DAVIDSON

CAVALRY RESERVE: COOKE

GEN. ROBERT E. LEE

The bloody stalemate of Seven Pines brought a momentous change: Johnston, wounded during the battle, was replaced by Robert E. Lee. With stunning speed and decisiveness, Lee reorganized the battered Rebel army and prepared to launch an offensive. Badly outnumbered, he summoned Stonewall Jackson's force from the Shenandoah. After repulsing a Federal attack on June 25, the next day Lee sparked the first major fight of what came to be called the Seven Days' Battles. Leaving only a thin screen of troops under John Magruder to defend Richmond, he boldly moved the bulk of his army northward to strike Fitz-John Porter's V Corps, isolated on the Federal right near Mechanicsville. Porter repulsed the attack but was ordered by McClellan to pull back to the vicinity of Gaines' Mill, where the following day he was hammered again *(next pages)* and forced to retreat south across the Chickahominy River. During the next three days an alarmed McClellan shifted his base of operations and his entire army southward to the James River, beating back Lee's attempts to cut him off at Savage's Station and around White Oak Swamp on June 29 and 30. On July 1, both sides girded for a climactic battle at Malvern Hill.

William F. Smith *(center, on horseback)* orders troops of the Vermont brigade to cover the withdrawal of a gun crew *(right)* during a rearguard action at White Oak Swamp on June 30. Smith's division, part of William Franklin's corps, played a vital role in slowing the advance of the Confederates under Jackson and D. H. Hill.

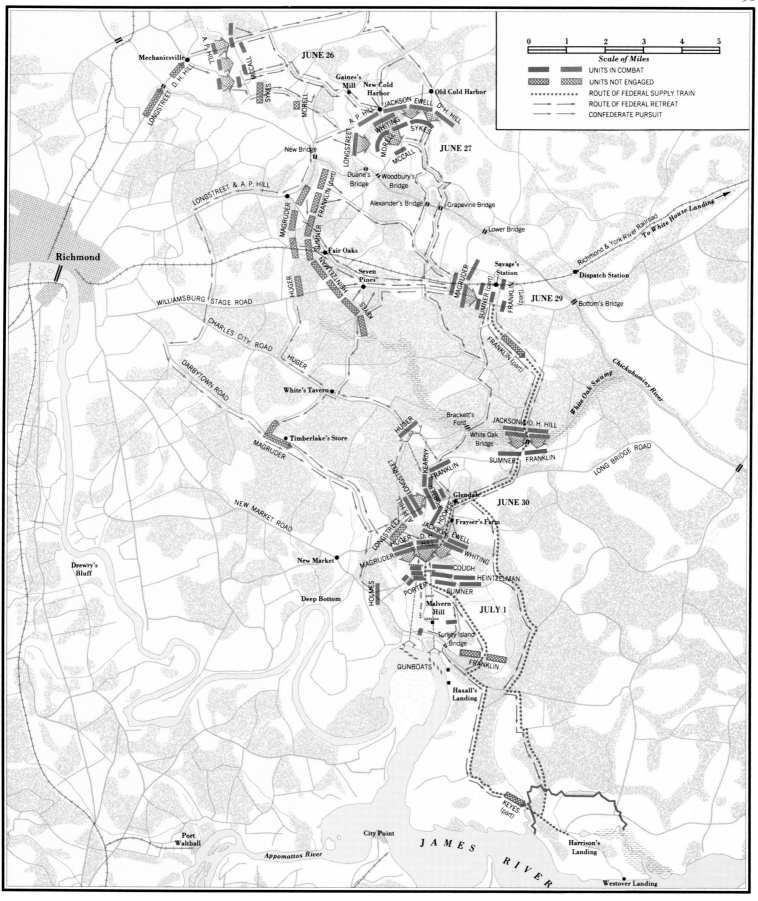

Scale of Miles

| 0 | 1 | 2 | 3 | 4 | 5 |

UNITS IN COMBAT

UNITS NOT ENGAGED

••••••••••• ROUTE OF FEDERAL SUPPLY TRAIN

——→ ROUTE OF FEDERAL RETREAT

——→ CONFEDERATE PURSUIT

Mechanicsville

JUNE 26

A. P. HILL

LONGSTREET D. H. HILL

McCALL

SYKES

Gaines's Mill

New Cold Harbor

MORELL

Old Cold Harbor

A. P. HILL

JACKSON EWELL D. H. HILL

LONGSTREET

WHITING

MORELL SYKES

McCALL

JUNE 27

New Bridge

LONGSTREET & A. P. HILL

Duane's Bridge

Woodbury's Bridge

MAGRUDER

FRANKLIN (part)

SUMNER

Alexander's Bridge

Grapevine Bridge

HUGER

HEINTZELMAN

Fair Oaks

Seven Pines

Lower Bridge

Richmond & York River Railroad

To White House Landing

Richmond

WILLIAMSBURG STAGE ROAD

KEYES

MAGRUDER

SUMNER (part)

Savage's Station

Dispatch Station

JUNE 29

Bottom's Bridge

CHARLES CITY ROAD

HUGER

FRANKLIN (part)

White Oak Swamp

Chickahominy River

DARBYTOWN ROAD

White's Tavern

Brackett's Ford

JACKSON & D. H. HILL

MAGRUDER

Timberlake's Store

HUGER

White Oak Bridge

SUMNER FRANKLIN

LONG BRIDGE ROAD

NEW MARKET ROAD

KEARNY

FRANKLIN

LONGSTREET

PORTER

HOOKER

Glendale

JUNE 30

A. P. HILL

Frayser's Farm

JACKSON EWELL

New Market

MAGRUDER

LONGSTREET

HUGER

D. H. HILL

WHITING

COUCH

HEINTZELMAN

HOLMES

PORTER

SUMNER

Deep Bottom

Malvern Hill

JULY 1

Drewry's Bluff

Turkey Island Bridge

GUNBOATS

FRANKLIN

Haxall's Landing

Port Walthall

City Point

Appomattox River

JAMES RIVER

KEYES (part)

Harrison's Landing

Westover Landing

In the midst of the desperate fighting on the Confederate left, Colonel Bradley Johnson halts his 1st Maryland Infantry of Richard Ewell's division and drills the ranks under fire after they faltered during a charge. The men quickly recovered, hurled themselves at the Union line, and drove it back.

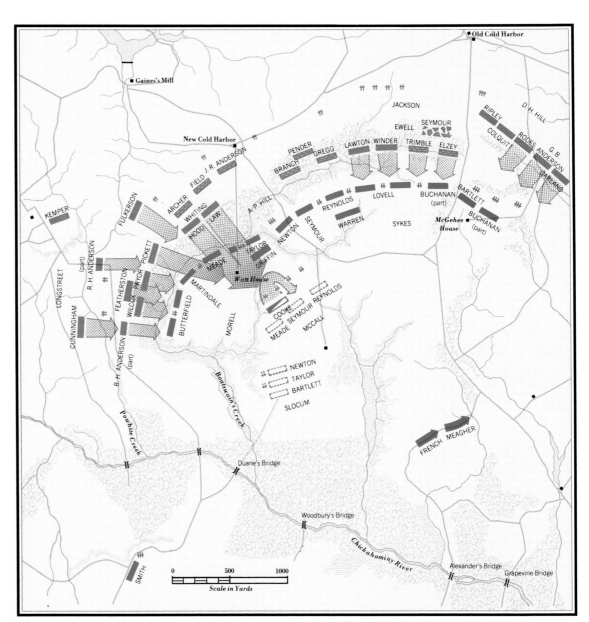

After an inconclusive fight at Mechanicsville on June 26, Lee attacked Fitz-John Porter's Federal V Corps the next day north of the Chickahominy River with Jackson's forces from the Shenandoah Valley and the divisions of James Longstreet, Ambrose Powell Hill, and D. H. Hill. A. P. Hill led off the battle around 2:00 p.m., pushing Porter's rear guard a mile southeastward from a large gristmill—Gaines' Mill—and then launching an attack on the Union center just past the village of New Cold Har-

bor. By midafternoon, Longstreet had come up on A. P. Hill's right, and Richard Ewell's division of Jackson's command later took positions to Hill's left. About 7:00 p.m., the Confederates, 56,000 strong, attacked all along the line. The decisive moment of the battle came when John Bell Hood's brigade of Whiting's division broke through and routed the Federal center, forcing the stubborn Porter to withdraw his entire corps across the Chickahominy during the night.

In a dramatic painting by William Trego, troopers of the 5th U.S. Cavalry, part of Cooke's cavalry reserve, make a desperate charge to rescue Federal artillery batteries threatened by the Rebel advance. The gallant try was futile. Hood's Confederate brigade beat off the attack in vicious fighting that killed or wounded more than half the Union horsemen.

MALVERN HILL

After falling back with Lee in hot pursuit, Mc-Clellan's army finally turned to stand and fight at Malvern Hill, a large plateau near the James River. The Federals formed up along the northern rim of the 100-foot-high hill, deploying most of their infantry and 250 guns. Lee, eager for the kill, massed the bulk of five divisions and attacked shortly after 4:00 p.m. on July 1. Despite the fact that their own artillery had been mauled by the mass of Federal cannon, Rebel infantrymen hurled themselves up the flanks of the hill— Magruder's six brigades on the right and D. H. Hill's and Huger's divisions on the left. Wave after Rebel wave attacked, only to be mowed down by the storm of Federal artillery and infantry fire. Not until nearly 9:00 p.m. did the Confederates give up their futile assaults. By then they had added more than 5,000 casualties to the 15,000 Lee had lost since June 26. Despite the bloody repulse of Lee at Malvern Hill, a nervous McClellan pulled back his army during the night to Harrison's Landing, where it sat for six weeks before being withdrawn from the Peninsula. The Seven Days' Battles had cost the Federals nearly 16,000 men and ended any chance for a quick capture of the Confederate capital.

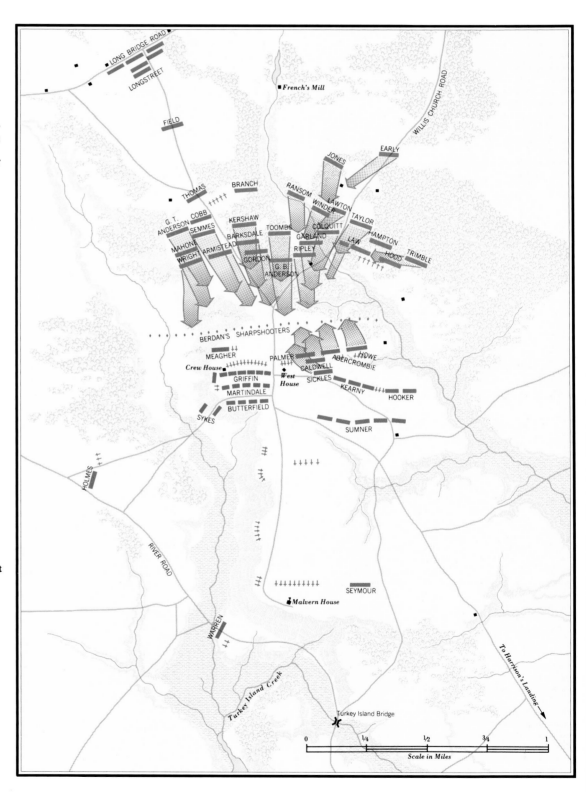

Firing over their own battle lines, Federal gunners on a slope of Malvern Hill blaze away at Confederate brigades advancing across open ground in the distance. One Union battery fired nearly 1,400 rounds during the battle, switching from shot and shell to shotgun-like loads of case and canister as the advancing Confederates closed the distance.

The U.S. Navy gunboats *Galena* (left) and *Mahaska* lob shells over Malvern Hill at Confederate positions beyond. A signalman atop the farmhouse at center wig-wagged firing directions to the ships while Union infantry waited in reserve on the near slope.

Following the Seven Days' Battles, Mc-Clellan's army, camped on the James River only 20 miles from Richmond, remained a threat to the Confederate capital. Nevertheless, in mid-July, Robert E. Lee reorganized his army into two commands under Jackson and Longstreet and embarked on a series of daring moves that took the War north, back to the doorstep of Washington. Counting on McClellan's continuing inertia, Lee first sent Jackson northwestward to block the advance of a Federal army from that quarter. Then he turned his back on McClellan entirely and launched an offensive with all his forces where the Federals least expected it, initiating a campaign that for a time reversed the tide of the War.

The Union army that Lee set out to attack was in effect a new one, although made of old parts. The Lincoln government, hoping to stir up some action, combined three Federal forces in northern Virginia—the corps of Irvin McDowell, Nathaniel Banks, and Franz Sigel—and gave them a new leader, Major General John Pope. Pope's mission was to protect Washington and the Upper Shenandoah and, if possible, sever Lee's connections with the Valley. But before Pope could concentrate his forces, he found himself facing Jackson advancing from the south. Within weeks, Pope was embroiled with Lee's entire army in a ferocious fight that resulted in a devastating Union defeat.

A Federal supply train pulls into the station at Culpeper Courthouse on the Orange & Alexandria Railroad in late July 1862. Much of Pope's command was strung along this rail line, which formed a vital link between the army and the huge Union supply depots at Manassas Junction and Alexandria. Lee's advance north from Gordonsville forced the Federals to abandon Culpeper in mid-August.

Major General John Pope was named commander of the Union's new Army of Virginia after leading Federal troops to victory at New Madrid and Corinth along the Mississippi River in the Western theater.

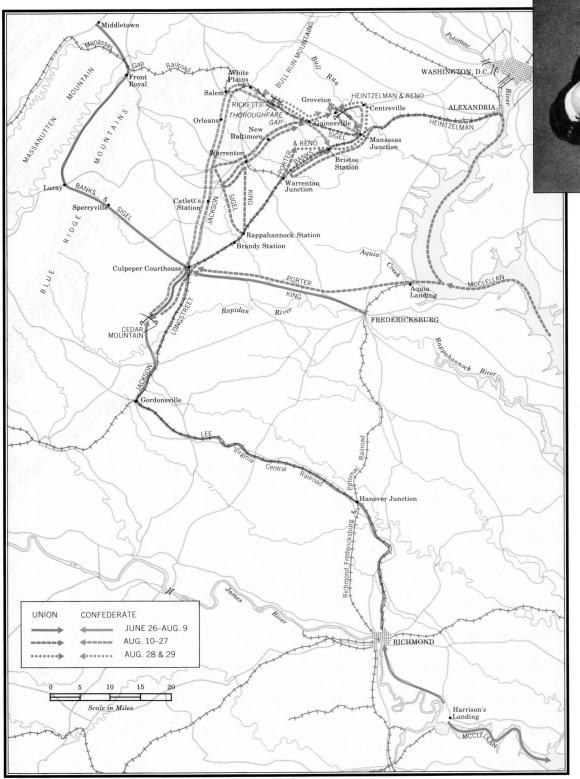

UNION	CONFEDERATE
→	← JUNE 26–AUG. 9
┈►	┈◄ AUG. 10–27
⋯►	⋯◄ AUG. 28 & 29

0   5   10   15   20
Scale in Miles

In the first stage of his advance from Richmond, Lee rushed Jackson's command to Gordonsville via the Virginia Central Railroad in mid-July. A. P. Hill followed and joined Jackson in repulsing the Federals at Cedar Mountain on August 9. Then Lee sent Jackson circling around Pope's army and into its rear via Thoroughfare Gap. After raiding the Union supply depot at Manassas Junction, Jackson took up positions northwest of Bull Run. Lee and Longstreet, following the same route, caught up on August 29, uniting the army's two wings. In mid-August, meanwhile, Pope had ordered the scattered corps of McDowell, Sigel, and Banks to concentrate north of the Rappahannock River. Pope also received reinforcements shipped up the Potomac—most notably Heintzelman's III Corps and Porter's V Corps from McClellan's army, which was now withdrawing from the Peninsula. But not until August 26, after Jackson's raid, did Pope come up with a plan. Believing he could destroy Jackson, he ordered his dispersed forces to find and attack the waiting Confederates.

Samuel Crawford's
Federals charge
through woods
and over a rail
fence at Cedar
Mountain, routing
Jackson's left
flank, including
the famed Stone-
wall Brigade,
which up to that
time had never
been driven from
the field.

In a sketch done for a Northern magazine, Federal ambulances line up near a farmhouse used
as a hospital at Cedar Mountain. The numbers keyed the scene for the magazine's editors;
for example, the *4* indicates Union guns firing at Confederate positions north of Cedar Run.

The first battle of the campaign flared at Cedar Mountain on the afternoon of August 9 when Jackson and A. P. Hill, probing northward from Gordonsville, ran into Nathaniel Banks' corps, which was leading Pope's slow, strung-out advance. The Federals, despite knowing they were outnumbered more than two to one, launched an attack—which nearly succeeded. Lying undetected in thick woods, Crawford's 1,700-man brigade suddenly burst upon the Confederate left, routing the brigades of Ronald, Garnett, and Taliaferro of Winder's division. But the Federals lacked the reserves to exploit Crawford's breakthrough. As the Union attack faltered, Jackson counterattacked with the brigades of Branch, Archer, and Pender of Hill's division, smashing Crawford's brigade and driving Banks' forces from the field. It was a badly mismanaged battle on both sides that left 3,700 dead and wounded.

General Charles Winder, one of Jackson's most trusted subordinates, was killed by a shell at Cedar Mountain shortly before the attack that shattered his division.

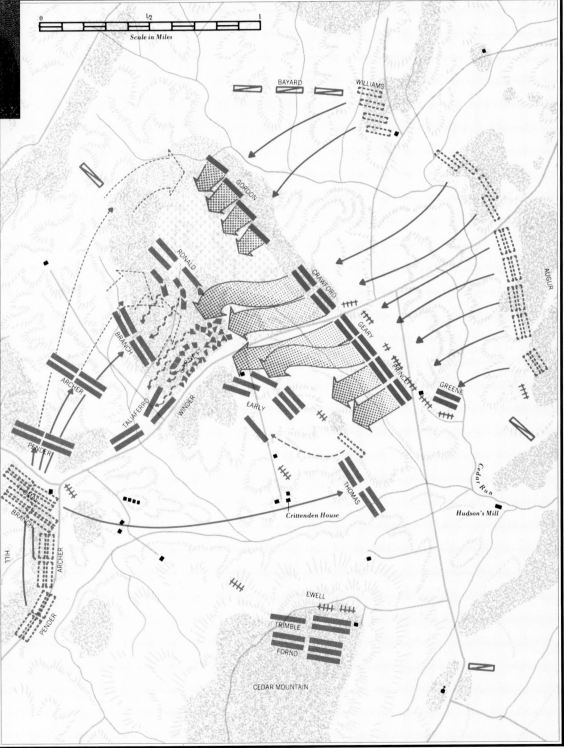

ORDER OF BATTLE

ARMY OF NORTHERN VIRGINIA
LEE
55,000 MEN

LEFT WING (FIRST CORPS)
JACKSON

W. B. TALIAFERRO'S DIVISION	A. P. HILL'S DIVISION	EWELL'S DIVISION
BAYLOR'S BRIGADE	BRANCH'S BRIGADE	LAWTON'S BRIGADE
JOHNSON'S BRIGADE	ARCHER'S BRIGADE	EARLY'S BRIGADE
A. G. TALIAFERRO'S BRIGADE	PENDER'S BRIGADE	TRIMBLE'S BRIGADE
STARKE'S BRIGADE	FIELD'S BRIGADE	STRONG'S BRIGADE
	GREGG'S BRIGADE	
	THOMAS' BRIGADE	

RIGHT WING (SECOND CORPS)
LONGSTREET

R. H. ANDERSON'S DIVISION	D. R. JONES' DIVISION	WILCOX'S DIVISION	HOOD'S/EVANS' DIVISION	KEMPER'S DIVISION
ARMISTEAD'S BRIGADE	BENNING'S BRIGADE	WILCOX'S BRIGADE	HOOD'S BRIGADE	CORSE'S BRIGADE
MAHONE'S BRIGADE	DRAYTON'S BRIGADE	PRYOR'S BRIGADE	LAW'S BRIGADE	JENKINS' BRIGADE
WRIGHT'S BRIGADE	G. T. ANDERSON'S BRIGADE	FEATHERSTON'S BRIGADE	STEVENS' BRIGADE	HUNTON'S BRIGADE

CAVALRY
STUART

HAMPTON'S BRIGADE   F. LEE'S BRIGADE

ROBERTSON'S BRIGADE

ARMY OF VIRGINIA
POPE
70,000 MEN

I CORPS SIGEL	II CORPS BANKS	III CORPS McDOWELL
FIRST DIVISION: SCHENCK *Brigades:* STAHEL, McLEAN	FIRST DIVISION: WILLIAMS *Brigades:* CRAWFORD, GORDON	FIRST DIVISION: KING *Brigades:* HATCH, DOUBLEDAY, PATRICK, GIBBON
SECOND DIVISION: VON STEINWEHR (KOLTES' BRIGADE ONLY)	SECOND DIVISION: GREENE *Brigades:* CANDY, SCHLAUDECKER, TAIT	SECOND DIVISION: RICKETTS *Brigades:* DURYEA, TOWER, STILES, THOBURN
THIRD DIVISION: SCHURZ *Brigades:* SCHIMMELFENNIG, KRZYZANOWSKI, MILROY	CAVALRY BRIGADE: BUFORD	REYNOLDS' DIVISION *Brigades:* MEADE, SEYMOUR, JACKSON
CAVALRY BRIGADE: BEARDSLEY		CAVALRY BRIGADE: BAYARD

RESERVE CORPS STURGIS
(PIATT'S BRIGADE ONLY)

from: ARMY OF THE POTOMAC

III CORPS HEINTZELMAN	V CORPS PORTER	IX CORPS (UNDER RENO'S COMMAND)
FIRST DIVISION: KEARNY *Brigades:* ROBINSON, BIRNEY, POE	FIRST DIVISION: MORELL *Brigades:* ROBERTS, GRIFFIN, BUTTERFIELD	FIRST DIVISION: STEVENS *Brigades:* CHRIST, LEASURE, FARNSWORTH
SECOND DIVISION: HOOKER *Brigades:* GROVER, TAYLOR, CARR	SECOND DIVISION: SYKES *Brigades:* BUCHANAN, CHAPMAN, WARREN	SECOND DIVISION: RENO *Brigades:* NAGLE, FERRERO
	VI CORPS (TAYLOR'S BRIGADE ONLY)	

Battle flag flying, jubilant Georgia infantrymen of Colonel Evander Law's brigade fire down on Ricketts' Federals, who had arrived to block Thoroughfare Gap in the Bull Run Mountains on August 28, two days after Jackson had gotten through. Law's Georgians reopened the gap, allowing Longstreet's command to pass through and join Jackson.

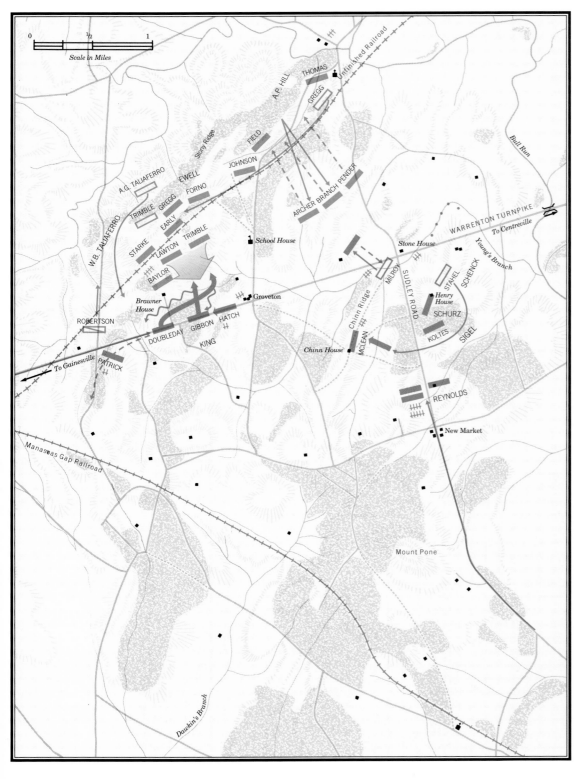

BRAWNER'S FARM, AUGUST 28

After falling back from Manassas Junction in three columns on August 27, Jackson reunited his force along Stony Ridge just north of the Warrenton Turnpike near Groveton. There he waited behind an unfinished railroad embankment for Lee and Longstreet. But, before their arrival, the combative Jackson touched off the battle on the afternoon of August 28 when the four Federal brigades of King's division, marching east along the turnpike to join Pope in Centreville, passed Jackson's hidden positions. Concerned that time was now on the side of Pope, Jackson decided to strike. He let the first Union brigade of John Hatch go by, then ordered his batteries to shell John Gibbon's brigade, which followed after. Gibbon sent a line of skirmishers advancing toward the guns up a slope on a farm owned by John Brawner—and found himself facing six Confederate brigades from Taliaferro's and Ewell's divisions. While the two forces traded volleys from lines only 75 yards apart, Abner Doubleday, whose Federal brigade had been following Gibbon's, rushed up to help. The battle sputtered out only when darkness came and the men found themselves aiming at each other's muzzle flashes. The Federals finally fell back, and the exhausted Confederates did not pursue. Casualties were heavy—about 1,300 on each side—with Gibbon losing more than 900 of his 2,100 men. Jackson also lost two division commanders, Generals Ewell and Taliaferro, both of whom were wounded.

FEDERAL ATTACKS, AUGUST 29

After Jackson revealed his position at Brawner's Farm, Pope ordered all available units to converge on the Bull Run battlefield. He failed, however, to outline a coherent plan of attack. The result was a series of piecemeal assaults that never employed more than a fraction of the Union strength. Most of the attacks were thrown back by murderous fire from Confederate infantry entrenched behind the ready-made bulwark of the railroad embankment. On the Federal right, Grover's brigade of Hooker's division cut through Lawton's first and second lines but, unsupported, was stopped by the third line. On the Federals' far right, Philip Kearny led a furious rush that nearly overwhelmed Gregg's South Carolinians, but the Federals were thrown back by A. P. Hill's reserves. Meanwhile, unknown to Pope, Longstreet's entire wing had arrived on the Confederate right, ready to outflank and roll up the Federal left. A late-afternoon probe by troops from Hood's division was met head-on in a brutal encounter with Hatch's division (formerly King's) that ended in a stalemate after sundown. South of the turnpike, Fitz-John Porter's V Corps remained inactive. Having belatedly received attack orders that arrived almost at dusk, Porter refused to advance, in part because of ominous signs that a huge force was massing on the Confederate right.

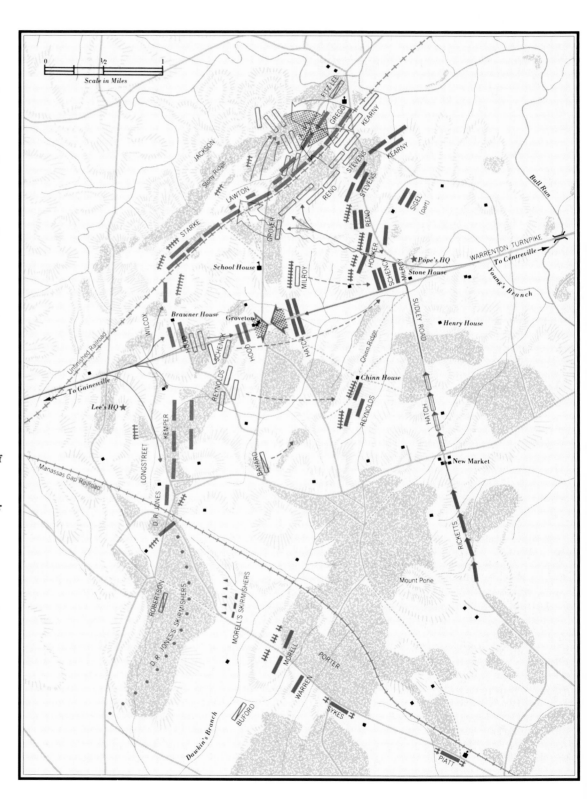

Confederate infantry, from the cover of the railroad embankment, hurl rocks into a wave of Federal attackers. The Confederates also had the advantage of the high ground provided by the ridge line that Jackson had chosen for his defensive position.

Philip Kearny, who led the attack on the Rebel left on August 29, was killed three days later in a brief, bloody fight that followed the main battle. Even the Confederates mourned the death of so gallant a man.

A photograph made after the battle shows the Warrenton Turnpike running past a farm *(foreground)* and the railroad cut atop the distant slope.

Confederate batteries under S. D. Lee, deployed on the far right of Jackson's line, fire furiously to stem the strong Federal attacks in the early afternoon of August 30. Lee and Longstreet, with their staffs *(on horseback, right)*, plan the assault on the Union left. Longstreet waited until the Federals were fully committed against Jackson's line before giving the order to attack.

LONGSTREET'S ATTACK, AUGUST 30

Pope, still unaware of Longstreet's presence, massed virtually his entire army north of the Warrenton Turnpike on the morning of the 30th for what, he thought, would be a final, crushing attack on Jackson's line. The leading Federal units were engaged in storming the railroad cut when Longstreet, shortly before 4:00 p.m., launched his massive and unexpected attack. Anderson's division and part of Hood's surged forward north of the turnpike, crossing in front of Jackson's embattled right. More of Hood's men smashed through Warren's New York brigade—virtually the only Federals still south of the pike. Farther south, Longstreet's divisions, led by Jones and Kemper, advanced unopposed toward Chinn Ridge in a dangerous flanking movement. By 5:00, Pope, at last realizing what was afoot, dispatched reinforcements, first from Sigel's and McDowell's corps, across the pike to Chinn Ridge and Henry House Hill to slow the Confederate attack. These and other troops put up a fighting withdrawal that slowed Longstreet's advance long enough to save the Federal army from annihilation.

In one of the last attacks by the Federals during the afternoon of August 30, Lieutenant Colonel William Chapman *(on horseback, right)* leads his Regular Army brigade in a charge on Jackson's line. "The slope was swept by a hurricane of death," a Union survivor said, "and each minute seemed 20 hours long."

A panoramic view of the battle sketched from the slope of Henry House Hill in midafternoon, August 30, shows Pope's line on the ridge in the middle distance facing Jackson's troops, in their positions on the wooded slope beyond. At right is the Stone House; at left, Milroy's brigade moves toward Chinn Ridge.

Federal infantrymen flee in panic from onrushing Confederates despite the efforts of a mounted officer to stem the rout.

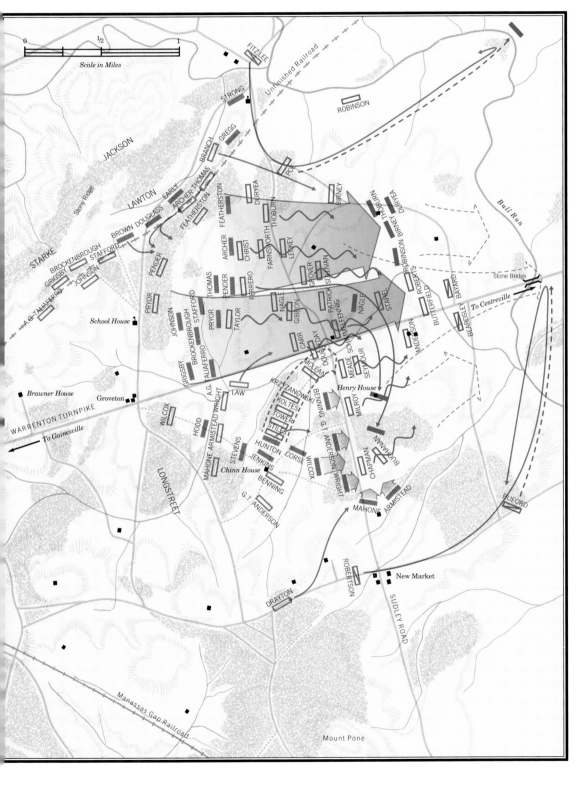

Scale in Miles

CONFEDERATE ATTACKS AND FEDERAL RETREAT

Shortly after 5:00 p.m., the bulk of Longstreet's command hurled itself against the hastily formed Federal line on Chinn Ridge. In less than an hour, despite a ferocious defense, the Confederates had control of the ridge. Now Pope's entire left began to give way, the troops retreating toward the turnpike. About 6:00, Jackson's troops attacked the center and right of Pope's army. Some Federal units, including Gibbon's brigade and Kearny's men, held for a time, but eventually they were driven back toward Bull Run and the Stone Bridge. Saving the Federals from complete disaster were brigades from the divisions of Reynolds, Sykes, Reno, and Schurz, who stubbornly held the Manassas-Sudley Road, then the slopes of Henry House Hill, preventing the Confederate right from reaching the turnpike and clamping shut the Federal line of withdrawal. As dusk fell, the Confederate attack ended, and Pope's army made an orderly retreat. By midnight, all but a few stragglers were across Bull Run and trudging toward Centreville and Washington. The casualties in the two-day battle were horrendous. Pope's ill-led army lost 14,462 men, Lee's forces 9,474.

ANTIETAM CAMPAIGN

Immediately after his stunning victory at Bull Run, Robert E. Lee decided to keep the initiative by thrusting into Maryland. Although his army was depleted and exhausted, its morale was soaring, and the plan offered several attractions. Northern Virginia had been stripped of foodstuffs; Maryland held the promise of a rich autumn harvest to feed the Confederate troops. Lee's move north would draw Federal forces away from war-ravaged Confederate territory and forestall any advance on Richmond. And, possibly, his invasion of the Union would so galvanize discontent over the War in the North that Lincoln would be forced to sue for peace.

Soon after Lee crossed the Potomac River into Maryland on September 4, the Union army, reorganized once again under George McClellan, moved westward to intercept the Confederates. Within two weeks, the rival forces would collide along Antietam Creek near the dusty village of Sharpsburg. The battle there would rank as the bloodiest one-day encounter of the entire Civil War.

A Federal scout shoots at men of Lee's army as they wade across the Potomac at White's Ford on the night of September 4, 1862.

After a final clash with John Pope's rear guard at Chantilly on September 1, Lee marched his army northward, crossing the Potomac at two fords near Leesburg and moving on to Frederick, in Maryland. There, on September 10, he daringly ordered a temporary four-way split of his army. James Longstreet and D. H. Hill headed north to threaten Hagerstown and southern Pennsylvania. Stonewall Jackson, John Walker, and Lafayette McLaws took three widely divergent routes to surprise the Federal garrison at Harpers Ferry, capture that Union outpost, and open a Confederate supply line through the Shenandoah Valley. On September 5, McClellan had taken up the pursuit, dividing his divisions into three wings that advanced toward Frederick on a front 25 miles wide. Ambrose Burnside and his column hooked northward to protect the Baltimore & Ohio tracks. Edwin Sumner marched his wing on two middle routes via Gaithersburg and Darnestown. William Franklin's wing hugged the Maryland shore of the Potomac. The advance guard approached Frederick on September 11, the day after Lee's divisions had left the city. There McClellan learned of the Confederate plans from a copy of Lee's orders that somehow had been lost, and he pushed his army westward hoping to catch the Rebels while they were still spread across the countryside. But Lee, suspecting the Federal intentions, ordered McLaws and Jackson to speed up the capture of Harpers Ferry, and Longstreet and D. H. Hill to block the Federal advance at South Mountain to gain time. After an opening clash there on September 14, Lee's army fell back toward Sharpsburg to await the oncoming Federals.

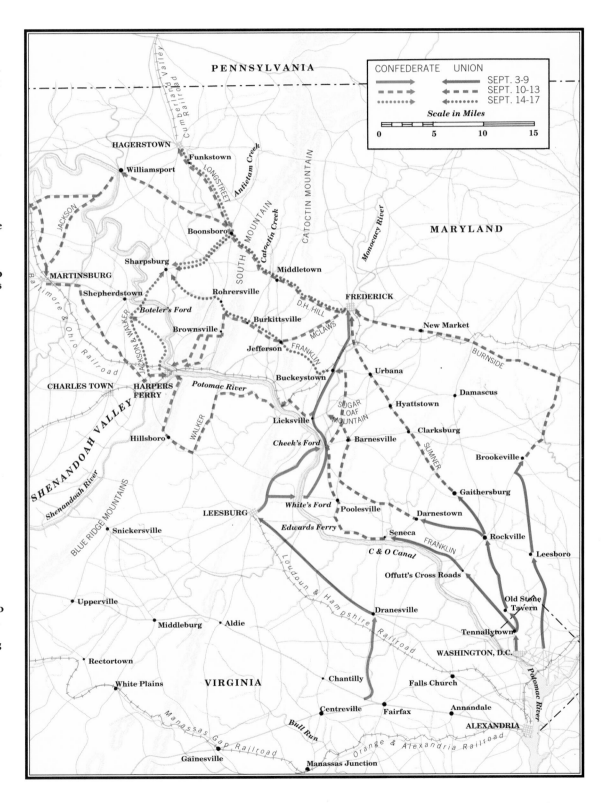

Troops of Jacob Cox's division storm a hill defended by Samuel Garland's Confederates during the Federal assault at Fox's Gap. In the left foreground, two soldiers attend their wounded regimental commander, Rutherford B. Hayes.

In a Federal assault at dusk on the north side of Turner's Gap, Pennsylvanians of John Hatch's division overrun Alabama troops who had been firing from behind stone outcroppings on the gap's wooded crest.

The first crisis of Lee's campaign came when McClellan arrived on September 14 with three Federal corps at South Mountain, a long ridge that stretched roughly 40 miles from the Potomac River to Pennsylvania. With Jackson absent at Harpers Ferry and other units still scattered, Lee ordered the few troops available to hold the South Mountain passes at all costs until he could reunite his army. The initial Federal attack came shortly after dawn, when Cox's division from Reno's IX Corps tried to outflank the Confederates holding Turner's Gap by taking nearby Fox's Gap. After a sharp two-hour battle, the Federals drove off Garland's brigade, and by midday the lead elements of Reno's corps had passed through the gap and were advancing north along a ridge toward Turner's Gap. The Federals were stopped, however, by D. H. Hill's division and just-arriving troops from Longstreet's command. This attack stymied, McClellan ordered Gibbon's brigade to march straight for Turner's Gap while the rest of Hooker's I Corps hit the Confederates from the north. Gibbon could make little progress, but eventually attacks by Hatch and Meade forced the Confederates from the pass—only to have darkness stop the fighting and allow the troops of Hill and Longstreet to withdraw in good order. The main Union success came at Crampton's Gap six miles to the south, where Franklin's VI Corps easily defeated a handful of Confederate defenders. But Franklin failed to follow up, losing a chance to hit McLaws' lone division marching up from Harpers Ferry.

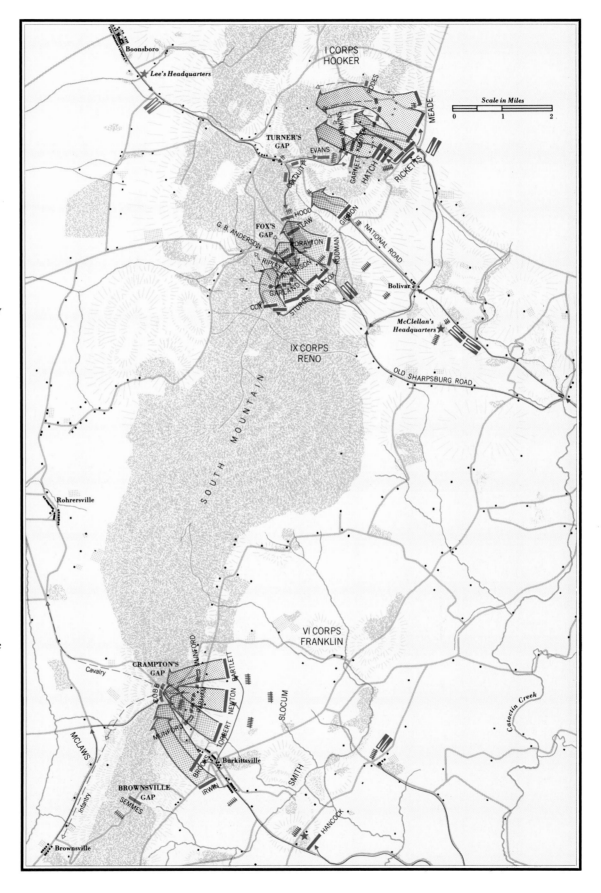

ORDER OF BATTLE
ARMY OF NORTHERN VIRGINIA
LEE
39,200 MEN

LONGSTREET'S CORPS

McLAWS' DIVISION	R. H. ANDERSON'S DIVISION	D. R. JONES' DIVISION	J. G. WALKER'S DIVISION	HOOD'S DIVISION
KERSHAW'S BRIGADE	CUMMING'S BRIGADE	TOOMBS' BRIGADE	MANNING'S BRIGADE	WOFFORD'S BRIGADE
MacRAE'S BRIGADE	POSEY'S BRIGADE	DRAYTON'S BRIGADE	RANSOM'S BRIGADE	LAW'S BRIGADE
SEMMES' BRIGADE	ARMISTEAD'S BRIGADE	GARNETT'S BRIGADE		EVANS' BRIGADE
BARKSDALE'S BRIGADE	PRYOR'S BRIGADE	KEMPER'S BRIGADE		
	PARHAM'S BRIGADE	J. WALKER'S BRIGADE		
	WRIGHT'S BRIGADE	G. T. ANDERSON'S BRIGADE		

JACKSON'S CORPS

LAWTON'S DIVISION	A. P. HILL'S DIVISION	J. R. JONES' DIVISION	D. H. HILL'S DIVISION
DOUGLASS' BRIGADE	BRANCH'S BRIGADE	GRIGSBY'S BRIGADE	RIPLEY'S BRIGADE
EARLY'S BRIGADE	GREGG'S BRIGADE	WARREN'S BRIGADE	RODE'S BRIGADE
J. A. WALKER'S BRIGADE	BROCKENBROUGH'S BRIGADE	PENN'S BRIGADE	McRAE'S BRIGADE
HAYS' BRIGADE	ARCHER'S BRIGADE	STARKE'S BRIGADE	G. B. ANDERSON'S BRIGADE
	PENDER'S BRIGADE		COLQUITT'S BRIGADE

CAVALRY
STUART

HAMPTON'S BRIGADE   MUNFORD'S BRIGADE

F. LEE'S BRIGADE

ARMY OF THE POTOMAC
McCLELLAN
70,000 MEN

I CORPS HOOKER

FIRST DIVISION: DOUBLEDAY
Brigades: PHELPS, HOFMANN, PATRICK, GIBBON

SECOND DIVISION: RICKETTS
Brigades: DURYEA, CHRISTIAN, HARTSUFF

THIRD DIVISION: MEADE
Brigades: SEYMOUR, MAGILTON, ANDERSON

II CORPS SUMNER

FIRST DIVISION: RICHARDSON
Brigades: CALDWELL, MEAGHER, BROOKE

SECOND DIVISION: SEDGWICK
Brigades: GORMAN, HOWARD, DANA

THIRD DIVISION: FRENCH
Brigades: KIMBALL, MORRIS, WEBER

V CORPS PORTER

FIRST DIVISION: MORELL
Brigades: BARNES, GRIFFIN, STOCKTON

SECOND DIVISION: SYKES
Brigades: BUCHANAN, LOVELL, WARREN

THIRD DIVISION: HUMPHREYS
Brigades: TYLER, ALLABACH

VI CORPS FRANKLIN

FIRST DIVISION: SLOCUM
Brigades: TORBERT, BARTLETT, NEWTON

SECOND DIVISION: SMITH
Brigades: HANCOCK, BROOKS, IRWIN

IX CORPS BURNSIDE

FIRST DIVISION: WILLCOX
Brigades: CHRIST, WELSH

SECOND DIVISION: STURGIS
Brigades: NAGLE, FERRERO

THIRD DIVISION: RODMAN
Brigades: FAIRCHILD, HARLAND

KANAWHA DIVISION: SCAMMON
Brigades: EWING, CROOK

XII CORPS MANSFIELD

FIRST DIVISION: WILLIAMS
Brigades: CRAWFORD, GORDON

SECOND DIVISION: GREENE
Brigades: TYNDALE, STAINROOK, GOODRICH

CAVALRY
PLEASONTON

FIRST BRIGADE: WHITING   SECOND BRIGADE: FARNSWORTH
THIRD BRIGADE: RUSH   FOURTH BRIGADE: McREYNOLDS

FIFTH BRIGADE: DAVIS

A photograph taken shortly after the battle shows Sharpsburg's modest Main Street leading west toward the woods on the horizon where Lee had established his headquarters.

OPENING SITUATION, SEPTEMBER 17

Lee was tempted to retreat into Virginia after the Federals broke through at South Mountain, but he became his usual combative self after receiving news that Jackson had triumphed at Harpers Ferry. Now determined to fight, Lee issued orders for all units to concentrate at the town of Sharpsburg. By first light on September 17, most of his army was ranged on a ridge north and east of the town, with Jackson on the left flank and Longstreet in the center. The right was left lightly defended in anticipation of the late arrival of A. P.

Hill's division from Harpers Ferry. Predictably, McClellan moved slowly, giving Lee time to concentrate and deploy. Not until the afternoon of September 16, 24 hours after reaching Antietam Creek, did McClellan begin issuing orders for an attack the next day. He moved two of his corps, commanded by Hooker and Mansfield, across Antietam Creek to the north to attack the Confederate left. Two other corps would hold the center to wait for developments while Burnside staged a diversion by advancing across the creek on Lee's right.

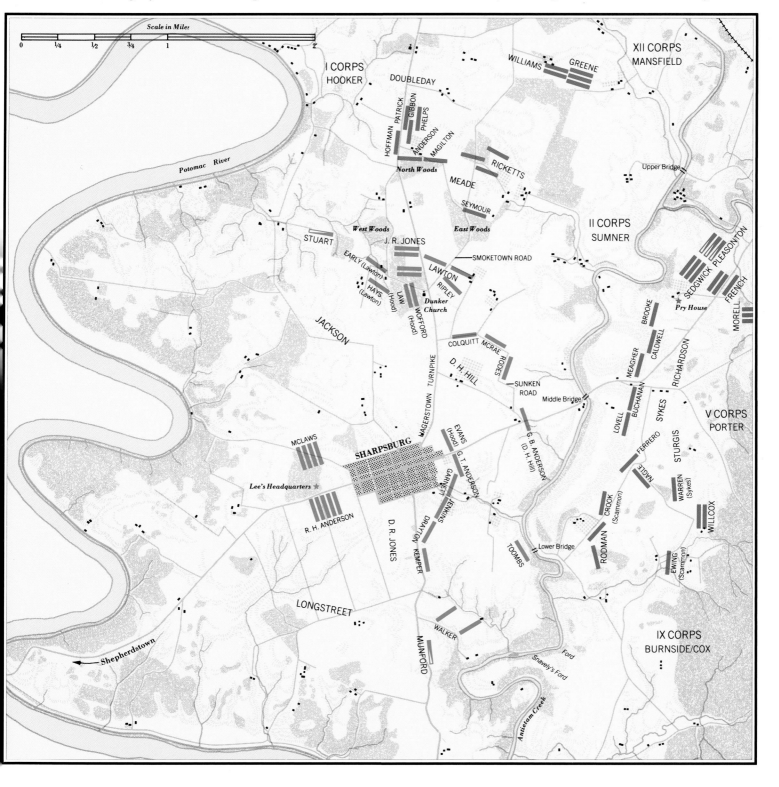

Brigadier General John Gibbon's troops earned the nickname Iron Brigade for their performance at Turner's Gap. On the morning of September 17, the reputation of his command was tested again in the bitter fighting along the Hagerstown Turnpike.

FEDERAL I CORPS ATTACK

Hooker's I Corps launched the Federal attack at 5:30 a.m. with Doubleday's division pushing south on the Federal far right, Ricketts' division advancing through the East Woods, and Meade's division attacking in the center. Savage fighting soon developed on Ricketts' front in the soon-to-be-infamous Cornfield. A Federal cannonade blasted the Confederates hidden in the head-high stalks, and the Union brigades rushed through—only to be met by deadly volleys from Alexander Lawton's Confederates. A ferocious seesaw fight continued around the East Woods and along the eastern edge of the Cornfield until 7:00 a.m., when the bloodletting finally forced a stalemate. A few hundred yards to the west, on the Federal right, Doubleday's division, with Gibbon's brigade in the lead, thrust a mile down both sides of the Hagerstown Turnpike but then was raked by Confederate fire from the brigades of David R. Jones' division positioned west of the turnpike. Supported by heavy artillery fire, Gibbon's men pushed the Rebels back. On all fronts, Jackson's Confederates teetered near collapse. Then Hood's division, which had been held in reserve, charged the Federals' right and center, while D. H. Hill's division attacked the Federal left. Hood's men sent the Yankees reeling until they were stopped by Meade's division at the Cornfield's northern edge.

Spearheading the opening assault, troops from the Federal I Corps charge through the bullet-swept Cornfield.

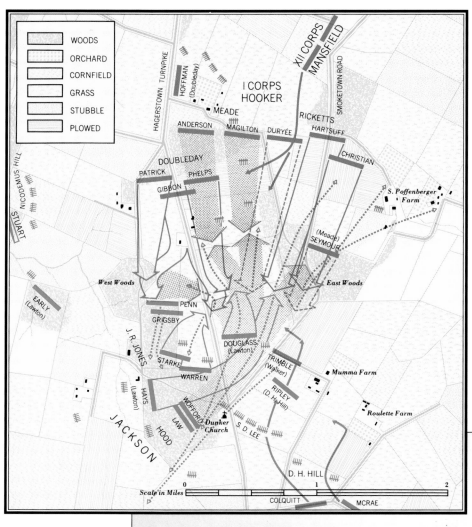

BRIG. GEN. WILLIAM E. STARKE

Dead Confederates of Starke's Louisiana Brigade lie in rows along the rail fence by the Hagerstown Turnpike, killed by the advancing troops of Abner Doubleday's division. General William Starke *(above, right)*, a rising star in the Army of Northern Virginia, was fatally wounded in the fight.

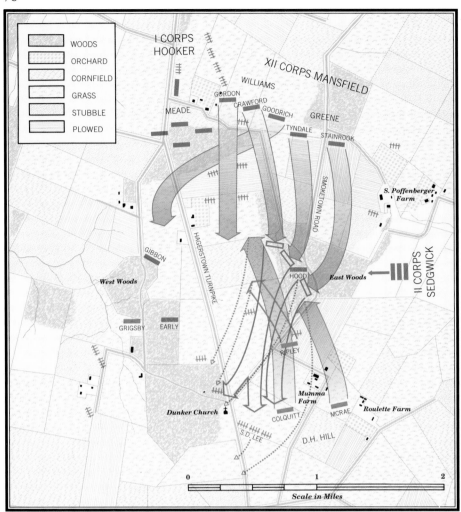

WOODS
ORCHARD
CORNFIELD
GRASS
STUBBLE
PLOWED

I CORPS HOOKER

XII CORPS MANSFIELD

WILLIAMS

GORDON

MEADE

CRAWFORD

GOODRICH

GREENE

TYNDALE

STAINROOK

SMOKETOWN ROAD

S. Poffenberger Farm

GIBBON

HAGERSTOWN TURNPIKE

West Woods

HOOD

East Woods

II CORPS SEDGWICK

GRIGSBY

EARLY

RIPLEY

Mumma Farm

Roulette Farm

Dunker Church

COLQUITT

MCRAE

S.D. LEE

D.H. HILL

0   1   2

Scale in Miles

FEDERAL XII CORPS ATTACK

Idle during Hooker's attack, Joseph Mansfield's XII Corps advanced around 7:30 a.m. After a confusing start, the two Federal divisions picked up momentum, first pushing Hood's exhausted troops from the East Woods and the Cornfield and then engaging D. H. Hill's brigades in a bloody standoff. Then a regiment in William McRae's Confederate brigade, about to be flanked, broke and ran, carrying most of the brigade with it. Through the gap poured 1,700 Federals of Tyndale's and Stainrook's brigades led by General George Greene. Soon Hood's and D. H. Hill's men were streaming back to the West Woods. But after reaching the high ground around the Dunker Church, Greene's Federals, now taking fire from the woods and low on ammunition, faltered—as did the entire XII Corps assault. Around 9:00 a.m., the fighting subsided, and a lull settled over the battlefield.

Troops from one of Greene's Federal brigades pause near the blazing ruins of the Mumma farmhouse and its outbuildings, torched by the retreating Confederates to prevent Federal sharpshooters from using them as cover.

Burning of Mr. mumma's houses and barns at the fight of the 17th Sept.

Deploying in dense
ranks near a corner of
the East Woods *(left)*,
troops from the Federal
XII Corps exchange
fire with Confederates
defending the north-
ern edge of the Corn-
field. The XII Corps
commander, Gener-
al Joseph Mansfield
(right), a Regular Army
engineer, had taken
command only two days
earlier. Shortly after
sending his men into
battle, he was mortally
wounded in the chest.

MAJ. GEN. JOSEPH MANSFIELD

Men of Greene's Federal division charge past the tiny, shell-shot Dunker Church after helping to drive Stonewall Jackson's troops from the hotly contested open fields to the northeast. The caisson at far left, abandoned by retreating gunners of Stephen D. Lee's Confederate batteries, marked the farthest Federal advance during the early-morning attacks on the Confederate left. After gaining the plateau near the church, Greene's troops were stopped by Rebel fire. But they managed to hold their position and later aided the attack by General William French's division (*next pages*).

80

FEDERAL II CORPS ATTACK

The last Federal assault on the Confederate left began about 9:15 a.m. as Sedgwick's division of Sumner's II Corps forded Antietam Creek and plunged straight for the West Woods, intending to turn the enemy flank and march south toward Sharpsburg. Suddenly, Sedgwick's Federals were hit on their left flank by reinforcements Lee had sent north—the divisions of Walker and McLaws plus a brigade led by George T. Anderson. Within minutes the Confederates had killed or wounded almost half of Sedgwick's troops. When Gordon's XII Corps brigade in the East Woods went to Sedgwick's aid, it, too, was shot to pieces by Walker's men. In the meantime, French's division followed Sedgwick across Antietam Creek, then inexplicably veered south—and ran into the brigades of Robert Rodes and George B. Anderson, both hidden in a sunken road that made an ideal rifle trench. Attacking in close order, the Federals were mowed down by Confederate volleys until, at about 10:30 a.m., Richardson's division arrived to reinforce French's left. Richardson's initial assault was likewise turned back, but the Confederates were wavering. The decisive moment came when two regiments of Caldwell's brigade gained the top of a knoll from which they could pour a deadly fire down the length of Sunken Road. When orders from Rodes to deal with this threat were mistaken for a command to retreat, the Confederate line gave way, Rodes' and Anderson's veterans fleeing to the rear. The Federals turned back several counterattacks and by noon had effectively cracked the Confederate center. But McClellan sent no fresh troops to French and Richardson. Their battered divisions were bombarded by guns Longstreet had rushed into action, and they pulled back to reorganize.

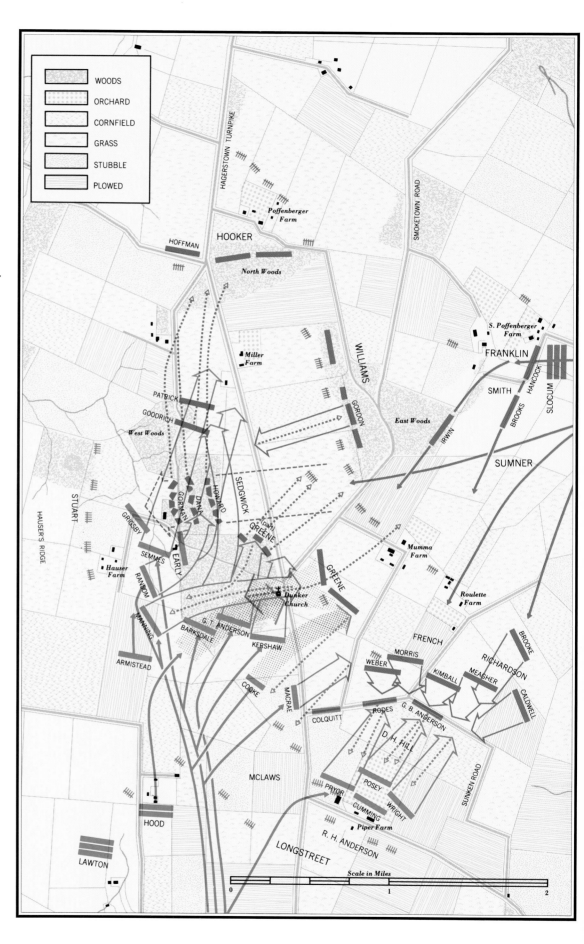

Federals of George Gordon's brigade, advancing to aid Sedgwick's battered division, are cut down as they charge toward unseen riflemen of John Walker's division, firing from dense cover at the edge of the West Woods beyond a wooden rail fence bordering the Hagerstown pike.

Confederate dead, probably artillerymen from one of Stephen D. Lee's batteries *(right),* sprawl by an abandoned caisson east of the Dunker Church. Below, Stephen Lee's guns fire at Sedgwick's division, advancing toward the Rebel-held West Woods.

A photograph taken five days after the battle shows the middle bridge over Antietam Creek and, at top left, the ridge crest just west of Sunken Road where the Federals formed up for their attacks on the Confederate center. Barely visible in the middle horizon are the much-fought-over East Woods.

Two Union soldiers, probably part of a burial detail, gaze at the piled and twisted dead of D. H. Hill's division lying in Sunken Road. The painting below gives a panoramic view of the same gruesome scene, showing Federals shot down before the Confederate positions and Rebel dead sprawled across the rail fence bordering the Piper cornfield.

Maj. Gen. Israel Richardson, the tough 46-year-old West Pointer whose brigades took Sunken Road, was mortally wounded while leading the Federal attack.

Brig. Gen. George B. Anderson, also fatally wounded at Sunken Road, led the Confederates who were attacked by Richardson and French.

84

A view from the high wooded bluff held by Robert Toombs' Georgians shows the Burnside Bridge, the east bank of Antietam Creek, and the open ground beyond that the Federal attackers had to cross under fire.

Colonel Robert B. Potter *(center)* leads his 51st New York up a steep slope west of the Burnside Bridge *(right)* in the successful Federal attack that finally pushed back Toombs' riflemen and opened the way for the main Federal assault.

**MAJ. GEN.
AMBROSE POWELL HILL**

FEDERAL IX CORPS ATTACK

Belatedly ordered to attack the Confederate right at 10:00 a.m., troops of Burnside's IX Corps were repeatedly thrown back as they tried to cross the narrow span over Antietam Creek—known ever since as Burnside Bridge—in the face of concentrated fire from Toombs' well-emplaced Georgia regiments. About 1:00 p.m., two regiments of Ferrero's brigade, the 51st New York and the 51st Pennsylvania, managed to storm across the bridge. Their crossing opened the way for a full-scale assault by brigades under Sturgis and Willcox. They linked up with Rodman's division, which had crossed downstream at Snavely's Ford. But as the Federals pushed toward Sharpsburg and tried to cut Lee's line of retreat, they were attacked suddenly on the left flank by A. P. Hill's troops, who had just reached the battlefield after marching from Harpers Ferry. The Federal left was shoved back, and General Jacob Cox, in charge at the front, ordered a withdrawal to the west bank of Antietam Creek. At about 5:30 p.m., the battle ended. McClellan had refused to commit two entire reserve corps that, Longstreet later said, could have "taken Lee's army and everything in it." The day's total loss for both sides was 22,726 dead, wounded, and missing; one out of every four men in action had become a casualty.

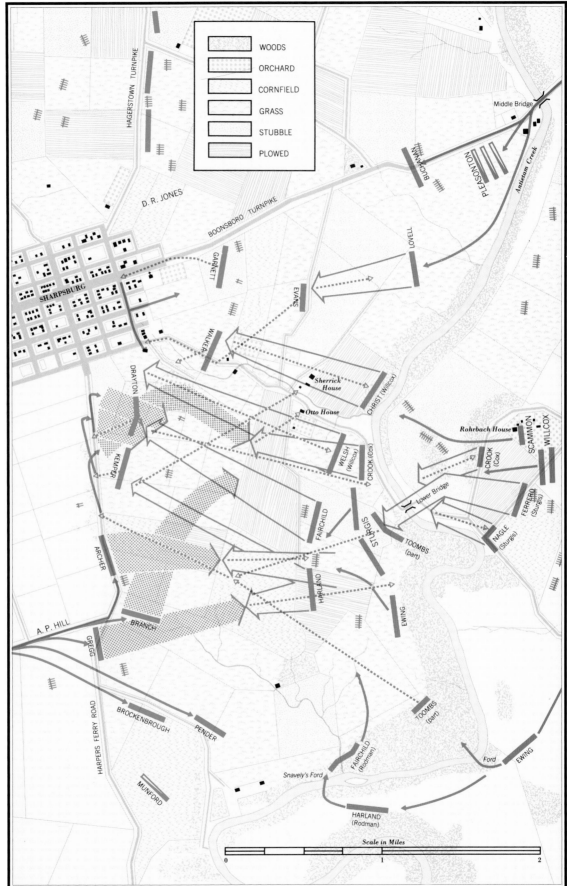

	WOODS
	ORCHARD
	CORNFIELD
	GRASS
	STUBBLE
	PLOWED

Scale in Miles

0   1   2

FREDERICKSBURG

Frustrated by McClellan's failure to pursue and attack Lee's army, Lincoln at last fired him in early November 1862 and replaced him with the elaborately whiskered Ambrose Burnside—not because Burnside had distinguished himself in any way at Antietam, but rather because there seemed to be no other viable candidate to head the Army of the Potomac.

To Lincoln's surprise, Burnside moved, and moved fast. Reorganizing his army into three "grand divisions," in mid-November he marched them swiftly from the vicinity of Warrenton to the north bank of the Rappahannock River near Fredericksburg. In the process, he left Lee's army well to the west, Longstreet's Corps at Culpeper, and Jackson's farther away in the Shenandoah. The lightly defended Fredericksburg was ripe for the taking and an avenue to Richmond wide open.

MAJ. GEN. AMBROSE E. BURNSIDE

But then Burnside hesitated—for three weeks. The river was too high to ford, and he had to wait for pontoon bridges whose arrival was delayed by bad weather and bureaucratic bungling. This interval was all that the Confederates needed. Within days Longstreet had hurried eastward, followed by Jackson. As their brigades arrived at Fredericksburg, Lee placed most of them in virtually impregnable positions on a high ridge that curved behind the town. But Burnside did not comprehend what he was facing and decided on a frontal attack. Having lost the opportunity for a quick victory, he sent his army against the waiting Confederate guns.

In Burnside's opening move on December 11, soldiers of the 7th Michigan and the 19th and 20th Massachusetts Infantry row pontoons across the Rappahannock to attack the town of Fredericksburg, while engineers *(left)*, working under Confederate fire, complete a pontoon bridge.

OPENING SITUATION, DECEMBER 13

On the afternoon of December 11, Burnside sent two of his grand divisions across the Rappahannock on pontoon bridges. Sumner's grand division with Couch's II Corps and Willcox's IX Corps crossed at Fredericksburg and deployed around the town. Franklin's grand division—Reynolds' I Corps and Smith's VI Corps—were delayed by a series of confusing orders from Burnside and finished crossing the next day a mile downstream. Observing these moves, Lee further improved his defenses. The troops of Longstreet's corps, centered on a part of the ridge behind Fredericksburg called Marye's Heights, bolstered the earthworks they had been digging since the first troops arrived on November 20. Their position was especially strong where a stone wall protected a sunken road. To Longstreet's right was Jackson's corps, strengthened by the last-minute arrival of Jubal Early's and D. H. Hill's divisions, which Lee retrieved from positions downriver now that he was sure Burnside intended a frontal attack. Jeb Stuart's cavalry secured the right flank. Lee's army was outnumbered—the Federal force totaled 116,600 men, the Confederate 72,500—but the Rebels enjoyed an immensely strong position on high ground with their artillery poised to fire down at the Federals.

ORDER OF BATTLE
ARMY OF NORTHERN VIRGINIA
LEE
72,500 MEN

FIRST CORPS
LONGSTREET

McLAWS' DIVISION	R. H. ANDERSON'S DIVISION	PICKETT'S DIVISION	HOOD'S DIVISION	RANSOM'S DIVISION
KERSHAW'S BRIGADE	WILCOX'S BRIGADE	GARNETT'S BRIGADE	LAW'S BRIGADE	RANSOM'S BRIGADE
BARKSDALE'S BRIGADE	FEATHERSTON'S BRIGADE	KEMPER'S BRIGADE	G. T. ANDERSON'S BRIGADE	COOKE'S BRIGADE
COBB'S BRIGADE	MAHONE'S BRIGADE	ARMISTEAD'S BRIGADE	ROBERTSON'S BRIGADE	
SEMMES' BRIGADE	WRIGHT'S BRIGADE	JENKINS' BRIGADE	BENNING'S BRIGADE	
	PERRY'S BRIGADE	CORSE'S BRIGADE		

SECOND CORPS
JACKSON

D. H. HILL'S DIVISION	A. P. HILL'S DIVISION	EARLY'S DIVISION	TALIAFERRO'S DIVISION
RODES' BRIGADE	BROCKENBROUGH'S BRIGADE	ATKINSON'S BRIGADE	PAXTON'S BRIGADE
DOLES' BRIGADE	GREGG'S BRIGADE	HOKE'S BRIGADE	J. R. JONES' BRIGADE
COLQUITT'S BRIGADE	THOMAS' BRIGADE	WALKER'S BRIGADE	WARREN'S BRIGADE
IVERSON'S BRIGADE	LANE'S BRIGADE	HAYS' BRIGADE	PENDLETON'S BRIGADE
GRIMES' BRIGADE	ARCHER'S BRIGADE		
	PENDER'S BRIGADE		

CAVALRY
STUART

HAMPTON'S BRIGADE	W. H. F. LEE'S BRIGADE
F. LEE'S BRIGADE	W. E. JONES' BRIGADE

ARMY OF THE POTOMAC
BURNSIDE
116,600 MEN

LEFT GRAND DIVISION FRANKLIN	CENTER GRAND DIVISION HOOKER	RIGHT GRAND DIVISION SUMNER
I CORPS REYNOLDS	**III CORPS STONEMAN**	**II CORPS COUCH**
FIRST DIVISION: DOUBLEDAY *Brigades:* PHELPS, GAVIN, ROGERS, MEREDITH	FIRST DIVISION: BIRNEY *Brigades:* ROBINSON, WARD, BERRY	FIRST DIVISION: HANCOCK *Brigades:* CALDWELL, MEAGHER, ZOOK
SECOND DIVISION: GIBBON *Brigades:* ROOT, LYLE, TAYLOR	SECOND DIVISION: SICKLES *Brigades:* CARR, HALL, REVERE	SECOND DIVISION: HOWARD *Brigades:* SULLY, OWEN, HALL
THIRD DIVISION: MEADE *Brigades:* SINCLAIR, MAGILTON, JACKSON	THIRD DIVISION: WHIPPLE *Brigades:* PIATT, CARROLL	THIRD DIVISION: FRENCH *Brigades:* KIMBALL, PALMER, ANDREWS
VI CORPS SMITH	**V CORPS BUTTERFIELD**	**IX CORPS WILLCOX**
FIRST DIVISION: BROOKS *Brigades:* TORBERT, CAKE, RUSSELL	FIRST DIVISION: GRIFFIN *Brigades:* BARNES, SWEITZER, STOCKTON	FIRST DIVISION: BURNS *Brigades:* POE, CHRIST, LEASURE
SECOND DIVISION: HOWE *Brigades:* PRATT, WHITING, VINTON	SECOND DIVISION: SYKES *Brigades:* BUCHANAN, ANDREWS, WARREN	SECOND DIVISION: STURGIS *Brigades:* NAGLE, FERRERO
THIRD DIVISION: NEWTON *Brigades:* COCHRANE, DEVENS, ROWLEY	THIRD DIVISION: HUMPHREYS *Brigades:* TYLER, ALLABACH	THIRD DIVISION: GETTY *Brigades:* HAWKINS, HARLAND
CAVALRY BRIGADE: BAYARD	CAVALRY BRIGADE: AVERELL	CAVALRY DIVISION: PLEASONTON

Men of Colonel J. M. Brockenbrough's 40th Virginia await the Federal attack on December 13 at a bend in the railroad near Hamilton's Crossing. These troops, along with Colonel Reuben L. Walker's artillery *(background),* helped beat back a Union assault through a gap in Jackson's line.

Charging into ferocious Rebel fire, Pennsylvania infantrymen of George Meade's division storm across the railroad embankment at the foot of the ridge. The usually dour Meade later praised his men, writing that "they went in *beautifully*" and were only stopped by "an overwhelming force of the enemy."

Confederate General Maxcy Gregg, whose brigade was positioned behind a gap in A. P. Hill's line between Lane's and Archer's brigades, made a fatal error in judgment. Believing the attacking Federals to be friendly troops, he ordered his South Carolinians not to fire. Gregg's brigade was overrun and he became an easy target for a Union Minié ball, which killed him.

FEDERAL I CORPS ATTACK

Burnside launched the Union assault against Jackson's line with elements of Franklin's grand division. Leading the attack at 8:30 a.m. was Meade's division, supported on the right by Gibbon's division and on the left by Doubleday's. Meade's three brigades had barely started forward when they were abruptly halted by furious Confederate cannon fire. The massed Federal guns replied, and an artillery duel ensued. By noon, Meade's men were moving again, and by 1:00 p.m., his brigades had charged past the railroad embankment and were clawing their way into a tangle of woods left unprotected because the Rebel commander, A. P. Hill, thought the area impassable. Piling through the gap, one Union brigade veered right and crashed into the flank of Lane's brigade, while the other two slammed into Archer's and Gregg's brigades and threatened to cut open Jackson's defenses. The Confederates responded sharply. Early's and Taliaferro's divisions, backing up Hill's first line, lunged forward, hitting Meade's attackers head-on and enfilading their flanks. Gibbon, on Meade's right, could offer no help; his division had been stopped cold at the rail line by Confederate artillery and small-arms fire. By midafternoon both Meade's and Gibbon's men, refused reinforcements by Franklin, who let 20,000 men stand idly by, had been driven back to their starting points by Rebel counterattacks.

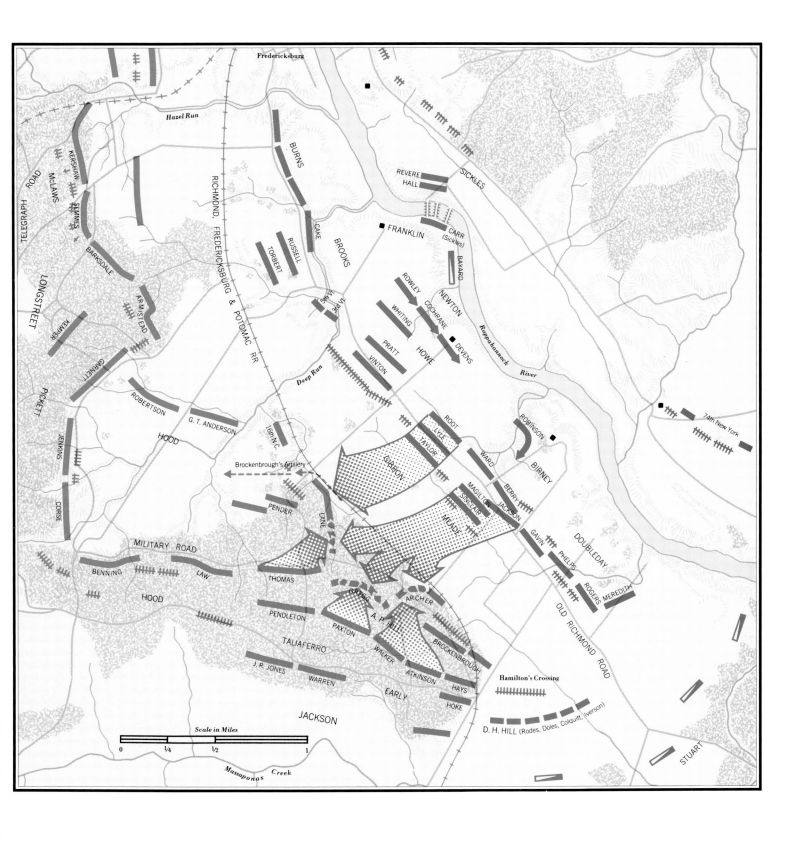

Fredericksburg

Hazel Run

TELEGRAPH ROAD

KERSHAW

McLAWS

SEMMES

BARKSDALE

BURNS

RICHMOND, FREDERICKSBURG & POTOMAC RR

CAKE

BROOKS

TORBERT

RUSSELL

REVERE

HALL

SICKLES

FRANKLIN

CARR
(Sickles)

BAYARD

LONGSTREET

ARMISTEAD

KEMPER

GARNETT

PICKETT

5th Vt.
3rd Vt.

ROWLEY

WHITING

COCHRANE

NEWTON

PRATT

HOWE

VINTON

DEVENS

Rappahannock River

ROBERTSON

G. T. ANDERSON

Deep Run

ROOT

LYLE

TAYLOR

ROBINSON

74th New York

HOOD

16th N.C.

Brockenbrough's Artillery

GIBBON

WARD

JACKSON

BERRY

BIRNEY

JENKINS

CORSE

PENDER

LANE

MEADE

MAGILTON

SINCLAIR

GAVIN

PHELPS

DOUBLEDAY

ROGERS

MEREDITH

MILITARY ROAD

BENNING

LAW

THOMAS

HOOD

GREGG

ARCHER

A. P. HILL

PENDLETON

PAXTON

WALKER

BROCKENBROUGH

TALIAFERRO

J. R. JONES

WARREN

EARLY

ATKINSON

HAYS

HOKE

Hamilton's Crossing

JACKSON

D. H. HILL (Rodes, Doles, Colquitt, Iverson)

STUART

Scale in Miles

0   1/4   1/2   1

Massaponax Creek

The 114th Pennsylvania Zouaves of Robinson's brigade charge into a Confederate counterattack, helping to save the Federal left from disaster after Meade's retreat. The Irish-born Colonel Charles Collis, who had raised the regiment, won the Medal of Honor for riding into the midst of his troops, waving the colors to spur them on.

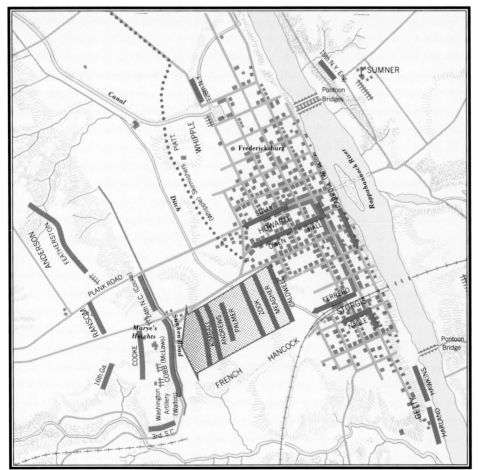

MARYE'S HEIGHTS, FIRST PHASE

Shortly before noon, Burnside launched a
second head-on assault, this one aimed at
Longstreet's corps, which held Marye's
Heights directly west of Fredericksburg.
The Federal troops, spearheaded by French's
division with Kimball's brigade in the lead,
were pounded by murderous Confederate
artillery fire as soon as they left the cover
of the town. Still they marched on, forming
lines of battle and advancing across the
mostly open plain until Kimball's men were
within 125 yards of the stone wall at the foot
of Marye's Heights. There the Federals were
met by lethal volleys from Cobb's infantry
hidden behind the stone wall, and from
Cooke's men farther up the slope. Kimball
lost a quarter of his command in minutes.
The same devastating fire chewed up the
brigades of Andrews and Palmer, which followed Kimball, as well as the three brigades
of Hancock's division that formed a second
wave. By midafternoon, the entire attack faltered and stopped, although many of the surviving Federals held their ground, desperately
trying to find cover on the fire-swept hillside.

As seen from behind Federal lines, regiments of Nathan Kimball's brigade lead the initial assault on Marye's Heights *(background)*. At far left, men of the 4th and 8th Ohio fire from a prone position. In the center, the 24th New Jersey advances amid bursting shells; on the right, the 28th New Jersey moves forward.

A photograph taken after the battle shows the northern end of Marye's Heights in the distance as well as some of the battered houses along Hanover Street that provided cover for a few of the advancing Federal units.

General Thomas R. R. Cobb *(right)* commanded the Georgia brigade that defended the stone wall on Marye's Heights *(above)*. Cobb formed his men in two ranks behind the wall so that they could alternately step up to fire and move back to reload. He was killed during the battle by a bullet that severed a leg artery.

Union Colonel Nelson A. Miles, commander of two regiments in John Caldwell's brigade, led his men within 40 yards of the stone wall on Marye's Heights before being driven back. Miles was wounded asking Caldwell for permission to make a bayonet charge.

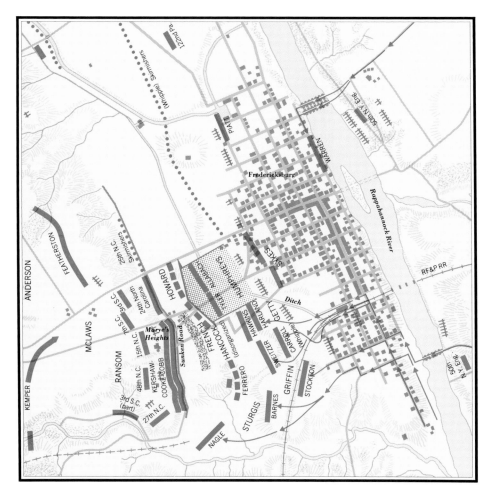

MARYE'S HEIGHTS, SECOND PHASE

Despite the slaughter in front of the stone wall, Burnside stubbornly ordered still more attacks against the Heights in the late afternoon. Howard's II Corps division advanced on the right, followed by a IX Corps division under Sturgis on the left. The result was the same: Confederate fire quickly tore apart the blue lines. Finally, as darkness was closing in, Burnside launched Butterfield's V Corps. Griffin's division went in on the left to relieve Sturgis' troops, followed by Humphreys' and Sykes' divisions, who attacked through the ravaged troops of the II Corps. But now the Confederate fire was even more devastating than before, Kershaw's Rebel brigade having reinforced the troops behind the stone wall. The Federal survivors of these futile attacks remained on the wintry slopes all night and throughout the next day, digging in amidst their wounded and dead comrades. Then, at the urging of his top commanders, Burnside ordered his army back across the Rappahannock. By the morning of December 16, the Federals were gone, leaving behind a total of 12,500 dead, wounded, and missing. Confederate losses amounted to about 5,000.

In earthworks above the stone wall on Marye's Heights, men of Robert Ransom's 24th North Carolina pour fire into dense lines of Federal troops struggling up the slope. The battle-field artist, an English journalist, made note of the shallow ravine in which some Union troops took cover.

Beneath a hill held by Jackson's artillery, Federal burial parties lay the dead to rest the day after the battle. Many of the corpses had been stripped of uniforms and shoes during the night by Confederate scavengers.

CHANCELLORSVILLE

The dreadful butchery at Fredericksburg ignited such an outcry in the North that Lincoln was again forced to change commanders. Out was Ambrose Burnside, in was one of his subordinates—and severest critics—Joseph Hooker. It was a controversial appointment. Hooker was thought to drink heavily and was known to be both arrogant and ambitious. But he had also shown signs of being an aggressive general who deserved his nickname, Fighting Joe.

Hooker energetically revitalized Burnside's tired and dispirited army. As the Union force spent the winter in quarters around Falmouth north of Fredericksburg, the new commander vastly improved sanitation, diet, and morale. By the early spring of 1863, he could boast that he had "the finest army on the planet," and added that he would soon lead it to Richmond and beyond.

Robert E. Lee's Army of Northern Virginia was, as usual, ill fed, ill shod, ill clothed, and generally miserable in its winter camps across the Rappahannock around Fredericksburg. It was also smaller than before; Lee had sent Longstreet south with two divisions to forage for provisions and keep an eye on the Federals along the Virginia-North Carolina coast. But even this reduced force could easily hold the vastly improved earthworks the men had been digging in and around Fredericksburg ever since the December battle. For the Federals, another frontal attack was out of the question. Hooker's only option was to outflank Lee, by moving up the Rappahannock.

Beginning in late April, Hooker marched the bulk of his army up the river. With admirable speed, his corps commanders got more than 70,000 men across several fords and moving smartly against the flank and rear of Lee's 40,000 men. But soon, in a monumental failure of nerve, Hooker drew back and went on the defensive around the crossroads of Chancellorsville. This was all Lee and Stonewall Jackson needed. Sending Jackson on a daring flank march, Lee contrived a battle considered his masterpiece. He so confounded Hooker that in three days the Federal army was speeding back across the Rappahannock. Lincoln had urged the boastful Hooker to "give us victories." Instead, he had delivered another ignominious defeat.

For Lee, however, the victory was sadly tainted by the loss of Jackson, who was mortally wounded by his pickets on the night after the great flank march. Lee lamented that he had lost his right arm.

MAJ. GEN. JOSEPH HOOKER

Hooker began his march around Lee's army by sending the corps of George Meade, Oliver Howard, and Henry Slocum northeast to cross the Rappahannock at Kelly's Ford on April 29. The three corps then crossed the Rapidan at Germanna and Ely's fords and turned southeast to converge on the crossroads called Chancellorsville. Hooker also ordered the corps of Darius Couch and Daniel Sickles to cross the Rappahannock at United States Ford and join the main force. In the meantime, John Sedgwick would lead his own VI Corps and John Reynolds' I Corps in a feigned attack south of Fredericksburg. Lee, slow to see the Federal threat, first sent only Richard Anderson's division west on the 29th, but soon dispatched Jackson with most of the Confederate army in the same direction. He left only Jubal Early's division and a brigade of Lafayette McLaws to guard Fredericksburg.

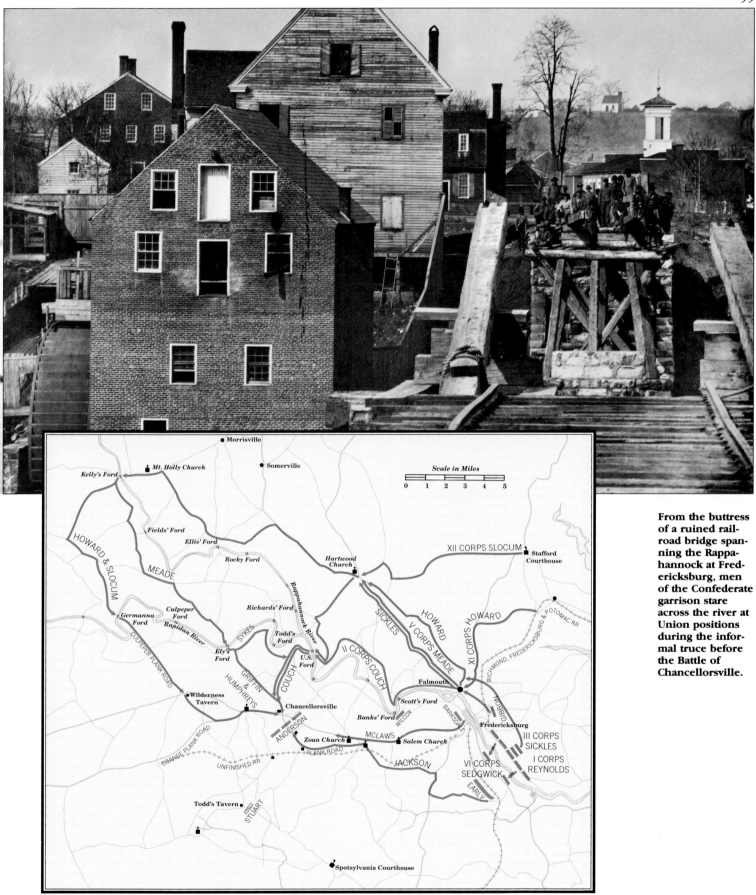

From the buttress of a ruined railroad bridge spanning the Rappahannock at Fredericksburg, men of the Confederate garrison stare across the river at Union positions during the informal truce before the Battle of Chancellorsville.

ORDER OF BATTLE

ARMY OF NORTHERN VIRGINIA
LEE
58,900 MEN

FIRST CORPS (LESS TWO DIVISIONS)
LONGSTREET (ABSENT)

McLAWS' DIVISION	ANDERSON'S DIVISION
WOFFORD'S BRIGADE	WILCOX'S BRIGADE
KERSHAW'S BRIGADE	MAHONE'S BRIGADE
SEMMES' BRIGADE	WRIGHT'S BRIGADE
BARKSDALE'S BRIGADE	POSEY'S BRIGADE
	PERRY'S BRIGADE

SECOND CORPS
JACKSON

A. P. HILL'S DIVISION	RODES' DIVISION	EARLY'S DIVISION	COLSTON'S DIVISION
HETH'S BRIGADE	RODES' BRIGADE	GORDON'S BRIGADE	PAXTON'S BRIGADE
McGOWAN'S BRIGADE	DOLE'S BRIGADE	SMITH'S BRIGADE	WARREN'S BRIGADE
THOMAS' BRIGADE	COLQUITT'S BRIGADE	HOKE'S BRIGADE	J. R. JONES' BRIGADE
ARCHER'S BRIGADE	IVERSON'S BRIGADE	HAYS' BRIGADE	NICHOLLS' BRIGADE
LANE'S BRIGADE	RAMSEUR'S BRIGADE		
PENDER'S BRIGADE			

CAVALRY
STUART

HAMPTON'S BRIGADE	W. H. F. LEE'S BRIGADE
F. LEE'S BRIGADE	W. E. JONES' BRIGADE

ARMY OF THE POTOMAC
HOOKER
134,600 MEN

I CORPS REYNOLDS

FIRST DIVISION: WADSWORTH
Brigades: PHELPS, CUTLER, PAUL, MEREDITH

SECOND DIVISION: ROBINSON
Brigades: ROOT, BAXTER, LEONARD

THIRD DIVISION: DOUBLEDAY
Brigades: ROWLEY, STONE

V CORPS MEADE

FIRST DIVISION: GRIFFIN
Brigades: BARNES, McQUADE, STOCKTON

SECOND DIVISION: SYKES
Brigades: AYRES, BURBANK, O'RORKE

THIRD DIVISION: HUMPHREYS
Brigades: TYLER, ALLABACH

II CORPS COUCH

FIRST DIVISION: HANCOCK
Brigades: CALDWELL, MEAGHER, ZOOK, BROOKE

SECOND DIVISION: GIBBON
Brigades: SULLY, OWEN, HALL

THIRD DIVISION: FRENCH
Brigades: CARROLL, HAYS, MacGREGOR

VI CORPS SEDGWICK

FIRST DIVISION: BROOKS
Brigades: BROWN, BARTLETT, RUSSELL

SECOND DIVISION: HOWE
Brigades: GRANT, NEILL

THIRD DIVISION: NEWTON
Brigades: SHALER, BROWNE, WHEATON

XII CORPS SLOCUM

FIRST DIVISION: WILLIAMS
Brigades: KNIPE, ROSS, RUGER

SECOND DIVISION: GEARY
Brigades: CANDY, KANE, GREENE

III CORPS SICKLES

FIRST DIVISION: BIRNEY
Brigades: GRAHAM, WARD, HAYMAN

SECOND DIVISION: BERRY
Brigades: CARR, REVERE, MOTT

THIRD DIVISION: WHIPPLE
Brigades: FRANKLIN, BOWMAN, BERDAN

XI CORPS HOWARD

FIRST DIVISION: DEVENS
Brigades: VON GILSA, McLEAN

SECOND DIVISION: VON STEINWEHR
Brigades: BUSCHBECK, BARLOW

THIRD DIVISION: SCHURZ
Brigades: SCHIMMELFENNIG, KRZYZANOWSKI

CAVALRY
STONEMAN

FIRST DIVISION: PLEASONTON	SECOND DIVISION: AVERELL	THIRD DIVISION: GREGG
Brigades: DAVIS, DEVIN	*Brigades:* SARGENT, McINTOSH	*Brigades:* KILPATRICK, WYNDHAM

Seated on hardtack boxes in the woods near Chancellorsville, Generals Lee *(left)* and Jackson quietly make plans to divide their forces and attack Hooker's Federals. Lee holds a map, sketched by Jackson's topographical expert Jedediah Hotchkiss, that charted the concealed route to the enemy's uncovered right flank. After learning that the Federal left and center were largely unassailable, Lee gave his approval to Jackson's bold proposal.

JACKSON'S FLANK MARCH AND ATTACK, MAY 2

In one of the great gambles of the war, Jackson set out on the morning of May 2 with the bulk of the Confederate force, about 26,000 men, on a furtive 14-mile march around the Federal right, leaving Lee with only 14,000 men to face Hooker's 70,000. The Federals spotted rear elements of Jackson's column passing an iron-works called Catherine Furnace, and two divisions of Sickles' III Corps attacked. Regiments from Anderson's and A. P. Hill's divisions threw the Federals back. Other Union officers also saw parts of Jackson's column along Brock Road toward the Orange Plank Road, but their warnings were ignored by Hooker, who by midday was convinced Lee was retreating. After nine hours of marching, Jackson deployed his troops in three lines perpendicular to the Turnpike and extending a mile on either side of it. At 5:00 p.m., the Confederates, with Robert Rodes' division leading, stormed over the Federal pickets and within half an hour had routed Howard's unprepared XI Corps.

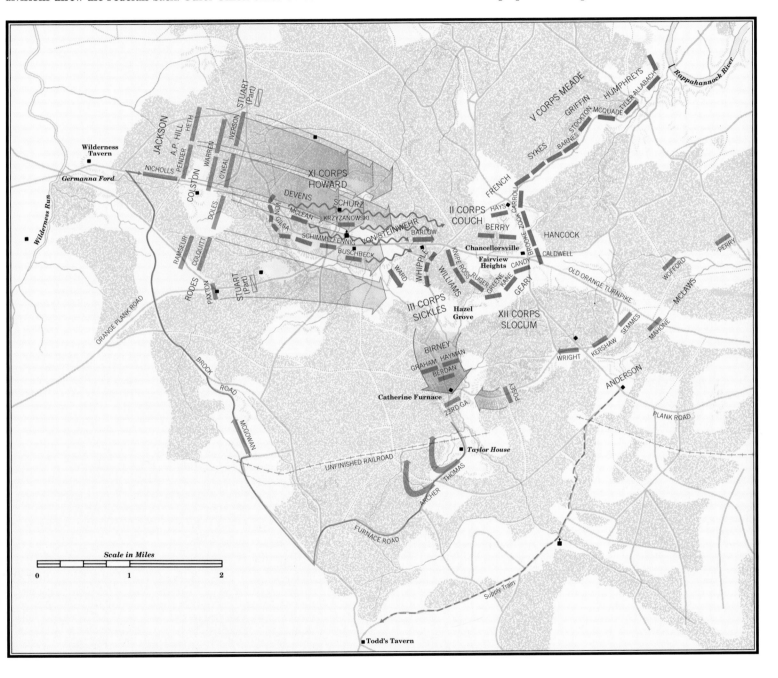

Brigadier General Robert Rodes, recovered from a thigh wound received at Antietam and now commanding a Confederate division, led the initial drive on Howard's corps. Howard, who had refused to believe an attack was imminent, later wrote that Rodes' assault was like "a terrible gale" with "quick lightning from a hundred points at once."

A brigade of Rodes' division, shouting the Rebel yell, storms a Federal breastworks on the Turnpike west of Chancellorsville, taking Union defenders by surprise. Only a handful of regiments managed to get off a few volleys before giving way. Echoes of the Confederate troops' wild scream, wrote a survivor of the battle, "swept the country for miles."

A Union officer brandishing pistol and saber *(right)* tries in vain to slow the stampede of the XI Corps down the Plank Road. The photograph below shows a stretch of the partially planked track where it met a side lane *(background)* down which Stonewall Jackson was riding when he was accidentally shot by Rebel pickets.

104

A fanciful painting of the Chancellorsville battle at sunset on May 2 shows the red brick Chancellor House at the intersection of the turnpike and Plank Road. Nearby, Federal infantry and artillery try to form a defensive perimeter while cavalrymen ride down the Plank Road to try to slow the oncoming enemy. Jackson's initial Confederate attack came out of the woods of the Wilderness to the west at upper left. In the foreground at right, Lee's troops charge from the southeast, an attack that actually came the next day.

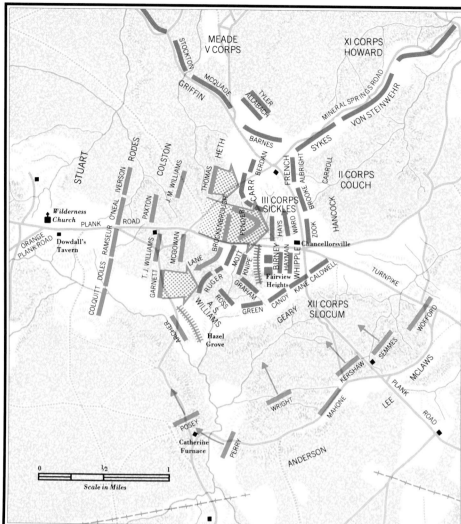

LT. GEN. JAMES EWELL BROWN "JEB" STUART

STUART'S ATTACK, MAY 3

During the night of May 2-3, the Federals frantically reorganized their lines, forming a loop around the Chancellor House with two wings extending northward in a crude V toward the Rappahannock. Jeb Stuart, who had assumed command after Jackson was wounded, sent his men forward at first light, with William Dorsey Pender's brigade of Henry Heth's division driving into the Federal perimeter from the west. The crucial moment came when James Archer's brigade charged virtually unopposed up the slopes of a key hill called Hazel Grove, abandoned by Sickles' men on the orders of Hooker, who thought the position too exposed. Colonel E. Porter Alexander immediately rushed 30 guns onto the knoll and began pouring a murderous fire on the brigades of Slocum's XII Corps and Sickles' III Corps. Soon Stuart renewed his attack while Lee began to close in from the southeast. By noon the Federal position had become untenable, and Hooker ordered his army to fall back to new positions north of Chancellorsville.

Winfield Scott Hancock, given command of the Federal rear guard, delayed the enemy pursuit with skill, allowing his corps commander, Darius Couch, to organize a defensive perimeter.

E. Porter Alexander, the brilliant Confederate artillerist, managed in the morning of May 3 to assemble the guns that whipsawed the Federal lines from Hazel Grove. He was credited by Lee with "the successful issue of the contest."

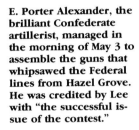

A Federal battle line covering the gradual retreat of Hooker's army from Chancellorsville bravely holds off attacks by the pursuing Confederates. Three of Hooker's subordinates, Meade, Reynolds, and Howard, wanted to fight it out south of the Rappahannock and even use the still-powerful Federal force to take the offensive, but Hooker ordered the entire army to withdraw.

108

Brigadier General Herman Haupt *(left),* field commander of U.S. military railroads, and an assistant survey wrecked Confederate caissons and dead horses on Marye's Heights at the Fredericksburg battlefield after Sedgwick's May 3 attack.

During the withdrawal of the Federal VI Corps to the Rappahannock on May 4, troops of the Vermont Brigade, part of Albion Howe's division, successfully held off Jubal Early's oncoming Confederates. Protecting the Federal left, Howe's stout defense enabled Sedgwick's corps to recross the river at Scott's Ford.

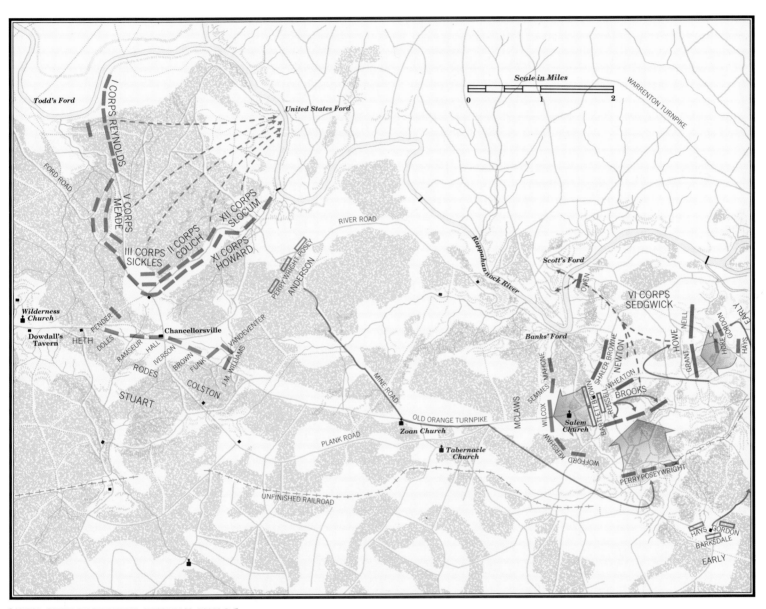

SALEM CHURCH/FEDERAL RETREAT, MAY 3-5

On the morning of May 3, Sedgwick, ordered by Hooker to march his 23,000 men to join the main Federal force, sent the divisions of John Gibbon and John Newton advancing by the most direct route westward from Fredericksburg—straight up Marye's Heights. As in December, the fighting was desperate and bloody, but in a final rush the Federals took the stone wall, sending Jubal Early's outnumbered defenders fleeing southward. That afternoon, however, Sedgwick's men, reaching Salem Church on the Turnpike, were brought to a standstill by Lafayette McLaws' division. The next

day Lee put in action a plan to annihilate Sedgwick's corps, bringing up artillery to support a three-pronged attack by McLaws, Richard Anderson, and Early, who had marched back into action. But through a combination of Confederate errors and a skillfully executed withdrawal, Sedgwick slipped out of the trap and during the night of May 4-5 got his force across the Rappahannock at Scott's Ford. By the morning of May 6, the six Federal corps north of Chancellorsville had also crossed, pressed by Stuart's force—which at 25,000 men was one-third of the fleeing Union army.

GETTYSBURG CAMPAIGN

Only days after his triumph at Chancellorsville, Robert E. Lee decided again to head for the rich farmlands of Pennsylvania. Lee intended to force the Army of the Potomac to engage him in a campaign of maneuver, the kind of war that afforded his outnumbered army its best hope of victory. At the same time, a successful invasion would surely encourage the North's Peace Democrats to demand an end to the fighting—with a treaty favorable to the South. It might also induce Britain and France to recognize the Confederacy and possibly intervene on its behalf.

Starting early in June 1863, Lee began slipping his army northwest toward the Shenandoah Valley. First to move were Jeb Stuart's horsemen, who soon became embroiled in a battle with Federal cavalry *(next two pages)*. Then came Stonewall Jackson's 2d Corps, now led by Richard Ewell, who had largely recovered from the loss of a leg at Second Manassas. Ewell quickly crossed the Blue Ridge into the Shenandoah and, trouncing a Federal force at Winchester, sped down the Valley. Next came Longstreet and his corps, followed by the newly created 3d Corps under A. P. Hill. Fording the Potomac, all three corps entered the Cumberland Valley—and immediately sent out foraging parties to scour the countryside. Elements of Ewell's corps reached the Susquehanna River; a cavalry detachment camped four miles from the Pennsylvania capital of Harrisburg.

On June 29, Lee sent urgent messages ordering all units to concentrate in the vicinity of Gettysburg to face the Federal army that had moved northward in pursuit with surprising swiftness. There, beginning on July 1, more than 160,000 Americans would fight a three-day battle that for its violence—and its importance—would forever be etched in the national memory. When silence fell over the Pennsylvania ridges and fields on July 3, Lee's cause had passed its high tide, and Confederate hopes had begun to fade.

Confederate troops, their trousers rolled, wade across the upper Potomac on their way to Pennsylvania.

After shifting his army west to Culpeper, Lee *(red lines)* marched through three gaps in the Blue Ridge and proceeded north, screened by the mountains. Once across the Potomac, his corps fanned out into the rich farmlands of the Cumberland Valley. On June 13, General Hooker started the Union army north on parallel routes *(blue lines)* from Fredericksburg through Northern Virginia and into Maryland. There General George Meade replaced Hooker and quickly hurried his new command into Pennsylvania to find and intercept Lee. Meanwhile, Jeb Stuart took three brigades of cavalry on a foray *(broken red lines)* that circled the Federal army—but left Lee without the scouts he needed to track Union movements.

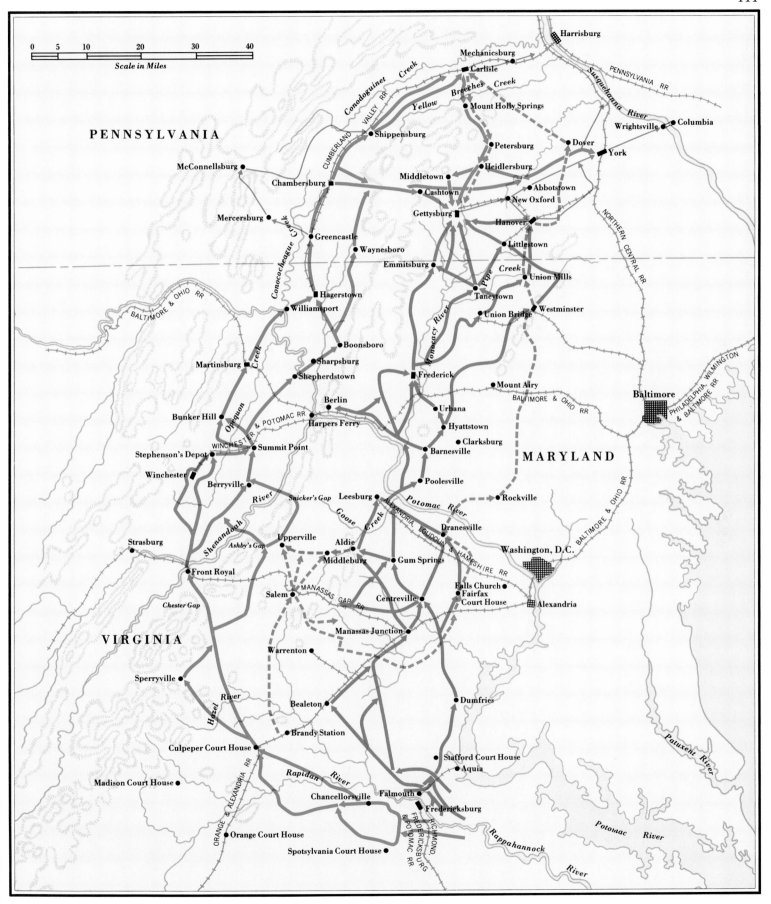

PENNSYLVANIA

Harrisburg

Mechanicsburg

Carlisle

Mount Holly Springs

Wrightsville Columbia

Shippensburg

Petersburg Dover York

Middletown Heidlersburg

McConnellsburg

Chambersburg Cashtown Abbotstown

New Oxford

Mercersburg Gettysburg Hanover

Greencastle

Waynesboro Littlestown

Emmitsburg

Taneytown Union Mills

Hagerstown Union Bridge Westminster

Williamsport

Boonsboro

Martinsburg Sharpsburg

Shepherdstown Frederick

Mount Airy

Berlin

Bunker Hill Urbana

Harpers Ferry Hyattstown

Stephenson's Depot Clarksburg

Summit Point Barnesville **MARYLAND**

Winchester

Berryville Poolesville

Baltimore

Leesburg

Strasburg Snicker's Gap Dranesville Rockville

Upperville Aldie Washington, D.C.

Front Royal Middleburg Gum Springs

Ashby's Gap

Salem Centreville Falls Church

Chester Gap Fairfax Alexandria

Court House

VIRGINIA Manassas Junction

Warrenton

Sperryville

Bealeton Dumfries

Brandy Station

Culpeper Court House Stafford Court House

Aquia

Madison Court House

Chancellorsville Falmouth

Orange Court House Fredericksburg

Spotsylvania Court House

Scale in Miles

BRANDY STATION

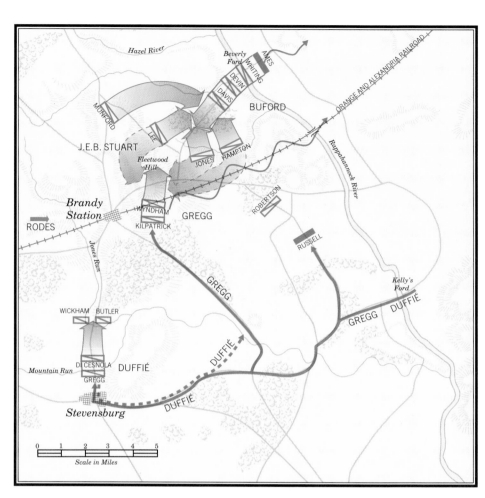

A few days after Hooker got wind of Lee's shift westward, he learned further that Jeb Stuart's cavalry was concentrated near Culpeper. Hooker ordered his own troopers, now massed in one large corps led by Brig. Gen. Alfred Pleasonton, to locate and attack Lee's horsemen. Early on June 9, after determining that the Confederates were camped near a hamlet called Brandy Station, Pleasonton sent Gen. John Buford's division across the Rappahannock to attack the northern end of the Confederate position. Buford's horsemen nearly broke through Wade Hampton's hastily improvised defenses in savage hand-to-hand fighting. Meanwhile, two divisions under David Gregg and Alfred Duffié circled via Kelly's Ford and hit Stuart in the right flank and rear. Duffié was slow in attacking, but Gregg's brigades under Hugh Judson Kilpatrick and the Englishman Sir Percy Wyndham cut their way into Stuart's main force east of Brandy Station. The Confederate defenses stiffened, and, by early evening, Pleasonton was forced to pull his various units back. But the Federal cavalrymen had given the vaunted Stuart a bad day. By holding their own in the War's largest all-cavalry battle, the Union horsemen had gained a new confidence that would last through the War.

In Buford's final attack, the 2d U.S. Cavalry gallops past two retiring Federal units toward W. H. F. Lee's Confederates on the rise in the distance.

ORDER OF BATTLE
ARMY OF NORTHERN VIRGINIA
LEE
75,000 MEN

FIRST CORPS
LONGSTREET

McLAWS' DIVISION

KERSHAW'S BRIGADE
SEMMES' BRIGADE
BARKSDALE'S BRIGADE
WOFFORD'S BRIGADE

PICKETT'S DIVISION

GARNETT'S BRIGADE
KEMPER'S BRIGADE
ARMISTEAD'S BRIGADE

HOOD'S DIVISION

LAW'S BRIGADE
ROBERTSON'S BRIGADE
G. T. ANDERSON'S BRIGADE
BENNING'S BRIGADE

SECOND CORPS
EWELL

EARLY'S DIVISION

HAYS' BRIGADE
SMITH'S BRIGADE
GORDON'S BRIGADE
AVERY'S BRIGADE

JOHNSON'S DIVISION

STEUART'S BRIGADE
WALKER'S BRIGADE
WILLIAMS' BRIGADE
JONES' BRIGADE

RODES' DIVISION

DANIEL'S BRIGADE
IVERSON'S BRIGADE
DOLES' BRIGADE
RAMSEUR'S BRIGADE
O'NEAL'S BRIGADE

THIRD CORPS
HILL

R. H. ANDERSON'S DIVISION

WILCOX'S BRIGADE
WRIGHT'S BRIGADE
MAHONE'S BRIGADE
LANG'S BRIGADE
POSEY'S BRIGADE

HETH'S DIVISION

PETTIGREW'S BRIGADE
BROCKENBROUGH'S BRIGADE
ARCHER'S BRIGADE
DAVIS' BRIGADE

PENDER'S DIVISION

PERRIN'S BRIGADE
LANE'S BRIGADE
THOMAS' BRIGADE
SCALES' BRIGADE

CAVALRY
STUART

HAMPTON'S BRIGADE
F. LEE'S BRIGADE
ROBERTSON'S BRIGADE
JENKINS' BRIGADE
JONES' BRIGADE
W. H. F. LEE'S BRIGADE

ARMY OF THE POTOMAC
MEADE
85,500 MEN

I CORPS REYNOLDS

FIRST DIVISION: WADSWORTH
Brigades: MEREDITH, CUTLER

SECOND DIVISION: ROBINSON
Brigades: PAUL, BAXTER

THIRD DIVISION: ROWLEY
Brigades: BIDDLE, STONE, STANNARD

II CORPS HANCOCK

FIRST DIVISION: CALDWELL
Brigades: CROSS, KELLY, ZOOK, BROOKE

SECOND DIVISION: GIBBON
Brigades: HARROW, WEBB, HALL

THIRD DIVISION: HAYS
Brigades: CARROLL, SMYTH, WILLARD

III CORPS SICKLES

FIRST DIVISION: BIRNEY
Brigades: GRAHAM, WARD, DE TROBRIAND

SECOND DIVISION: HUMPHREYS
Brigades: CARR, BREWSTER, BURLING

V CORPS SYKES

FIRST DIVISION: BARNES
Brigades: TILTON, SWEITZER, VINCENT

SECOND DIVISION: AYRES
Brigades: DAY, BURBANK, WEED

THIRD DIVISION: CRAWFORD
Brigades: McCANDLESS, FISHER

VI CORPS SEDGWICK

FIRST DIVISION: WRIGHT
Brigades: TORBERT, BARTLETT, RUSSELL

SECOND DIVISION: HOWE
Brigades: GRANT, NEILL

THIRD DIVISION: NEWTON
Brigades: SHALER, EUSTIS, WHEATON

XI CORPS HOWARD

FIRST DIVISION: BARLOW
Brigades: VON GILSA, AMES

SECOND DIVISION: VON STEINWEHR
Brigades: COSTER, SMITH

THIRD DIVISION: SCHURZ
Brigades: SCHIMMELFENNIG, KRZYZANOWSKI

XII CORPS SLOCUM

FIRST DIVISION: WILLIAMS
Brigades: McDOUGALL, LOCKWOOD, RUGER

SECOND DIVISION: GEARY
Brigades: CANDY, COBHAM, GREENE

CAVALRY CORPS PLEASONTON

FIRST DIVISION: BUFORD
Brigades: GAMBLE, DEVIN, MERRITT

SECOND DIVISION: GREGG
Brigades: McINTOSH, HUEY, GREGG

THIRD DIVISION: KILPATRICK
Brigades: FARNSWORTH, CUSTER

At the height of his reputation in the summer of 1863, Robert E. Lee was beloved by his countrymen, feared by his enemies, and respected by both. His careworn, grandfatherly face disguised the grim determination and fierce combativeness that for a second time compelled him to carry the War north.

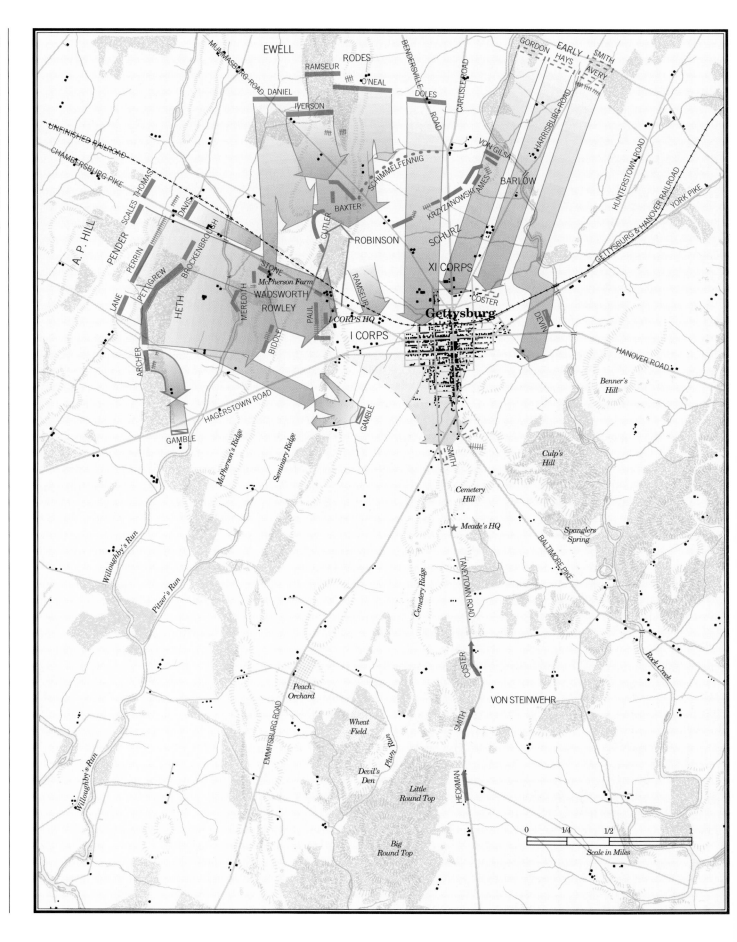

John Reynolds, one of the Union's finest generals, was shot from his horse while organizing the defense of McPherson's Ridge. In the photograph below, the white-shirted figure points to the edge of McPherson's Woods where Reynolds was killed; visible beyond the rise at upper left is Seminary Ridge.

OPENING CONFEDERATE ATTACKS, JULY 1

The Battle of Gettysburg began by accident on July 1 when General Henry Heth's division of A. P. Hill's 3d Corps, marching up the Chambersburg Pike toward Gettysburg at dawn, unexpectedly ran into elements of John Buford's Federal cavalry division. A vicious fight ensued for possession of McPherson's Ridge, and the sound of battle soon brought larger forces to the field. Brigades from General John Reynolds' I Corps joined in the fighting piecemeal through the late morning to help Buford's men hold the McPherson woods and farm against Heth's attacks. During a two-hour lull at midday, both sides rushed in reinforcements: Howard's Federal XI Corps fanned out north of Gettysburg while Heth was joined by Pender, and Rodes' division of Ewell's corps took up positions northwest of the town. Rodes attacked around 2:30 p.m. but was repulsed with heavy losses. Shortly thereafter, however, Ewell's division under Jubal Early hit Howard's weak right flank and sent the Federals streaming southward. At about the same time, Heth and Pender surged forward and the Federal I Corps also gave way, falling back through Gettysburg to the high ground of Cemetery and Culp's hills.

Maj. Gen. Henry Heth, whose troops sparked the battle when seeking shoes from a warehouse, ranked last in his West Point class but proved an able field commander. At left, John Brockenbrough's brigade attacks along the Chambersburg Pike toward McPherson's barn and woods.

A photograph taken on Seminary Ridge after the battle shows the view of Gettysburg that confronted A. P. Hill's troops when they drove eastward toward the town in a second series of assaults on the afternoon of July 1. The embankment of an unfinished railroad is at left, the Chambersburg Pike at right.

Federal reinforcements move up through the casualties of earlier fighting toward the embattled McPherson farm to help hold off Heth's attacking Confederates. In the foreground, litter-bearers carry off the body of General Reynolds.

Maj. Gen. George Gordon Meade, initially reluctant to command the Army of the Potomac, responded with decisiveness, moving swiftly to block Lee in Pennsylvania. On the evening of July 1, Meade decided momentously to stay and defend the high ground south of Gettysburg. Throughout the battle, an aide said, he was "quick, bold, cheerful, and hopeful."

OPENING SITUATION, JULY 2

Stubbornly determined to attack despite Longstreet's urgent advice to sideslip past the Federals and fight on more favorable ground, General Lee redeployed his army on the morning of July 2 for a complex echeloned assault that would move in stages from south to north along the Union line. He first sent Longstreet's I Corps three miles to the south, where the Federal left was exposed and lightly held. There John Bell Hood's division would lead off with an assault on two strategically valuable hills, Big Round Top and Little Round Top. Lafayette McLaws would attack next into an area marked by a large wheat field and a peach orchard. After cracking the Union front, both divisions would turn north and roll up the Federal line, supported by attacks by A. P. Hill from the west and Ewell from the north. If all went by plan, the multiple attacks would crush the Federal defenses in a huge pincers. To face Lee, General Meade crowded five entire corps with two in reserve—more than 85,000 men—in a tight horseshoe that reached from Culp's Hill around Cemetery Hill and on down Cemetery Ridge. Since most of the Confederates were evidently to the north and northeast, that is where Meade concentrated his army. On his left, where the Rebels who were to deliver the first blows were hidden by ridges and woods, his line was stretched thin.

A shattered stone wall and dead horses show the effects of Confederate artillery fire on Taneytown Road, which ran just behind the Union defensive line on Cemetery Ridge. General Meade made his headquarters in the Leister farmhouse (center).

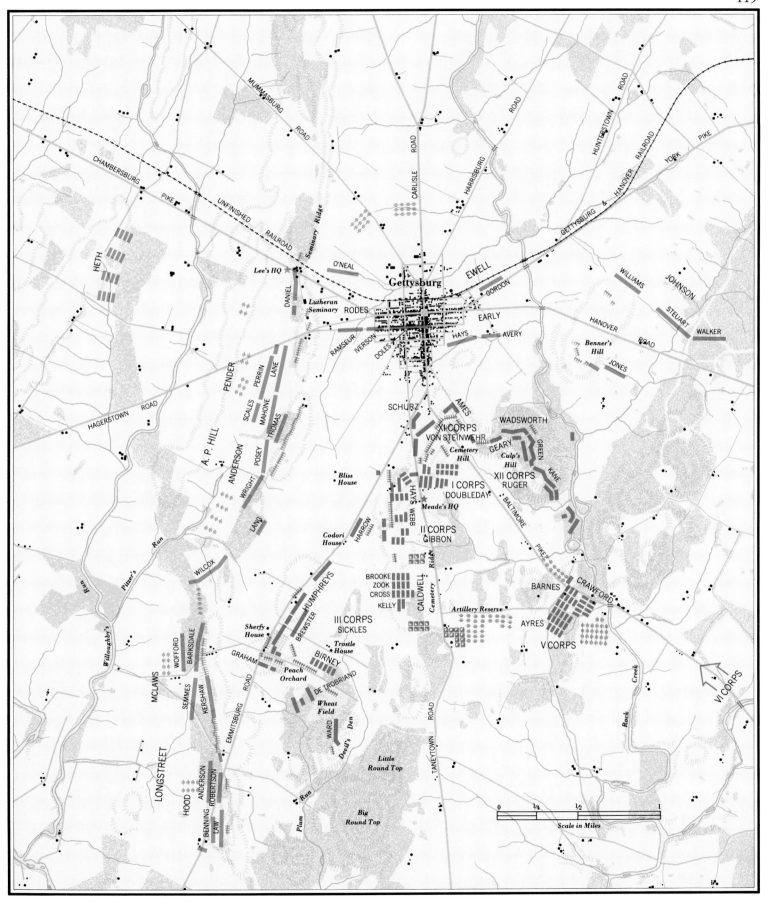

MUMMASBURG ROAD

CHAMBERSBURG PIKE

UNFINISHED RAILROAD

HARRISBURG ROAD

CARLISLE ROAD

HUNTERSTOWN ROAD

GETTYSBURG & HANOVER RAILROAD

YORK PIKE

HETH

Seminary Ridge

O'NEAL

Lee's HQ

EWELL

Gettysburg

Lutheran Seminary

DANIEL

RODES

WILLIAMS

JOHNSON

GORDON

EARLY

STEUART

WALKER

RAMSEUR

IVERSON

DOLES

HAYS

AVERY

HANOVER ROAD

Benner's Hill

JONES

PENDER

PERRIN

LANE

A. P. HILL

SCALES

MAHONE

THOMAS

POSEY

ANDERSON

WRIGHT

LANG

HAGERSTOWN ROAD

SCHURZ

AMES

WADSWORTH

XI CORPS
VON STEINWEHR

Cemetery Hill

GEARY

GREEN

Culp's Hill

XII CORPS
RUGER

KANE

Bliss House

HAYS

WEBB

I CORPS
DOUBLEDAY

Meade's HQ

HARROW

BALTIMORE PIKE

Pitzer's Run

Willoughby's Run

Codori House

II CORPS
GIBBON

Cemetery Ridge

WILCOX

HUMPHREYS

BROOKE

ZOOK

CROSS

KELLY

CALDWELL

BARNES

CRAWFORD

Rock Creek

Artillery Reserve

AYRES

V CORPS

BREWSTER

III CORPS
SICKLES

Sherfy House

WOFFORD

BARKSDALE

GRAHAM

Trostle House

BIRNEY

MCLAWS

SEMMES

KERSHAW

EMMITSBURG ROAD

Peach Orchard

DE TROBRIAND

Wheat Field

WARD

Devil's Den

VI CORPS

LONGSTREET

HOOD

ANDERSON

ROBERTSON

BENNING

LAW

Plum Run

Little Round Top

TANEYTOWN ROAD

Big Round Top

0   1/4   1/2   1

Scale in Miles

John Bell Hood, a Kentucky-born West Pointer, was an implacable warrior who had led his famed Texas brigade in the fighting at the Seven Days' Battles, Second Bull Run, and Antietam. A division commander at Gettysburg, he was severely wounded early in the fighting on July 2 and replaced by Evander Law. Hood had, said one contemporary, "a sad Quixote face, the face of an old crusader."

Troops of Ward's Federal brigade begin to give way as Hood's Confederates scramble into the Devil's Den, a labyrinth of huge boulders and rock-walled passages. Ward lost one-third of the men in his brigade of New York, Pennsylvania, Indiana, and Maine regiments, but his troops inflicted heavy losses on the attacking Rebels.

ROUND TOP—DEVIL'S DEN, FIRST PHASE

Longstreet's attack against the Federal left got under way around 4:00 p.m. when Hood sent Law's and part of Robertson's brigades toward Big Round Top and Plum Run Valley. Encountering only light fire from skirmishers and a single artillery battery, the Confederates easily reached the entrance to the valley and the summit of Big Round Top. But when they pushed on toward Little Round Top, they were stopped by Vincent's Federal brigade, dispatched to the hill at the last minute by General Meade's chief engineer, Gouverneur Warren. Meanwhile, the rest of Robertson's brigade, along with Anderson's and Benning's Georgia brigades, advanced into Plum Run Valley from the west and quickly found themselves in a bloody fight for the boulder-strewn cul-de-sac dubbed the Devil's Den. There the Confederates finally hammered back Ward's Federal brigade, which was trying to hold the left flank of Sickles' exposed III Corps.

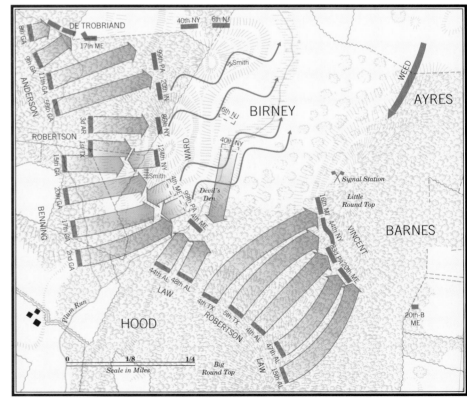

After the battle, the rock-strewn Plum Run Valley was soon to become known as the Valley of Death. In the background are the humps of Big Round Top on the right, Little Round Top on the left.

122

ROUND TOP—DEVIL'S DEN, SECOND PHASE

Attacking up the saddle between Big Round Top and Little Round Top, Alabamians and Texans of Robertson's and Law's brigades repeatedly charged the Federal line on Little Round Top through the waning hours of July 2. Several times they almost broke through, but were stopped by murderous Federal fire and desperate local counterattacks by Vincent's and Weed's brigades. Meanwhile, Benning's Georgians held their hard-won ground around the Devil's Den while Anderson's troops wheeled north to support McLaw's attack into the Wheat Field.

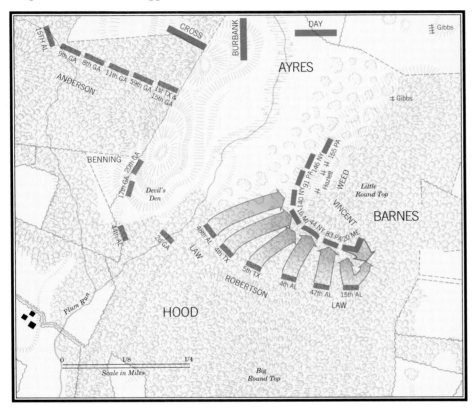

Col. Joshua Chamberlain left a professorship at Maine's Bowdoin College to serve in the Union army, eventually taking command of the 20th Maine. His bold coun- terattack on Little Round Top won him the Medal of Honor.

Parrott guns of Lt. Charles Hazlett's Battery D, 5th U.S. Artillery, fire from their commanding position on the summit of Little Round Top.

Dashing down the south slope of Little Round Top, the 20th Maine, led by Col. Joshua Chamberlain *(sword raised, right of center)*, attacks the 15th Alabama under Col. William Oates *(right foreground)*, who tries to rally his men. Chamberlain ordered the bayonet attack as a last resort after his men had run out of ammunition.

Dozens of Confederate dead, probably killed by Union fire from Little Round Top, can be seen sprawled amid the open rocky area east of Plum Run and the Devil's Den that came to be known as the Slaughter Pen.

MAJ. GEN. DANIEL E. SICKLES

WHEAT FIELD—PEACH ORCHARD, FIRST PHASE

In late afternoon, Anderson's brigade on Hood's left drove back the left wing of Sickles' III Corps, then slammed into Caldwell's division from the II Corps that had moved up into the Wheat Field. Around 5:30, just as Anderson was forced to fall back, Longstreet ordered McLaws' division into the fight, with Kershaw's brigade first and Semmes' brigade following. After taking heavy fire from Federal artillery on their left flank, McLaws' men engaged elements of three Federal divisions in a vicious seesaw battle for control of the Wheat Field, which changed hands six times.

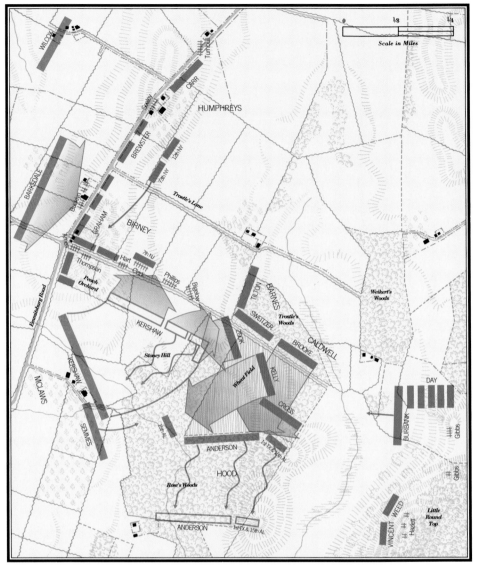

General Sickles (*center*) gallops to inspect Federal troops waiting near the Peach Orchard (*right*) for Confederates to attack from the distant trees.

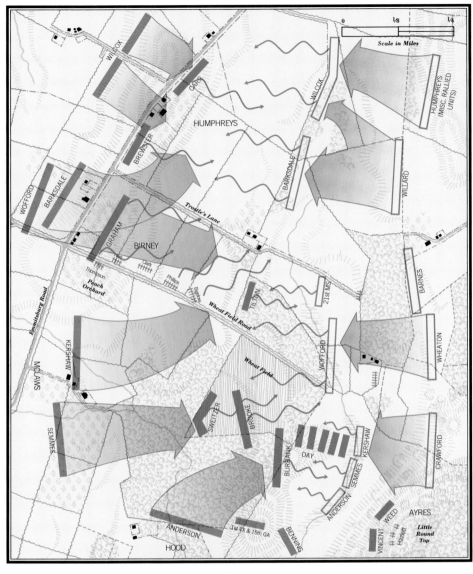

MAJ. GEN. LAFAYETTE McLAWS

WHEAT FIELD—PEACH ORCHARD, SECOND PHASE

While the fighting raged on in the Wheat Field, McLaws launched the brigades of Barksdale and Wofford against Graham's brigade, which held the apex of Sickles' salient at the Peach Orchard. The Federals were swept away in a matter of minutes, and soon the whole Union line gave way in a general retreat back across Plum Run. But after a final attack to the north by elements of A. P. Hill's corps, the Confederates' ground assault sputtered to a halt in the face of darkness, mounting casualties, and stiffening Federal resistance on Cemetery Ridge.

Union dead, probably from Sickles' III Corps, litter a trampled meadow as a burial detail gathers in the distance. The bodies are without shoes, indicating that the Confederates who held the area after the fighting on July 2 had scavenged equipment from the dead.

Urged on by Col. William Colvill *(with arm upraised at center),* troops of the 1st Minnesota make a headlong countercharge into Cadmus Wilcox's Confederates near Cemetery Ridge. Wilcox, exploiting a gap left in the Federal III Corps line during the confused fighting in the Wheat Field and Peach Orchard, threatened momentarily to crack the main Union defenses. Colvill's Minnesotans threw the Confederates back—at a cost of 82 percent of the regiment's men.

General Samuel Crawford's Pennsylvania Reserve Division charges across Plum Run Valley and into Longstreet's Confederates, who had paused on the valley's western side after chasing the last of the Federals from the Wheat Field. Crawford's assault was one of several local Federal counterattacks launched at dusk that checked the advance of the exhausted Rebels.

128

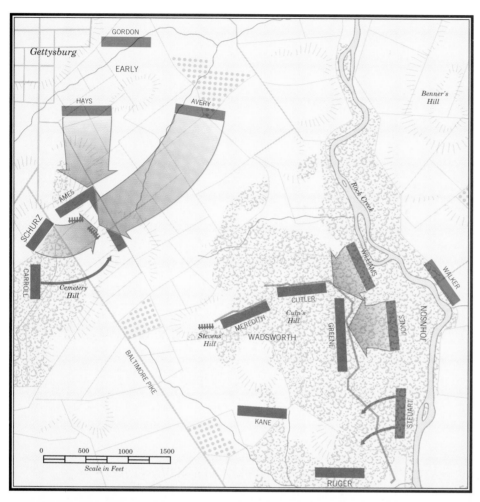

CULP'S HILL—CEMETERY HILL

Lacking precise orders from Lee and displaying little initiative, Richard Ewell failed to attack the northern end of the Federal line until around 6:30 p.m. His twilight assaults, however, threatened to overwhelm the Union defenses. Moving against Culp's Hill from the east, the brigades of Steuart, Jones, and Williams clawed their way to the summit, only to be stopped by Greene's Federals firing from behind hastily erected but formidable breastworks. Attacking from the north, around 8:00 p.m., Hays' Louisiana brigade and Avery's North Carolinians routed a line of Federals behind a stone wall, burst over the brow of Cemetery Hill, drove back still more defenders, and swarmed into the forwardmost Union artillery positions. But the Rebels, now disorganized, shot up, and fighting in pitch darkness, were driven back down the hill by Federal counterattacks spearheaded by Carroll's and Schurz's brigades. The next morning, Ewell renewed his attacks against Culp's Hill only to be repulsed a second time.

Taking cover behind boulders and trees, Confederates of J. M. Williams' brigade advance up Culp's Hill toward Federal positions on the summit.

A postbattle photograph taken from the position of the 5th Maine Battery on Stevens Hill shows the ground crossed by Avery's brigade during its attack on Cemetery Hill *(left)*. The battery's six 12-pounders tore huge gaps in the North Carolinians' ranks as they advanced from right to left across the field of view.

Troops of Hays' 9th Louisiana charge the battery of Capt. R. Bruce Ricketts on the crest of Cemetery Hill. The Louisiana Tigers nearly overran Ricketts' guns before they were forced to retreat.

BRIG. GEN. HARRY THOMPSON HAYS

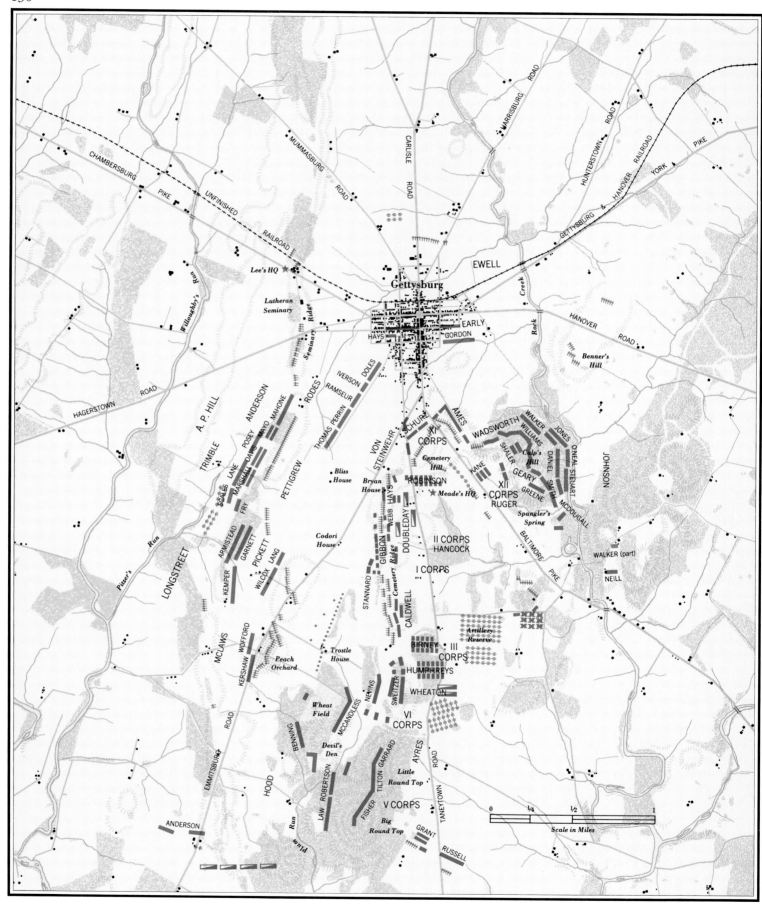

Lee's HQ ★

Gettysburg

EWELL

Lutheran
Seminary

HAYS
GORDON
EARLY

Benner's
Hill

IVERSON DOLES
RODES
RAMSEUR
A. P. HILL
ANDERSON
THOMAS PERRIN

SCHURZ
AMES
XI
CORPS
WADSWORTH
WALKER
WILLIAMS
JONES
O'NEAL STEUART

VON
STEINWEHR
Cemetery
Hill
SHALER
Culp's
Hill
DANIEL
SMITH
JOHNSON

TRIMBLE
POSEY MAHONE
MAYO
LANE
MARSHALL
DAVIS
FRY
PETTIGREW
Bliss
House
Bryan
House
ROBINSON
KANE
GEARY
GREENE
McDOUGALL

SCALES
HAYS
WEBB
Meade's HQ ★
XII
CORPS
RUGER
Spangler's
Spring

ARMSTEAD
GARNETT
PICKETT
Codori
House
GIBBON
Cemetery Ridge
DOUBLEDAY
II CORPS
HANCOCK

Pitzer's Run
LONGSTREET
KEMPER
WILCOX LANG
STANNARD
I CORPS
WALKER (part)

Run
Cemetery Ridge
CALDWELL
NEILL

Artillery
Reserve
✕✕✕
✕✕✕
✕✕✕

MCLAWS
WOFFORD
Trostle
House
BIRNEY
III
CORPS

KERSHAW
Peach
Orchard
HUMPHREYS
SWEITZER
WHEATON

Wheat
Field
NEVINS
VI
CORPS

BENNING
McCANDLESS
Devil's
Den

EMMITSBURG ROAD
HOOD
LAW
ROBERTSON
FISHER TILTON GARRARD
Little
Round Top
AYRES
V CORPS

ANDERSON
Plum Run
Big
Round Top
GRANT
RUSSELL

TANEYTOWN ROAD

BALTIMORE PIKE

0   1/4   1/2   1
Scale in Miles

CHAMBERSBURG PIKE
UNFINISHED
RAILROAD
Willoughby's Run

MUMMASBURG ROAD

CARLISLE ROAD

WARRISBURG ROAD

HUNTERSTOWN ROAD

GETTYSBURG & HANOVER RAILROAD

YORK PIKE

HANOVER ROAD

Rock Creek

HAGERSTOWN ROAD

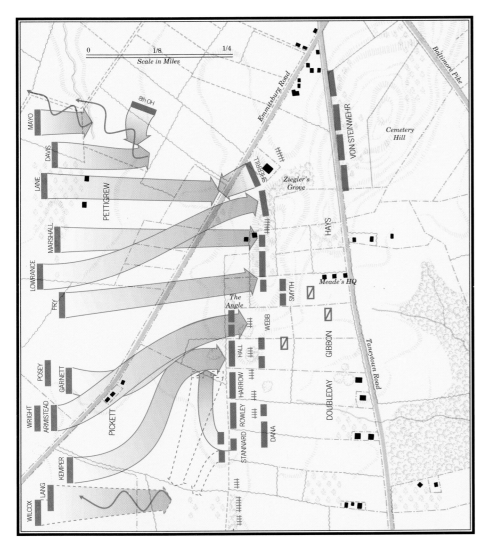

George Pickett, who lost 3,000 men in the doomed charge, uttered a simple but moving epitaph when asked to prepare his division for a Federal countercharge. "General Lee," he said, "I have no division now."

PICKETT'S CHARGE, JULY 3

After two days of fighting, the Confederates retained the initiative, but the costly attacks against the Federal flanks had failed to dislodge Meade's army. Still grimly determined to force the issue at Gettysburg, Lee deployed his forces on the third day, this time on the weakened center of the Union line *(map, left)*. Making the attack would be the fresh troops of General George Pickett's division along with already battered units from Hill's corps, including the wounded Henry Heth's division, now led by James Pettigrew, plus two of Pender's brigades under Isaac Trimble. Facing the Confederates on Cemetery Ridge were elements of the I and II Corps under Hancock's command with reserves posted nearby. After a two-hour artillery bombardment that inflicted little damage on the Federal front line, the Confederate infantry started forward at 3:00 p.m. *(map,*

above). The brigades of James Kemper, Richard Garnett, and Lewis Armistead advanced obliquely to their left to close up with Pettigrew, exposing their right flanks to fire from Union guns. Pettigrew's men were similarly mauled by batteries on Cemetery Hill. As the flanks of both divisions contracted, the Federals overlapped the Confederates and poured in a terrible fire. Despite dreadful losses, Pettigrew's men rushed the Federal line defended by Hays' division—and were staggered by musket and cannon fire. Most of the survivors of Pickett's brigades attacked the Angle, a jog in a stone wall, where they were pulverized by fire from Gibbon's division. The Rebels flooded over the wall but were blasted back by Union reserves. With that repulse, the Confederates began streaming to the rear. The charge—and the Battle of Gettysburg—was over.

Brig. Gen. James Johnston Pettigrew, commanding Heth's division, was wounded during the charge but was one of the last to leave the field. Two weeks later he was killed during the retreat from Gettysburg.

The painting below portrays the climactic moment when the Confederates, now led by Lewis Armistead, the last of Pickett's brigadier generals still on his feet, swarmed over the wall near the Angle. They were met by murderous fire from Federal reinforcements, who then charged and hurled back the attackers. As the battered survivors staggered back to Seminary Ridge, Lee rode among them *(right)* offering encouragement and accepting the blame for the failure of the attack. The next evening he set his army in motion toward Virginia, starting a painful 10-day retreat during which he managed to hold off Meade's delayed, ineffective pursuit and withdraw his forces across the Potomac River. Lee's losses at Gettysburg were catastrophic: about 28,000 men, or nearly 40 percent of his force, compared with about 25 percent for the Federals. But Lee's army had survived to fight again.

WILDERNESS CAMPAIGN

On March 8, 1864, a journalist attending a White House reception for Ulysses S. Grant described the heralded honoree as a "little, scared-looking man." When the unassuming lieutenant general took command of all Union forces four days later, his troops were similarly unimpressed. President Lincoln, however, knew Grant for a fighter and was convinced he would achieve what a succession of Union generals had not—the destruction of the Confederate armies and the conquest of the Confederacy. The president's confidence would be put to the test that spring as his new commander led the Union forces against the army of the formidable and brilliant Robert E. Lee in a series of battles whose names would live in history: the Wilderness, Spotsylvania, and Cold Harbor.

Grant reorganized and reequipped the Army of the Potomac, which awaited the coming Wilderness campaign in winter quarters at Brandy Station, Virginia, and reinforced its ranks with idle troops from Washington and other garrisons. His orders to General George Meade, commander of the Army of the Potomac, were succinct:

In the opening move of the Federal offensive in the Wilderness, troops of Gen. John Sedgwick's VI Corps cross a pontoon bridge over the Rapidan River at Germanna Ford on May 4.

"Lee's army will be your objective point. Wherever Lee goes, there you will go also." General Grant would map the strategy and General Meade the tactics in a series of flanking maneuvers that would culminate in a climactic drive on Richmond.

Blocking the path to the Confederate capital was Lee's Army of Northern Virginia, which had pulled back south of the Rapidan River after being defeated at Gettysburg the year before. Heavy casualties and a rash of desertions had sapped the strength of the Rebels, and the South, with its smaller population, was hard-pressed to replace the losses.

Counting on the Union's superior reserves of men and matériel, Grant was confident that he could defeat Lee's forces by grinding them down in a war of attrition. In the spring of 1864, as the nation entered the final and most bitter year of the Civil War, Grant crossed the Rapidan and met his adversary in the tangled thickets of the Wilderness. In the series of close-range, bloody battles that followed, the new commander learned that there would be no easy victories.

Ulysses S. Grant, whose usual dress consisted of a private's blouse with shoulder straps tacked on to indicate his rank, is shown wearing his lieutenant general's uniform with his customary casual air. Col. Charles Wainwright of the V Corps complained that the Union commander "rode along the line in a slouchy, unobservant way, with his coat unbuttoned and setting anything but an example of military bearing to the troops."

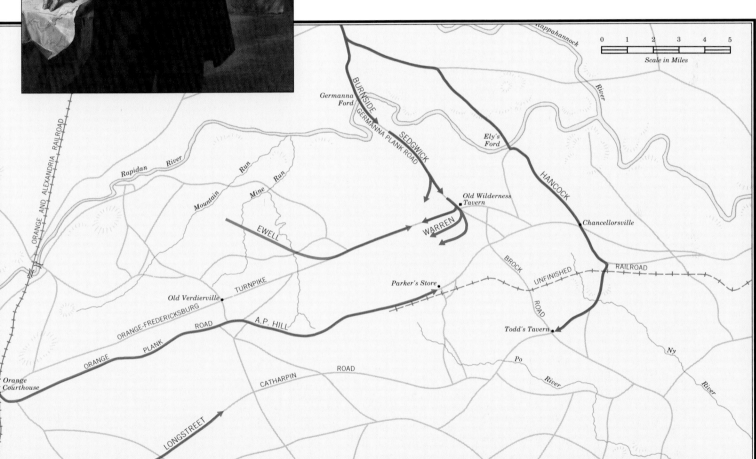

INTO THE WILDERNESS, MAY 4-5

Just after midnight on May 4, 1864, Meade's Army of the Potomac left its camps around Culpeper and soon began crossing the Rapidan in two columns, intending to envelop Lee's right flank. Warren's V Corps crossed first at Germanna Ford and headed southwest, followed by Sedgwick's VI Corps. Hancock's II Corps crossed at Ely's Ford, six miles east of Germanna, and reached Chancellorsville by the afternoon of May 5. That afternoon Ambrose Burnside's IX Corps, originally held in reserve to guard the Orange & Alexandria Railroad, was ordered to cross the river and join the army. By 9:00 a.m. on May 4, Lee had received scouting reports that confirmed his suspicions of a crossing on the Confederate right. Although the Army of Northern Virginia was outnumbered nearly two to one—with 61,000 men to the Union's 118,000—it enjoyed the advantage of experienced commanders operating in familiar territory. To counter the Federal attack, Lee moved Ewell's 2d Corps from the vicinity of Mine Run eastward along the Orange-Fredericksburg Turnpike. A. P. Hill's 3d Corps, camped upstream on the Rapidan and south of Ewell, was instructed to advance along Orange Plank Road. Stationed to the south, Longstreet received orders to move his 1st Corps up Catharpin Road.

General Charles Griffin, whose division opened the fighting on May 5, was one of the most seasoned Federal commanders. Gruff and bellicose, he harangued Meade in the presence of Grant after Griffin's failed attack.

ORDER OF BATTLE

ARMY OF NORTHERN VIRGINIA
LEE
61,000 MEN

FIRST CORPS
LONGSTREET

KERSHAW'S DIVISION	FIELD'S DIVISION
HENAGAN'S BRIGADE	JENKINS' BRIGADE
HUMPHREYS' BRIGADE	G. T. ANDERSON'S BRIGADE
WOFFORD'S BRIGADE	LAW'S BRIGADE
BRYAN'S BRIGADE	GREGG'S BRIGADE
	BENNING'S BRIGADE

SECOND CORPS
EWELL

EARLY'S DIVISION	JOHNSON'S DIVISION	RODES' DIVISION
HAYS' BRIGADE	J. A. WALKER'S BRIGADE	DANIEL'S BRIGADE
PEGRAM'S BRIGADE	STEUART'S BRIGADE	RAMSEUR'S BRIGADE
GORDON'S BRIGADE	JONES' BRIGADE	DOLES' BRIGADE
	STAFFORD'S BRIGADE	BATTLE'S BRIGADE
		JOHNSTON'S BRIGADE

THIRD CORPS
HILL

R. H. ANDERSON'S DIVISION	HETH'S DIVISION	WILCOX'S DIVISION
PERRIN'S BRIGADE	DAVIS' BRIGADE	LANE'S BRIGADE
MAHONE'S BRIGADE	KIRKLAND'S BRIGADE	McGOWAN'S BRIGADE
HARRIS' BRIGADE	COOKE'S BRIGADE	SCALES' BRIGADE
WRIGHT'S BRIGADE	H. H. WALKER'S BRIGADE	THOMAS' BRIGADE
PERRY'S BRIGADE	ARCHER'S BRIGADE	

CAVALRY CORPS
STUART

HAMPTON'S DIVISION	F. LEE'S DIVISION	W. H. F. LEE'S DIVISION
YOUNG'S BRIGADE	LOMAX'S BRIGADE	CHAMBLISS' BRIGADE
ROSSER'S BRIGADE	WICKHAM'S BRIGADE	GORDON'S BRIGADE
BUTLER'S BRIGADE		

ARMY OF THE POTOMAC
GRANT/MEADE
118,000 MEN

II CORPS HANCOCK	V CORPS WARREN	VI CORPS SEDGWICK
FIRST DIVISION: BARLOW *Brigades:* MILES, SMYTH, FRANK, BROOKE	FIRST DIVISION: C. GRIFFIN *Brigades:* AYRES, SWEITZER, BARTLETT	FIRST DIVISION: WRIGHT *Brigades:* BROWN, UPTON, RUSSELL, SHALER
SECOND DIVISION: GIBBON *Brigades:* WEBB, OWEN, CARROLL	SECOND DIVISION: ROBINSON *Brigades:* LEONARD, BAXTER, DENISON	SECOND DIVISION: GETTY *Brigades:* WHEATON, GRANT, NEILL, EUSTIS
THIRD DIVISION: BIRNEY *Brigades:* WARD, HAYS	THIRD DIVISION: CRAWFORD *Brigades:* McCANDLESS, FISHER	THIRD DIVISION: RICKETTS *Brigades:* MORRIS, SEYMOUR
FOURTH DIVISION: MOTT *Brigades:* McALLISTER, BREWSTER	FOURTH DIVISION: WADSWORTH *Brigades:* CUTLER, RICE, STONE	

IX CORPS BURNSIDE	CAVALRY CORPS SHERIDAN
FIRST DIVISION: STEVENSON *Brigades:* CARRUTH, LEASURE	FIRST DIVISION: TORBERT *Brigades:* CUSTER, DEVIN, MERRITT
SECOND DIVISION: POTTER *Brigades:* BLISS, S. G. GRIFFIN	SECOND DIVISION: D. M. GREGG *Brigades:* DAVIES, J. I. GREGG
THIRD DIVISION: WILLCOX *Brigades:* HARTRANFT, CHRIST	THIRD DIVISION: WILSON *Brigades:* BRYAN, CHAPMAN
FOURTH DIVISION: FERRERO *Brigades:* SIGFRIED, THOMAS	

137

OPENING ACTION, MAY 5

The battle started shortly after noon on May 5, when Griffin's V Corps division attacked Johnson's division of Ewell's corps positioned along the western side of Sanders' Field. Johnson's left held against repeated assaults, but Griffin, along with a brigade from Wadsworth's division, broke through the Rebel center south of the turnpike. The Federals were soon forced to fall back from lack of support after Confederate counterattacks drove back Wadsworth's left and Wright's division of

Sedgwick's VI Corps was held up by dense undergrowth and skirmishers from the 1st North Carolina Cavalry. Farther south, Getty's Federal division, holding the intersection of Brock and Orange Plank roads, was attacked by A. P. Hill's 3d Corps. The brigades of Henry Heth's division slowly pushed the Federals back until Hancock's II Corps arrived to reinforce Getty's left flank. A stalemate ensued as nightfall brought an end to the fighting.

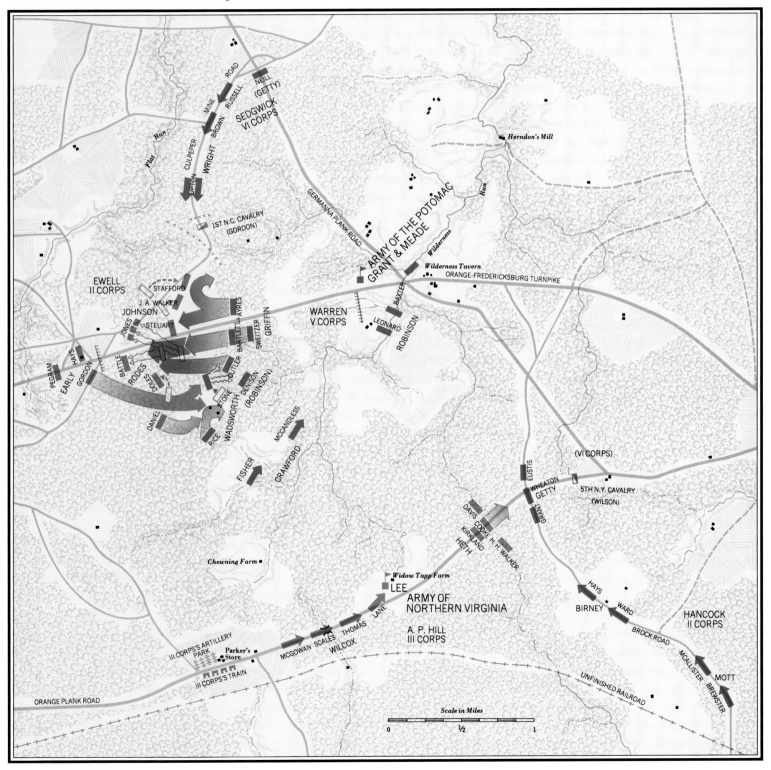

138

Maj. Gen. Gouverneur K. Warren *(near right)* was a capable but irascible commander, whose V Corps troops fought Richard Ewell's Confederates to a standoff on May 5. Brig. Gen. John Marshall Jones *(far right)* was killed along Orange Turnpike while trying to rally his crumbling brigade against Warren's V Corps. Ewell called the loss of Jones "an irreparable one to his brigade."

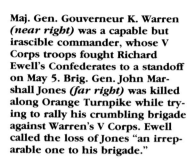

Men of John Sedgwick's VI Corps trade fire with Confederates while at their feet wounded comrades try to crawl to safety. The scrub forest and nearly impenetrable brush of the Wilderness impeded battle lines and the use of artillery, forcing the armies to fight at close range.

Skirmishers of Sedgwick's VI Corps probe for their foe as a brigade draws up behind them in this painting by Civil War veteran Julian Scott.

FINAL ACTION, MAY 6

On the morning of May 6, Hancock's Federals seized the initiative and shattered A. P. Hill's line across Orange Plank Road, throwing the Rebels back to Tapp's farm until stopped by Longstreet's troops, who arrived to relieve Hill's exhausted corps. Longstreet's men struck the Federal flank and rolled up the Union line "like a wet blanket," in the words of Hancock. The Confederates had advanced nearly to Brock Road by early afternoon when Longstreet was wounded by friendly fire and the attack faltered. Lee launched a second assault against Hancock at about 4:00 p.m., but by that time, Burnside's troops had arrived to shore up Hancock's right. Brush fires and Union reserves helped stymie the Confederate advance. Farther north, Early's division launched a surprise attack on the Union right at about 6:00 p.m., throwing Sedgwick's right flank into disarray, but darkness and Federal reserves put an end to the assault. In two days' fighting, Lee's army had sustained at least 7,500 casualties; Grant had lost 17,666 men killed, wounded, and missing.

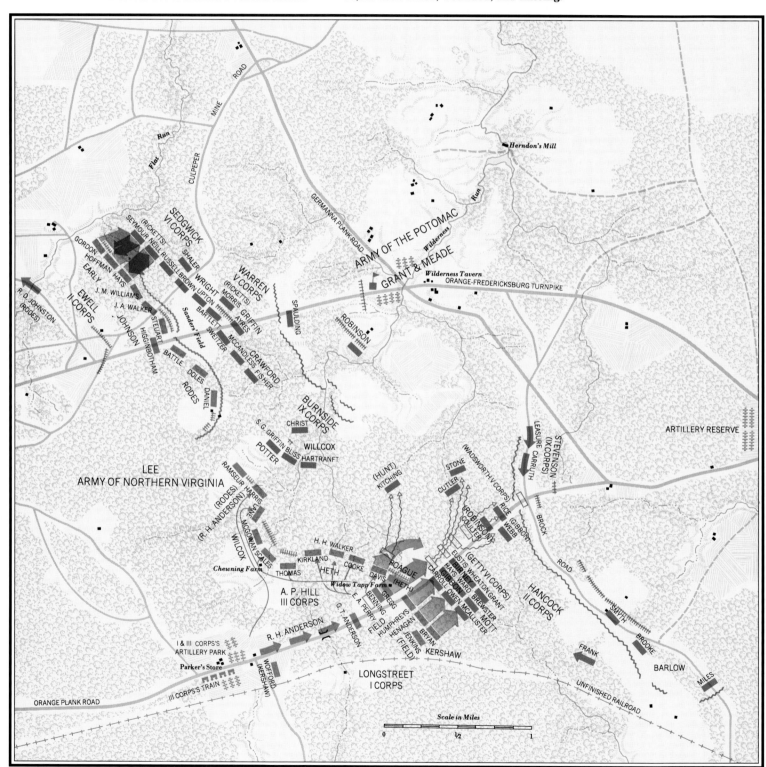

Hastily thrown up by Ewell's men on May 5, these Confederate breastworks were the first to be erected in the campaign.

Troops of Brig. Gen. James Wadsworth's division exchange fire with Confederates in the woods by Orange Plank Road on May 6 *(inset)*. Later that day, Lee's men *(bottom)* momentarily gain the smoldering Union breastworks along Brock Road in an incorrectly dated sketch showing the height of the Rebel assault. Musket flashes ignited the tinder and dead leaves that blanketed the woods, aggravating the already grueling conditions at the front.

Ignoring orders to keep silent lest the Confederates hear them, Federal troops cheer General Grant *(center, on horse)* for his decision to press on to Richmond rather than withdraw after the Battle of the Wilderness.

Todd's Tavern, at the intersection of Brock, Catharpin, and Piney Branch roads, was the scene of some of the first fighting of the Spotsylvania campaign.

WILDERNESS TO SPOTSYLVANIA, MAY 7-9

Despite heavy losses in the Wilderness, Grant continued to press the Confederates toward Richmond. At 8:30 p.m. on May 7, the Army of the Potomac began moving southeast toward Spotsylvania courthouse. Warren's V Corps marched southward along Brock Road, passing behind the smoldering breastworks of Hancock's men, who held their position to cover the army's shift southward before following. Sedgwick and his VI Corps headed east and then turned south, followed by Burnside's corps. Apprised of Grant's intentions, Lee ordered Richard Anderson, who had taken over from the wounded Longstreet, to withdraw from his position on Orange Plank Road and lead his men on a night march to Spotsylvania, where they arrived just in time to block Warren's advance. Ewell's 2d Corps and Hill's 3d Corps, now commanded by Jubal Early while Hill was on sick leave, followed close behind. The Confederates spent the morning of May 9 throwing up earthworks, waiting for the Federal assault that was sure to come.

Gen. John Sedgwick, affectionately known as Uncle John, was killed by a sniper's bullet at Spotsylvania while directing the emplacement of artillery before the battle on May 10. Just as he was reassuring his front-line troops that Confederate sharpshooters "couldn't hit an elephant at this distance," a bullet slammed into Sedgwick's face below his left eye.

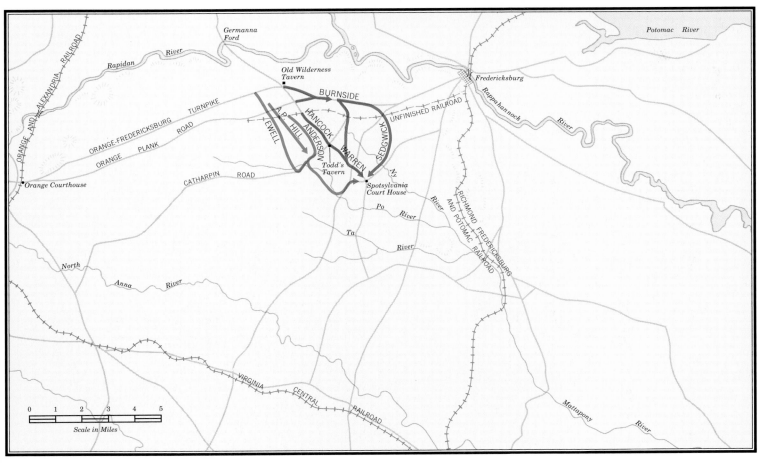

For his boldly conceived assault on the Mule Shoe salient, Colonel Emory Upton, 24 years old *(above)*, was promoted to brigadier general.

The Federals marveled at the speed with which their foe threw up defensive obstacles, such as these abatis (felled trees with sharpened branches) in the Wilderness *(above)*. At Spotsylvania near the Bloody Angle, the Confederates also constructed log-and-earth breastworks *(right)*, which became sites for some of the deadliest close-range fighting of the war.

General Richard (Fighting Dick) Heron Anderson, whose troops beat the Federals in the race to Spotsylvania, was one of the South's most popular leaders. When he replaced Longstreet as 1st Corps commander, Anderson's new men tossed their caps in the air, moving the general to tears.

OPENING FEDERAL ATTACKS, MAY 10

By May 10, the entrenched Confederate front resembled a ragged V, with a strong salient—known as the Mule Shoe by its defenders—that protruded northward in the center. At 4:00 p.m., Warren's V Corps launched an attack on Anderson's corps on the left flank of the V, but the Federals gained no ground and lost about 3,000 men. Two hours later, a scratch brigade of Wright's VI Corps—12 regiments under Col. Emory Upton—spearheaded an attack directly on the Mule Shoe. Upton's concentrated force, striking three regiments wide and four lines deep, pierced Ewell's line just west of the salient's apex and tore a narrow but deep gap in the Confederate defenses. Catching the defenders unaware, Upton's attackers clawed their way through tangled abatis and sent Gen. George Doles' Georgia brigade running. The Federal regiments, however, could not keep the fissure open without help and were forced to withdraw when reinforcements promised from Mott's division of II Corps failed to appear.

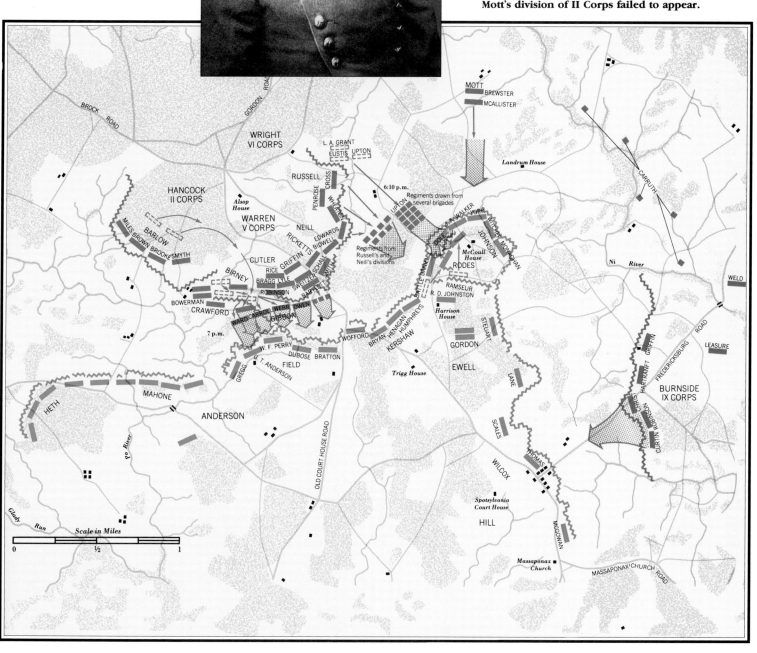

146

BLOODY ANGLE, MAY 12

After pausing on May 11 to regroup his forces, Grant launched 20,000 men of Hancock's II Corps against the apex of the Mule Shoe in an attempt to repeat Upton's attack on a massive scale. Led by Francis Channing Barlow's division, the Federals penetrated the Confederate line, routing the brigades of Gen. Edward Johnson's division at the toe of the salient. In an effort to stem the Union tide, John Gordon shifted his three brigades from the west side of the salient to confront the Federals. Supported by Rodes and Early, Gordon forced the Federals out of much of the Mule Shoe but failed to reclaim it. Meanwhile, Burnside had hit the eastern face of the salient, where he met with some initial success but was eventually driven back. At 6:00 a.m., Wright's VI Corps joined the attack from the northwest—throwing his men against Rodes' in the so-called Bloody Angle, where brutal fighting raged and ended inconclusively. The toll for two days at Spotsylvania: more than 10,000 casualties for each side.

Gen. John B. Gordon saved the day for the Confederates with a daring counterattack. "With that splendid audacity which characterized him," one of Lee's staff officers explained, Gordon rushed his men from the west side of the Mule Shoe salient into the path of the oncoming Federals.

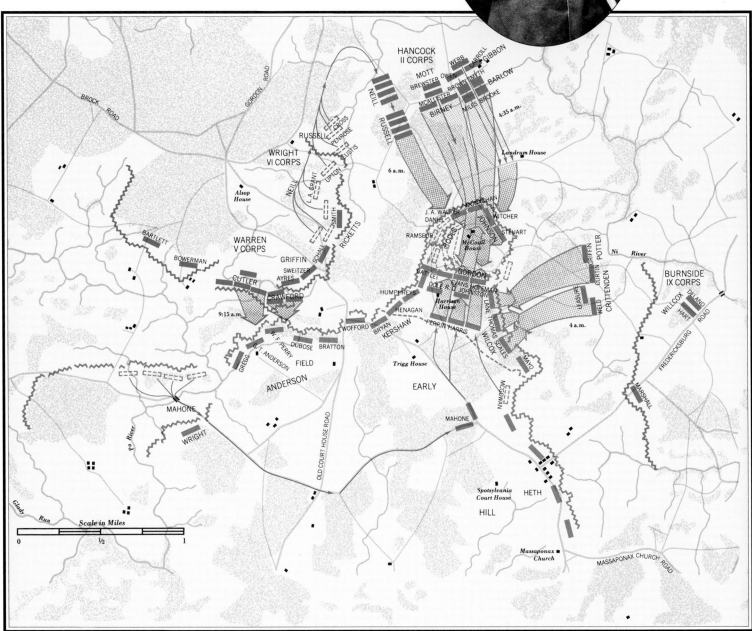

Attacking near Spotsylvania courthouse early on May 12, Hancock's Federals surge over breastworks ready to grapple with Confederates in a salient known thereafter as the Bloody Angle for the savage fighting that raged there *(above)*. At left, opposing ranks face each other on opposite sides of an earthwork near the Bloody Angle, at such close range that men can be seen attempting to draw fire with hats held up on ramrods. An officer wrote in horror of the "mass of torn and mutilated corpses" strewn over the field of battle here.

A 160-foot pontoon bridge spans the North Anna River at Jericho Mill about two miles north of Hanover Junction, where an attack by Gen. A. P. Hill's Confederates surprised troops of the V Corps on May 23. Panicking Federals rushed across to the safety of the north bank *(background)*.

On the grounds of the Massaponax Baptist Church, General Grant, smoking a cigar, sits in a pew directly beneath the trees, and General Meade, reading a map, sits at the far end of the pew at left. The Union's commanding generals held an impromptu war council in the churchyard on the afternoon of May 21 on their way from Spotsylvania to Guiney's Station.

SPOTSYLVANIA TO COLD HARBOR, MAY 9-31

On the morning of May 9, Union cavalry commander Philip Sheridan swung his column to avoid the brewing battle at Spotsylvania and looped to the southwest to strike at Jeb Stuart *(dashed lines)*. Stuart's cavalry followed and the two forces met at Yellow Tavern on May 11, where the Confederates broke and Stuart was mortally wounded. Sheridan then regained Grant along the North Anna on May 24. The fighting continued at Spotsylvania Courthouse until May 20, when Grant attempted to turn the Confederate right flank by sending Hancock's II Corps to Milford Station, with the other Federal corps following. As soon as Lee detected the Federal movement, he dropped back to the south and headed for the banks of the North Anna near Hanover Junction, where the two armies collided on May 23. After four days of skirmishes, the Federal army went on the march again, crossing the Pamunkey at Hanovertown. Learning of the Federal movement early on May 27, Lee marched 18 miles south to Atlee's Station and then to positions at Cold Harbor to block the approaches to Richmond.

In a May 19 attack that marked the end of
the fighting around Spotsylvania, Ewell's
2d Corps was turned back by a division of
former heavy artillerymen on the fields of
Alsop's farm *(dotted line on map, below)*.
In the photograph at right, Confederate
dead are laid out for burial near the farm.
Standing by are the men of the 1st Massachusetts Heavy Artillery, who were
assigned the grim duty of burying the
fallen of both sides.

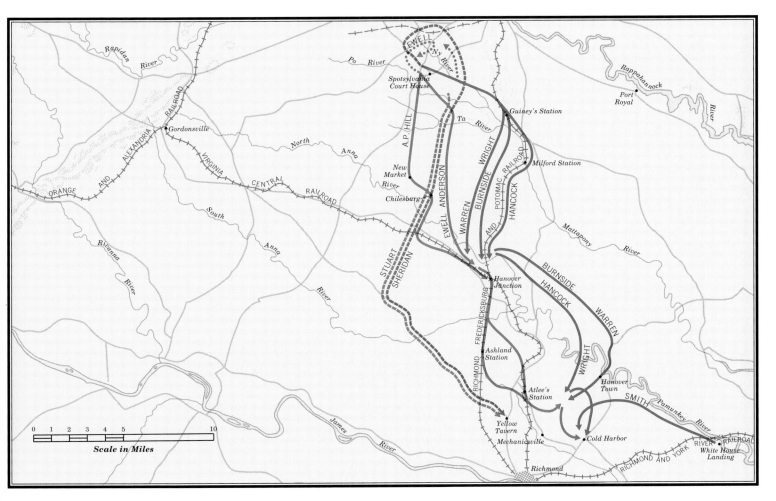

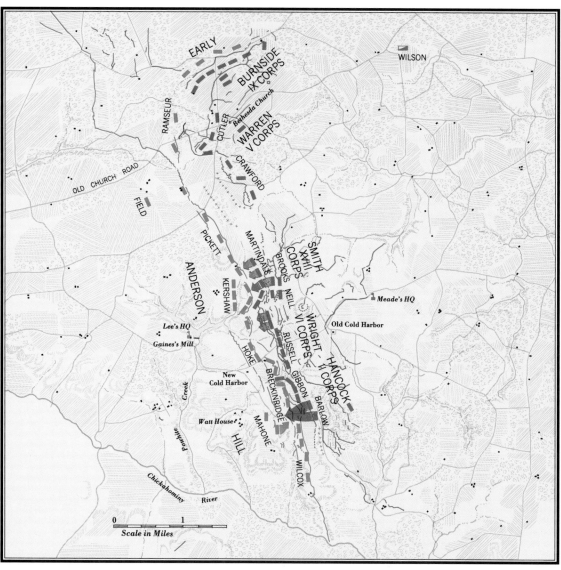

After three days of inconclusive sparring for control of the vital crossroads of Cold Harbor, Grant decided to launch a massive head-on attack, hoping to drive the dug-in Confederates back to the Chickahominy River. At 4:30 a.m. on June 3, the II, VI, and the newly arrived XVIII Corps under Gen. William Smith—together totaling 50,000 men—advanced on the lines of Hill and Anderson and reached to within 50 yards of the Confederate breastworks before heavy fire forced the Federals to the ground. In furious fighting on the extreme left of the Union line, Barlow's division of II Corps overran the lines held by Breckinridge and captured an advance position, but was repulsed trying to carry Hill's main breastworks. By the end of the day, the opposing lines had stabilized within 100 yards of each other. Bitter static fighting continued until June 12. The cost of one month of campaigning had been staggering. Grant had lost 50,000 men, Lee about 30,000. Grant's fourth major thrust toward Richmond was thwarted, and now he set his sights on Petersburg.

An April 1865 photograph *(left)* shows what remained of the Confederate breastworks after Cold Harbor. As depicted in the sketch below, these obstacles halted the disastrous June 1 and 3 Federal XVIII Corps attacks on Joseph Kershaw's division.

1864 VALLEY CAMPAIGN

In the spring of 1864, the fertile Shenandoah Valley once again became a battleground. As part of General Ulysses S. Grant's grand strategy to grind down the Confederacy with relentless multifront offensives, he was determined to wrest control of this vital region away from his hard-pressed foe.

Mastery of the Shenandoah Valley was critical to Grant's plans not only because the Valley was a rich breadbasket for the South. But it also provided Confederate General Robert E. Lee's army with an invasion route into the states of Maryland and Pennsylvania, and, conversely, the Valley lay on the flank of a Federal advance on Richmond. An advance into the Shenandoah would force Lee to further stretch his already-thinned-out forces to defend it.

The first Union attempt, led by the bumbling General Franz Sigel, was turned back by General John Breckenridge's patchwork Rebel army at New Market in May. Breckenridge's departure to reinforce Lee, however, left the Valley open to Federal depredations, and Lee was forced to send in Jubal Early's Corps to chase the Yankees out. Shortly after, the Confederates took the offensive: Early invaded Maryland and threatened Washington before returning to defend the Valley. Shaken, the Federals put Grant's personal choice, General Philip H. Sheridan, in command of the Army of the Shenandoah, setting the stage for the confrontation that would climax in the Battle of Cedar Creek on October 19.

Running broad and straight, northeast to southwest, the Valley Turnpike with its macadam surface was the main thoroughfare for the armies vying for control of the region.

153

In May 1864, the Union forces of Franz Sigel met the Confederates of John C. Breckinridge in scattered actions that culminated in a Federal defeat at New Market on May 15. Sigel and Breckinridge then both left the Valley, and, on May 19, David Hunter ordered the burning of farms and other property. The new, scorched-earth tactics compelled Lee to dispatch Jubal Early from his own forces north of Richmond to defend the Valley. Early defeated Hunter at Lynchburg on June 18, then invaded Maryland. He defeated Gen. Lew Wallace at Monocacy and advanced on Washington, turning back before the guns of Fort Stevens on the outskirts of the Federal capital. But with Early still at large in the Valley, Grant named Philip Sheridan on August 1 to head a newly unified command of all Federal forces from Washington to West Virginia; his orders were to "drive Early out of the Valley." In September and October, Sheridan and Early clashed at Winchester, Fishers Hill, and Cedar Creek. This last engagement placed the Valley in Federal control.

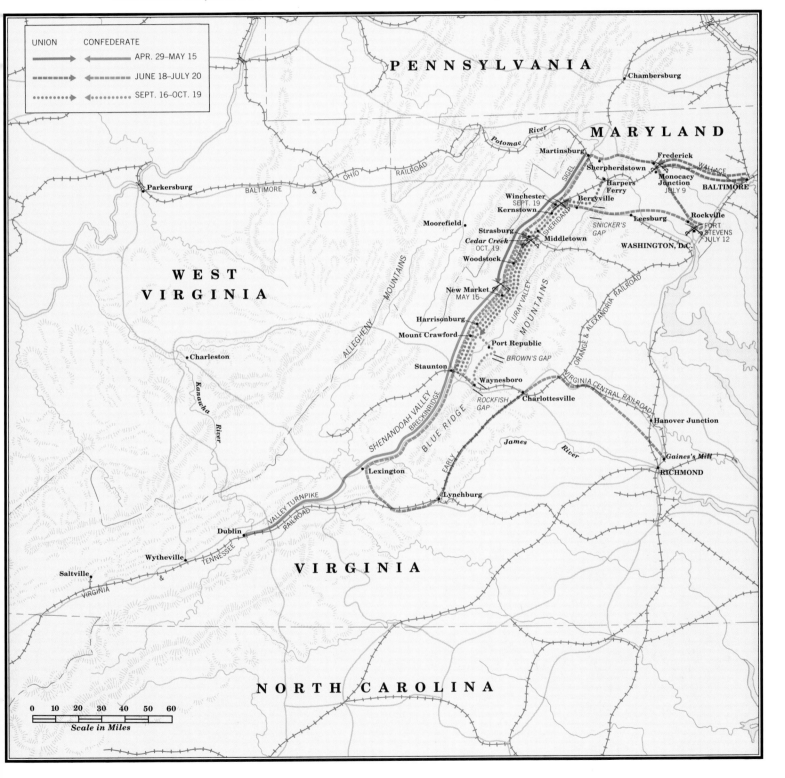

In early May of 1864, as Franz Sigel's 6,500 Federals moved southward up the Shenandoah Valley, Confederate Maj. Gen. John C. Breckinridge prepared to meet them with his army of 5,000. Late on the morning of May 15, with Sigel's army sitting north of New Market, Breckinridge attacked, forcing the Federal vanguard on Manor's Hill under Augustus Moor to fall back. Sigel re-formed his line on Bushong's Hill, with Thoburn's brigade on the right, Stahel's cavalry on the left, and Moor's brigade in the Valley between the hills. Around 2:00 p.m., the Rebels struck again, scattering Moor's troops and pushing on to Bushong's Hill. There the two sides shot it out for nearly two hours, the battle hanging in the balance until a climactic charge by the whole Confederate line forced Sigel to withdraw north, with a loss of 831 men. Four days later, both commanders left the Valley. Breckinridge joined Lee, while Sigel—replaced by Gen. David Hunter—was posted to a minor command in West Virginia.

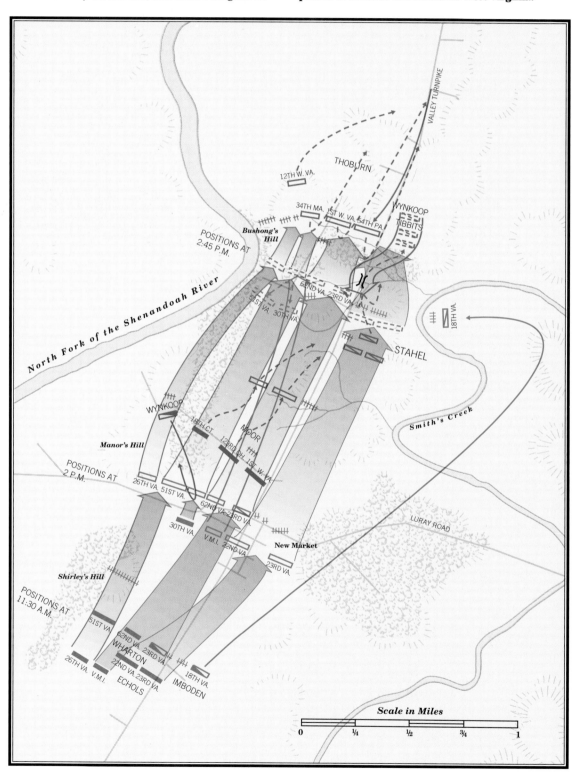

German-born Gen. Franz Sigel was awarded promotions in the Federal army, not because he deserved them, but to induce other Germans to enlist. His timid, clumsy, and negligent leadership in the Valley campaign, said one Union officer, "bred in everyone the most supreme contempt."

Amid bursting shells and lightning flashes, cadets from the Virginia Military Institute charge a Federal battery during the fight for Bushong's Hill. The cadets captured a gun but lost 50 of their 200 young men.

A former U.S. vice president, branded a traitor in the North, Gen. John Breckinridge defended the Confederacy's Department of Western Virginia in early 1864.

On a wooded ridge overlooking the Shenandoah Valley, Col. John S. Mosby and his Rangers prepare for an attack on the Federals. Their swift, plundering forays harassed Sigel and drove Hunter to try to suppress their activity with harsh reprisals.

David Hunter, quick-tempered and contentious, waged a ruthless campaign in the Valley. On the march from Winchester to Lexington, Hunter reduced military and civilian property to charred ruins, prompting his troops to dub him Black Dave.

Jubal Early returned to the Valley in mid-June with orders from Lee to clear it of Federal forces in time for the harvest, and, if possible, to strike northward and force Grant to loosen his grip on Richmond and Petersburg. Early commanded an underfed, tattered corps, numbering barely 8,000 men. But many were seasoned Valley campaigners who had marched with Stonewall Jackson two years before.

Lexington citizens go about their daily business on the town's main street after a three-day Federal occupation. Union soldiers reduced the Virginia Military Institute *(on the horizon)* to ruins, and destroyed all the food and supplies they could not carry off.

Lew Wallace estimated that his improvised army was "probably too small to defeat the Confederates at Monocacy" but strong enough to gain time. "I made up my mind to fight."

Infantrymen of the 10th Vermont retreat gingerly over the railroad bridge across the Monocacy River near the end of the daylong battle. In a show of chivalry that was rare this late in the War, the Confederate artillery held its fire while the Union soldiers crossed the open span.

Union artillerymen prepare for drill inside Fort Stevens, where Jubal Early's offensive ended after two days four miles from the White House. The fort's "position was naturally strong," Early wrote, "and every possible approach was raked by artillery."

In the first major engagement of his invasion of the North, Jubal Early faced Lew Wallace on July 9 at Monocacy Junction, 45 miles west of Baltimore. Here, where a B & O railroad bridge crossed the Monocacy River, Wallace had determined to delay Early's advance on Washington. Early's Confederates found Wallace's smaller force of Federals entrenched behind the river. At noon, as Rodes threatened the Federal right about two miles north of the bridge and Ramseur pressed the Federal skirmish line defending Monocacy Junction, Gordon's division crossed the river and attacked the Union left. Gordon drove back Ricketts' VI Corps division, forcing Wallace to retreat toward Baltimore. At a cost of 1,294 casualties, he had won 24 hours for the assembly of defenses at the Federal capital and had cost Early some 700 men. After his defeat, Wallace was stripped of his Middle Department command. But he was soon reinstated by Grant, who noted that in defeat, Wallace had given more service to the Federal cause than many commanders rendered in victory.

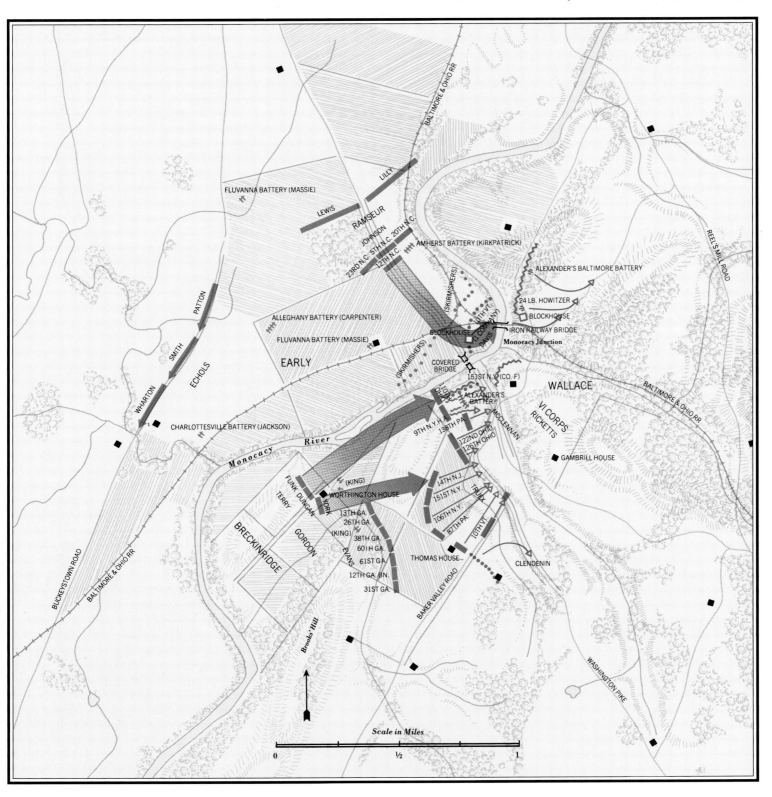

Led by skirmishers, Ricketts' 3d division charges up a wooded hill near Berryville Road about noon on September 19, 1864. The Union attack faltered when XIX Corps, on Ricketts' right, failed to advance.

On August 7, 1864, Grant placed energetic and capable Philip Sheridan, standing at left in this postwar group portrait, in command of the Army of the Shenandoah, with orders to dispose of Early. His able subordinates included *(left to right)* Wesley Merritt, George Crook, James W. Forsyth, and George A. Custer.

Confederate Gen. Robert E. Rodes, mortally wounded, is helped aboard an ambulance amid his division's retreat from the Federals along the Berryville road.

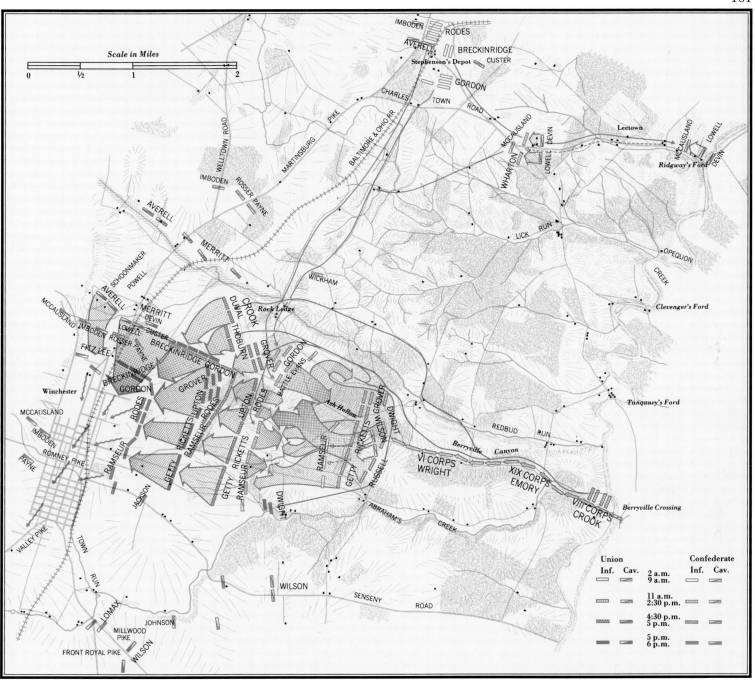

	Union			Confederate	
	Inf.	Cav.		Inf.	Cav.
2 a.m. 9 a.m.					
11 a.m. 2:30 p.m.					
4:30 p.m. 5 p.m.					
5 p.m. 6 p.m.					

With the Army of the Potomac now pressing hard on Lee's defenses around Richmond and Petersburg, Grant was confident that Lee would soon be forced to recall reinforcements he had sent to Early, now back in the Valley after his abortive raid. A week after Grant had instructed Sheridan to be ready to exploit such a development, Early was ordered to give up Kershaw's division, reducing his strength to about 14,000 men. When, on September 17, Early boldly took Gordon's and Rodes' divisions north from Winchester to threaten Maryland, Sheridan seized the opportunity to attack the forces left behind under Ramseur and Wharton. Sheridan proposed a classic double envelopment, using Wright's VI Corps and Emory's XIX Corps to attack and hold from the east, while Sheridan's cavalry swept around from the north and Crook's VIII Corps struck from the south. On September 18, as Sheridan prepared his attack, Early, 20 miles away at Martinsburg, learned of Grant's recent visit to Sheridan; he took the two

divisions with him on a forced march back to Winchester. Sheridan's predawn attack on the 19th met with some success but was hampered by the Federal troops in the rear. Early thus gained time to reunite his command around Winchester, but Sheridan, with more than 30,000 men, still outnumbered him. By 11:00 a.m., after nearly eight hours of seesaw fighting, the Confederate divisions of Breckinridge, Rodes, Gordon, and Ramseur had been forced back into an L-shaped defensive line north and east of Winchester. Their lines held until midafternoon, when a prolonged lull made Early believe he had won "a splendid victory." But at about 4:30 p.m., all three Federal corps, supported by the cavalry divisions of Merritt and Averell, attacked along the entire line. A half-hour later, Merritt's charge broke through Early's left flank, precipitating a Confederate rout. Winchester had changed hands for the 73d and last time, and Early's forces fled in disarray, having suffered 4,000 casualties to Sheridan's 5,000.

Confederates of Joseph Kershaw's division overrun a Federal camp at Cedar Creek in a surprise dawn attack on October 19. Stripped of anything that might rattle or clink, the attackers had crept into position in the darkness. Many Union soldiers fled before them without their guns, hats, or shoes. A few Union units managed to form battle lines, but most were, as one Federal officer put it, "stolidly, doggedly determined to go to the rear."

Maj. Gen. Stephen D. Ramseur, one of Early's youngest and ablest division commanders, hoped a victory at Cedar Creek would enable him to take leave to visit his wife and new baby daughter. Instead, he was mortally wounded while trying to rally his men during Sheridan's counterattack in the afternoon.

ORDER OF BATTLE
ARMY OF THE VALLEY
EARLY
21,000 MEN

WHARTON'S DIVISION
READ'S BRIGADE
LOGAN'S BRIGADE
SMITH'S BRIGADE

KERSHAW'S DIVISION
GOGGIN'S BRIGADE
HUMPHREYS' BRIGADE
WOFFORD'S BRIGADE
SIMMS' BRIGADE

"SECOND CORPS"
GORDON

PEGRAM'S DIVISION
HOFFMAN'S BRIGADE
JOHNSTON'S BRIGADE
DAVIS' BRIGADE

RAMSEUR'S DIVISION
GRIMES' BRIGADE
COX'S BRIGADE
COOK'S BRIGADE
BATTLE'S BRIGADE

GORDON'S DIVISION (EVANS)
LOWE'S BRIGADE
TERRY'S BRIGADE
PENDLETON'S BRIGADE

CAVALRY

LOMAX'S DIVISION
McCAUSLAND'S BRIGADE
JOHNSON'S BRIGADE
JACKSON'S BRIGADE
IMBODEN'S BRIGADE

ROSSER'S DIVISION
FUNSTEN'S BRIGADE
WICKHAM'S BRIGADE
PAYNE'S BRIGADE

ARMY OF THE SHENANDOAH
SHERIDAN/WRIGHT
31,000 MEN

VI CORPS WRIGHT/RICKETTS
FIRST DIVISION: WHEATON
Brigades: PENROSE, HAMBLIN, EDWARDS
SECOND DIVISION: GETTY
Brigades: WARNER, GRANT, BIDWELL
THIRD DIVISION: KEIFER
Brigades: EMERSON, BALL

VIII CORPS CROOK
(ARMY OF WEST VIRGINIA)
FIRST DIVISION: THOBURN
Brigades: WILDES, CURTIS, HARRIS
SECOND DIVISION: HAYES
Brigades: DEVOL, COATES
PROVISIONAL DIVISION: KITCHING

XIX CORPS EMORY
FIRST DIVISION: McMILLAN
Brigades: DAVIS, THOMAS, CURRIE
SECOND DIVISION: GROVER
Brigades: BIRGE, MOLINEUX, MACAULEY, SHUNK

CAVALRY CORPS TORBERT
FIRST DIVISION: MERRITT
Brigades: KIDD, DEVIN, LOWELL (RESERVE)
SECOND DIVISION: POWELL
Brigades: MOORE, CAPEHART
THIRD DIVISION: CUSTER
Brigades: PENNINGTON, WELLS

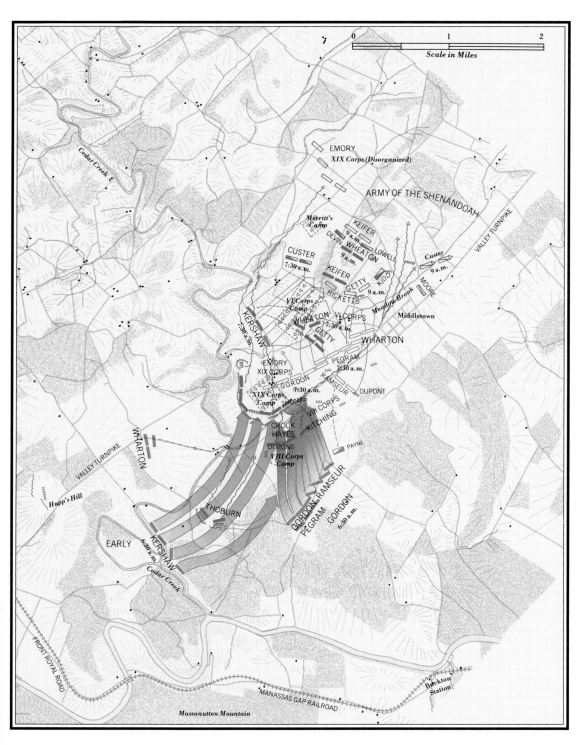

Scale in Miles

0   1   2

CONFEDERATE ATTACK

Sheridan pursued Early up the Valley, defeating him again at Fishers Hill on September 22. Then, believing his enemy had fled east across the Blue Ridge, the Federal commander gave up the chase and kept his troops busy laying waste to the Upper Valley between Strasburg and Staunton. Early's army, however, demoralized but still full of fight, had only fallen back to Port Republic and then to Waynesboro. Lee, meanwhile, returned Kershaw's division, plus an artillery battalion and a cavalry brigade, to Early's main force. On October 1, the Confederates, now more than 20,000 strong and enraged by Sheridan's wanton destruction, slipped back into the Valley. After nearly three weeks of probing and heavy skirmishing, Early decided to strike the still-unsuspecting Federals encamped along Cedar Creek, just north of Strasburg. At first light on October 19, the Rebels crossed Cedar Creek and stormed the Federal tent lines, catching the Union troops entirely by surprise. Gordon's three Confederate divisions swept through the camps of Crook's VIII Corps, and Kershaw's division routed Thoburn's two brigades that had been posted about a mile south of the main Federal encampment. The Confederates, pressing their advantage, drove the XIX Corps from an entrenched position near Belle Grove plantation; but between 7:00 and 9:00 a.m., they were slowed by the dogged resistance of the Federal VI Corps. Sheridan, absent when the battle began, arrived at 10:30 a.m. and began rallying his scattered troops on a line north of Middletown.

FEDERAL COUNTERATTACK

By midday, the battle had reached a critical juncture. The Federals had been dealt a heavy blow, but the bulk of the army had taken up solid defensive positions about a mile north of Middletown. The expended Confederates were now attacking piecemeal and were easily repulsed. Concerned about the condition of his command and the Federal cavalry massed beyond his right flank, Early ordered a fateful pause to rest his exhausted men, many of whom had already stopped fighting to plunder food and clothing from the Federal camps. While the Rebels waited, Sheridan formed the largely intact VI and XIX Corps, along with his cavalry, and shortly after 4:00 p.m., he attacked. At first, the Confederates blocked the advance. But when the Federals flanked Gordon's division on the Confederate left, Early's line began to crumble and soon was in retreat, despite a heroic stand by Ramseur's division in the center. Fierce pursuit by Federal cavalry under Custer and Merritt turned the retreat into a rout that continued until the Confederates halted four miles south of Cedar Creek. By nightfall, Early's shattered army had fallen back to New Market. Sheridan's victory was complete. The Army of the Valley was finished as a fighting force, and despite having suffered around 3,000 casualties to the Federal 5,665, it was still outnumbered two to one. The devastated Valley was Confederate no more.

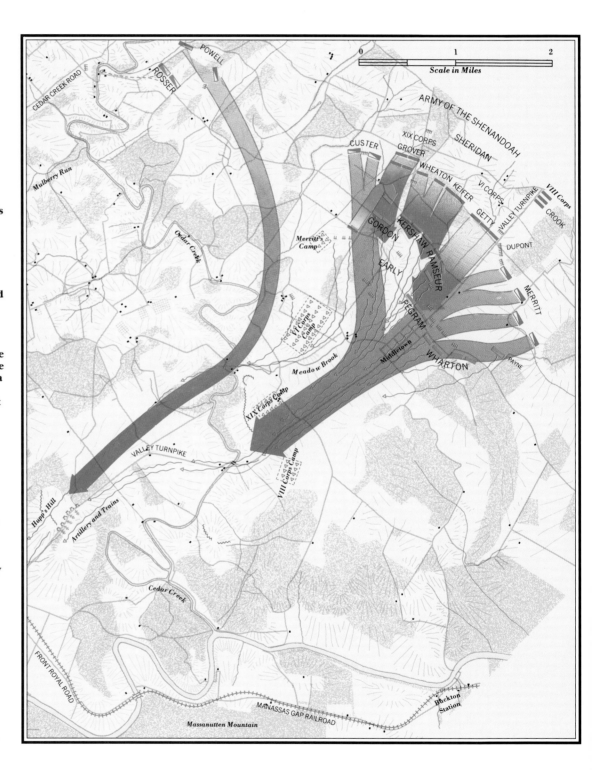

Waving his hat, Philip Sheridan urges men of Crook's shattered VIII Corps forward, shouting, "Follow me! We'll sleep in the old camp tonight!" Artist-correspondent James E. Taylor, who witnessed this scene and later drew it, added, "The responsive shout from the enthusiastic Blue Coats was like a thunder peal, for there was no resisting the magnetism of the man."

Invigorated by Sheridan's arrival on the battlefield, Gen. Lewis Grant's Vermont brigade forms for a counterattack at Cedar Creek as Confederate prisoners *(left foreground)* are hustled away. The Vermonters had given ground grudgingly during the morning action. During the counterattack, they helped break the back of Stephen Ramseur's division.

Horsemen of George Custer's 3d Cavalry Division run down retreating Confederate foot soldiers on Hupp's Hill.

PETERSBURG TO APPOMATTOX

"This is likely to prove a very tedious job," Ulysses S. Grant wrote to his wife, Julia, on June 6, 1864, "but I feel very confident of ultimate success." In spite of the recent bloodbath at Cold Harbor, Grant was optimistic about his new strategy for a Federal victory. After a spring of relentless flanking maneuvers in the Wilderness, the Union commander determined to seize the initiative, pin Lee down, and sever the supply lines that fed his army. On June 12, Grant began to move the Army of the Potomac—and the venue of battle—across the Chickahominy River and south of the James to seize the key rail center of Petersburg. Through this city passed Lee's lifelines: four railroads that linked the Confederate capital of Richmond with the Deep South.

Grant's flanking march to Petersburg was nearly flawless, but it ended in frustration. General William Smith, commander of the XVIII Corps, grew cautious about attacking Petersburg, giving away valuable time to his adversary, General P. G. T. Beauregard. On the night of June 15, with only 2,200 soldiers, Beauregard mounted a valiant defense of Petersburg against an onslaught of 14,000. Although the Confederates lost a portion of the city's defenses, they were able to withdraw and improvise a new line. Thus began the Siege of Petersburg, which would last until the closing days of the War.

By the spring of 1865, after almost nine months of siege, attrition had taken its toll on the weary Confederate forces. The Union war machine was well supplied from its prodigious depot of matériel housed up the James River at City Point, Virginia, while the Confederates—ill-fed, exhausted, and hopelessly outnumbered— lost men they could not replace. As one Southern general remarked, "However bold we might be, however desperately we

GEN. PIERRE GUSTAVE TOUTANT BEAUREGARD

might fight, we were sure in the end to be worn out. It was only a question of a few months, more or less."

When Lee was finally forced from his trenches at Petersburg on April 2, 1865, he led the remnant of his army westward on a desperate quest for food. Lee entertained hopes of marching southwestward to hook up with General Joseph Johnston in the hills of North Carolina, but he could never break contact with the Federals who were in constant pursuit. Although loath to admit it, Lee knew that the end was nigh. The North had almost a million men bearing arms; the south had fewer than 100,000. "There is nothing left for me to do," he told his aides, "but to go and see General Grant and I had rather die a thousand deaths." The two generals signed the surrender document at Appomattox Courthouse on the afternoon of April 9, 1864, and the proud Army of Northern Virginia laid down its arms.

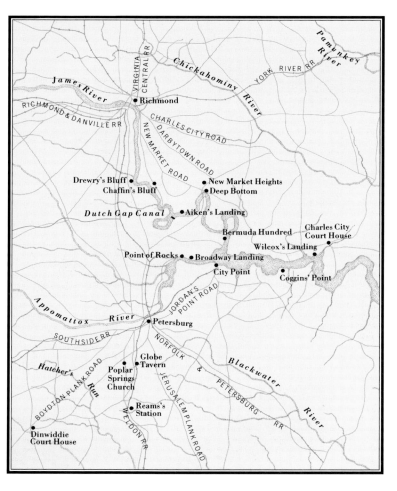

Instead of continuing sledgehammer blows against the Confederates, Grant decided to seize Petersburg, the vital rail hub 23 miles south of Richmond. His plan was fraught with peril. To reach Petersburg, Grant would have to disengage his 100,000-man army from contact with the enemy at Cold Harbor. Then he would have to march south through swampland on either side of the Chickahominy River, cross the broad, tidal James River, and deploy 40 miles away in the Confederate rear. If Lee were to detect the plan, he could launch an assault on the flank of the strung-out Federals, and the result might be an unmitigated Union disaster. Grant therefore took pains to distract his adversary. He ordered Benjamin Butler to demonstrate against Richmond and Petersburg from a position at Bermuda Hundred. Grant would also send some forces on a feint from Cold Harbor to Richmond. Through such subterfuge, he hoped to achieve the near impossible—outwitting Robert E. Lee.

From the depot at Petersburg, rail lines stretched to Richmond and Norfolk, as well as west to Tennessee and south to the Carolinas. The irregularly laid rails attest to the Confederates' inability to maintain adequately their transportation system.

On May 16, after vacillating for 10 days, Gen. Benjamin Butler struck north at the Confederate bastion of Fort Darling on Drewry's Bluff *(above)*. By that time, the Rebels had rushed in reinforcements to bolster the already-formidable defenses, which included gun emplacements, bombproofs, and a well *(left)*.

The inept Benjamin Butler *(above)* sits in his tent near Petersburg in the summer of 1864. An astute attorney and politician in civilian life, he was too influential to be relieved of command even after his bungling at Bermuda Hundred.

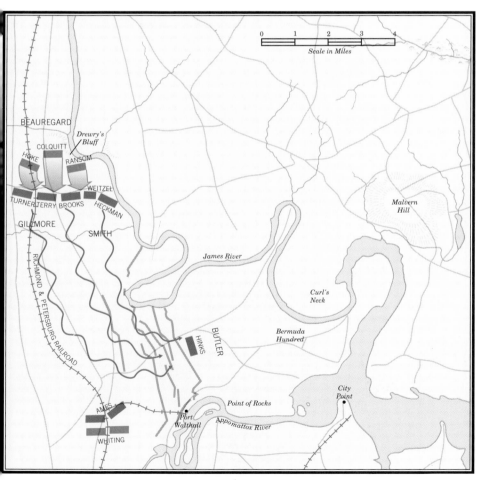

As part of his overall strategy for the final phase of the War, Grant ordered Butler to take his 33,000-man army up the James on transports and debark at Bermuda Hundred, a peninsula some 15 miles southeast of Richmond. Once there, the troops were to seize the Richmond & Petersburg Railroad and then advance on either Petersburg or Richmond. When Butler reached Bermuda Hundred on May 5, there were fewer than 2,000 Confederates defending Petersburg. Yet Butler hesitated for 10 days while his men dug trenches, conducted reconnaissances, and probed the flimsy Confederate line. Then, on May 16, Butler changed direction toward Richmond. By this time, the Confederates, under the command of Beauregard, had mustered 20,000 reinforcements. Spearheaded by the division of Gen. Robert Ransom *(above),* the Rebels forced Butler to withdraw. His Army of the James was then bottled up on the peninsula.

CROSSING THE JAMES

Photographed from atop a canvas-covered supply wagon, Federal troops cross the James River on a 2,100-foot-long pontoon bridge installed by Army of the Potomac engineers on June 14, 1864. The bridge was a masterpiece of military engineering.

An oil painting by Edward Henry, a Union recruit, depicts the Federals' supply base at City Point, Virginia. As Grant's line of operations moved south, the Union army transformed this quiet hamlet at the confluence of the James and Appomattox rivers into a bustling seaport and railhead.

As early as June 9, Beauregard predicted that Grant would cross the James and advance on Petersburg. Lee disagreed, insisting that the Federal army could never cross the river undetected and that Richmond was the more likely target. Lee was wrong on both counts. Federal boats began taking Winfield Scott Hancock's II Corps across the James on June 14. That same day, engineers under Capt. George Mendell finished erecting a half-mile-long bridge at Wilcox's Landing, and at midnight, Ambrose Burnside's IX Corps led the way across the span, followed by Gouverneur K. Warren's V Corps. James Wilson's cavalry division crossed on June 16, followed by Horatio G. Wright's VI Corps, which had stayed on the north side of the James to cover the crossing. By the 17th, all of the army except some wagons and guards were on the south side. The plan, though complicated and dangerous, was flawlessly executed.

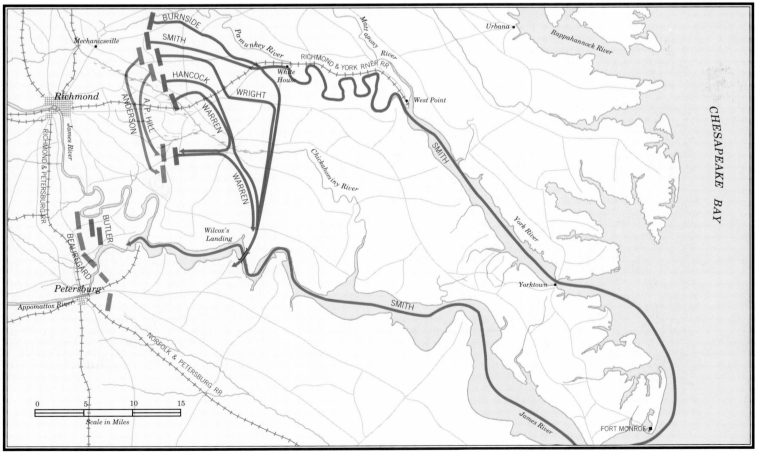

Men of the 22d U.S. Colored Troops capture a Confederate entrenchment on the Dimmock Line outside Petersburg on June 16, 1864. During the siege of Petersburg and Richmond, 38 black regiments served with the Union armies, more than in any other campaign of the Civil War.

A regiment of Smith's XVIII Corps overruns a portion of the Confederate defenses at Petersburg on the night of June 15. Woefully short of troops, Beauregard had to space his infantrymen at intervals of 10 feet along the eastern four miles of the line.

On June 14, as the Federals crossed the James River, Beauregard had only Henry Wise's Virginia Brigade and the local militia, a total of about 2,200 men, to defend Petersburg. The Confederate commander did possess extensive fortifications. Called the Dimmock Line for the engineer who designed it, this chain of redans—triangular projections open in the rear and designed to allow for both frontal and flanking fire—was connected by almost 10 miles of entrenchments. Ditches and felled trees, or abatis, fronted the redans to obstruct any hostile advance. But the strength of the line depended on sufficient forces to man it, something Beauregard sorely lacked. William Farrah "Baldy" Smith's XVIII Corps, supported by August Kautz's cavalry, attacked Petersburg at 7:00 p.m. on June 15 with a force some 14,000 strong and quickly rolled over a mile-long section of Beauregard's works, from redans 3 through 11. Meanwhile, additional reinforcements had arrived in the form of Hancock's II Corps. The road to Petersburg was wide open—yet Smith stopped short. Trying to explain one of the War's gravest errors of generalship, he reported the next day, "Deeming that I held important points of the enemy's line of works, I thought it prudent to make no further advance." Smith's poor performance stood in contrast to that of his opponent, General Beauregard. Fiery and flamboyant, he served the Confederacy brilliantly that night by feverishly building a new line of defenses that would hold off the Union siege for almost 10 months.

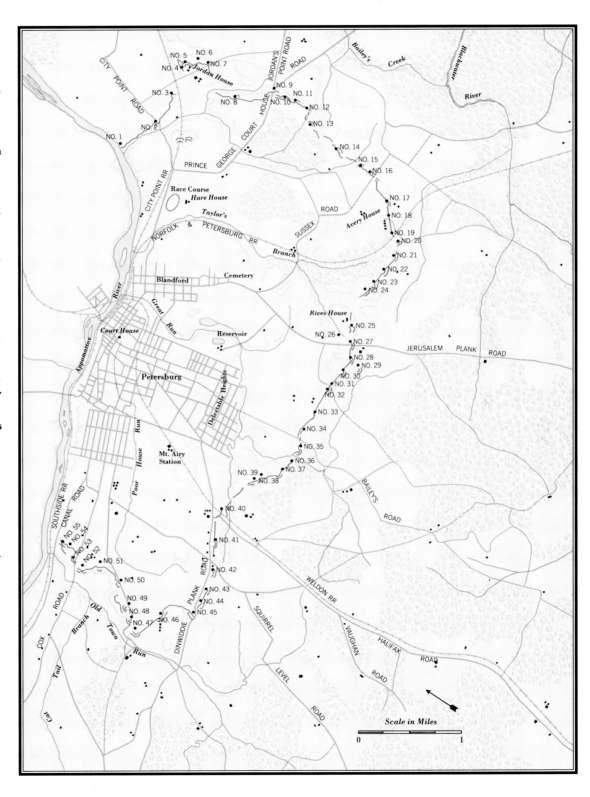

Troops of Burnside's IX Corps, supported by artillery, charge the Confederate defenses at the crater shortly after the July 30 explosion *(above)*. Eight hours later, Gen. William Mahone's men drove the Federals back in bitter hand-to-hand combat *(left)*. The Union lost some 4,400 men at the Crater in what Grant called "the saddest affair I have ever witnessed in the War." He labeled the attack a "stupendous failure—and all due to inefficiency on the part of the corps commander and the incompetency of the division commander who was sent to lead the assault."

In July 1864, frustrated by efforts to take Petersburg, General Meade accepted Lt. Col. Henry Pleasants' scheme to breach the defenses. Pleasants' 48th Pennsylvania, made up mostly of coal miners from Schuylkill County, dug a 511-foot tunnel to a salient in the Confederate line, where a cross shaft was dug and loaded with four tons of gunpowder. The mine was blown early on July 30, and the way was opened for the attack. Spearheaded by Gen. James Ledlie's division, four divisions in Burnside's corps were to pour through the gap and assault the Rebels. But the blast stunned the soldiers, and they became confused in the debris-filled trenches that surrounded the 30-foot-deep, 70-foot-wide crater. Many rushed into the fissure rather than around it. The rear lip of the crater, backed by a Confederate earthwork, proved insurmountable. At a time when the Federals most needed leadership, General Ledlie huddled with a jug of rum in a rear bombproof. The widespread confusion gave the Confederates time to recover from the assault and shore up their defenses. By 9:00 a.m., when Edward Ferrero's black division joined the battle, the Rebels were fending off attacks on both sides of the crater. Confederate Gen. William Mahone began a counterattack about 1:00 p.m. David Weisiger's Virginia Brigade met the front line of Ferrero's troops west of the crater and repulsed them, dashing hopes for a Union breakthrough.

ELLETT & LETCHER'S BATTERIES

56th N.C.

MACON'S BATTERY

JOHNSON

WRIGHT'S BATTERY

35th N.C.

Picket Line

DUNCAN

CARR (XVIII CORPS)

2ND ME. ART.

Covered Way

MCAFEE

25th N.C.

HASKELL (COEHORNS)

ORD XVIII CORPS

Picket Line

JERUSALEM PLANK ROAD

LAMKIN'S BATTERY (COEHORNS)

(HASKELL)

64th Ga.

WRIGHT

9th N.C.

2nd N.Y. M.R.

36th Mass. (BLISS)

STEWART

STEDMAN

FAIRCHILD

19TH N.Y. ART. (COEHORNS)

48th Ga.

22nd Ga.

ELLIOTT

3rd Ga.

25th S.C.

49th N.C.

98th Pa.

48th N.Y.

76th Pa.

41th N.Y.

TURNER (IX CORPS)

3rd N.Y.

169th N.Y.

9th N.H.

4th N.H.

13th Ind.

COAN

17th N.Y.

1ST CONN. H.A. (MORTARS)

AMES (XVIII CORPS)

LEE

MAHONE

WEISIGER

61st N.C.

41st Va.

26th S.C. (Hoke)

17th S.C.

16th Va.

23rd S.C.

BELL

17th N.Y.

112th N.Y.

CURTIS

(BLISS)

BURNHAM (XVIII CORPS)

STEVENS

Gee House

6th Va.

4th R.I.

(BLISS)

POTTER

42th N.Y.

7th R.I. Eng.

HENRY

2nd

(WILLCOX)

SGFRIED

FLANNER'S BATTERY

THOMAS

27TH ME. ART.

BURNSIDE IX CORPS

Griffith House (ruins)

22nd S.C. (ELLIOTT)

LEDLIE

FERRERO

Taylor House (ruins)

59th Va.

26th Va.

DAVIDSON'S BATTERY (1 GUN)

2ND PA. (PROV.) H.A.

1ST CONN. H.A.

(ELLIOTT) 23rd S.C.

28th U.S.C.T.

JOHNSON

GOODE

46th Va.

WILLCOX

HUMPHREY

2ND PA. (PROV.) H.A.

2ND MICH.

20th Mich.

60th Ohio

LANGHORNE'S BATTERY

BAXTER ROAD

46th N.Y.

2ND PA.

27th N.Y.

NORFOLK & PETERSBURG RAILROAD

Covered Way

DAVIDSON'S BATTERY

CULLEN (BURNHAM)

34th Va.

Picket Line

Picket Line

Picket Line

Scale in Feet

0   250   500   1,000

By summer 1864, the fighting around Petersburg had settled into a pattern. Assaults north of the James, at Deep Bottom, and south of the river, at the Weldon Railroad, Reams' Station, and Poplar Springs Church, had tightened the Federals' noose. Yet when the chance for a breakthrough came at the end of September, the Yankees faltered. The Rebels held a fortified camp north of the James at Chaffin's Bluff, eight miles from Richmond. Grant planned to threaten the Confederate capital and tie down en-

emy troops that might be needed to reinforce Jubal Early, who was raising havoc in the Shenandoah Valley. Grant ordered Maj. Gen. Ord's XVIII Corps (Ord had replaced Smith) to assail Fort Harrison, on the camp's southeast corner. On the morning of September 29, the Federals swiftly overwhelmed the garrison and its 800 inexperienced artillerists. The way to Richmond was nearly open—but Ord's men fell into disorder and Confederate reinforcements arrived to stall the Federal drive.

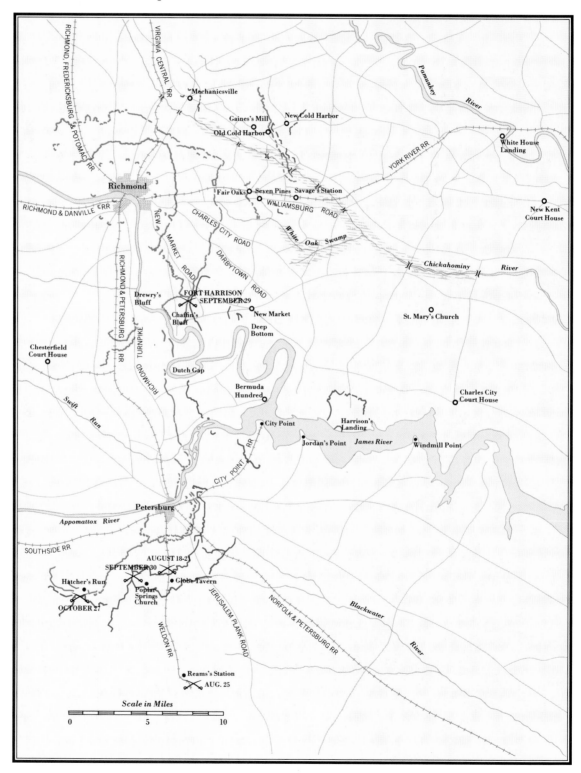

The Federals attacking Fort Harrison faced a daunting obstacle: a parapet with enclosed gun positions, fronted by a fraise—a row of sharpened stakes to frustrate charging infantry.

MAJ. GEN. EDWARD ORD

After destroying track along the Weldon Railroad, Hancock's II Corps *(foreground)* came under assault at Reams' Station by A. P. Hill on August 25. Hill's Confederates pushed the Federals back.

FORT STEDMAN

Three hundred Confederates, a select force from Maj. Gen. John Gordon's 2d Corps, pour through openings cut by axmen in the abatis shielding Fort Stedman, a redoubt in the Federal line besieging Petersburg.

The 3d Division of Parke's IX Corps (previously Burnside's), led by Brig. Gen. John F. Hartranft, launches the charge that recaptured Fort Stedman on March 25. The Confederates, Hartranft said, "were forced back into the works in such masses that the victors were scarcely able to deploy among the crowds of prisoners."

Federal gun positions reinforced by gabions—earth-filled baskets—remain standing after the Battle of Fort Stedman. It was nearly impossible for the Confederates to maintain formation within the earthworks, connecting trenches, and dugouts.

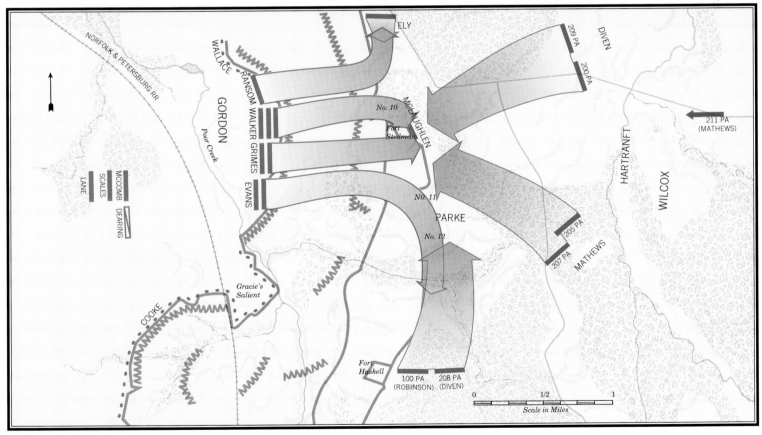

Union success on all fronts forced Lee to stage a desperate attack on Fort Stedman, a Union strong-point east of Petersburg. Striking before dawn on March 25, Gen. John Gordon's men captured the fort and adjoining batteries: nos. 10, 11, and 12. The Confederates then moved beyond Stedman to seize smaller works and widen the gap in the enemy line.

At 7:30 a.m., however, John Hartranft's 3d Division led a spirited countercharge that forced Gordon back into Fort Stedman. When Lee sent orders to withdraw at 8:00, many Confederates chose to surrender because their line of retreat was threatened by cross fire. The Union had turned aside Lee's last, great effort to break its grip on Petersburg.

FIVE FORKS

In what was the final major battle of the Petersburg campaign, Grant sent Philip Sheridan's cavalry, along with some infantry units, to envelop the Confederate right flank southwest of Petersburg. Grant hoped not only to cut the Southside Railroad, a vital Confederate supply line, but to block Lee's escape to the west. Lee dispatched George Pickett's division and W. H. F. Lee's cavalry corps to counter the Federals. By 1:00 p.m. on April 1, Sheridan had deployed Wesley Merritt's cavalry division to expel Pickett's Confederates from their entrenched position at Five Forks. Sheridan planned to pin down Pickett with the cavalry while Gouverneur Warren's V Corps assaulted the Confederate left. It was 4:00 p.m. before Warren came into action, and because of faulty deployment, V Corps nearly missed its objective, striking 800 yards too far to the east. Although Sheridan had agonized over the delay, it proved beneficial. Lulled by the failure of the Federals to attack, Pickett and W. H. F. Lee had left the field just after 2:00 p.m. to enjoy a shad bake on the north bank of Hatcher's Run. Meanwhile, Warren redirected his attack and struck Pickett on his left flank and rear, just as Merritt hit Pickett's front and Mackenzie circled his left. By 7:00 p.m., the Rebels had been decimated in what a Confederate commander later called the "Waterloo of the Confederacy."

Lee chose his nephew, Maj. Gen. Fitzhugh Lee, to lead the cavalry forces countering Sheridan's attack at Five Forks.

Ranald Mackenzie commanded the cavalry division of the Army of the James during the battle.

Two brigades of Gen. George Armstrong Custer's 3d Cavalry Division charge a line of Virginians on the Confederate far right at Five Forks. Because of the difficult terrain, the remainder of Custer's brigades fought on foot.

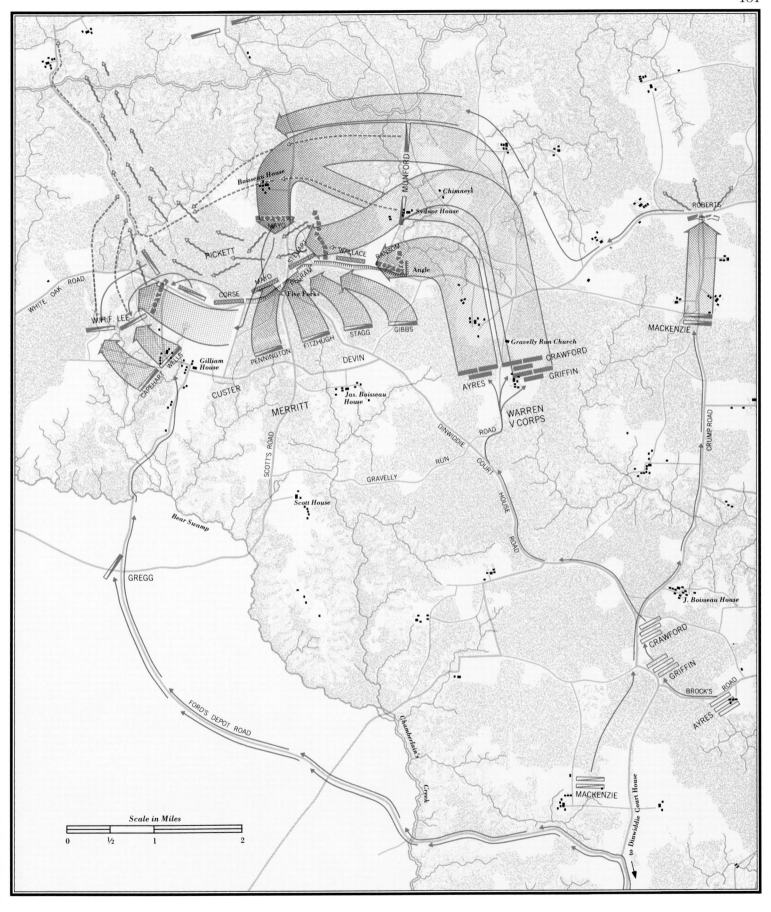

181

COLLAPSE AT PETERSBURG

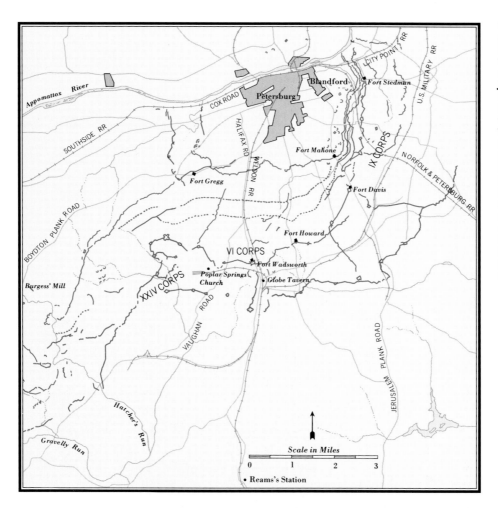

Galvanized by word of Sheridan's success at Five Forks, Grant's forces at Petersburg launched a concentrated assault on the weakened Confederate defenses at dawn on April 2. On the Union right, Maj. Gen. John Parke's IX Corps captured—but failed to hold—Fort Mahone, known to the Federals as Fort Damnation. Elsewhere, however, Maj. Gen. Horatio Wright's VI Corps broke through A. P. Hill's lines west of Petersburg, cutting Boydton Plank Road and the Southside Railroad. Hill was killed in the assault. On hearing of his trusted commander's death, a desolate Lee murmured, "He is at rest now and we who are left are the ones to suffer." In desperation, Lee withdrew to the innermost line of defense. By nightfall, Maj. John Gibbon's XXIV Corps had taken Fort Gregg and forced the evacuation of Fort Mahone. Lee had no choice but to evacuate Petersburg.

Standing atop a breastwork at Petersburg, a lone Confederate invites enemy fire in this 1864 painting by Winslow Homer. Although Homer used his imagination here, such acts were not uncommon. One man in the trenches pondered whether those who took such risks were seeking a swift end to their ordeal: "It was enough to make men mad and reckless."

LT. GEN. AMBROSE POWELL HILL

Pushing aside chevaux-de-frise, the 2d Division of Parke's IX Corps storms Fort Mahone during the climactic Federal attack on the works around Petersburg *(bottom)*. The following morning, a Confederate soldier lies dead among the scattered detritus of war.

Brig. Gen. Henry E. Davies' cavalry, fighting dismounted and on horseback, capture men and guns escorting the main Confederate supply train near Painesville on April 5. The attack not only robbed Lee of vital ammunition but left one of his escape routes blocked with wreckage.

After abandoning Richmond and Petersburg on April 2, Lee moved west, planning to turn south and meet up with Gen. Joseph Johnston in North Carolina. To avoid jamming the roads, the corps traveled different routes to Amelia Courthouse, the designated assembly point, some 35 miles west of Petersburg. Lee had ordered food sent to Amelia to supply his army but because of a staff mixup, it never arrived. The starving Confederates resumed their march on April 5. Grant hurled his armies in pursuit, sending Sheridan's troops to block Lee until the Federal infantry could bring the Confederates to bay. Amid continuous fighting, Lee managed to elude the Federals but was constantly forced farther west. After severe clashes on April 6 and 7, at Sayler's Creek and around Farmville, Lee turned toward Lynchburg, only to have his way blocked at Appomattox.

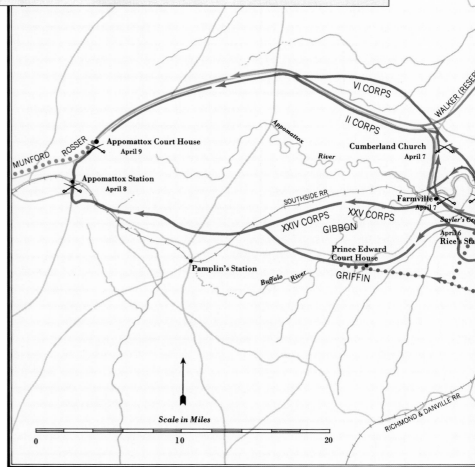

Scale in Miles

0   10   20

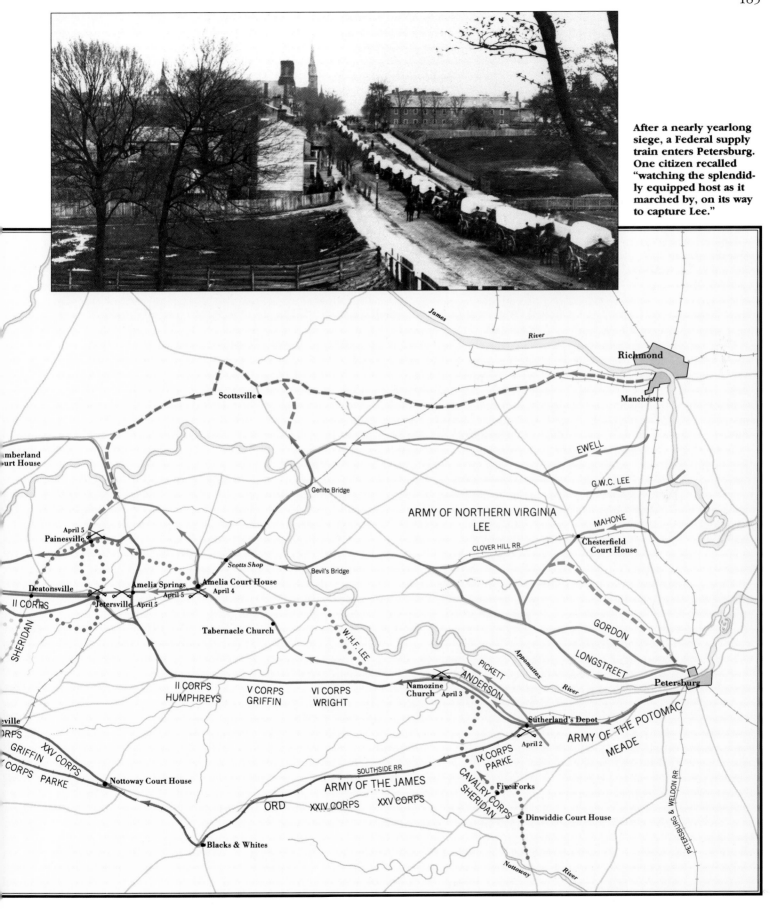

After a nearly yearlong siege, a Federal supply train enters Petersburg. One citizen recalled "watching the splendidly equipped host as it marched by, on its way to capture Lee."

James River

Richmond

Manchester

Scottsville

EWELL

G.W.C. LEE

mberland urt House

Genito Bridge

ARMY OF NORTHERN VIRGINIA
LEE

MAHONE

April 5
Painesville

CLOVER HILL RR

Chesterfield
Court House

Scotts Shop

Deatonsville

Amelia Springs
April 5

Amelia Court House
April 4

Bevil's Bridge

II CORPS

Jetersville   April 5

GORDON

SHERIDAN

Tabernacle Church

W.H.F. LEE

Appomattox

LONGSTREET

II CORPS
HUMPHREYS

V CORPS
GRIFFIN

VI CORPS
WRIGHT

Namozine
Church   April 3

PICKETT

ANDERSON

River

Petersburg

ville
ORPS

GRIFFIN   XXV CORPS

CORPS   PARKE

Nottoway Court House

SOUTHSIDE RR

Sutherland's Depot

April 2

ARMY OF THE POTOMAC

MEADE

IX CORPS
PARKE

ARMY OF THE JAMES

ORD   XXIV CORPS   XXV CORPS

CAVALRY CORPS
SHERIDAN

Five Forks

PETERSBURG & WELDON RR

Dinwiddie Court House

Blacks & Whites

Nottoway   *River*

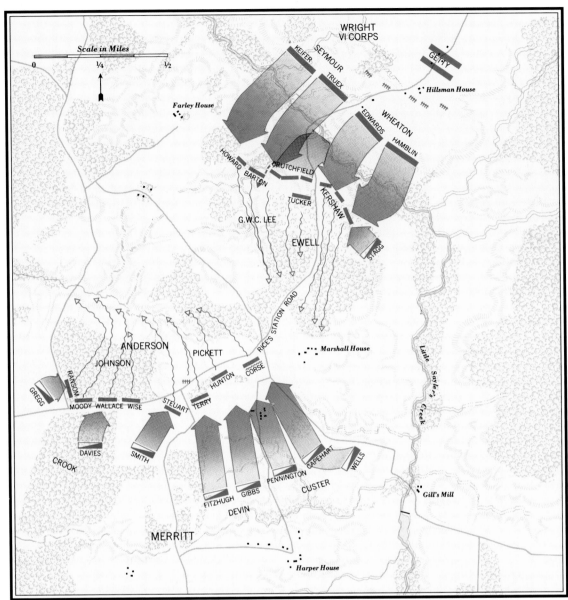

The Confederate commanders, their men at the point of starvation and total exhaustion, allowed their columns to become strung-out and disorganized as they approached the two forks of Sayler's Creek, a tributary of the Appomattox River, on the afternoon of April 6. There the Federals attacked. Wesley Merritt's cavalry halted the advance of Anderson's corps, on its way to Rice's Station three miles to the southwest. Ewell formed behind Little Sayler's Creek to face Wright's pursuing VI Corps. After a heavy bombardment, VI Corps divisions led by Seymour and Wheaton attacked across the shallow creek. Despite a brief check in the center by Crutchfield's Confederates, the brigades of Hamblin and Keifer enveloped the Confederate battle line, routing Ewell's men. At the same time, Merritt's cavalry overran Anderson's line when it began to withdraw. Lee's haggard men fought with stunning desperation against insurmountable odds. "I saw numbers of men kill each other with bayonets and the butts of muskets and even bite each other's throats and ears and noses, rolling on the ground like wild beasts," a Confederate officer later recalled. In spite of their valor, some 8,000 men—accounting for approximately one-fourth of Lee's army—were lost or taken prisoner.

Brigadier General Frank Wheaton, a Rhode Islander leading the 1st Division of VI Corps, accepted the surrender of 2,000 men at Sayler's Creek.

Major General Joseph P. Kershaw, the capable South Carolinian, was taken prisoner at Sayler's Creek along with Richard Ewell and six other generals.

Confederate Gen. Henry A. Wise led his brigade in halting momentarily the Federal pursuit at Sayler's Creek before withdrawing to Farmville.

Troops of Richard Ewell's corps raise their muskets in surrender on April 6 after the Battle of Sayler's Creek.

Confederate artillery-men of Gen. R. Lindsay Walker's brigade dismantle a cannon on the night of April 8 to prevent it from falling intact into the hands of Gen. George Armstrong Custer's cavalry. Behind them, other soldiers destroy the railroad track leading west from Appomattox to Lynchburg.

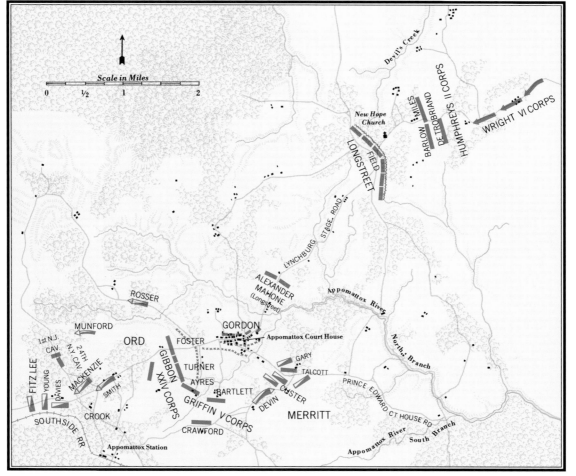

After capturing the Confederate supply train at Appomattox Station on April 8, Sheridan's cavalry pushed on toward Appomattox Courthouse to cut Lee's route to Lynchburg. The next morning, Gordon's corps and Fitzhugh Lee's cavalry successfully attacked Sheridan's positions along Bent Creek Road, but the arrival of Ord's infantry and the envelopment of Gordon's left by Merritt's Federal cavalry divisions, under Devin and Custer, forced the Confederates to fall back to the courthouse. Three miles to the northeast, at New Hope Church, Lee's rear guard, under Longstreet, turned to engage Humphreys' II Corps and Wright's VI Corps. As the morning wore on, Lee realized that further resistance was futile and ordered that a white flag be carried through the lines with a request for a cease-fire until terms of surrender could be worked out with Grant.

Seated in the parlor of Wilmer McLean's house at Appomattox, Lee signs the terms of surrender at 3:00 p.m. on April 9, 1865. The document, written in Grant's own hand, allowed all Confederate officers and men to return to their homes without the taint of treason.

Grieving Confederate soldiers cluster around Robert E. Lee as he returns from his fateful meeting with Grant. "Not an eye that looked on that scene was dry," one correspondent reported.

In the autumn of 1861, Brigadier General William Tecumseh Sherman completed a round of travels in the Western theater, having drawn an indelible military conclusion. Whichever side gains control of the Mississippi River and its tributaries, he maintained, "will control the continent."

Several other shrewd men in the Union camp had already decided as much. Among them was commander in chief of the Union army, General Winfield Scott, who had proposed using the Mississippi to defeat the Confederacy. As part of his so-called Anaconda Plan, Federal forces would strike south along the river, split the Confederacy, and, together with a coastal blockade, strangle it section by section. The quest to control the Mississippi, in fact, would dictate the strategies of the war in the West and give the campaigning there a character radically different from that of the Eastern conflict.

In the vast field of operations that lay between the Appalachian Mountains and the Mississippi, rivers were important for their great length and direction of flow. Eastern waterways tended to flow from west to east and were navigable only for short distances. They were less valuable as thoroughfares than as barriers to invading troops. The Western rivers, on the other hand, flowed from north to south as well as east to west, reaching deep into the Confederacy. These rivers more than made up for the West's inadequate roads and railroads.

The vital core of the Western river system was the 250-mile stretch of the Mississippi between St. Louis and Memphis. Here the great river was joined by the Ohio, which drained all the way from the Appalachian Mountains, making it an important route for men and arms moving from the industrial East to the Western war zone. The Ohio's two main tributaries were crucial as well. The Tennessee penetrated deep enough into Al-abama to enable an invading force to attack the Confederacy from the rear; and the Cumberland snaked through Tennessee to the major industrial and rail center of Nashville.

Altogether, the branches of the Mississippi system drained more than 1.2 million square miles of terrain and, being navigable over most of their lower courses, could quickly deliver troops and supplies to much of the central valley. Thus the fighting in the West became a far-flung war of movement as opposed to the more static war of position in the East, where the armies fought most of their battles on the 100 miles or so of terrain between Washington and Richmond.

The great distances also put an indelible stamp on the Western theater. To the despair of generals who fought in the West, their remoteness from Washington and Richmond made for neglect; they received manpower and supplies only after the needs of the forces in the East had been met. So they fought campaigns that were often haphazard and makeshift. In turn, their ability to improvise, and their sheer aggressiveness, earned more than a few Federal generals—notably Ulysses S. Grant—a reputation as men who were always ready to fight.

The campaigns that moved up and down the Western rivers featured several pivotal battles. In the winter of 1862, Grant led a combined naval and land assault that claimed Forts Henry and Donelson—Confederate strongholds on the Tennessee and Cumberland that protected the interior of the middle South. When the Confederate commander at Donelson proposed an armistice, Grant offered "no terms except unconditional and immediate surrender," sounding the theme for the punishing war in the West.

Caught off balance, Albert Sidney Johnston, Confederate commander in the West, ordered a sweeping withdrawal that opened all of Kentucky and much of western

Tennessee—including thriving Nashville—to Federal occupation. And in April, Johnston's forces met the Federals under Grant and Don Carlos Buell in a savage struggle that raged for two days along the Tennessee River near a Methodist meeting house called Shiloh Church. The battle cost Johnston his life, and the bloodletting at Shiloh—each side lost more than 10,000 men killed, wounded, and missing—shocked the nation. The sacrifice of more American lives than had been lost in all of the country's previous battles destroyed any notion of a negotiated peace. After Shiloh, wrote a captain from Illinois, "all sentimental talk of easy conquest ceased upon both sides."

Through the spring and summer of 1862, Federal forces solidified their hold on the Mississippi Valley. In April, Admiral David Farragut's flotilla claimed New Orleans and pushed up the river, capturing Baton Rouge and Natchez before being stopped by Vicksburg's big guns. By June, Union troops had occupied Memphis.

Determined to reverse the tide, President Jefferson Davis changed commanders, replacing P. G. T. Beauregard with Braxton Bragg. But the unpopular Bragg failed to make a difference, fighting costly but inconclusive battles at Perryville, Kentucky, and at Stones River in Tennessee.

The Confederates were dealt another calamitous blow in the summer of 1863 when Grant, after an extended siege, captured Vicksburg, the last major Rebel stronghold on the Mississippi. Jefferson Davis had referred to the port as "the nailhead that held the South's two halves together." The nail had been pulled, and Union forces were soon in possession of the mighty Mississippi.

Having split the Confederacy, the Federals pushed east, into the Confederate heartland, and in the autumn met Bragg's Confederates in a series of battles for Chattanooga, the mountain gateway to the deep South. Bragg's forces stunned the Federals under William Rosecrans at Chickamauga. But in late November, Grant's troops swept the Confederates from Lookout Mountain and Missionary Ridge and forced them into Georgia.

Early in 1864, Grant was elevated to commander in chief of the Federal armies and left the Western forces in the hands of his able subordinate, William T. Sherman. In May, Sherman struck out over the mountains of northern Georgia for the strategic hub of Atlanta. The Confederate commander, Joseph E. Johnston, was woefully outnumbered and could do little more than fight delaying actions, none of which held up Sherman for long. Atlanta, the most important Confederate city after Richmond, fell in late summer. By taking Atlanta, Sherman had deprived the Confederacy of a vital arsenal and rail hub. His stunning victory also electrified the North, giving its war-weary people renewed faith that the conflict could be won and making President Lincoln's reelection in November a near certainty. Gloom spread through the South. The diarist Mary Boykin Chesnut, a volunteer nurse, summed up the despair of Southerners everywhere: "Atlanta is gone. That agony is over. There is no hope, but we will try to have no fear."

The dynamic Sherman then embarked on one of the epic marches in the chronicles of war. Resolving to cut Georgia and the Confederacy in half, he led his troops to the sea, capturing Savannah in December, then storming through South Carolina. In March, Sherman's troops rolled into North Carolina, and the small Confederate force there under Joseph Johnston was unable to stop them. When word of Lee's surrender at Appomattox filtered south, Johnston reported to President Davis that his army was "melting away like snow before the sun," and he finally surrendered to Sherman on April 26.

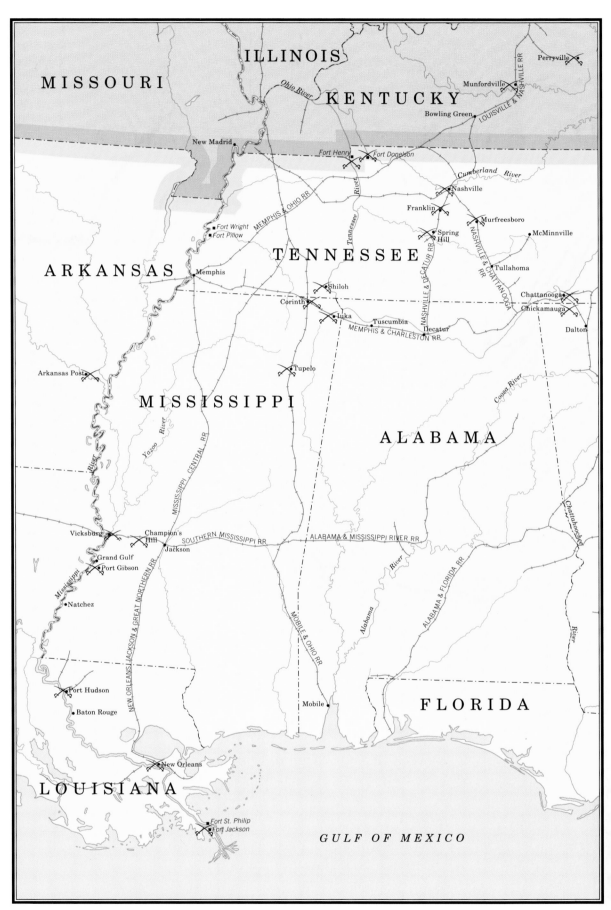

BATTLEFIELDS OF THE WESTERN THEATER

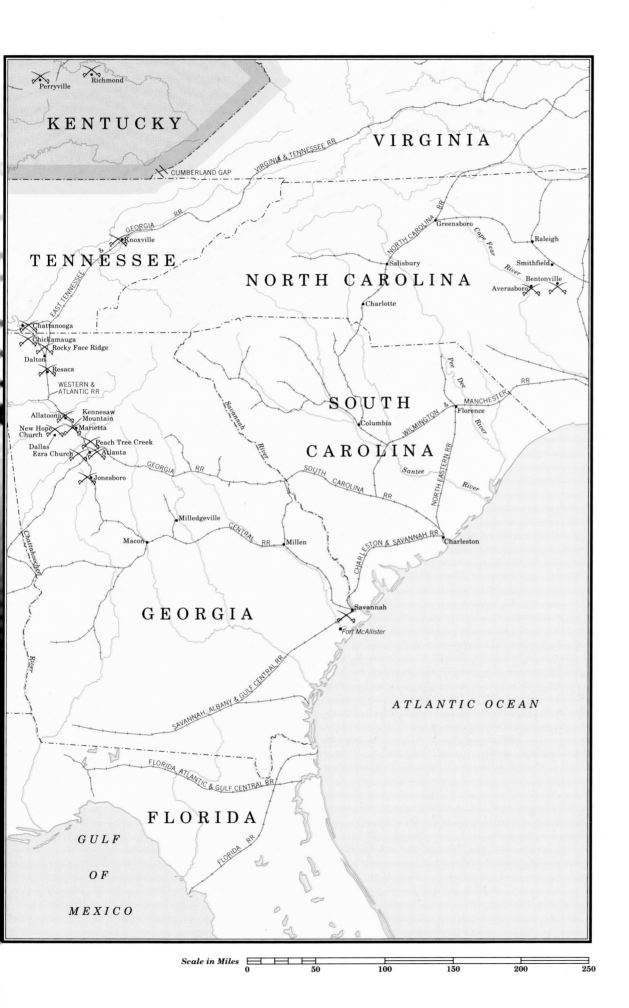

KENTUCKY

VIRGINIA

Perryville

Richmond

×CUMBERLAND GAP

VIRGINIA & TENNESSEE RR

TENNESSEE

GEORGIA   RR

Knoxville

EAST TENNESSEE &

NORTH CAROLINA

NORTH CAROLINA   RR

Greensboro

Cape Fear

Raleigh

Salisbury

Smithfield

River

Bentonville

Averasboro

Charlotte

Chattanooga

Chickamauga
Rocky Face Ridge

Dalton

Resaca

WESTERN &
ATLANTIC RR

SOUTH

Pee

Dee

RR

MANCHESTER

Florence

Allatoona

Kennesaw
Mountain

New Hope
Church

Marietta

CAROLINA

Columbia

WILMINGTON &

River

Dallas

Peach Tree Creek

Ezra Church

Atlanta

GEORGIA   RR

Santee

NORTH EASTERN RR

River

Jonesboro

SOUTH   CAROLINA   RR

Milledgeville

CENTRAL   RR

Millen

Chattahoochee

Macon

CHARLESTON & SAVANNAH RR

Charleston

GEORGIA

Savannah

Fort McAllister

River

SAVANNAH, ALBANY & GULF CENTRAL RR

ATLANTIC OCEAN

FLORIDA

FLORIDA, ATLANTIC & GULF CENTRAL RR

GULF

OF

FLORIDA   RR

MEXICO

Scale in Miles

0   50   100   150   200   250

SHILOH

The first major Federal campaign in the Western theater was a thrust south along the Tennessee River, one of several rivers that would become key avenues of invasion for Union forces attempting to gain control of the Mississippi Valley. The campaign began with the capture of Confederate Forts Henry and Donelson by a Federal force under a newly minted brigadier general named Ulysses S. Grant, aided by a flotilla of Union ironclad gunboats under Commander Andrew H. Foote. The army and the naval flotilla then proceeded 100 miles up the Tennessee, aiming to capture the important rail junction at Corinth, Mississippi. The Confederates, who had combined their forces at Corinth, suddenly turned on the Union army near Shiloh Church, setting off the West's first big battle and one of the most violent and bloody fights of the entire War.

ULYSSES S. GRANT

Three Federal gunboats shell Fort Henry on February 6, 1862, while a fourth, the *Essex (far right)*, takes a hit in its boiler.

Grant's swift capture in February 1862, of Forts Henry and Donelson shattered the defensive line that the Confederate commander in the West, Gen. Albert Sidney Johnston, had hoped to hold in northern Tennessee and Kentucky. The center of his line broken, Johnston abandoned Bowling Green and Nashville and headed for Corinth. At Corinth, Johnston was reinforced by Daniel Ruggles' 5,000 men from New Orleans and Braxton Bragg's 10,000 troops from Mobile, Alabama. Gen. Henry W. Halleck, now in overall command of Federal forces in the West, ordered Grant's army of 40,000 south to the big bend in the Tennessee, where Grant was joined by the man who would become his most trusted subordinate, William Tecumseh Sherman. Grant began concentrating his forces at Pittsburg Landing to await the arrival of Gen. Don Carlos Buell and his 55,000-man army, marching southwest from recently captured Nashville. While Grant paused, General Johnston—knowing he must strike before Buell arrived—launched the Battle of Shiloh.

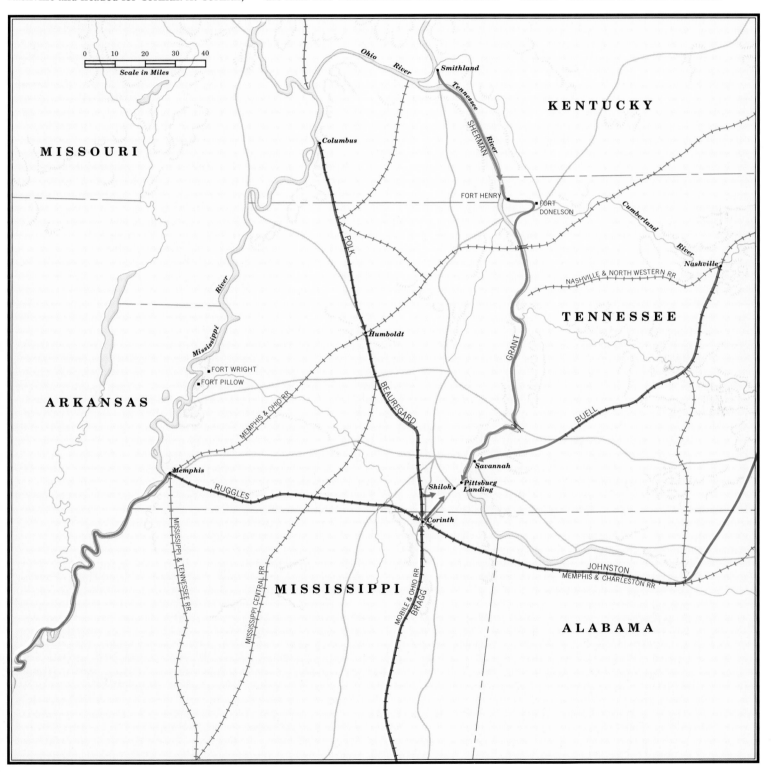

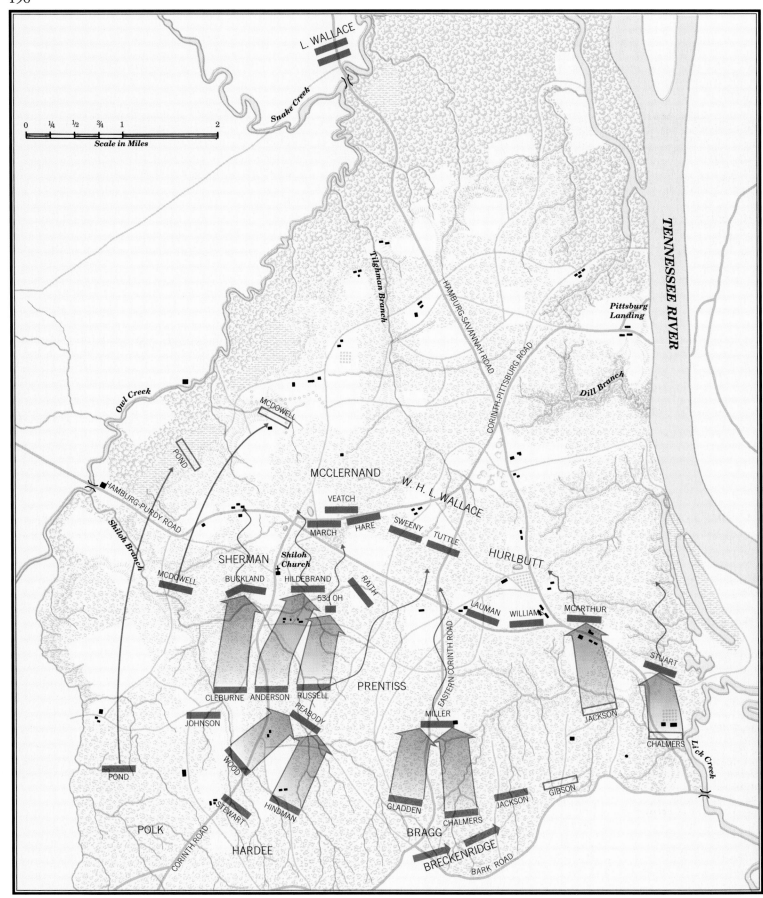

196

Albert Sidney Johnston, shown in 1860 wearing his U.S. Army uniform, was extravagantly admired in the South as both a gentleman and a soldier. His death at Shiloh from a freak wound was considered a catastrophe throughout the Confederacy.

ORDER OF BATTLE

ARMY OF THE MISSISSIPPI
JOHNSTON / BEAUREGARD
44,700 MEN

I CORPS POLK
FIRST DIVISION: CLARK
Brigades: RUSSELL, STEWART

SECOND DIVISION: CHEATHAM
Brigades: JOHNSON, STEPHENS

II CORPS BRAGG
FIRST DIVISION: RUGGLES
Brigades: GIBSON, ANDERSON, POND

SECOND DIVISION: WITHERS
Brigades: GLADDEN, CHALMERS, JACKSON

RESERVE CORPS BRECKINRIDGE
Brigades: TRABUE, BOWEN, STATHAM

III CORPS HARDEE

Brigades: HINDMAN, CLEBURNE, WOOD

ARMY OF THE TENNESSEE
GRANT
48,000 MEN

FIRST DIVISION: McCLERNAND
Brigades: HARE, MARSH, RAITH

THIRD DIVISION: L. WALLACE
Brigades: SMITH, THAYER, WHITTLESEY

FIFTH DIVISION: SHERMAN
Brigades: McDOWELL, STUART, HILDEBRAND, BUCKLAND

SECOND DIVISION: W. H. L. WALLACE
Brigades: TUTTLE, McARTHUR, SWEENY

FOURTH DIVISION: HURLBUT
Brigades: WILLIAMS, VEATCH, LAUMAN

SIXTH DIVISION: PRENTISS
Brigades: PEABODY, MILLER

ARMY OF THE OHIO
BUELL
17,900 MEN

SECOND DIVISION: McCOOK
Brigades: ROUSSEAU, KIRK, GIBSON

FOURTH DIVISION: NELSON
Brigades: AMMEN, HAZEN, BRUCE

FIFTH DIVISION: CRITTENDEN
Brigades: BOYLE, SMITH

SIXTH DIVISION: WOOD
Brigades: GARFIELD, WAGNER

OPENING CONFEDERATE ATTACKS, APRIL 6

Johnston attacked at dawn on April 6 and, catching the Federals off guard, swiftly devastated their first line of defense. Within minutes, a half-dozen Confederate brigades under Polk and Hardee *(red arrow)* had smashed their way into the Union camps, sending two of Sherman's brigades under Cols. Jesse Hildebrand and Ralph P. Buckland reeling backward. At the same time, Braxton Bragg's brigades hit the scattered units of Gen. Benjamin Prentiss' green division, which also retreated northward. The Federals refused, however, to collapse completely. Sherman, riding back and forth among his disorganized units, managed to cobble together a makeshift defensive line on the crest of a small hill. The bulk of Prentiss' men, giving ground but fighting stubbornly, also threw up a temporary line two miles to the rear. Shortly, Gens. John McClernand and William H. L. Wallace, whose units had been camped farther to the north, formed battle lines that helped slow the now badly disorganized Confederate assault.

Attacking at dawn on April 6, Confederates charge into the camps of Prentiss' startled Federals.

Brigadier General William T. Sherman, shown in this picture taken about the time of Shiloh, was praised as a "gallant and able officer" in Grant's official battle report and was soon promoted to major general. Sherman would remain in the Western theater and lead some of the Union's most effective campaigns there.

THE HORNET'S NEST, FIRST PHASE

The Confederates suffered heavy losses during the attack, and their units became intermixed and out of control. Some of the hungry Rebels even stopped in the Federal camps to eat their enemy's breakfasts. General Prentiss patched together a line on a sunken road with the 1,000-man remnant of his division. He was supported by Capt. Andrew Hickenlooper's 5th Ohio Battery and reinforced by W. H. L. Wallace's fresh division and two of Stephen Hurlbut's brigades. By 10:30 a.m., the Federals were formed up in a strong natural position that was dubbed the Hornet's Nest for the furious fighting that raged there through the day. Across the open field before the Hornet's Nest, the Confederates launched several uncoordinated and unsuccessful attacks. Despite these failures, Braxton Bragg ordered Col. Randall Gibson to make a head-on attack, and then another and then two more between 12:30 and 2:30, until Gibson's four regiments had been virtually wiped out by furious blasts of canister from two Union batteries and volleys from Prentiss' troops and the Union infantry on both sides. Other Confederate attacks made progress, however. By late afternoon, two Federal brigades holding the left of the Hornet's Nest, as well as David Stuart's isolated troops, came under pressure from the brigades of James R. Chalmers, John S. Bowen, and John K. Jackson. Polk's division pressed Sherman and McClernand on the Federal right.

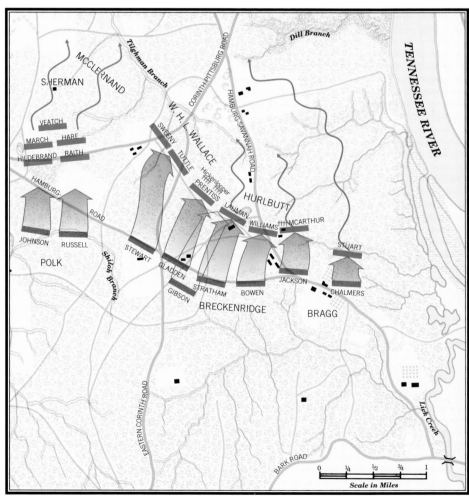

Arkansas and Louisiana troops of Confederate Col. Randall L. Gibson's brigade make the fourth of their desperate attacks on the Hornet's Nest. A Federal soldier likened Gibson's Confederates to "maddened demons."

General Benjamin Prentiss, on horseback at right, directs the troops defending the Hornet's Nest against one of the Confederate attacks during the afternoon of April 6. At left, an officer of Capt. Andrew Hickenlooper's 5th Ohio Battery shouts orders as his gunners fire their 6-pounders at point-blank range into Confederate infantry charging through the scrub oak.

Colonel Randall Lee Gibson, a 29-year-old, Yale-educated lawyer, was enraged by Bragg's orders to continue attacking the impregnable Hornet's Nest—and by Bragg's charging him with cowardice when he failed to capture it. Gibson was later exonerated and promoted to the rank of general.

Brigadier General Benjamin M. Prentiss, an Illinois lawyer and Mexican War veteran, helped give Grant time to form a new line by holding the Hornet's Nest all afternoon, surrendering only when his men were surrounded and almost out of ammunition.

Confederate Gen. Daniel Ruggles, commander of Bragg's first division, saw that infantry charges against the Hornet's Nest were suicidal and brought up artillery, finally massing 62 guns to blast the Federal position.

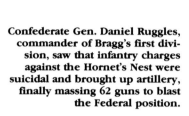

THE HORNET'S NEST, SECOND PHASE

Finally realizing his army was being wasted in futile attacks on the Hornet's Nest, Johnston ordered a brigade of Breckinridge's corps to attack the Federals holding a 10-acre peach orchard just to the east of the Hornet's Nest. Leading the assault, Johnston was mortally wounded by a Minié ball that nicked a leg artery, and he bled to death on the field. He was replaced by his second-in-command, Gen. P. G. T. Beauregard. Breckinridge's attack continued, however, sending the troops of Hurlbut's division tumbling back toward Pittsburg Landing; at about 4:00 p.m., the Federal positions came under heavy fire from Gen. Daniel Ruggles' artillery. The Union line began to waver, the troops on both sides of Prentiss' division falling back under new attacks by Breckinridge's troops and elements of Bragg's corps. On the Federal far right, Sherman and McClernand, also pressed, retreated toward Pittsburg Landing. The survivors in the Hornet's Nest found their flanks being hammered backward into the shape of a horseshoe; soon they were surrounded, and Prentiss was forced to surrender. By 5:45, the Federal line had disintegrated. Throughout the bloody afternoon, however, Grant had been forming a new defensive front running west from Pittsburg Landing toward Owl Creek. In the line, Grant placed Sherman's and McClernand's divisions and other regiments and brigades that had withdrawn more or less intact as well as stragglers. Grant also added Gen. Lew Wallace's 6,000-man division of fresh troops that arrived late on the battlefield from their position at Crump's Landing about 7:00. By then, the first units of Buell's army, led by Gen. William Nelson, had arrived on the eastern bank of the Tennessee, to be ferried across during the evening. The Confederates had lost their chance to destroy Grant before Buell's reinforcements arrived.

Fleeing from the battlefield, terrified Federal troops stream toward the Tennessee River. Thousands of Union recruits at Shiloh fled after the first Confederate attack, hiding under the bluffs and refusing to rejoin their units.

The peach orchard, devastated by gunfire during the battle, lies overgrown beyond the plowed field and rail fence in this postwar photograph taken from the roof of a barn. The tangled trees and brush of the Hornet's Nest can be seen at upper right. Breckinridge's Confederates attacked through the orchard from left to right, hitting Hurlbut's defenders in the flank.

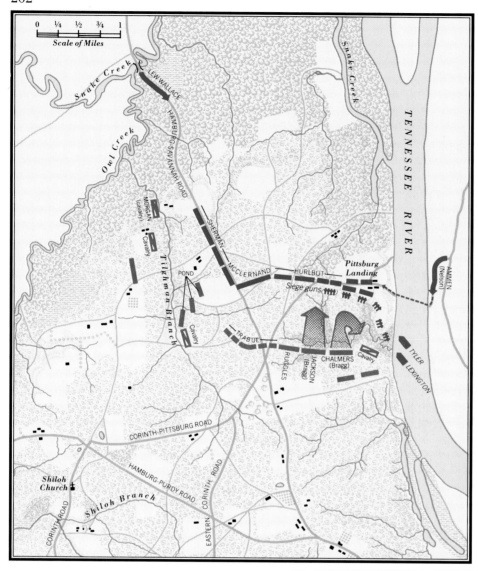

FINAL CONFEDERATE ATTACKS

Having taken the peach orchard and the Hornet's Nest, the Confederates continued pushing northward for a time, but then many of the famished, exhausted troops stopped to rummage the well-stocked camps of the Federals. Thousands started fires and began cooking their suppers. Sensing that victory might be slipping away, several of the Confederate commanders prodded their men to make a last drive to capture Pittsburg Landing. On the left, Hardee and Polk continued to press slowly after Sherman and McClernand. On the right, a furious Braxton Bragg mustered two brigades, commanded by James Chalmers and John Jackson, and sent them forward—across a ravine cut by a stream called Dill's Branch. The Confederates bravely waded the stream and clambered up the ravine's far side, but were met there by steady and murderously accurate fire from Federal artillery, including five heavy siege guns that Grant had massed on the left side of his new line. At last, General Beauregard, thinking that the battle was won—he wired news to Richmond of "a complete victory"—ordered Bragg to retire and instructed the rest of the Confederate army to disengage for the night.

Firing from high ground on the northern edge of the Dill Creek ravine *(right),* Federal infantry and artillery pour fire into the brigades of Chalmers and Jackson as they make their last attack at sunset on April 6.

On a bluff near Pittsburg Landing, crewmen of Battery B, 2d Illinois Light Artillery, stand at their five guns for a picture taken a few days after the Battle of Shiloh. The big 24-pounder guns, intended for siege operations against Corinth, point south in the direction of the last Confederate attack.

The *Tyler* and *Lexington* shell Confederate positions on April 6 while transports *(background)* land reinforcements of Gen. Don Carlos Buell.

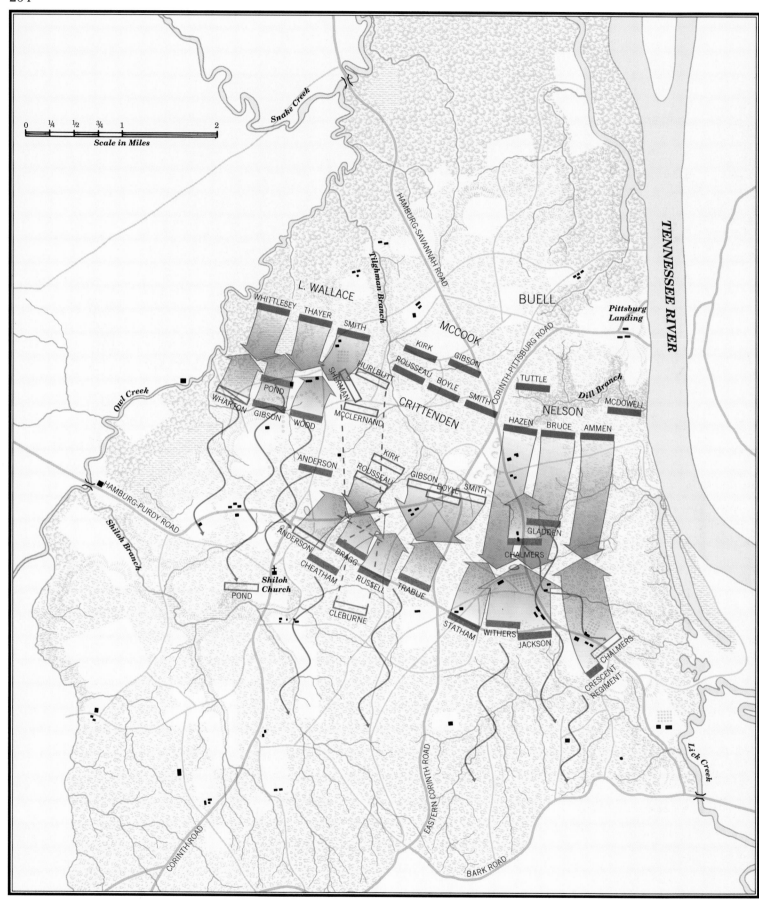

BRIG. GEN. DON CARLOS BUELL

FEDERAL COUNTERATTACK, APRIL 7

Believing that victory was his and that Grant was about to flee across the Tennessee, Beauregard made no attempt during the night of April 6-7 to form a defense or to replenish his ammunition. But Grant was shuffling Buell's brigades into his line and preparing to counterattack. At dawn on the seventh, Federal skirmishers moved forward, followed by the bulk of both Union armies, about 45,000 men versus only 20,000 Confederates still able to fight. As the Union attack ground ahead, several Confederate units made desperate charges into the Federal front. Taking the initiative when Federal progress slowed, Patrick Cleburne's brigade of Hardee's corps smashed into the Union center near the road to Corinth—and lost 1,700 men killed or wounded. Benjamin Cheatham's brigade reinforced Cleburne to attack Gen. Thomas Crittenden's division in the Federal center. Around Shiloh Church, remnants of Gen. Dan Ruggles' division and Gen. Sterling A. M. Wood's brigade put up savage resistance. But as more Federal brigades came into action, the Confederates were pushed back. Shortly after 2:30, Beauregard ordered a withdrawal, forming a rear guard and sending the rest of his army trudging toward Corinth, burning the captured Federal camps as they withdrew. The Federals, also spent, and bogged down by heavy rains, did not pursue. The casualties for the two-day battle were shocking and nearly equal: Each side lost about 1,700 killed and roughly 8,000 wounded. Grant, criticized for the near defeat, was briefly shunted to a meaningless post, and Gen. Henry Halleck, commander in chief in the West, took over the Federal army. Halleck did not push the Confederate army out of Corinth until May 29.

GEN. P. G. T. BEAUREGARD

Beauregard *(second from the right)* reins up with his staff next to Shiloh Church about 2:00 p.m. on April 7. He soon sent aides to the Confederate corps commanders with orders to retreat. At top right are the tents of Sherman's camp, overrun on the battle's first day.

After Shiloh, the war in the West split into two loosely interdependent campaigns. One was the long, arduous Federal attempt, overseen by Ulysses S. Grant, to gain control of the Mississippi River. The other was a sprawling contest for control of middle and eastern Tennessee. It began with an ambitious Confederate invasion of Kentucky—a campaign of marching and countermarching that ranged from the Alabama-Tennessee border northward 350 miles to the Ohio River.

The campaign began when General Don Carlos Buell's Army of the Ohio began a slow advance from Corinth, Mississippi, toward another vital Confederate rail junction at Chattanooga. To divert Buell from this target, General Edmund Kirby Smith, clever and ambitious commander of Confederate forces in East Tennessee, boldly decided to strike north into Kentucky with a small army from his base at Knoxville. After vacillating for several weeks, General Braxton Bragg decided to join in the action, bringing his army from its base at Tupelo, Mississippi, to Chattanooga, and then northward on a parallel track. Bragg, initially reluctant to move, soon embraced the campaign with fervor, believing that thousands of pro-Southern Tennesseans and Kentuckians would flock to join his army and that a successful invasion would not only force Buell's army out of Tennessee but maybe even bring Kentucky into the Confederacy.

Buell was compelled to pursue Bragg and Kirby Smith. His progress was slow; Buell was methodical to a fault and his supply lines were constantly beset by bands of Confederate cavalry. But in September he reached Louisville, then doubled back to meet Bragg. At Perryville, in October, the two forces collided violently. Bragg, realizing he was seriously outnum-

General Braxton Bragg was given command of the Confederate army in northern Mississippi in June 1862, replacing General Beauregard, who had abandoned Corinth without a fight.

bered, broke off the fight and retreated 200 miles to Knoxville. At the end of the month, President Jefferson Davis, concerned about the mounting criticism of Bragg's abilities, summoned the general to Richmond. Davis was satisfied with Bragg's explanation that the retreat had been a military necessity, but the rift between Bragg and his generals would never heal. Back in Tennessee, the army commander prepared his forces for an advance on Nashville, while John Hunt Morgan's Rebel cavalry played havoc with Union supply lines.

At length, the Federals under General William S. Rosecrans, who had replaced the timid Buell, caught up with Bragg again, this time near Murfreesboro, Tennessee, where the Confederate general had gathered his forces in late November and December. There, at year's end, on the banks of Stones River, Bragg attacked with a ferocity that nearly won a decisive victory. But showing a strange loss of nerve and judgment, the general failed to press his advantage and retreated once more. The battle ended as a major victory for the North. Kentucky was safe at last and Nashville made secure as a base for future Federal operations.

Taking the offensive in mid-August 1862, Kirby Smith first sent Gen. Carter Stevenson to pry a Federal force under George Morgan from the Cumberland Gap; then both Stevenson and Kirby Smith, with 20,000 men, marched on to Lexington and Frankfort. Later that month, Bragg, with about 30,000 men, moved north along a parallel route to the west, intending to join Kirby Smith in capturing the vital Union supply center at Louisville. Forced to abandon the drive on Chattanooga, the 55,000-man Federal army under Buell started in pursuit over several routes, reuniting in Kentucky and managing to reach Louisville before the Confederates arrived. Once there, Buell turned his divisions about and collided with part of Bragg's Confederate army at Perryville on October 8. After the inconclusive battle, Bragg, outnumbered and fearful for his supply lines, headed back to Tennessee, eventually concentrating at Murfreesboro. The Federals returned to Nashville where they gathered their strength under their new commander, Gen. William S. Rosecrans. On December 26, they marched out to the southeast looking for a fight with General Bragg.

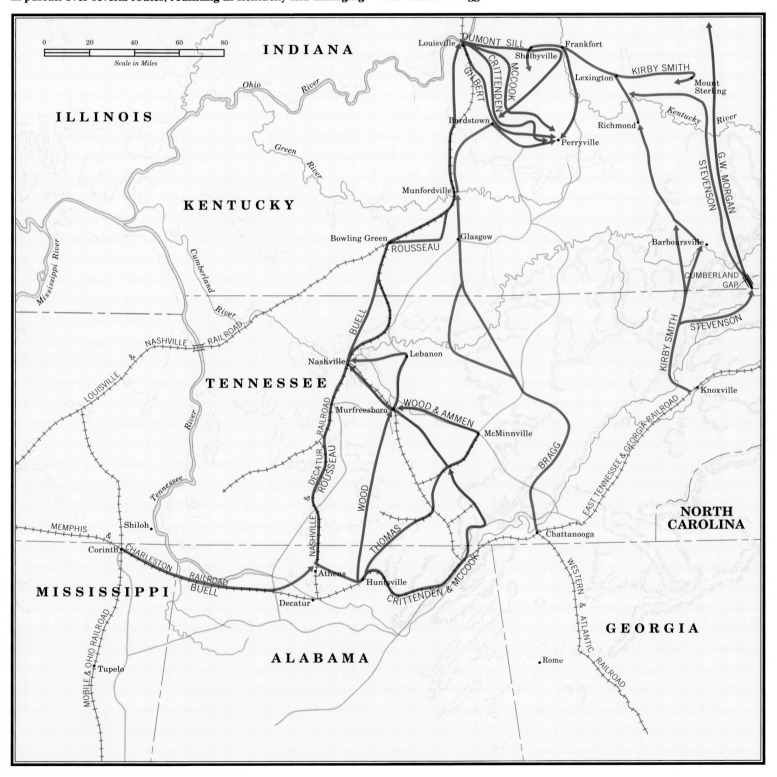

General William Rufus Terrill, disowned by his Virginia family for remaining faithful to the Union, was killed by a Confederate shell while urging his brigade to hold the Federal left at Perryville.

Major General Benjamin Franklin Cheatham, though distrusted by Bragg as an incompetent political appointee, led his Tennessee infantry in a disciplined attack at Perryville. "Cheatham's noble division," one officer recalled, "moved forward as if on dress parade."

In a cornfield on the Federal left, men of Col. John C. Starkweather's brigade level a volley at George Maney's Confederates advancing through the stalks. Starkweather's grim defense prevented Benjamin Cheatham's division from turning the Federal flank.

A log house stands among meadows on the high ground near the intersection of Benton Road and Mackville Pike, where McCook's Federals were finally able to stem the Confederate advance.

The Battle of Perryville nearly ended in disaster for General Bragg, who, believing that most of the Federal army was far to the north, marching from Louisville toward Frankfort, sent 16,000 Confederates under Leonidas Polk into the path of Buell's entire force of some 60,000 men. At 2:00 p.m. on October 8, Bragg ordered Cheatham's division across the Chaplin River to attack the Federal left. Cheatham's rush broke Jackson's division, and follow-up attacks by Buckner's and part of Anderson's divisions drove back the rest of McCook's corps. But in the center, Sheridan repulsed Anderson's other two brigades, and by nightfall, the exhausted Confederates halted their attacks. Bragg, at last realizing that he was vastly outnumbered, broke off the battle and retreated, saved from possible annihilation by the failure of General Crittenden to advance his Federal II Corps and envelop the Confederate left.

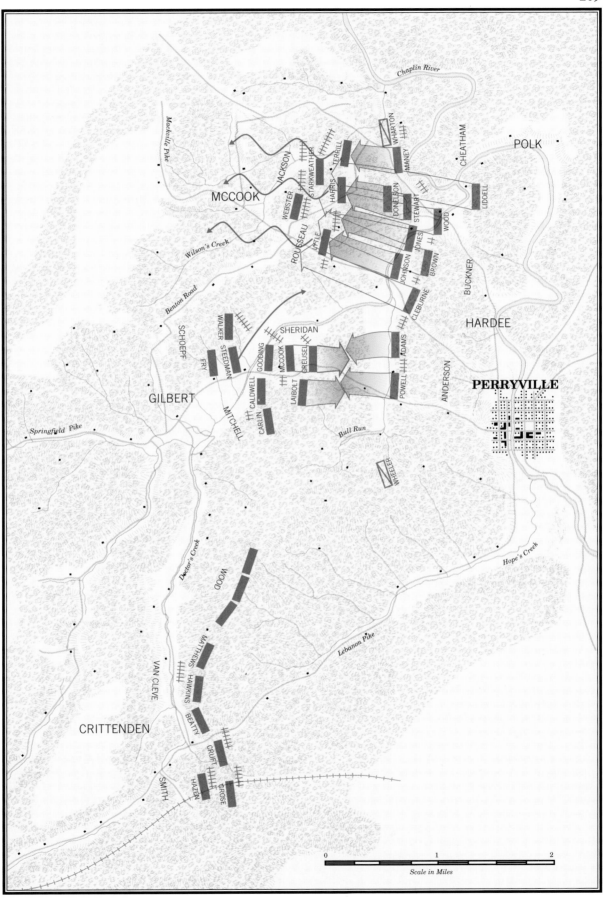

GEN. LEONIDAS POLK

GEN. WILLIAM J. HARDEE

ORDER OF BATTLE
ARMY OF TENNESSEE
BRAGG
34,700 MEN

POLK'S CORPS

FIRST DIVISION: CHEATHAM
Brigades: DONELSON, STEWART, MANEY, VAUGHN

SECOND DIVISION: WITHERS
Brigades: LOOMIS, CHALMERS, ANDERSON, MANIGAULT

HARDEE'S CORPS

FIRST DIVISION: BRECKENRIDGE
Brigades: ADAMS, PALMER, PRESTON, HANSON, JACKSON

SECOND DIVISION: CLEBURNE
Brigades: L. E. POLK, LIDDELL, JOHNSON, WOOD

McCOWN'S DIVISION
Brigades: ECTOR, RAINS, McNAIR

CAVALRY
WHEELER

WHEELER'S BRIGADE	PEGRAM'S BRIGADE
BUFORD'S BRIGADE	WHARTON'S BRIGADE

ARMY OF THE CUMBERLAND
ROSECRANS
41,400 MEN

LEFT WING CRITTENDEN

FIRST DIVISION: WOOD
Brigades: HASCALL, WAGNER, HARKER

SECOND DIVISION: PALMER
Brigades: CRUFT, HAZEN, GROSE

THIRD DIVISION: VAN CLEVE
Brigades: BEATTY, FYFFE, PRICE

CENTER THOMAS

FIRST DIVISION: ROUSSEAU
Brigades: SCRIBNER, BEATTY,
STARKWEATHER, SHEPHARD

SECOND DIVISION: NEGLEY
Brigades: SPEARS, STANLEY, MILLER

THIRD DIVISION: FRY
WALKER'S BRIGADE ONLY

FOURTH DIVISION (two regiments only)

FIFTH DIVISION (not engaged)

RIGHT WING McCOOK

FIRST DIVISION: DAVIS
Brigades: POST, CARLIN, WOODRUFF

SECOND DIVISION: JOHNSON
Brigades: WILLICH, KIRK, BALDWIN

THIRD DIVISION: SHERIDAN
Brigades: SILL, SCHAEFER, ROBERTS

CAVALRY
STANLEY

CAVALRY DIVISION: KENNETT
Brigades: MINTY, ZAHM

OPENING CONFEDERATE ATTACKS, DECEMBER 31, 1862

For two months after the Battle of Perryville, fighting between the armies was limited to heavy skirmishing along Federal supply lines. Gen. William Rosecrans *(right),* having taken over from the slow-moving Buell, holed up in Nashville reorganizing his new command. Bragg, who had retreated into Tennessee, advanced north in early November to the Murfreesboro's area—and waited for Rosecrans to move. On the day after Christmas, Rosecrans started his advance toward Murfreesboro; by December 30, the two armies were drawn up for battle along the icy Stones River with each commander planning to attack the other's right flank. Needing a quick victory, Bragg struck first, sending Hardee's 10,000 men on the Confederate left dashing forward at dawn on the 31st in a sustained assault against Mc-

Cook's corps. By 8:00 a.m., Gen. John Mc-Cown's Rebels had shattered Johnson's division on the Union far right. At the same time, Cleburne's division hammered away at Davis' three Federal brigades, who put up a stiff fight until they were outflanked. General Polk's corps also advanced, attacking the Federal center held by Sheridan's, Palmer's, and Negley's divisions, but Polk's assaults failed to break through, and the battered Union troops were able to fall back and form a new line to face the threat to their flank. Meanwhile, on the Federal left, Rosecrans had initiated his own attack, sending Van Cleve's division across Stones River. But before the next units could cross, frantic appeals from McCook and the sound of heavy fighting to the south forced him to call off the attack to deal with the threat to his right.

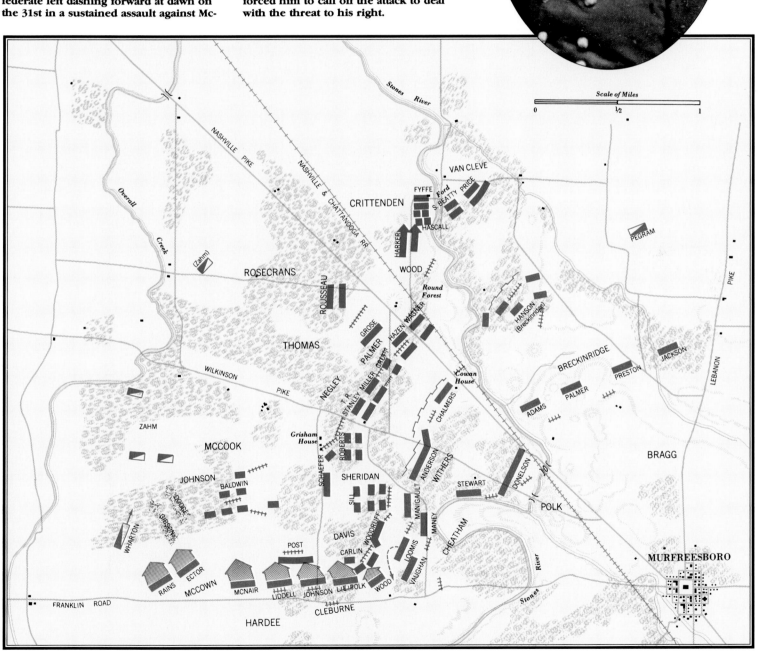

Colonel William P. Hazen, a West Pointer who had commanded the 41st Ohio at Shiloh and Perryville, held the Round Forest with his four-regiment brigade of Palmer's division for most of December 31, forming the pivot of the Federal defense.

In one of a series of remarkably accurate pictures of the battle done by a Union soldier, Pvt. Alfred Mathews, Confederate troops *(background, right)* advance in disciplined lines. They were slaughtered by fire from Federal infantry and artillery, drawn up north of the Round Forest between the Nashville Pike *(right)* and the railroad.

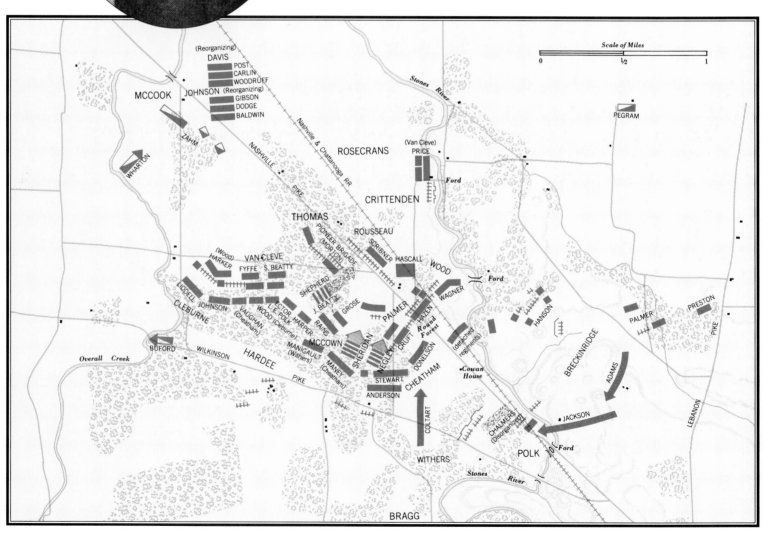

FINAL CONFEDERATE ATTACKS

By midmorning on December 31, the Federal right had been jackknifed almost 90 degrees from its original position by Hardee's continuing assaults. The Federal center had also been driven in by the furious attacks of Cheatham's and Withers' divisions against Sheridan's and Palmer's positions. The Confederate assaults were slowed, however, as General Rosecrans, riding forward to take charge of the Federal defense, funneled reinforcements to the threatened parts of his line. Giving up his original idea of having Crittenden's corps cross Stones River to attack Bragg's right flank, Rosecrans began stripping his left, sending parts of Van Cleve's and Wood's divisions across the rear of the battlefield to help the remnants of McCook's men hold their line. At the same time, Rosecrans moved Rousseau's division into position along Nashville Pike to back up Sheridan and Negley. He also deployed other units to reinforce Palmer and brought up battery after battery of guns to support the infantry. Despite the stiffening resistance, Polk continued to attack, hammering back Sheridan's and Negley's weary troops. This exposed Palmer's division in the nose of the salient formed by the V-shaped Federal line. Particularly vulnerable was the brigade under William Hazen that was holding a grove called the Round Forest. Beginning around 2:00 p.m., Hazen's position was attacked first by two brigades from Polk's corps and finally just before dark by four brigades from Breckinridge's division brought over from the Confederate right. But all the assaults were thrown back, the attackers scythed down by furious fire from Hazen's troops and supporting units, and from the Federal guns lined up virtually hub-to-hub. As night fell, Bragg, his army having suffered dreadful losses, ended the battle for the day.

In another of Private Mathews' pictures, the Ohio, Indiana, and Kentucky troops of Samuel Beatty's brigade *(foreground)*, moving quickly to reinforce the Federal right, stagger Patrick Cleburne's attacking Confederates with a sharp volley about noon on the first day of the battle.

BRECKINRIDGE'S ATTACK, JANUARY 2, 1863

Certain he had scored a crushing victory that would send the Federals fleeing to Nashville, Bragg was shocked to find Rosecrans' army still firmly in place on January 1 and ready to fight. The shock produced a strange lethargy, and for the entire day, Bragg did virtually nothing. Finally, on the afternoon of January 2, he impulsively ordered Breckinridge's division to attack four Union brigades under General Beatty that Rosecrans had sent to occupy a ridge just east of Stones River. At precisely 4:00 p.m., Breckinridge's troops stormed the height and in 45 minutes of furious fighting, drove Beatty's men back across the river. But the advance exposed the Confederates to murderous fire from Maj. John Mendenhall's 58 Federal guns massed on the river's west bank. Shortly, elements of Negley's division, followed by Palmer's, counterattacked across the river and swept Breckinridge back to his starting point. With this dismal failure, Bragg ended the battle. The next day, he began a retreat into southern Tennessee, leaving the field—and most of the state—securely in Union hands.

General James S. Negley, whose Federal division counterattacked across Stones River on January 2, was a stout, affable 36-year-old who had served as a private in the Mexican War. In civilian life, Negley had been a well-known horticulturist.

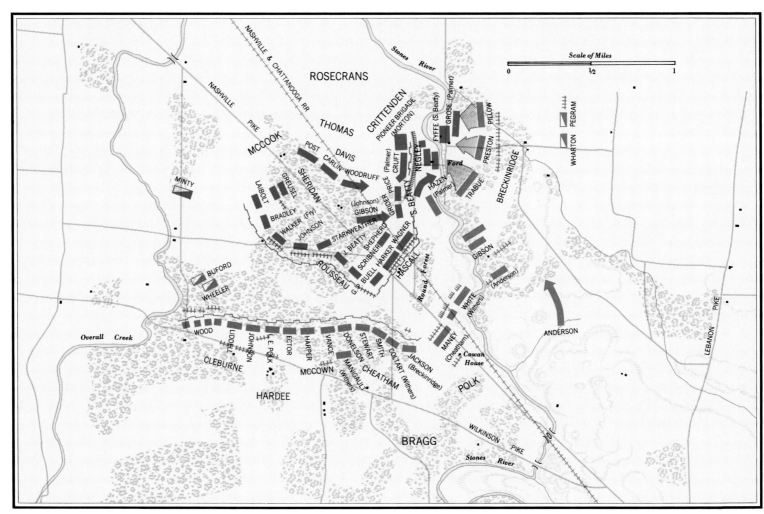

The 2,200 men of Col. John Miller's brigade of Negley's division ford Stones River to pursue the remnants of Breckinridge's Confederates. The headlong Federal counterattack was halted only by the early-winter darkness.

A view looking west across Stones River shows the hill where Crittenden's chief of artillery, Maj. John Mendenhall, placed his guns to repel Breckinridge's assault. When the Federals opened fire, one observer wrote, it must have seemed to the Confederate troops that they had "opened the door of Hell, and the devil himself was there to greet them."

MISSISSIPPI RIVER CAMPAIGN

In the spring of 1862, the Union army and navy together began one of the most difficult as well as important campaigns of the War—the long, arduous effort to seize control of the lower Mississippi River, cut the Confederate supply lines across it, and open the great waterway to Northern commerce moving from the Midwest to New Orleans and the sea.

The first moves went well for the Federals, a fleet under Admiral David Glasgow Farragut rather handily taking New Orleans. But the navy and a Union army under Ulysses S. Grant found the main upriver Confederate stronghold of Vicksburg extraordinarily hard to crack. Bombardments by gunboats achieved nothing.

Equally fruitless were Grant's repeated attempts through the fall and winter of 1862-1863 to take the city from the rear. Finally, in the spring, the determined Grant managed to move down the Mississippi past Vicksburg's guns and land his army on the river's east bank. From there, he pushed northward, battling Confederate forces at Port Gibson, Champion's Hill, and Jackson before at last closing in on Vicksburg itself and beginning a long siege that ultimately forced the city's surrender. With that stunning blow to the Southern cause, the defenders of the other Rebel citadel at Port Hudson also gave up, prompting a satisfied President Lincoln to remark: "The Father of Waters again goes unvexed to the sea."

Having secured most of the lower Mississippi, Farragut sailed his fleet upriver, bombarding Vicksburg in June with no success. Grant, trying to drive on the city from the north, was delayed by two Confederate thrusts *(red lines)* at his supply lines led by Earl Van Dorn and Nathan B. Forrest. But in late 1862, Grant had two Union corps moving down the Mississippi River: John McClernand's taking a Confederate fort at Arkansas Post en route and William T. Sherman's making a first failed attack on Vicksburg's outer defenses at Chickasaw Bluffs. By January 1863, the bulk of Grant's army was at Milliken's Bend, ready to begin the main struggle for Vicksburg.

Dominated by its Greek revival courthouse, which was completed in 1860, Vicksburg looks westward over a wide stretch of the Mississippi. The city, constructed on a series of bluffs, loomed like a fortress over the river; to the north and east it was protected by a maze of bayous and bogs.

Confederate Brig. Gen. Johnson K. Duncan salutes as he boards the Federal gunboat *Harriet Lane* to surrender Forts Jackson and St. Philip to Cdr. David Porter, who waits at the top of the gangway. The fall of the forts on April 28, 1862, left New Orleans defenseless, and the city was occupied the next day.

Farragut's fleet, one of the largest ever assembled in the United States, blasts past Fort Jackson *(foreground)* and Fort St. Philip before dawn on April 24, 1862. Earlier, two Federal gunboats had opened the way by cutting a passage through the massive iron chains *(bottom right)* the Confederates had strung as a barrier across the river. Despite furious fire from the two forts' heavy batteries and attacks by a small Confederate flotilla, Farragut's losses were amazingly light—one ship sunk and 37 men killed. By midday, the Union fleet was steaming upriver unchallenged.

To pry open the lower reaches of the Mississippi, David Farragut assembled a fleet at Ship Island off Biloxi and sailed toward the river's delta in March 1862. The smaller ships, including a flotilla of 19 mortar-carrying schooners led by Cdr. David D. Porter, made it through the Pass à l'Outre; Farragut's larger vessels bulled their way through the deeper Southwest Pass. On April 18, Porter's schooners began lobbing shells into Forts Jackson and St. Philip, the Confederate bastions guarding the river. The bombardment did only superficial damage to the formidable stone ramparts, however, and after five days, Farragut, weary of waiting, boldly sailed his heavy sloops of war and gunboats clear past the forts. Both strongholds surrendered when an 18,000-man Union army under Gen. Benjamin F. Butler, landing on the shore of Isle au Breton Sound, threatened to take them from the rear. By April 25, Farragut's fleet had passed New Orleans' last puny defenses and in May took Baton Rouge.

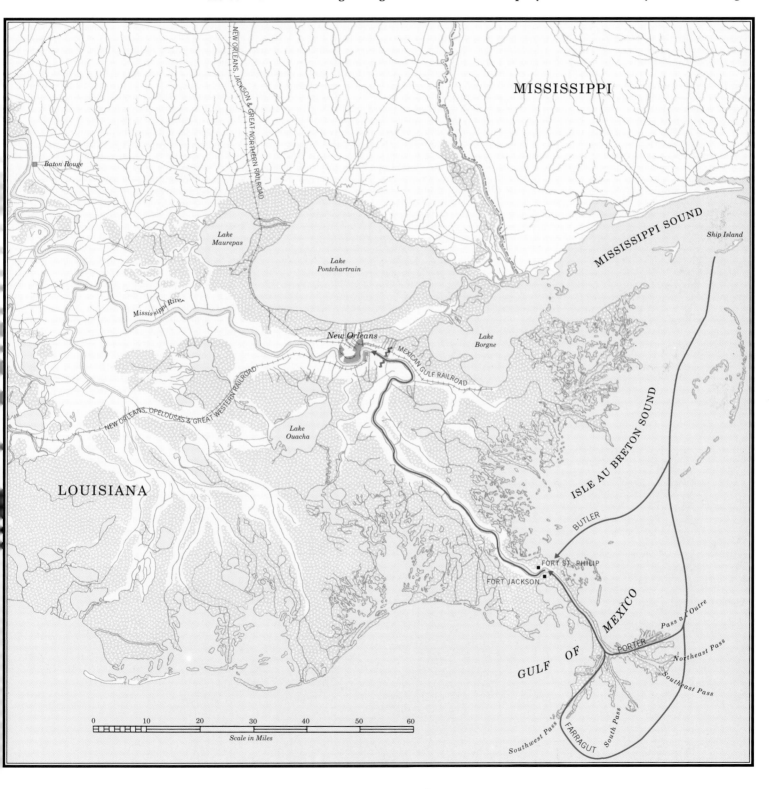

MAJ. GEN. EARL VAN DORN

Attempting to break Grant's hold on northern Mississippi before the Federals could drive on Vicksburg, Confederate Gen. Earl Van Dorn moved north with 10,000 troops and joined a force of 17,000 led by Sterling Price for an attack on the key Union supply depot at Corinth. On October 3, 1862, three of Van Dorn's divisions swiftly pushed back the first Union line. But the town's Federal defenders, led by Gen. William Rosecrans, re-formed and stubbornly held a second line of recently dug earthworks until darkness brought an end to the fighting. The next morning, Van Dorn's Confederates attacked again, his regiments smashing into the center of the Federal entrenchments. Col. William Rogers' Texans broke through only to be slaughtered by volleys from Rosecrans' reserves. By 11:30 a.m., the battle was over and Van Dorn's crippled force was in full flight.

Earl Van Dorn, a 42-year-old West Pointer *(below left)*, rashly sent his Confederate troops in head-on attacks against the Federals' strong inner earthworks at Corinth on October 3 and 4, 1862. The scene at left shows Col. William Rogers, whose 2d Texas spearheaded the disastrous assault, being shot dead while waving the regiment's colors from the parapet of a Union strongpoint called Battery Robinett. In the photograph below, Federal soldiers survey the carnage after the battle, including Rogers' body, which lies just left of the tree stump at center.

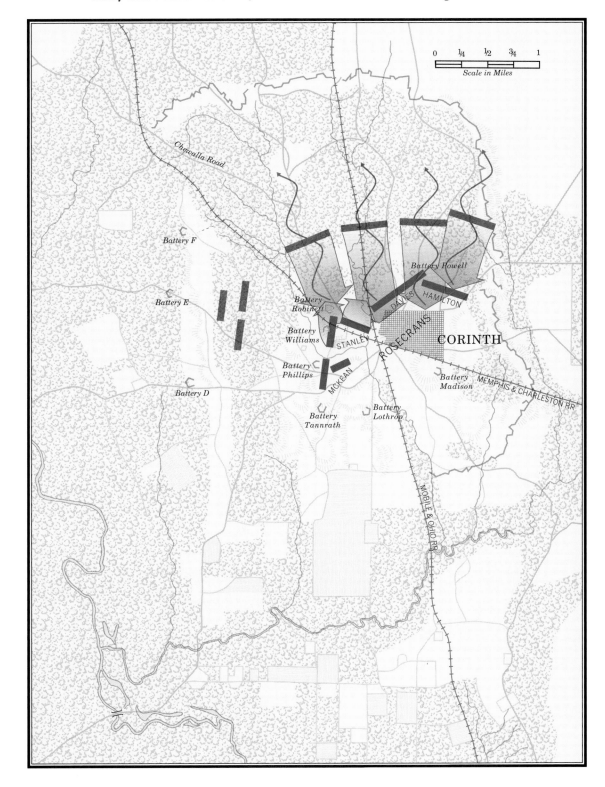

David Porter's Federal flotilla braves Confederate fire from batteries along the shore and on the bluffs at Vicksburg during a daring night run on April 16, 1863. Barges and transports, lashed to the gunboats for protection, carried men and supplies to landing sites downriver for Grant's assault on Vicksburg from the south.

Federal troops engage in the grueling task of dredging a canal across a bend in the Mississippi opposite Vicksburg that would have given Porter's ships a detour past the fortress' guns. Grant had little faith that this and other amphibious schemes would work but thought them worth a try. They also kept the soldiers busy during the rainy, muddy winter when offensive operations on land were impossible. "I let the work go on," he wrote, "believing employment was better than idleness."

FLANKING ATTEMPTS, DECEMBER 1862-MARCH 1863

On the west bank of the Mississippi, Grant began building a canal across from Vicksburg. Farther north, James McPherson cut a passage to Lake Providence, ships could navigate the bayous south to the Red River. On the east bank, 325 miles above the city, Union engineers breached a levee at Yazoo Pass, letting Mississippi water flood the Yazoo, making it navigable. The scheme was foiled when Gen. W. W. Loring's Confederates built Fort Pemberton at a bend in the river. To support the expedition, Sherman and his naval ally David Porter tried pushing up the lower Yazoo into Steele's Bayou, but low water nearly bottled up Porter's fleet. The Union's plans failed, forcing Porter and Grant to run their boats at night past Vicksburg.

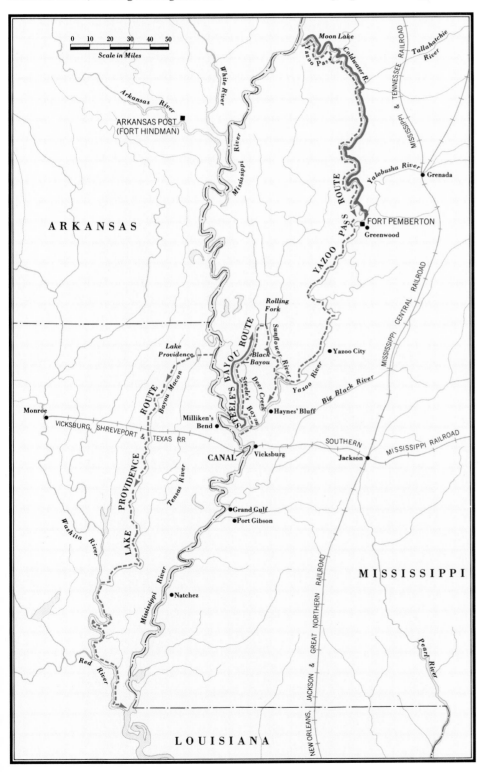

MAJ. GEN. ULYSSES S. GRANT

REAR ADM. DAVID DIXON PORTER

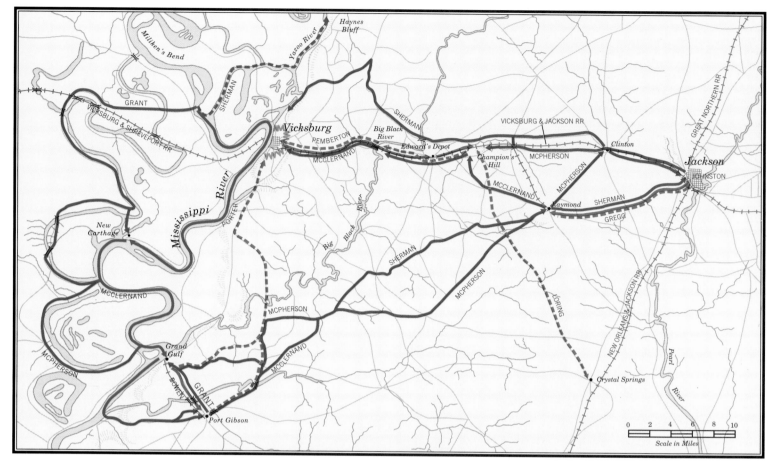

MARCH ON VICKSBURG, APRIL-MAY

As Porter's ships landed some of Grant's troops south of Vicksburg at New Carthage, others marched down muddy roads on the Mississippi's west bank. Then, while Sherman distracted Gen. John C. Pemberton, commander of Vicksburg's defenses, with a feint at Haines' Bluff, Grant sent both McClernand's and McPherson's corps across the river to the east bank. There on May 1 they beat back a small but stubborn Confederate force led by Brig. Gen. John S. Bowen at Port Gibson. With Sherman's corps now across the river as well, Grant marched swiftly to get between Pemberton's forces near Vicksburg and strong Rebel reinforcements gathering at Jackson. Near Raymond, McPherson's corps overcame Gen. John Gregg's troops. With McPherson's and Sherman's troops, Grant defeated Joseph E. Johnston at Jackson, taking the town on May 14. Grant then turned west, overcoming Pemberton's three divisions in a fierce battle at Champion's Hill. By May 18, the Federals were in the outskirts of Vicksburg.

MAJ. GEN. JOHN S. BOWEN

MAJ. GEN. JOHN McCLERNAND

CHAMPION'S HILL, MAY 16

Trying to cut Grant's communications and strike his rear, Pemberton sent three divisions westward to intercept the Federals at Champion's Hill. Gen. Alvin Hovey's Union brigade seized the hill on May 16 but was soon flung back in furious fighting by John Bowen's Confederates. Bowen was shortly in trouble, however, as William Loring failed to advance in support. Federal brigades under John Logan and Marcellus Crocker smashed into Carter L. Stevenson's division on the Confederate left flank, and McClernand belatedly ordered Osterhaus' brigade forward to assail the Rebel right. By late afternoon, Pemberton's bloodied troops were in retreat toward Baker's Creek and the roads to Vicksburg.

Braving rounds of double-shotted canister, Indiana troops of Gen. George McGinnis' brigade overwhelm a Confederate battery on the crest of Champion's Hill. In spite of a subsequent Rebel counterattack, Pemberton's army was eventually routed at a cost of 3,839 casualties.

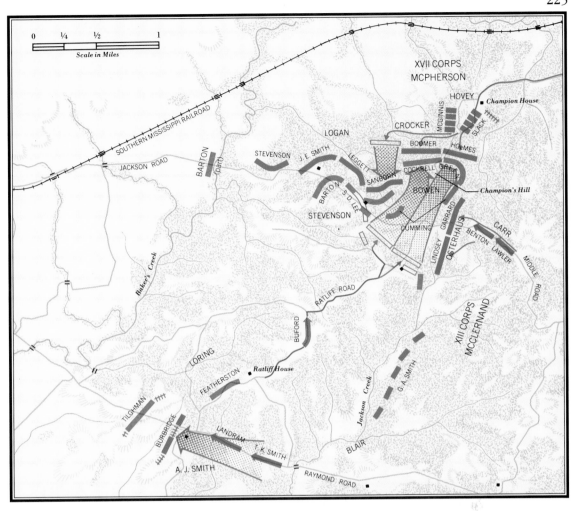

General John C. Pemberton confirmed his reputation as a cautious commander by concentrating his army for a static defense of Vicksburg, rather than boldly driving eastward to link up with another Confederate force under Joseph Johnston and fighting Grant in open battle.

VICKSBURG BESIEGED, MAY-JULY

Having pushed the Rebels back to Vicksburg's defenses, Grant ordered an assault on May 19 that met a violent reception. McPherson and McClernand could not advance through ravines choked with felled trees. Only Sherman on the north made progress, Col. Giles A. Smith storming the Stockade Redans. But Smith was pinned down and escaped only after dark. On May 22, Grant tried again. Some of McClernand's troops, including Lawler's and Landrum's men, reached the top of the Railroad Redoubt only to be beaten back. Grant settled for a siege. On June 25, the Federals tried again, detonating a mine beneath the Jackson Road defenses. McPherson's troops charged through the resulting crater, but made little headway. Vicksburg was taken only after 48 days of shelling and near starvation convinced Pemberton that resistance was futile.

Staggered by a hail of Minié balls and grapeshot, troops of the 22d Iowa struggle up the steep ramparts of the Confederate Railroad Redoubt on May 22, their color sergeant bravely leading the way. All the day's Union attacks were driven back with heavy losses totaling 3,199 men.

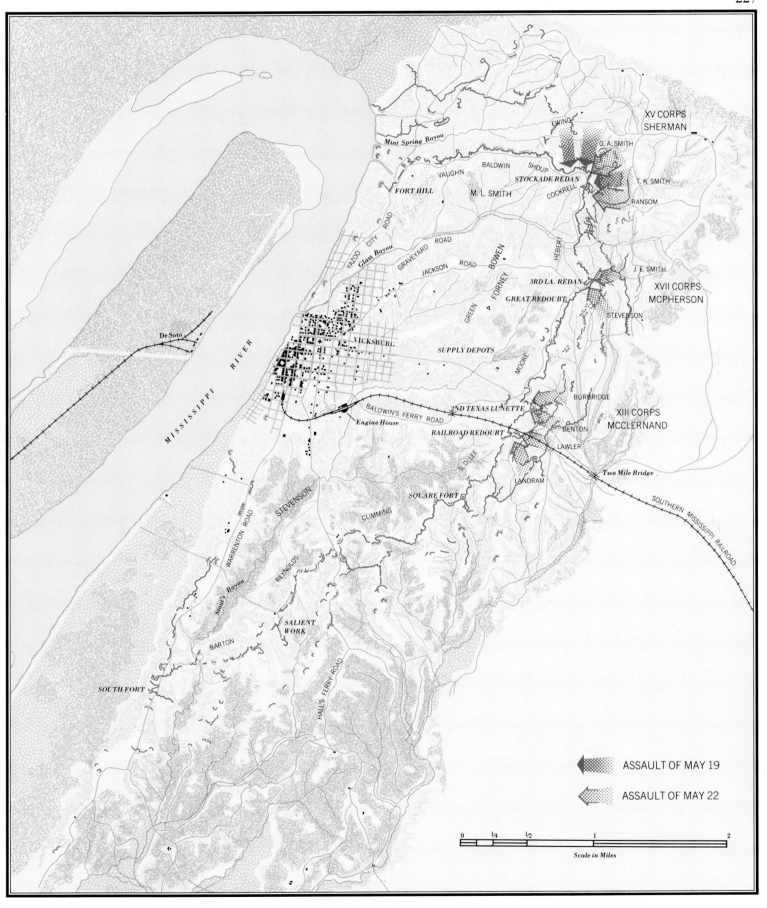

XV CORPS
SHERMAN

EWING

G. A. SMITH

T. K. SMITH

RANSOM

Mint Spring Bayou

BALDWIN SHOUP

VAUGHN

STOCKADE REDAN

COCKRELL

FORT HILL M. L. SMITH

HEBERT

J. E. SMITH

XVII CORPS
MCPHERSON

YAZOO CITY ROAD

Glass Bayou

GRAVEYARD ROAD

JACKSON ROAD

BOWEN

FORNEY

GREEN

3RD LA. REDAN

GREAT REDOUBT

STEVENSON

De Soto

MISSISSIPPI RIVER

VICKSBURG

SUPPLY DEPOTS

MOORE

BALDWIN'S FERRY ROAD

2ND TEXAS LUNETTE

BURBRIDGE

XIII CORPS
MCCLERNAND

Engine House

RAILROAD REDOUBT

BENTON

LAWLER

S. D. LEE

Two Mile Bridge

STEVENSON

SQUARE FORT

LANDRAM

WARRENTON ROAD

CUMMING

SOUTHERN MISSISSIPPI RAILROAD

REYNOLDS

Stout's Bayou

**SALIENT
WORK**

BARTON

SOUTH FORT

HALL'S FERRY ROAD

ASSAULT OF MAY 19

ASSAULT OF MAY 22

0   1/4   1/2   1   2

Scale in Miles

In the painting at left, soldiers of the 45th Illinois charge through a trench into the crater made by the explosion of 2,200 pounds of gunpowder under a Confederate redoubt near the Jackson Road. The blast blew away much of the redoubt but killed few defenders. Most of them, anticipating the explosion, had pulled back to a new line—from which they mowed down the Federals with cannon and musket fire before counterattacking. The photograph, taken after the siege, shows the same sections of Union trench and the crater *(upper right)* as well as a curious structure made of railroad ties that was built and used by a celebrated sharpshooter of the 23d Indiana named Henry C. Foster. Because Foster favored a coonskin cap, his perch was dubbed Coonskin Tower.

Accepting the Confederate surrender on July 4, 1863, Grant and his staff approach the Vicksburg house used by Pemberton as his headquarters. Grant's terms were generous—he paroled the entire Confederate garrison instead of making the men prisoners—and he rushed in food to relieve the half-starved city. Despite the bombardments, fewer than a dozen civilians were known to have been killed and about three times that number injured. The news of Vicksburg's surrender caused shock in the South, especially since it came on the same day that Robert E. Lee retreated after the defeat at Gettysburg.

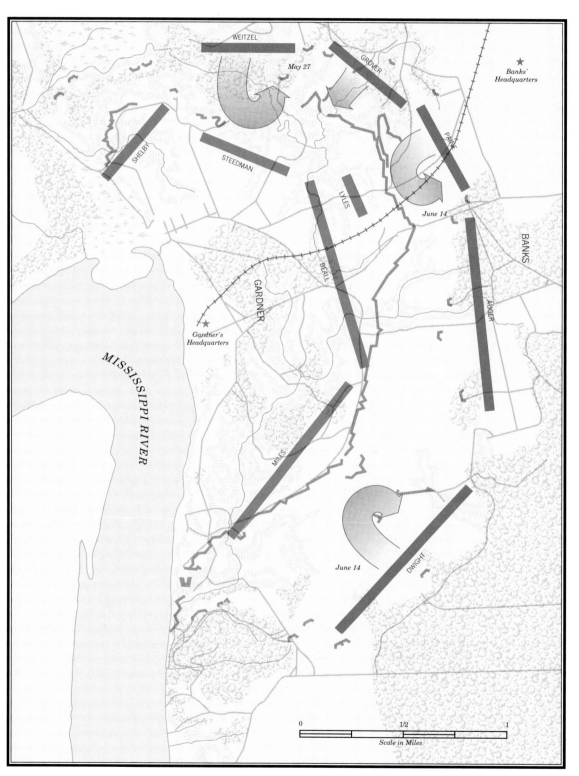

WEITZEL

May 27

GROVER

Banks'
Headquarters

SHELBY

STEEDMAN

PAINE

LYLES

BANKS

June 14

BEALL

GARDNER

ADGER

Gardner's
Headquarters

MISSISSIPPI RIVER

MILES

June 14

DWIGHT

0   1/2   1
Scale in Miles

Like Vicksburg 120 miles to the north, Port Hudson was situated on high bluffs overlooking a sharp bend in the Mississippi and was protected inland by bayous, thickets, and gullies. The Confederates, 16,000 strong, under Maj. Gen. Franklin Gardner, fortified the town with 19 heavy guns commanding the river and the same number of lighter artillery pieces on the landward side. In the spring of 1863, Gen. Nathaniel P. Banks besieged Port Hudson with 24,000 men and then, becoming impatient, attacked head-on. On May 27, troops from the divisions of Weitzel and Grover advanced, but soon became entangled in dense thickets and mazes of fallen trees and were easily repulsed by the Confederates of Col. I. G. W. Steedman. A two-pronged attack on June 14, by troops under Paine and Dwight, was also a catastrophe for the Federals. Banks' total losses in the two assaults came to nearly 4,000 men. But the Confederates were also in trouble as sickness spread and supplies ran desperately low. When word came that Vicksburg had fallen, Gardner gave up hope and surrendered on July 9.

Federal infantrymen clamber over fallen timbers during one of Banks' attacks on the Port Hudson defenses. Thrown back with heavy losses, the Union troops cursed the entire operation, one officer fuming that "the affair was a gigantic bushwhack." In the two failed attacks, the Federals lost 4,000 dead and wounded. By mid-June, another 7,000 men had fallen ill, many suffering dysentery or sunstroke in the stifling heat of Port Hudson's swamps. By that time, General Gardner's garrison had been reduced to 6,000 men, units having been sent north to help defend Vicksburg.

After the siege, a section of the defensive line called Fort Desperate by the Confederates is a shambles of broken timbers and wrecked cannon. Gardner's men survived bombardment by heavy 20-pounder Parrott rifles by burrowing dugouts in the earth that protected against all but a direct hit. When the surrender finally came, the men from both sides crawled from their trenches and redoubts to shake hands. Port Hudson was especially valuable to the South because its guns blocked Federal river traffic and also guarded the nearby mouth of the Red River, an avenue for goods flowing from the West that helped sustain the Confederacy.

CHATTANOOGA CAMPAIGN

Following the Battle of Stones River, the armies of Braxton Bragg and William Rosecrans sat 30 miles apart in central Tennessee for six months, idle except for cavalry raids on each other's supply lines. Bragg, who had been defeated at Perryville and Stones River, was now the most maligned general in the Confederacy. The soldiers of his Army of Tennessee resented his severe discipline, his officers questioned his competence, and the public despised him for his retreats. It was said that Bragg retreated whether he won or lost; a Confederate joke had it that he would never get to heaven because the moment he was invited to enter he would fall back.

As winter changed to spring, Rosecrans, too, drew criticism—for his failure to take his Army of the Cumberland on the offensive. Despite goading from the Union high command, it was not until June that Rosecrans bestirred himself. When he did, to the surprise of many, Rosecrans acted with boldness and confidence. Maneuvering skillfully, he threatened to outflank Bragg and forced the Confederates to retreat again, this time to Chattanooga.

Geography and the Southern rail system dictated that Chattanooga, an otherwise unremarkable settlement of 3,500 people, play a key role in the War. But when Federal troops closed around this transportation hub on September 6, 1863, the Confederates evacuated it without a fight. Again Bragg was outmaneuvered and had to move his army south or risk being cut off.

Convinced that the Confederates were fleeing, Rosecrans swiftly pursued them into Georgia. But rather than retreat, Bragg stood and fought at Chickamauga Creek, inflicting a stunning blow and sending the Federals reeling. Bragg declined to pursue the Union army. His men were exhausted and both sides had suffered heavy casualties—the Rebels lost 18,454 and the Yankees 16,179 in the bloodiest two days of the War. When Rosecrans' forces withdrew into Chattanooga, Bragg bottled them up and severed their supply lines, imposing a state of siege.

Now it was Rosecrans' turn to be discredited. Remarking that the general was "stunned and confused, like a duck hit on the head," Lincoln relieved him of command and placed the perilous situation in the hands of the North's most trusted leader, Ulysses S. Grant. Losing no time, Grant launched assaults that cleared the Confederates from their positions on the heights of Lookout Mountain and Missionary Ridge. The South would never recover from the loss of Chattanooga, which brought Bragg's dismissal and opened the gateway to the Confederate heartland.

In January 1863, after the repulse at Murfreesboro, Braxton Bragg withdrew to positions around Tullahoma. Pursuing in mid-June with a series of bold flanking moves, William S. Rosecrans forced Bragg to retreat across the Tennessee River to Chattanooga. Rosecrans, after several weeks of delay, advanced to the river, and by early September, most of his army was across the river below Chattanooga and pushing east in three columns. Bragg evacuated the town on September 7, fell back south, and then turned to fight. After botching several attempts to smash Thomas and Crittenden as they emerged from the mountains (inset), the Confederates girded for battle along Chickamauga Creek.

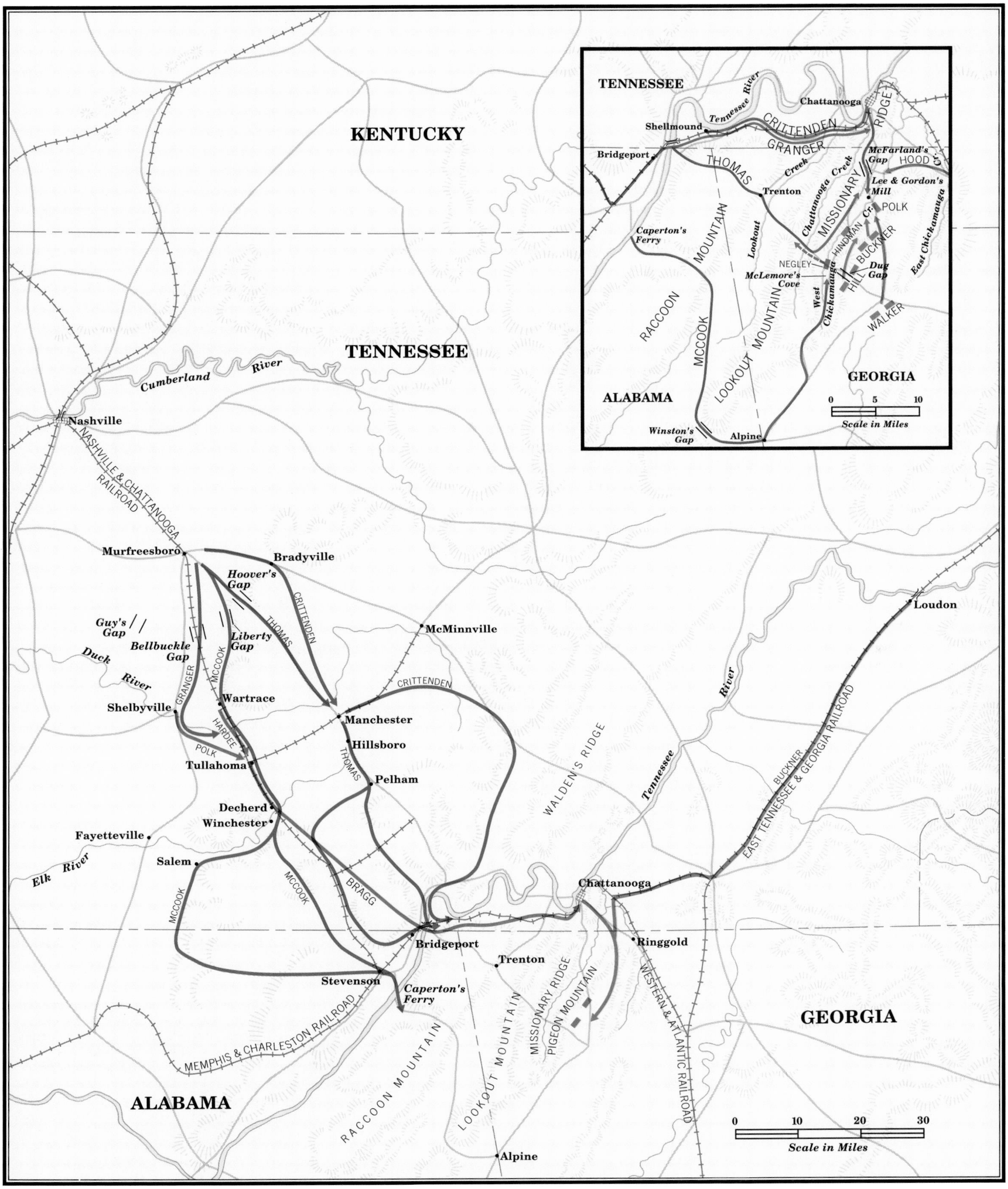
KENTUCKY
TENNESSEE
Cumberland River
Nashville
NASHVILLE & CHATTANOOGA RAILROAD
Murfreesboro
Bradyville
Hoover's Gap
Liberty Gap
Guy's Gap
Bellbuckle Gap
Duck River
Shelbyville
Wartrace
GRANGER
MCCOOK
THOMAS
CRITTENDEN
HARDEE
POLK
Tullahoma
McMinnville
Manchester
Hillsboro
Pelham
Decherd
Winchester
Fayetteville
Salem
Elk River
BRAGG
Bridgeport
Stevenson
Caperton's Ferry
Trenton
Chattanooga
Ringgold
Loudon
BUCKNER
EAST TENNESSEE & GEORGIA RAILROAD
Tennessee River
WALDEN'S RIDGE
MEMPHIS & CHARLESTON RAILROAD
RACCOON MOUNTAIN
LOOKOUT MOUNTAIN
MISSIONARY RIDGE
PIGEON MOUNTAIN
WESTERN & ATLANTIC RAILROAD
Alpine
ALABAMA
GEORGIA
0 10 20 30
Scale in Miles
TENNESSEE
Tennessee River
Chattanooga
Shellmound
Bridgeport
CRITTENDEN
GRANGER
THOMAS
RIDGE
MISSIONARY
McFarland's Gap
HOOD
Lee & Gordon's Mill
POLK
Trenton
Chattanooga Creek
Lookout
Caperton's Ferry
NEGLEY
McLemore's Cove
HINDMAN
BUCKNER
HILL
Dug Gap
West Chickamauga
East Chickamauga Cr.
WALKER
RACCOON MOUNTAIN
MCCOOK
LOOKOUT MOUNTAIN
GEORGIA
ALABAMA
0 5 10
Scale in Miles
Winston's Gap
Alpine

OPENING ACTION, SEPTEMBER 19

By September 13, Rosecrans realized that his three scattered corps were in grave danger. Bragg was clearly massing for a fight, and alarming rumors, soon proved true, were circulating that the Confederates were being reinforced. The Federal commander ordered Mc-Cook and Thomas to close up with Crittenden, who had reached Lee and Gordon's Mill after passing through Chattanooga. Bragg, after having missed numerous opportunities to attack, decided to strike Crittenden's left and cut off the three Union corps from Chattanooga. He ordered Bushrod Johnson, Hood (newly arrived from Virginia), Walker, and Buckner to cross to the west bank of the Chickamauga, a stream whose Cherokee name meant River of Blood. The advance got under way on

the afternoon of September 18, but skirmishes with Union cavalry and rough mountain roads made the Confederates' progress slow. The fighting began almost by accident on the morning of September 19, when Thomas sent John Brannan's division, followed by Absalom Baird's, to reconnoiter the Chickamauga. There Brannan's Federals drove back Forrest's cavalry until the Yankees were hit hard by States Rights Gist's division from W. H. T. Walker's Corps. Thomas threw in Baird's division to steady the line until it, too, was beaten back by Walker's other division, under St. John Liddell. The seesaw battle grew furious, but neither side could gain an advantage. "The Chickamauga lived up to its name that day," later wrote Col. Thomas Berry, one of Forrest's officers. "It ran red with blood."

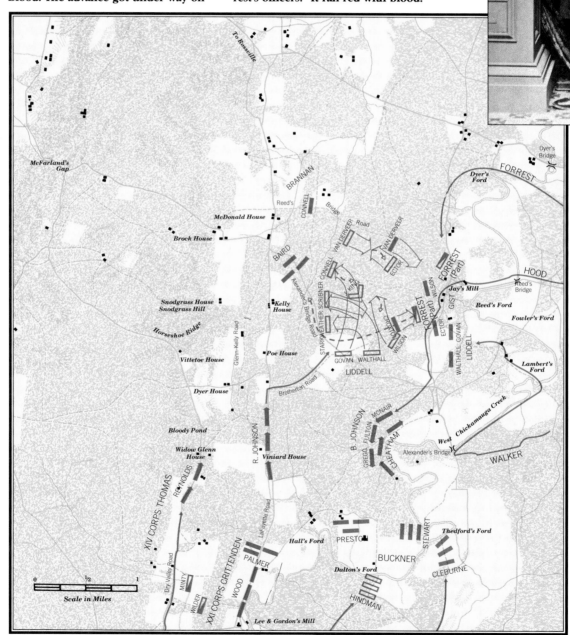

Colonel John T. Wilder commanded the Federal "Lightning Brigade," named for its swift, decisive movements at Stones River. At Chickamauga Creek, Wilder's outnumbered cavalrymen valiantly defended Alexander's Bridge, slowing the advance of William Walker's Confederate corps and buying precious time for the Federal army to consolidate its forces.

ORDER OF BATTLE

ARMY OF THE TENNESSEE
BRAGG
66,300 MEN

RIGHT WING
POLK

POLK'S CORPS
CHEATHAM'S DIVISION

JACKSON'S BRIGADE
MANEY'S BRIGADE
SMITH'S BRIGADE
WRIGHT'S BRIGADE
STRAHL'S BRIGADE

HILL'S CORPS
CLEBURNE'S DIVISION

WOOD'S BRIGADE
L. E. POLK'S BRIGADE
DESHLER'S BRIGADE

BRECKINRIDGE'S DIVISION

HELM'S BRIGADE
ADAMS' BRIGADE
STOVALL'S BRIGADE

WALKER'S CORPS
GIST'S DIVISION

COLQUITT'S BRIGADE
ECTOR'S BRIGADE
WILSON'S BRIGADE

LIDDELL'S DIVISION

GOVAN'S BRIGADE
WALTHALL'S BRIGADE

LEFT WING
LONGSTREET

BUCKNER'S CORPS

STEWART'S DIVISION

BATE'S BRIGADE
CLAYTON'S BRIGADE
BROWN'S BRIGADE

PRESTON'S DIVISION

GRACIE'S BRIGADE
KELLY'S BRIGADE
TRIGG'S BRIGADE

HINDMAN'S DIVISION

ANDERSON'S BRIGADE
DEAS' BRIGADE
MANIGAULT'S BRIGADE

HOOD'S CORPS

KERSHAW'S DIVISION

KERSHAW'S BRIGADE
HUMPHREYS' BRIGADE

JOHNSON'S DIVISION

FULTON'S BRIGADE
GREGG'S BRIGADE
McNAIR'S BRIGADE

LAW'S DIVISION

SHEFFIELD'S BRIGADE
ROBERTSON'S BRIGADE
BENNING'S BRIGADE

CAVALRY

WHEELER'S CORPS

WHARTON'S DIVISION

CREWS' BRIGADE
HARRISON'S BRIGADE

MARTIN'S DIVISION

MORGAN'S BRIGADE
RUSSELL'S BRIGADE
RODDEY'S BRIGADE

FORREST'S CORPS

ARMSTRONG'S DIVISION

J. T. WHEELER'S BRIGADE
DIBRELL'S BRIGADE

PEGRAM'S DIVISION

DAVIDSON'S BRIGADE
SCOTT'S BRIGADE

ARMY OF THE CUMBERLAND
ROSECRANS
58,200 MEN

XIV CORPS THOMAS

FIRST DIVISION: BAIRD
Brigades: SCRIBNER, STARKWEATHER, J. KING

SECOND DIVISION: NEGLEY
Brigades: J. BEATTY, STANLEY, SIRWELL

THIRD DIVISION: BRANNAN
Brigades: CONNELL, CROXTON, VAN DERVEER

FOURTH DIVISION: REYNOLDS
Brigades: WILDER, E. KING, TURCHIN

XX CORPS A. McCOOK

FIRST DIVISION: DAVIS
Brigades: POST, CARLIN, HEG

SECOND DIVISION: JOHNSON
Brigades: WILLICH, DODGE, BALDWIN

THIRD DIVISION: SHERIDAN
Brigades: LYTLE, LAIBOLDT, BRADLEY

XXI CORPS CRITTENDEN

FIRST DIVISION: WOOD
Brigades: BUELL, WAGNER, HARKER

SECOND DIVISION: PALMER
Brigades: CRUFT, HAZEN, GROSE

THIRD DIVISION: VAN CLEVE
Brigades: S. BEATTY, DICK, BARNES

RESERVE CORPS GRANGER

FIRST DIVISION: STEEDMAN
Brigades: WHITAKER, J. MITCHELL

CAVALRY
R. MITCHELL

FIRST DIVISION: E. McCOOK
Brigades: CAMPBELL, RAY, WATKINS

SECOND DIVISION: CROOK
Brigades: MINTY, LONG

General Nathan Bedford Forrest, the Confederate cavalry commander, was a self-taught military strategist whose very simple but effective maxim was "to get there first with the most men." The first shots of the Battle of Chickamauga were fired when John Croxton's brigade of the Federal XIV Corps encountered Forrest's mounted troops and opened fire. After Chickamauga, Forrest had a clash with the fractious Bragg and was transferred.

236

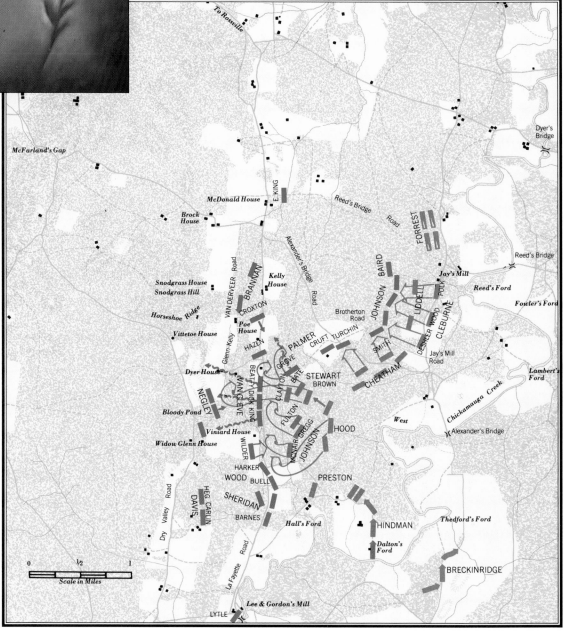

Patrick Cleburne, who emigrated from Ireland at the age of 21, was one of only two foreign-born officers to attain the rank of major general in the Confederate army. Known as the Stonewall Jackson of the West, he led a division of Hill's Corps at Chickamauga.

AFTERNOON ACTION

Through the rest of the day on September 19, the two armies surged back and forth, roughly along the lines shown here. The Confederates launched an attack against Horatio Van Cleve's division, which had marched north to reinforce the Union line. The assault bent back the center of the Federal line, but counterattacks by the divisions of Brannan and James Negley in the center, and Philip Sheridan and Thomas Wood on the right, halted the Confederate advance. Cleburne's division attacked on the Federal left in the late afternoon but was repulsed by the divisions of Richard W. Johnson and Baird. Later that evening, Longstreet, with most of his men, arrived to reinforce Bragg.

Newly arrived from Virginia, troops of Longstreet's 1st Corps detrain at Ringgold, Georgia, to join Bragg's army in the fighting at Chickamauga Creek. "Never before," recorded a staff officer, "were so many troops moved over such worn-out railways. Never before were such crazy cars—passenger, baggage, mail, coal, box, platform—used for hauling such good soldiers."

At twilight on September 19, Cleburne's division surges forward through the woods to attack the Federal line, visible under the trees in the distance. As night fell, troops of both sides had to aim their weapons by sound and muzzle flashes—occasionally firing on their comrades in error.

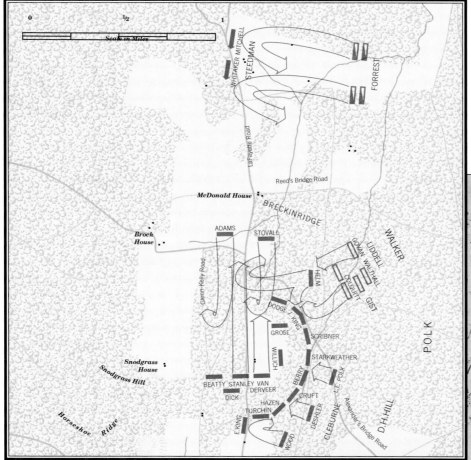

POLK'S ATTACK, SEPTEMBER 20

On the night of September 19, the leaders
of both armies drew up orders for the next
day's battle. Rosecrans opted to assume a
defensive stance, placing Thomas in charge
of the left, McCook the right, with Crittenden in reserve. Bragg meanwhile reorganized his army into two wings, giving
Polk command of the right and Longstreet
the left. Adhering to the original plan of
first assailing the Union left with Polk's
command, Breckinridge's division of Walker's Corps attacked at 9:30 a.m. on September 20, attempting to envelop Thomas'
flank and seize the LaFayette Road. By
10:15 a.m., elements of Negley's and Brannan's divisions had driven back the Rebel
attack. Cleburne attacked next, at about
10:00 a.m., but his men were also
repulsed. At 11:00 a.m., the Federals managed to turn back additional assaults by
two of Liddell's brigades, and later Steedman's two brigades stopped a flanking attempt by Forrest's cavalry. As the fighting
shifted down the Confederate line to
Bragg's center and left, the troops on the
north end of the battlefield traded long-
range fire for the rest of the morning.

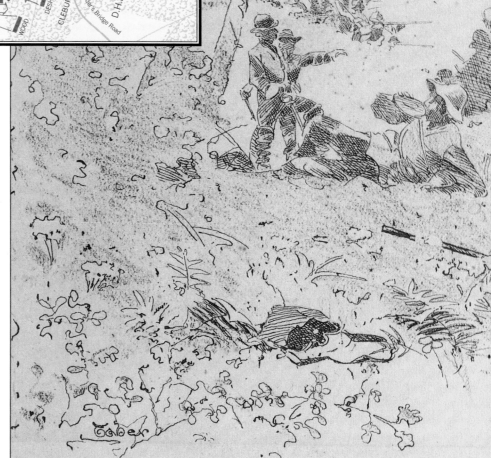

Confederates load and fire their rifles in the tangled woodland along Chickamauga Creek. The heavily thicketed terrain, noted a Union officer, made for a "mad, irregular battle, very much resembling guerrilla warfare on a vast scale, in which one army was bushwhacking the other."

Confederate Brig. Gen. Bushrod Johnson led the September 20 attack of Longstreet's wing that sent the Yankees running. He had the capacity in battle, noted a superior, to assess a situation at a glance and to exploit it.

General William Lytle, a popular author and poet turned capable commander, was killed leading a desperate charge against thousands of Confederates at Chickamauga on September 20.

With his arm in a sling from a wound at Gettysburg, Gen. John Bell Hood reels in the saddle as he is struck by a Minié ball while rallying his Texas troops at Chickamauga. Some of his men tenderly bore him to the rear, where his leg was amputated.

241

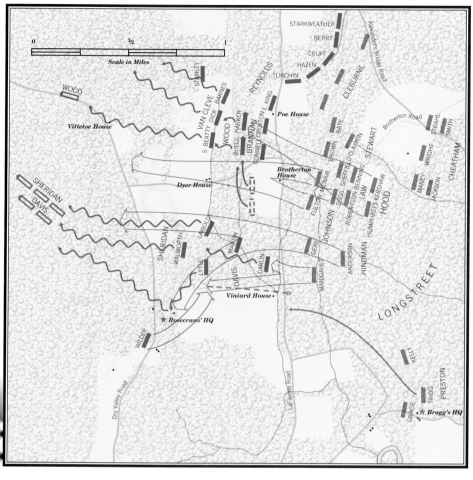

LONGSTREET'S ATTACK

At 11:30 a.m., Longstreet's wing moved forward against the Federal right with a juggernaut of 23,000 men from Johnson's, Kershaw's, and Law's divisions. At the same time, Thomas, under heavy attack to the north, was clamoring for reinforcements, and in response, Rosecrans shifted several Federal units, including Wood's division. The reason for this fateful decision is unclear, but apparently Rosecrans believed, in error, that Brannan had either withdrawn or pulled back his right, thus exposing Wood's left flank. When Wood received the order to "close in on Reynolds," the only way he could do so was to withdraw from the line and move to the rear of Brannan. Wood dutifully obeyed the order, leaving a gaping hole in the Union line through which the Confederates poured like a tidal wave. To the south Hindman routed Sheridan and Davis, completing the collapse of the Federal right. Despite Wilder's counterattack against the flank of the Rebel onslaught, nearly half of Rosecrans' command was streaming for the rear.

This small pond behind Rosecrans' headquarters, established at the house of a widow named Eliza Glenn, was one of the only sources of water available to the fighting men in the Federal line. The watering hole was known as Bloody Pond because of the injured horses and wounded soldiers who dragged themselves to it and died while drinking.

242

This painting of the Battle of Chickamauga captures the critical action on Snodgrass Hill during the afternoon of September 20, 1863. Gesturing from his horse in the middle distance *(center)*, Gen. George Thomas rallies John Brannan's bloodied division against the unceasing assaults of Longstreet's Confederates *(background)*. Only the arrival of James Steedman's reserves *(far right)* averted a Federal rout.

General George Thomas was left in sole command of the battlefield when roughly half of the Union army retreated to Chattanooga. A dispatch later informed Rosecrans that Thomas was "standing like a rock," a fact that earned the doughty corps commander the honorific "Rock of Chickamauga."

SNODGRASS HILL

After the Federal army's center collapsed and its right wing disintegrated, Thomas formed a south-facing defensive line on Snodgrass Hill and along adjacent high ground known as Horseshoe Ridge. Against this line Longstreet threw four divisions—Kershaw's, Hindman's, Bushrod Johnson's, and finally Preston's. All afternoon the troops defending the ridge, and those still holding out on the Federal left, repulsed attack after attack. Critical in checking Johnson's many assaults was the arrival of Steedman's reserve division on Brannan's right flank. On the night of September 20, Thomas disengaged, aided by Sheridan and Davis, who had returned to the field of battle at about 7:00 p.m. The Federals withdrew to Rossville through Mc-Farland's Gap. Bragg, skeptical of reports of a Federal retreat, decided not to pursue.

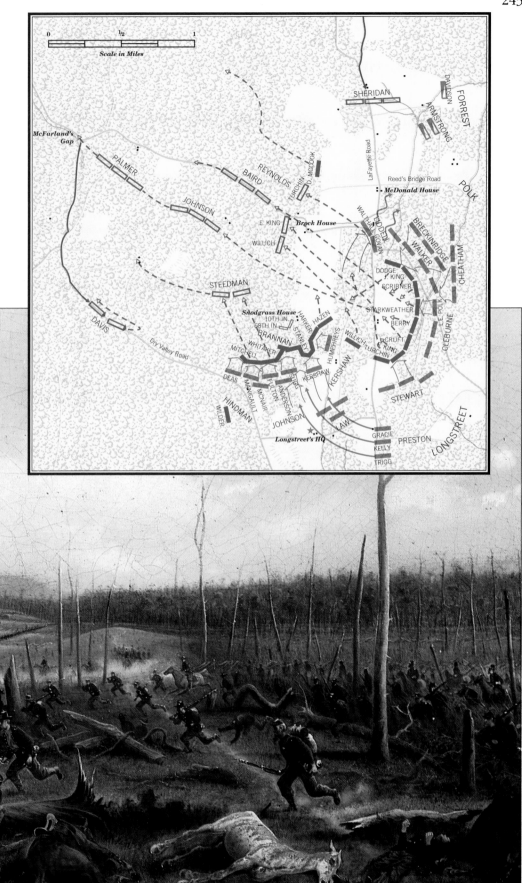

Hooker's men charged up the rugged terrain of Lookout Mountain *(inset)* to seize the Confederate position on the afternoon of November 24. In the painting below, three Union divisions advance toward the mountain, while Hooker, riding a white horse at center, directs artillery fire on Rebel emplacements low on the fog-shrouded slopes.

245

Following the Union defeat at Chickamauga, Rosecrans withdrew to Chattanooga. Bragg moved up
to occupy Missionary Ridge and Lookout Mountain, placing the Federals virtually under siege. In
November, Ulysses S. Grant dispatched reinforcements under Hooker and Sherman to launch a
three-pronged attack against the Confederates. On
November 24, Hooker's forces cleared the Confederates from Lookout Mountain and proceeded to

Rossville to threaten Bragg's left and rear. On the
25th, Sherman's troops attacked the Rebel right at
Tunnel Hill but were stopped cold by Cleburne's
and Stevenson's divisions. That same day, Thomas'
divisions under Johnson, Sheridan, Wood, and
Baird advanced up Missionary Ridge and routed
the Confederate center as Hooker pummeled
Bragg's left. The Confederate front dissolved, and
Bragg prepared to retreat deep into Georgia.

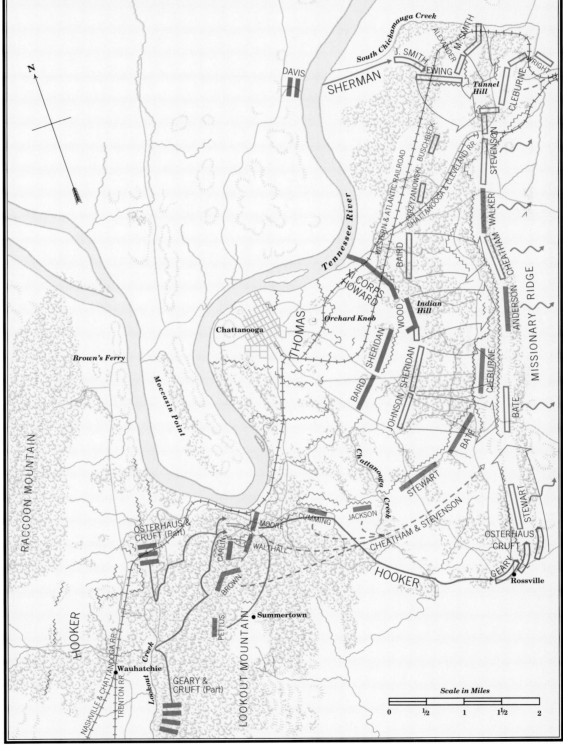

The Confederate lines of defense are just visible in the distance along the crest of Missionary Ridge. Bragg established three parallel lines of entrenchments—one along the base, one halfway up the slope, and a third along the crest.

Patrick Cleburne's infantrymen and gunners fire into William Sherman's onrushing line at Missionary Ridge. Against overwhelming odds, Cleburne held off the Union force even after the rest of the Confederate defenses on the ridge had crumbled.

Granger, Grant, and Thomas, on a ledge at left, watch from Orchard Knob as their troops swarm up Missionary Ridge in the background. "What was on the summit they knew not," Granger wrote, "and did not inquire. The enemy was before them; to know that was to know sufficient."

Captured Confederate soldiers are held under guard outside Chattanooga's train station as they wait to be sent north to prison camps. According to Grant, more than 6,000 Confederates were taken prisoner in the action at Chattanooga, many during Sheridan's dogged pursuit after the capture of Missionary Ridge.

ATLANTA CAMPAIGN

In March 1864, Ulysses S. Grant, newly named chief of all the Union armies, and his most trusted subordinate, William Tecumseh Sherman, planned a new, coordinated strategy to cripple the Confederacy and win the War. Grant would smash Robert E. Lee's army in Virginia and head for Richmond. At the same time, Sherman would destroy the other main Confederate force, the Army of Tennessee, and seize the key city of Atlanta. Calling itself the Gate City of the South, Atlanta was in fact the strategic back door to the central Confederacy. It was the South's most productive arsenal after Richmond and a critical transportation hub: Four railroads radiating from the city carried supplies to the principal Confederate armies.

Bristling with confidence, Sherman set out from Chattanooga, site of resounding Federal victories the previous November, with no fewer than three armies. The largest was the 60,000-man Army of the Cumberland led by the reliable George Thomas. Smallest was the 14,000-man Army of the Ohio under General John M. Schofield. As his "whiplash," Sherman had his old fast-moving Army of the Tennessee, 24,000 men commanded by the brilliant young James B. McPherson. Facing Sherman were two daunting obstacles. One was the canny Confederate general Joseph E. Johnston with a revitalized army that, when reinforced by General Leonidas Polk's corps, would number more than 60,000 troops. The second was a 120-mile stretch of some of the roughest, most easily defended country in the South—rocky spurs of the Appalachians, swift rivers, and deep valleys murky with dense forest and swamp.

Sherman moved out on May 7, pushing southeast down the Western & Atlantic Railroad with Thomas' army and capturing the critical rail tunnel at Tunnel Hill. Scho-field and Thomas advanced toward Dalton, Georgia, while McPherson marched on a parallel route to the west *(map, right)*. The first significant clash came at Dalton, where the Confederates were dug in on a craggy wall of quartz aptly called Rocky Face Ridge and on hills commanding nearby Mill Creek Gap *(overleaf)*. Sherman attacked, but his movements against Johnston's defenses were merely feints. In a tactic that he would use repeatedly, Sherman sent McPherson and, shortly afterward, the bulk of his army on a wide flanking maneuver that threatened the Confederate rear and forced Johnston to retreat.

Johnston stood again at Resaca, where after sharp clashes on May 14 and 15, he found himself outflanked once more and was forced to withdraw. The pattern was repeated at Allatoona Pass, then at Dallas and the nearby crossroads of New Hope Church. Finally Johnston spread his three corps under Polk, William Hardee, and John Bell Hood along formidable Kennesaw Mountain and its foothills. Here Sherman mounted a frontal assault—and saw his army being chewed to bits. Resorting again to a flanking maneuver, he pried Johnston from the hilltops and at last shoved the Confederates back past Smyrna and across the Chattahoochee River into the outskirts of Atlanta.

There the entire campaign changed character as Johnston, who had retreated 100 miles but had kept his army intact, was replaced by General Hood. Immediately, Sherman found his forces assailed by furious attacks, including Hood's climactic effort at the Battle of Atlanta. But in almost two months of marching and fighting, Hood wore his army out and was obliged to retreat with the survivors south of the city. Sherman had Atlanta and a significant victory in the West for the Union.

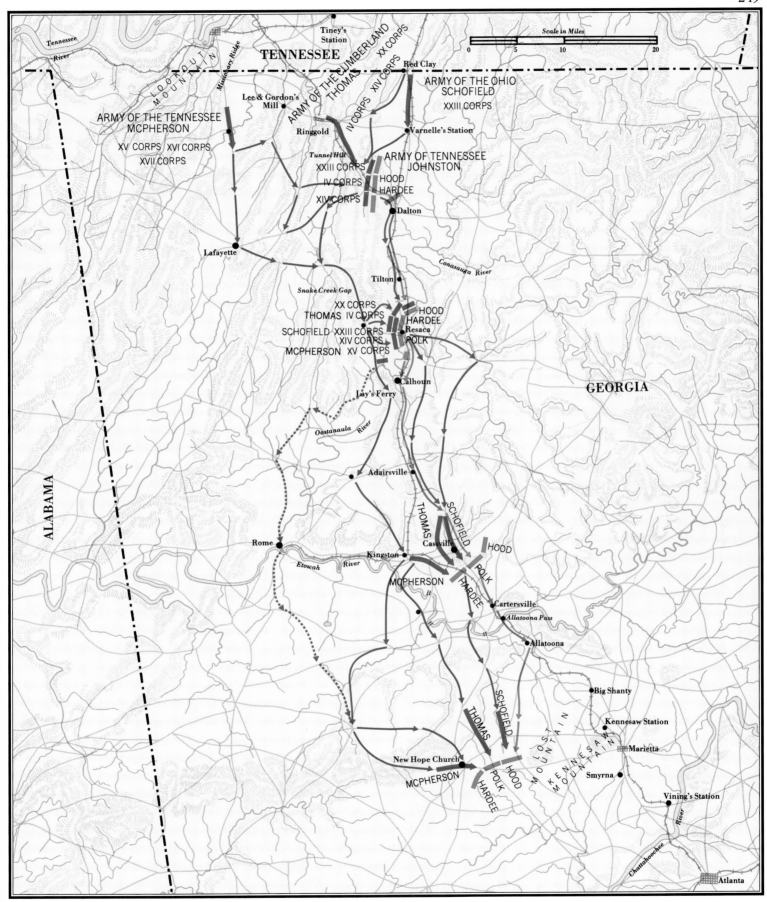

Scale in Miles

0   5   10   20

TENNESSEE

Tiney's Station

Tennessee River

LOOKOUT MOUNTAIN

Missionary Ridge

Lee & Gordon's Mill

ARMY OF THE TENNESSEE
MCPHERSON

XV CORPS   XVI CORPS
XVII CORPS

Ringgold

Tunnel Hill

XXIII CORPS
IV CORPS
XIV CORPS

ARMY OF THE CUMBERLAND
THOMAS

XX CORPS

IV CORPS   XIV CORPS

Red Clay

ARMY OF THE OHIO
SCHOFIELD

XXIII CORPS

Varnelle's Station

ARMY OF TENNESSEE
JOHNSTON

HOOD
HARDEE

Dalton

Lafayette

Conasauga River

Tilton

Snake Creek Gap

XX CORPS
THOMAS IV CORPS

SCHOFIELD XXIII CORPS
XIV CORPS

MCPHERSON XV CORPS

HOOD
HARDEE

Resaca

POLK

GEORGIA

Calhoun

Lay's Ferry

Oostanaula River

Adairsville

Rome

Etowah River

Kingston

Casville

THOMAS

SCHOFIELD

HOOD

POLK

MCPHERSON

HARDEE

Cartersville

Allatoona Pass

Allatoona

Big Shanty

Kennesaw Station

SCHOFIELD

THOMAS

Marietta

ALABAMA

New Hope Church

MCPHERSON

POLK

HOOD

HARDEE

LOST MOUNTAIN

KENNESAW MOUNTAIN

Smyrna

Vining's Station

Chattahoochee River

Atlanta

**MAJ. GEN.
WILLIAM T. SHERMAN**

**LIEUT. GEN.
JOSEPH E. JOHNSTON**

ORDER OF BATTLE

ARMY OF THE TENNESSEE
JOHNSTON
62,000 MEN

HARDEE'S CORPS

CHEATHAM'S DIVISION	CLEBURNE'S DIVISION	WALKER'S DIVISION	BATE'S DIVISION
MANEY'S BRIGADE	L.E. POLK'S BRIGADE	J. JACKSON'S BRIGADE	LEWIS' BRIGADE
CARTER'S BRIGADE	LOWREY'S BRIGADE	GIST'S BRIGADE	TYLER'S BRIGADE
STRAHL'S BRIGADE	GOVAN'S BRIGADE	STEVENS' BRIGADE	FINLEY'S BRIGADE
VAUGHN'S BRIGADE	GRANBURY'S BRIGADE	MERCER'S BRIGADE	

HOOD'S CORPS

HINDMAN'S DIVISION	STEVENSON'S DIVISION	STEWART'S DIVISION
DEAS' BRIGADE	BROWN'S BRIGADE	STOVALL'S BRIGADE
MANIGAULT'S BRIGADE	CUMMING'S BRIGADE	CLAYTON'S BRIGADE
TUCKER'S BRIGADE	A. REYNOLDS' BRIGADE	BAKER'S BRIGADE
WALTHALL'S BRIGADE	PETTUS' BRIGADE	GIBSON'S BRIGADE

POLK'S CORPS

LORING'S DIVISION	FRENCH'S DIVISION	CANTEY'S DIVISION
FEATHERSTON'S BRIGADE	ECTOR'S BRIGADE	QUARLES' BRIGADE
ADAMS' BRIGADE	COCKRELL'S BRIGADE	D. REYNOLDS' BRIGADE
SCOTT'S BRIGADE	SEARS' BRIGADE	CANTEY'S BRIGADE

CAVALRY
WHEELER

MARTIN'S DIVISION	KELLY'S DIVISION	HUMES' DIVISION	W. JACKSON'S DIVISION
MORGAN'S BRIGADE	ALLEN'S BRIGADE	J.T. WHEELER'S BRIGADE	ARMSTRONG'S BRIGADE
IVERSON'S BRIGADE	DIBRELL'S BRIGADE	HARRISON'S BRIGADE	ROSS' BRIGADE
	HANNON'S BRIGADE	GRIGSBY'S BRIGADE	FERGUSON'S BRIGADE

FEDERAL GRAND ARMY
SHERMAN
98,000 MEN

ARMY OF THE CUMBERLAND
THOMAS

IV CORPS HOWARD	XIV CORPS PALMER	XX CORPS HOOKER	CAVALRY CORPS ELLIOT
FIRST DIVISION: STANLEY
Brigades: CRUFT, WHITAKER, GROSE	FIRST DIVISION: JOHNSON
Brigades: CARLIN, KING, SCRIBNER	FIRST DIVISION: A. WILLIAMS
Brigades: KNIPE, RUGER, ROBINSON	FIRST DIVISION: E. McCOOK
Brigades: DORR, LA GRANGE
SECOND DIVISION: NEWTON
Brigades: F. SHERMAN, WAGNER, HARKER	SECOND DIVISION: DAVIS
Brigades: MORGAN, MITCHELL, D. McCOOK	SECOND DIVISION: GEARY
Brigades: CANDY, BUSCHBECK, IRELAND	SECOND DIVISION: K. GARRARD
Brigades: MINTY, LONG, WILDER
THIRD DIVISION: T. WOOD
Brigades: WILLICH, HAZEN, BEATTY	THIRD DIVISION: BAIRD
Brigades: TURCHIN, VAN DERVEER, ESTE	THIRD DIVISION: BUTTERFIELD
Brigades: WARD, COBURN, J. WOOD	THIRD DIVISION: KILPATRICK
Brigades: KLEIN, C. SMITH, MURRAY

ARMY OF THE TENNESSEE
McPHERSON

XV CORPS LOGAN	XVI CORPS DODGE	XVII CORPS BLAIR
FIRST DIVISION: OSTERHAUS
Brigades: WOODS, WILLIAMSON, WANGELIN	SECOND DIVISION: SWEENEY
Brigades: RICE, BURKE, BANE	THIRD DIVISION: LEGGETT
Brigades: FORCE, SCOTT, MALLOY
SECOND DIVISION: M. SMITH
Brigades: G. SMITH, LIGHTBURN	FOURTH DIVISION: VEATCH
Brigades: FULLER, SPRAGUE, GROWER	FOURTH DIVISION: GRESHAM
Brigades: POTTS, LOGAN, HALL
FOURTH DIVISION: HARROW
Brigades: R. WILLIAMS, WALCUTT, OLIVER		

ARMY OF THE OHIO
(XXIII CORPS)
SCHOFIELD

| FIRST DIVISION: HOVEY
Brigades: BARTER, McQUISTON | THIRD DIVISION: COX
Brigades: REILLY, MANSON, McLEAN, CRITTENDEN |
|---|---|
| SECOND DIVISION: JUDAH
Brigades: McLEAN, HASCALL, STRICKLAND | CAVALRY DIVISION: STONEMAN
Brigades: I. GARRARD, BIDDLE, CAPRON, HOLEMAN |

The road south from Ringgold, Georgia, toward Dalton and the first of General Johnston's fortified positions leads through desolate Mill Creek Gap. On May 8, General Sherman moved troops into the heavily defended gap, then veered around the position when McPherson's army turned the Confederate left.

Federal troops swarm up a slope of Rocky Face Ridge in a strong feint that kept the Confederates locked in their defenses just west of Dalton while McPherson rounded their position. McPherson's lead division had an opportunity to dash into Resaca and cut Johnston's line of retreat, but the action was thwarted by units from Polk's corps, which reached the town just in time. Given a reprieve, Johnston swiftly fell back to Resaca after his cavalry reported that the bulk of Sherman's army was marching around his flank.

Major General Joseph Wheeler, nicknamed Fightin' Joe, ably led his four divisions of Confederate cavalry during the Atlanta campaign. Hailed for his dogged aggressiveness, he kept Johnston informed of Sherman's flanking movements.

Infantry and artillery open up on Federals advancing up a slope *(left)* on the first day of the Battle of Resaca. "A roaring fire of artillery burst from the enemy's works on the margin of the woods on our front," wrote Federal Lieut. John Joyce of Gen. Jacob Cox's division. "We charged across an open field interspersed with dead trees that flung out their ghostly arms to welcome us to the shadows of death."

Reaching Resaca, Johnston deployed his army on a ridge in a four-mile arc anchored on the left by the Oostanaula River and on the right by the Conasauga. Sherman, in hot pursuit, decided to probe the enemy line with part of his force while again sending McPherson to turn Johnston's flank. On the first day of fighting, May 14, two of Schofield's divisions led by Jacob Cox and Henry Judah attacked Thomas Hindman's division of Hood's Corps, only to be stopped cold by murderous Confederate fire. Johnston quickly struck back, ordering Hood to drive at elements of Oliver Howard's IV Corps. Darkness ended the fighting. That night, Johnston learned that part of McPherson's force was about to cross the Oostanaula, and he sent William H. T. Walker's division to head off McPherson. Sherman was also busy, moving Joseph Hooker's XX Corps around the rear of the Federal line to strike Hood and buttress Howard's embattled troops. Just before noon on May 15, Hooker launched his attack with William Ward's brigade of Butterfield's division in the lead. Ward's Indianans stormed trenches strongly defended by Carter Stevenson's division but were halted by fire from a second line. A Confederate counterthrust by Alexander Stewart's division was also repulsed by Alpheus Williams' Federals. While this fighting was in progress, the battle was being settled elsewhere. By the afternoon of the 15th, McPherson's spearhead was across the Oostanaula and beating back Walker's men. Outflanked again, Johnston had to withdraw his army and head down the railroad to Allatoona.

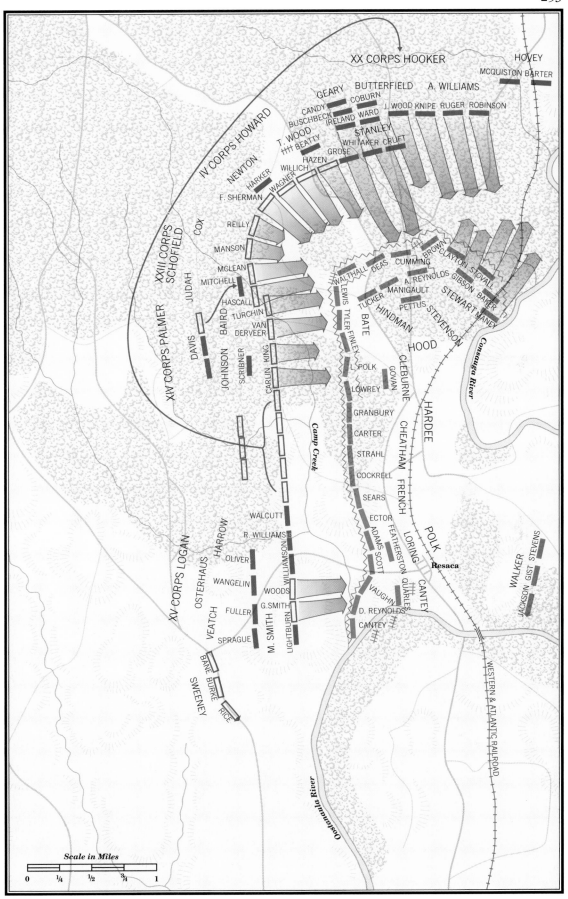

Western & Atlantic tracks snake through Allatoona Pass, a gorge commanded by a Confederate fort on the hilltop at left. Knowing a frontal assault would be suicidal, Sherman swung his entire force away from the tracks toward Dallas and New Hope Church.

Rifle pits buttressed by log traverses enabled troops of both sides to repulse all attacks during the murderous battles at Dallas and New Hope Church. Dense woods made the fighting especially nightmarish; Union troops called the area the Hell Hole.

Pursuing from Resaca, Sherman evaded a strong Rebel position at Allatoona Pass and followed Johnston to the area of Dallas—to find the Confederates again strongly entrenched on wooded ridges between the town and a Methodist chapel to the north called New Hope Church. Here the two armies slugged it out in three battles. In the Federal attack on May 25, three divisions of Hooker's corps hit an angle near the church held by Alexander Stewart's Confederates. Flailing through dense stands of pine, the attacking Yankees were cut to pieces. Two days later, Howard's IV Corps probed for the far right of Johnston's line, but the Federals were blasted back by Cleburne's crack division of Hood's Corps. On May 28, Johnston tried his own assault to turn the Union right. William Bate's division, leading the attack, was butchered, losing almost half its men. On June 1, McPherson disengaged and began another flanking move, forcing the Confederates to withdraw once more.

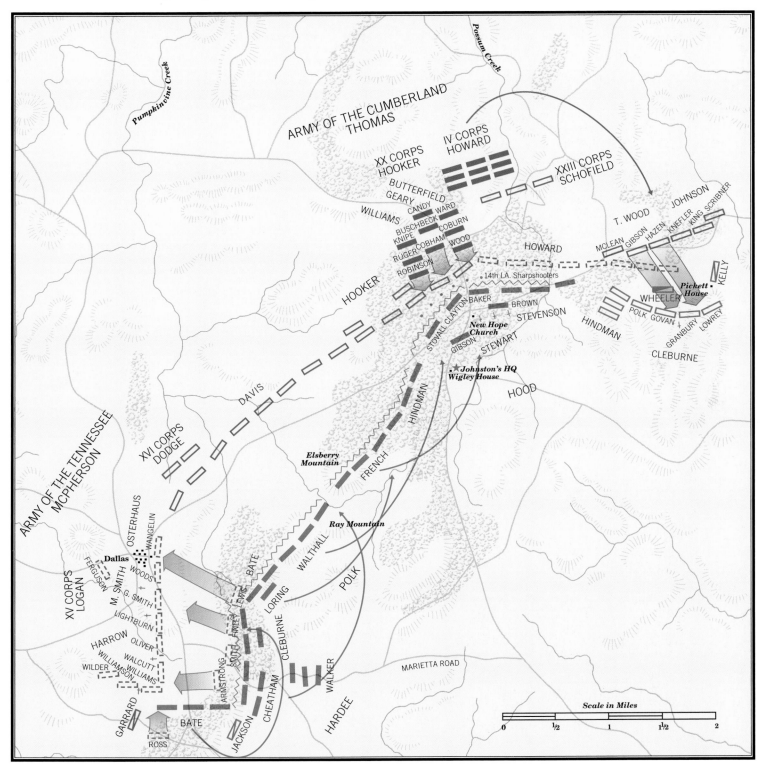

Confederate artillerymen *(left)* drag their guns up a slope of Kennesaw Mountain too steep and rocky for horses. The guns were placed in elaborate earthworks, some seven feet high and nine feet thick, that had been constructed in advance by gangs of slaves on Big Kennesaw and on its foot-hills to the south, Little Kennesaw and Pigeon Hill. "The whole country is one vast fort," Sherman wired Washington, "and Johnston must have at least 50 miles of trenches and abatis and finished batteries." In the picture below, Gen. John A. Logan, astride a black charger *(left center),* watches as his Federal XV Corps starts its advance toward the smoke-wreathed heights. Logan's objective during the June 27 attack was to drive a wedge between Little Kennesaw on the left and Pigeon Hill, thus splitting the Confederate line.

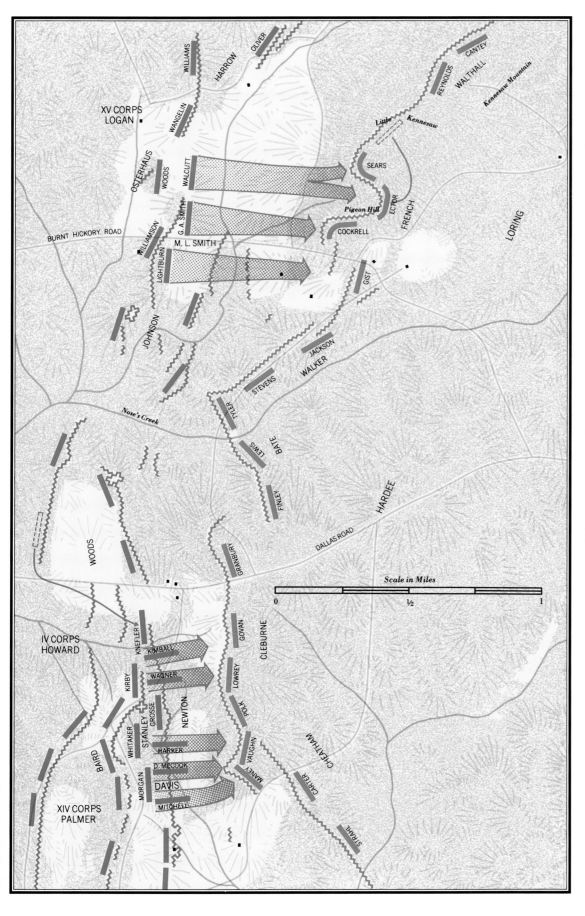

By early June, Sherman was only 30 miles from Atlanta, but he faced the most daunting obstacle so far, 700-foot-high Kennesaw Mountain, whose wooded slopes were laced with trenches and bristling with cannon. After probing attacks produced no result, Sherman decided on an all-out frontal assault. At 8:30 a.m. on June 27, John Logan's XV Corps—comprising 5,500 men—hit the Confederate right center held by the corps of William Loring (the replacement for Polk, who had been killed during a Union bombardment). The Federal attackers overran the first rifle pits but were slowed by the steep, rough terrain, then stopped by savage fire from Samuel French's division and its supporting guns. A mile and a half to the south, meanwhile, two divisions from Thomas' Army of the Cumberland, led by Gens. John Newton and Jefferson Davis, smashed at the center of the Confederate line. The fighting reached a climax at a salient held by Alfred Vaughan's and George Maney's brigades of Cheatham's division—an area soon to be called the Dead Angle—but nowhere could the Federals crack Johnston's defenses. By noon, the battle was over, with about 3,000 Union dead and wounded and no gains to show for them. Soon, however, Schofield's Army of the Ohio crossed a creek well to the south of Kennesaw Mountain, forcing Johnston to retreat yet again. By July 2, Sherman was in pursuit, heading for the Chattahoochee.

Federal troops take a break near a captured railroad bridge across the Chattahoochee River *(background)*. On reaching the Chattahoochee, virtually the entire Federal army went for a swim, including Sherman, who stripped off his uniform and plunged in along with his men.

Sherman *(center, on horseback),* accompanied by an aide using field glasses, receives a report from the chief of an artillery battery during a bombardment. Determined to "make the inside of Atlanta too hot to be endured," Sherman shelled the city repeatedly.

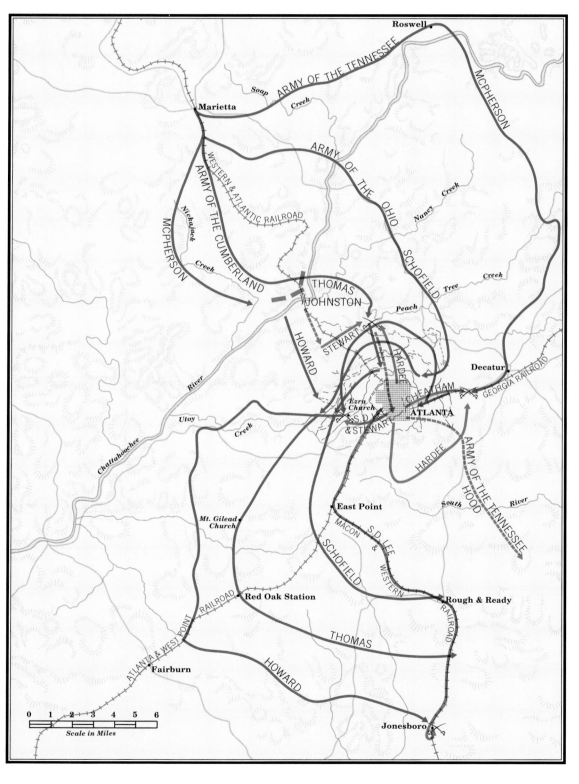

Using his well-practiced flanking maneuver, Sherman in early July nudged Johnston's army from another set of prepared defenses at Smyrna, near Marietta, then made a double end run to force the Confederates from entrenchments astride the rail line on the banks of the Chattahoochee. McPherson feinted at the Confederate defenses, then followed Federal cavalry that had hurried upstream to take the town of Roswell and secure a river crossing there. At the same time, Schofield and his Army of the Ohio marched to where Soap Creek met the Chattahoochee, forded the river, and secured a mile-deep bridgehead on the other side. On the night of July 9-10, Johnston abandoned his last earthworks and retreated across the river, moving southeast onto a ridge behind Peachtree Creek. Sherman quickly expanded the bridgeheads and by July 17 had almost his entire force marching on Atlanta. McPherson and Schofield made wide wheeling maneuvers to bear down on the city from the north and east and to cut supply lines while Thomas' army marched on the Peachtree defenses. That same night, Johnston was replaced in command by General Hood, who soon counterattacked with vigor. Hood struck Thomas' army first, doubled back to attack McPherson east of Atlanta, then maneuvered to hit the Federals again at Ezra Church. The last of the battles came on September 1, south of Atlanta at Jonesboro. Defeated there, Hood retreated south to restore his battered forces.

Hood lashed out at the Federals on July 20, only three days after taking command. His plan was to surprise Thomas' advance units while they were crossing Peachtree Creek, then wheel and crush the rest of Thomas' army in the pocket where the creek and the Chattahoochee met. But Hood's attack was delayed until 4:00 p.m., when most of Thomas' troops were well across the creek. Still, Hardee's Corps hit the four divisions on Thomas' left a ferocious blow. John Newton's men were attacked in front by William Walker's Confederates and on the flank by William Bate's. Thomas quickly ordered up artillery that stopped Bate. But then he faced another assault by five divisions of Polk's old corps— now led by the popular Alexander Stewart *(left)*. Maney's and Loring's Confederate divisions made a dangerous thrust into a gap in Hooker's corps, created when William Ward's division failed to come up. Two of Ward's brigades, under Coburn and Harrison, dashed forward to fill the breach. Nonetheless, Thomas' army was in peril until Hardee, about to launch another attack on the Union left, was ordered by Hood to detach Cleburne's division to block McPherson, who was approaching from the east with alarming speed. This move—and darkness—ended the battle, which had cost Hood 3,000 men and gained nothing.

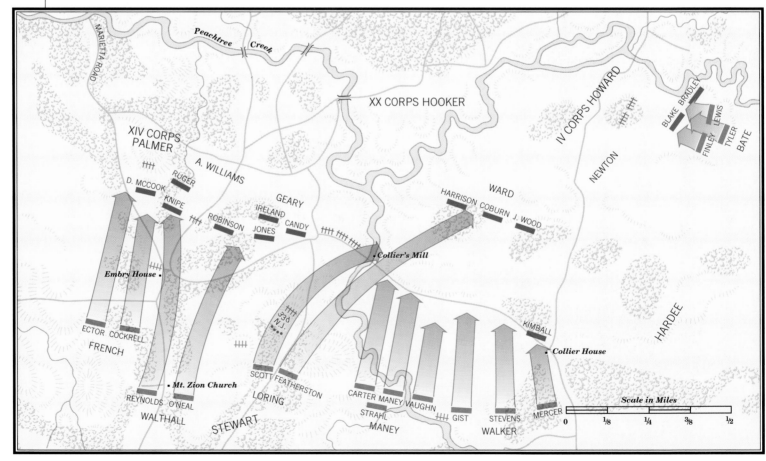

3284 ✓   #14

Hardee   Stewart.

Battle of Peachtree Creek July 20th, 64
General Jo Hookers 20th Corps

Atlanta Campaign

attack of Hardee & Stewarts Corps
on the army of the Cumberland
4 miles north of Atlanta

A sandbagged redoubt for cannon *(above, foreground)* gets added protection from rows of the spiked logs called chevaux-de-frise on the northern perimeter of Atlanta's defenses. The outbuildings of the nearby Potter farm have been stripped to provide timber for the palisade that snakes away into the distance. So formidable was the city's 12-mile defensive ring that Sherman never considered attacking it. Instead, he concentrated on severing the rail lines that supplied Atlanta. In the tattered sketch at left, Gen. Joseph Hooker watches as brigades of his XX Corps form up on the south bank of Peachtree Creek to meet the attacking Rebels seen in the distance.

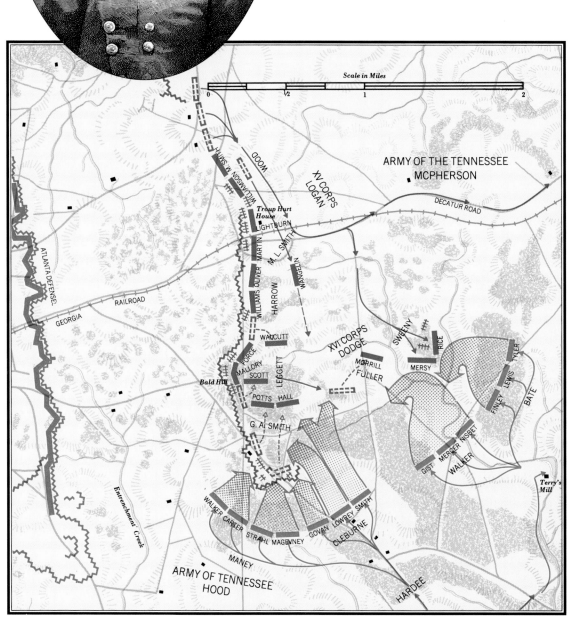

HARDEE'S ATTACK

Hood saw another chance to smash the Federals when, the day after Peachtree Creek, units of McPherson's army took Bald Hill, a crest commanding the eastern approach to the city. Hood detected that the Federals had failed to protect their left flank. To attack the weak spot, he rushed Hardee's Corps south through Atlanta in the night, then northeast past McPherson's flank. At 12:15 p.m. on July 22, Bate's and Walker's divisions lunged forward—though without the able Walker *(left)*, who had been killed by a Federal picket. The attackers nearly succeeded in rolling up the Federal flank but met unexpected resistance from part of Grenville Dodge's XVI Corps, which McPherson had hurried south that morning. More successful were Cleburne's and Maney's divisions on the Confederate left. Together, they shattered Giles A. Smith's Federal division. Some of Cleburne's troops dashed into a gap between two Federal corps and pushed north almost to Bald Hill before being checked in desperate fighting by the divisions of Fuller and Leggett.

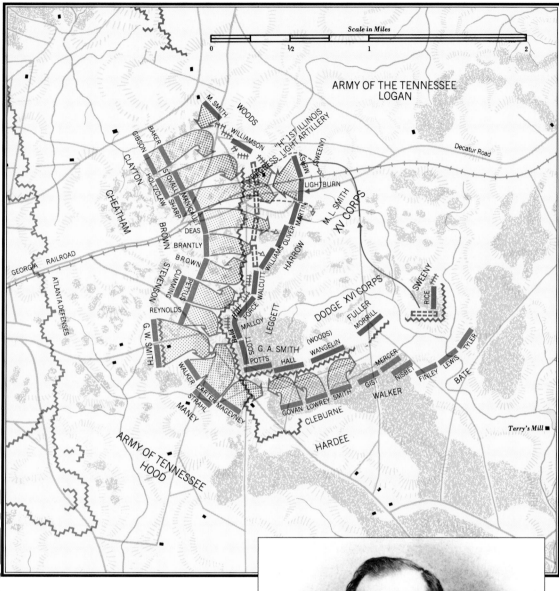

CHEATHAM'S ATTACK—FEDERAL COUNTERATTACK

With Hardee's attacks stalled, Hood at 3:30 p.m. committed Benjamin Cheatham's Corps to the offensive. The new attacks hit the main north-south line of the Army of the Tennessee, now led by General Logan, who had replaced McPherson *(right)*, killed earlier by a Confederate skirmisher. Carter Stevenson's divisions pressed the Federals near Bald Hill. Farther north, Arthur Manigault's brigade, followed by others, broke through the XV Corps' line straddling the Georgia Railroad. In the crisis, Sherman himself mounted a fierce seven-brigade counterstrike that sent the Confederates reeling. At dusk, the fighting sputtered out after a last attack by Cleburne, who had lost 40 percent of his men. In two battles, Hood had suffered 8,000 casualties, more men than Johnston had lost in 10 weeks.

264

Part of a huge cyclorama depicting the crucial moments of the Battle of Atlanta shows Manigault's Confederates, after their breakthrough, firing fr

In another part of the enormous painting, Carter Stevenson's Confederates *(background, left)* charge over open ground toward the wooded slope

brick Troup Hurt House and from behind logs and cotton bales at counterattacking Federals from Mersy's brigade.

Hill, while at right, Federals in several ragged lines desperately try to beat back a charge by a Georgia brigade emerging from a line of trees.

To lead the Army of the Tennessee, Sherman named West Point-trained Oliver Howard *(left)* to replace the hard-fighting, but less professional, interim commander, John Logan. Howard was soon tested at Ezra Church—and passed.

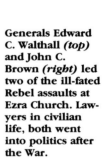

Generals Edward C. Walthall *(top)* and John C. Brown *(right)* led two of the ill-fated Rebel assaults at Ezra Church. Lawyers in civilian life, both went into politics after the War.

Less than a week after the Battle of Atlanta, Hood saw another chance to cripple the Federals when Sherman, intent on driving south to cut the last railroad supplying Atlanta, the Macon & Western, began to shift his forces, moving the Army of the Tennessee from Bald Hill east of the city to a spot several miles west near a rural chapel called Ezra Church. To surprise the Federals in transit, Hood dispatched four divisions, two of them from his own old corps, now led by Stephen D. Lee, and two from Alexander Stewart's Corps. But when the Confederates attacked on the morning of July 28, the Federals were prepared. Now commanded by the careful Oliver O. Howard, who foresaw trouble, the Army of the Tennessee troops had piled up temporary breastworks of logs, fence rails, even church pews. From behind the breastworks, they shattered John Brown's division of Lee's Corps as it tried to storm the Federal right held by Logan. Undeterred, Lee sent Henry Clayton's division forward—with the same disastrous result. Stewart, coming up, saw that Lee needed help and threw his division under Edward Walthall into a second attack on the Union right. Despite Walthall's personal bravery—he led successive charges himself, riding almost into the enemy works—the attack also failed. After Stewart was wounded, Walthall took charge. Judging further attacks suicidal, he ordered a withdrawal, leaving another 5,000 Confederate casualties on the field.

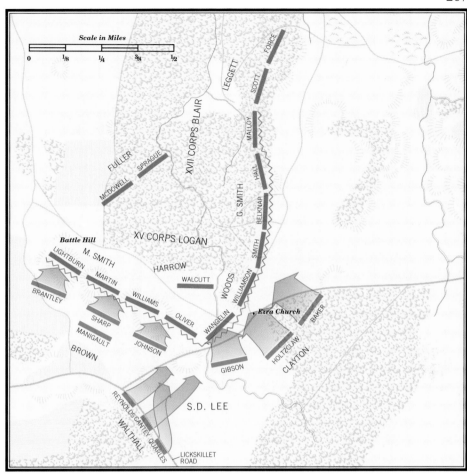

Sheltered by a crude fence, Union troops of John Logan's XV Corps deliver enfilading fire on advancing Confederates near Ezra Church. The fallen Rebel attackers, an Illinois soldier recalled, were piled "in windrows, sometimes two or three deep."

JONESBORO

A Georgia woman offers a drink to a man in a column of Confederate prisoners *(left)* being led to Union-held Atlanta after the Battle of Jonesboro. In the photograph below, scattered axles and blasted track testify to the force of the explosions that ripped through a Confederate ordnance train loaded with shells on the night of September 1, leveling the walls of the plant in the background. Set off by Hood's men as they prepared to abandon Atlanta, the blasts helped obliterate Atlanta's main industrial area.

For weeks, Hood's army prevented the Federals from severing Atlanta's last lifeline, the Macon & Western. To break the stalemate, Sherman concentrated most of his force and sent it south toward the tracks at Jonesboro. By August 31, two corps of Howard's army were only a mile or so from the rail line. There the Federals were suddenly assailed by 24,000 Confederates, under Hardee and Stephen Lee, "with orders to drive the Yankees back across the Flint River." Lee's divisions under Stevenson and Anderson attacked first, charging head-on at Logan's corps before being repulsed. Next Hardee's three divisions commanded by Cleburne, wheeled into the Federal right but were thrown back by Logan and Blair. Meanwhile, in Atlanta, a poorly informed Hood was convinced that the Union presence at Jonesboro was a diversion and ordered Lee's Corps north to help defend the city against an imagined Federal assault. The next day, September 1, Howard's and Thomas' men attacked all along Hardee's hastily fortified line. After taking heavy casualties, Davis' XIV Corps smashed through the tip of the salient and forced Cleburne's troops to fall back. Darkness ended the battle, but that night, Hood began a general withdrawal from Atlanta. On September 2, Sherman entered the city at last.

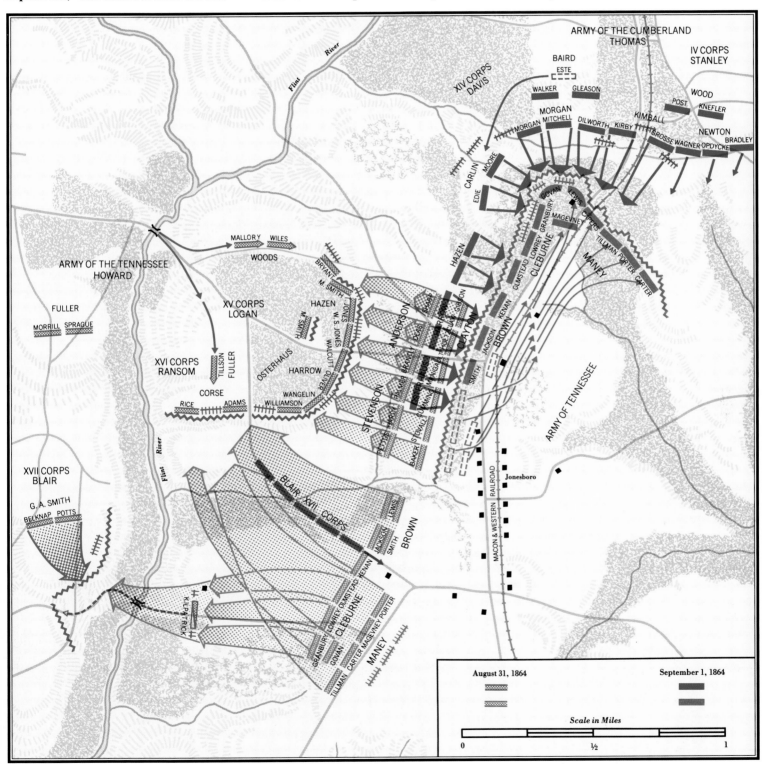

By the first week of September 1864, the Confederate Army of Tennessee had been driven from Atlanta after losing more than one-third of its men. Hood's aggressive, almost suicidal tactics had left him with fewer than 40,000 troops, who lacked everything from shoes to cartridges. Many of his bloodied veterans deeply resented the departure of Hardee, whom Hood tried to blame for their defeats, and they loathed their current commander for sacrificing so many lives in the reckless attacks on Sherman. Desertion had quickly become a chronic problem. Many men, though fully endowed with courage, deemed it pointless to continue the struggle after three years of frustration and continual retreat.

While the battered Confederates licked their wounds 30 miles south of Atlanta, Sherman's 80,000 Federals celebrated the city's capture and enjoyed what their commander dubbed "a period of repose." Even with the victor's laurels, however, Sherman recognized that sitting in Atlanta would contribute little to final victory. So, keeping a wary eye on the ever-bellicose Hood, Sherman began formulating plans to burn his way across Georgia to the sea.

Hood, too, realized that little was to be gained by continued inaction, especially with the steadily declining morale of his already-dispirited army. True to his reputation as a bold commander, he decided to go back on the offensive. But with a Federal force in Atlanta twice the size of his and already hard at work transforming the city into a Union bastion, a head-on attack against Sherman was out of the question. Hood's solution was daring but not without merit: He would ravage the vulnerable Yankee supply line stretching back across northern Georgia and into Tennessee, forcing Sherman to backtrack and eventually abandon Atlanta. If he could "draw Sherman back into the mountains, then beat him in battle," Hood might even invade Tennessee, where, like other Confederate generals before him, he believed he would find mountains of enemy stores and thousands of sympathizers to rejuvenate his army and reverse the tide of the War.

Three years of war had left John Bell Hood a virtual invalid. Missing a leg, and with a shattered arm, he led his army strapped to the saddle. In addition, Hood's mind was often befuddled by the laudanum that he took to numb his almost constant pain.

271

Hood wasted little time putting his ambitious designs into motion. On September 29, his army crossed the Chattahoochee River, and by the first week of October, the Rebels were tearing up track and overrunning Federal outposts along the Western & Atlantic Railroad. Sherman had already sent Gen. George Thomas to Nashville to organize the defenses in Tennessee; he was followed by two divisions earmarked for the protection of Chattanooga.

Then Sherman set out in pursuit of Hood with the bulk of his army. Meanwhile, the Confederate commander's plan quickly unraveled. Rebuffed by the Federal garrisons at Allatoona and Resaca, Hood's generals now balked at the prospect of engaging Sherman's army again. In late October, Hood withdrew west into Alabama, and Sherman, tired of the chase, returned to Atlanta after detaching two corps under John Schofield and David Stanley

to reinforce Thomas. But Hood set out north into Tennessee on November 21 with Forrest's cavalry and Cheatham's, S. D. Lee's, and Stewart's corps, after regrouping in Tuscumbia for three weeks and waiting for the weather to clear. Failing to cut off Schofield's Federals at Spring Hill and at Franklin, Hood's dwindling command was overwhelmed by Thomas' combined forces at Nashville on December 16 and driven into headlong retreat from the state.

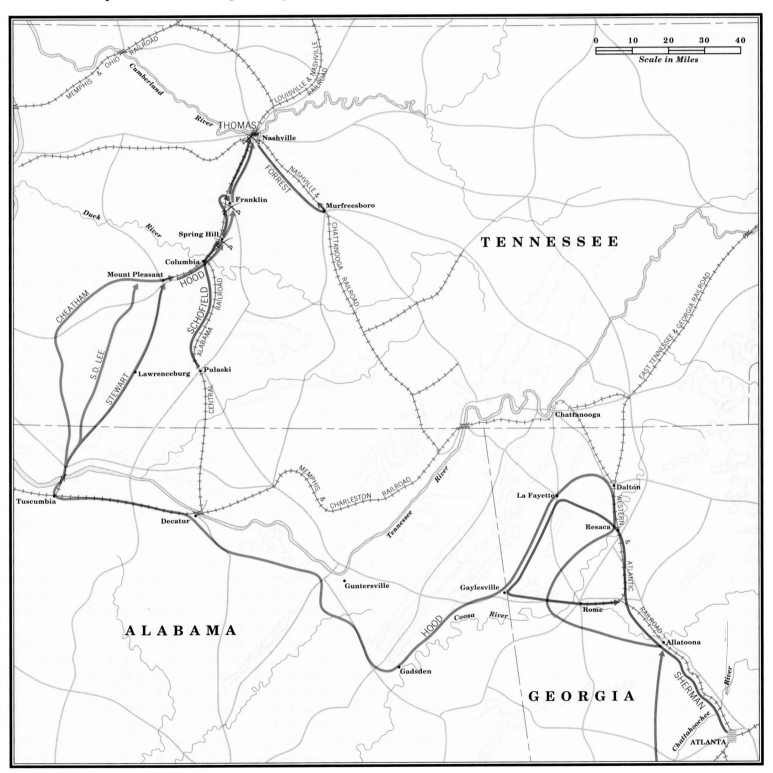

Hoping to defeat the scattered elements of Thomas' command before they could reunite, Hood targeted Schofield's 30,000 Federals at Pulaski. To cut them off from Nashville, the Rebel army, 38,000 strong, marched north past Pulaski toward Columbia, which lay astride Schofield's line of communications with Thomas. But Schofield got wind of the Confederate movements and, on November 22, ordered his five divisions to fall back. They narrowly beat Hood to Columbia and promptly dug in. Not to be denied, Hood left S. D. Lee's corps to pin down the Federals and sent the bulk of his army on a flanking march to Spring Hill, 18 miles to the north. Once again, Schofield had to withdraw. Early on November 29, he sent Wagner's division from Stanley's corps ahead to Spring Hill just in time to beat back Forrest's cavalry. A poorly planned attack by Cleburne's division later that day also failed. During the night, the rest of Schofield's force slipped past the Confederates and headed northward to Franklin.

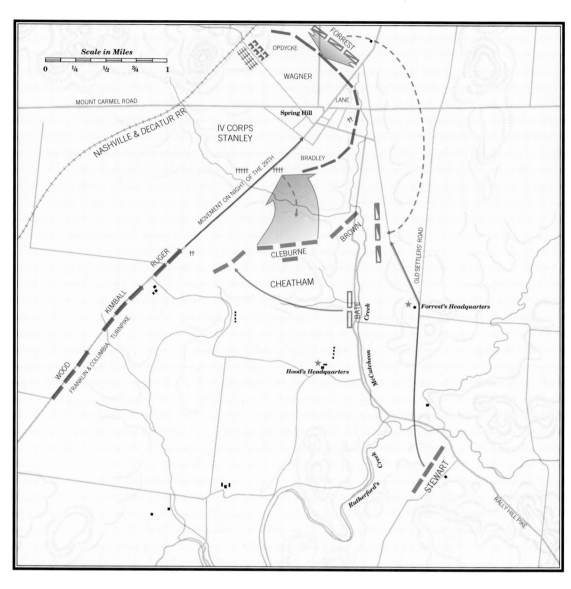

With sword drawn, Maj. Gen. Benjamin Cheatham urges troops of his Confederate corps forward during the campaign. A division commander for three years before taking over William Hardee's corps, Cheatham was incensed when Hood tried to blame him for the escape of the Federals at Spring Hill. In fact, Hood himself seemed strangely unconcerned about cutting Schofield's line of retreat on the night of November 29, a lapse that probably cost his army its only chance for victory.

Protected by hastily dug earth-works, Federal infantrymen from Wagner's division unleash a volley at Forrest's charging cavalry outside Spring Hill on the afternoon of November 29. Emerson Opdycke's brigade, marching in the van of Wagner's column, deployed on the run and hurled back Forrest's initial attack. The Federals then formed up in a semicircle around the village and drove off a series of assaults that lasted until about 3:00 p.m., when the Confederates, having suffered heavy losses and low on ammunition, withdrew to the south.

Major General John Schofield was a talented but contentious officer who, like his West Point classmate John Bell Hood, was often on worse terms with his officers than with the enemy. He was quick to criticize his commander, George Thomas, and distrusted the scouting reports of his cavalry chief, Gen. James Wilson.

A view looking south from the position held by Wagner's Yankees at Franklin surveys the open ground crossed by the Rebels; they attacked, said a Federal officer, with "red, tattered flags, as numerous as though every company bore them, flaring in the sun's rays."

Sword outthrust, Confederate Brig. Gen. John Adams gains the breastworks at Franklin moments before he was killed; he was the only one of the six generals slain that day known to have died in the saddle. The others were killed on foot, beside their men.

Well before dawn on November 30, Schofield's rear guard had cleared Spring Hill, and by early morning, most of the small Federal army was intact eight miles to the north in Franklin. Schofield had wanted to push on the final 18 miles to Nashville but feared that he would not be able to get his wagon trains across the Harpeth River before Hood caught up. He ordered Cox's and Ruger's divisions from his own corps to dig in on either side of the Franklin & Columbia Turnpike and posted Kimball's division from Stanley's IV Corps to cover the Union right. Wood's division forded the Harpeth and took up positions to protect the Federal rear, while Wagner's three brigades served as a rear guard, slowly giving ground in the face of the Rebel army advancing from the south. By 2:00 p.m., the Confederates had driven Wagner's division off the last high ground before Franklin, about two miles south of the town. Hood, still fuming over the Spring Hill fiasco, ordered an immediate attack despite the absence of S. D. Lee's corps, the open ground his troops would have to cross, and the strength of the Federal positions. Stewart's corps, with French's, Walthall's, and Loring's divisions, would assail the far left of the Union line. Cheatham's two divisions, under Brown and Cleburne, were to attack along either side of the turnpike, while Bate was sent off to the left to advance with a division of Forrest's cavalry. A half-hour before sunset, more than 25,000 Confederates moved out across the open plain and, about a half-mile from the Federal earthworks, formed up into battle lines and charged. The Confederates were met by a hail of fire, but pressing on, the Rebel center routed two of Wagner's brigades that had mistakenly stayed out in front of the main Union line. Brown's and Cleburne's men, shielded by their fleeing enemy, broke through the outer Federal works only to be thrown back when Opdycke's brigade counterattacked. Elsewhere, the attackers had been cut to pieces and pinned down. Darkness halted the slaughter, and overnight, Schofield's troops slipped away to Nashville. In the morning, Hood claimed victory, but the 7,000 casualties—including six dead generals, Cleburne among them—told a different story.

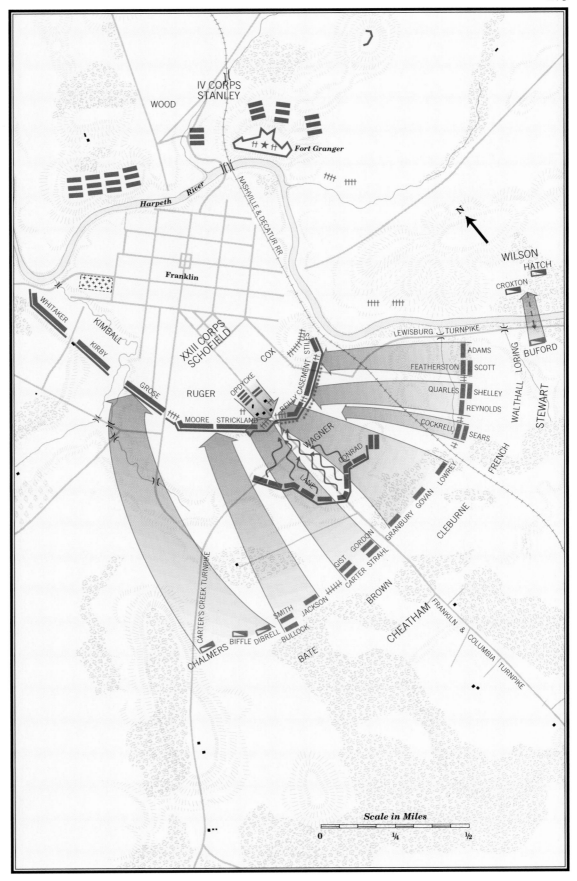

A Union sentry stands guard inside one of the casemates that commanded the eastern approaches to Nashville, between the Nolensville Pike and the Franklin & Columbia Turnpike. The extensive fortifications erected at Nashville during two and a half years of Federal occupation boasted heavy garrison artillery and steep ramparts reinforced with railroad iron.

Hood's battered army reached the outskirts of Nashville on the evening of December 1. The Confederate commander now had fewer than 25,000 men. Too weak to attack and too stubborn to withdraw, he deployed his forces in a thin, four-mile-long line south of the city that left both flanks in the air. Here the Confederates sat, entertaining vague hopes of reinforcements. Thomas, with 50,000 Federals secure behind their defenses, saw the opportunity to destroy the Rebel army once and for all. Nearly cashiered for delaying the assault while he made his preparations and waited for warmer weather, Thomas struck on the morning of December 15. Steedman's division moved first on the left, attacking Cheatham to divert attention from the main thrust to the southwest. There, at midday, the bulk of Thomas' army attacked Stewart's strung-out line. Wood's IV Corps took Montgomery Hill while elements of Smith's XVI and Schofield's XXIII Corps, along with Wilson's cavalry, enveloped Hood's left flank, sending the Confederates reeling. By evening, Hood had patched together a line stretching from Shy's Hill to Overton Hill, but his army was near collapse. The next day, the opening Federal attack against S. D. Lee's position on Overton Hill was repulsed. But at 3:30 p.m., a massive assault routed the Confederates on Shy's Hill and sent the remnants of Hood's army streaming south. The battle had cost Hood 6,700 dead, wounded, and captured. The Army of Tennessee was finished, and the war in the west was nearly over.

Colonel Sylvester Hill is shot from his horse while his brigade, part of John McArthur's division, storms Confederate Redoubt No. 3 on December 15. His men overwhelmed the defenders so quickly that only Hill and one enlisted man were killed.

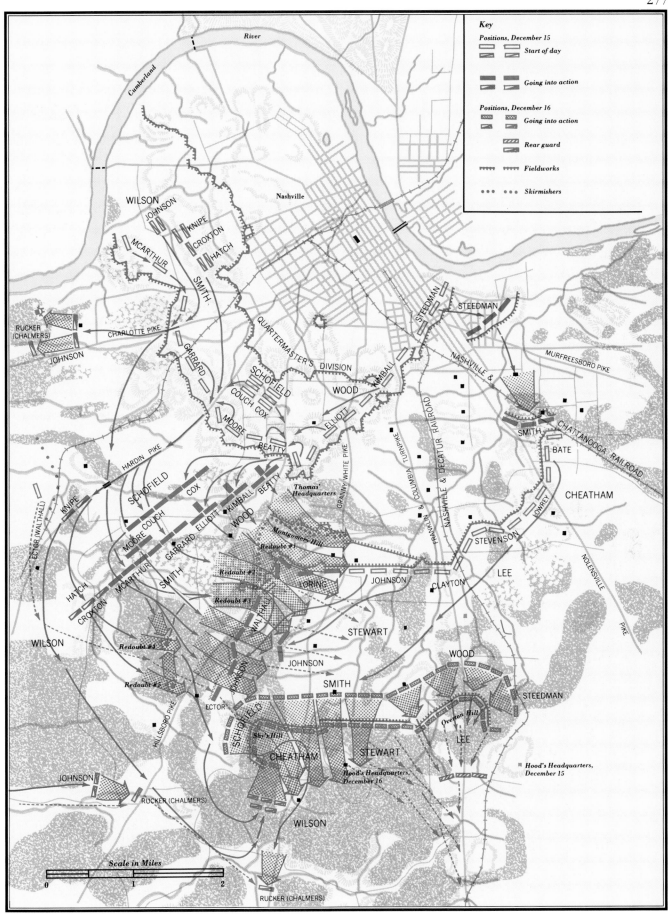

Key

Positions, December 15
Start of day

Going into action

Positions, December 16
Going into action

Rear guard

Fieldworks

Skirmishers

River

Cumberland

WILSON

JOHNSON

KNIPE

CROXTON

HATCH

MCARTHUR

SMITH

RUCKER
(CHALMERS)

JOHNSON

CHARLOTTE PIKE

GARRARD

Nashville

QUARTERMASTER'S DIVISION

SCHOFIELD

COUCH COX

MOORE

BEATTY

WOOD

KIMBALL

ELLIOTT

STEEDMAN

STEEDMAN

NASHVILLE &

MURFREESBORO PIKE

SMITH

BATE

CHEATHAM

HARDIN PIKE

SCHOFIELD

COX

KNIPE

MOORE COUCH

GARRARD ELLIOTT

KIMBALL

BEATTY

Thomas'
Headquarters

WOOD

Montgomery Hill

Redoubt #1

GRANNY WHITE PIKE

FRANKLIN & COLUMBIA TURNPIKE

NASHVILLE & DECATUR RAILROAD

CHATTANOOGA RAILROAD

LOWREY

STEVENSON

LEE

NOLENSVILLE PIKE

ECTOR (WALTHALL)

HATCH

CROXTON MCARTHUR

SMITH

Redoubt #2

Redoubt #3

WALTHALL

LORING

JOHNSON

CLAYTON

STEWART

PIKE

WILSON

Redoubt #4

Redoubt #5

JOHNSON

ECTOR

SCHOFIELD

Sby's Hill

SMITH

JOHNSON

WOOD

STEEDMAN

Overton Hill

LEE

Hood's Headquarters,
December 15

JOHNSON

RUCKER (CHALMERS)

SCHOFIELD

CHEATHAM

STEWART

Hood's Headquarters,
December 16

WILSON

Scale in Miles

0   1   2

RUCKER (CHALMERS)

278

Brigadier General John McArthur, who
launched the Federal assault on Shy's Hill,
fought in the headdress of his native Scotland.
On December 16 at Nashville, wrote one of
his officers later, McArthur sent his men into
battle "with orders to fix bayonets, not to fire
a shot and neither to halt nor cheer until
they had gained the enemy's works."

A South Carolinian who took part in the siege
of Fort Sumter, Gen. Stephen D. Lee distinguished himself as an artillery commander
early in the War. Defending Overton Hill on
the second day of fighting, he massed 28 guns
behind formidable barricades and stopped the
Federal assault with a devastating barrage.

McArthur's Minnesotans forge ahead to pierce Confederate defenses on Shy's Hill. They

met fierce resistance, corps commander Andrew J. Smith wrote, "but nothing save annihilation could stop the onward progress of that line."

SHERMAN'S MARCH

The launching of Sherman's epic march through Georgia to the sea was delayed when he was forced to backtrack from Atlanta and pursue John Bell Hood, who had shot off on his own desperate campaign to ravage Federal supply lines. But by November 15, 1864, all was in readiness and Sherman, boldly severing all contact with the rear by cutting telegraph lines and ripping up track, led his columns of blue-clad veterans swinging southeastward. Sherman's purpose, as one soldier put it, was "to play smash with the Confederacy," to prove to the people of the South by marching an army across their heartland that it was futile to carry on the War any longer.

For the 275-mile trek, Sherman streamlined his force to 62,000 of his best, fittest troops and 2,500 light wagons, which carried only essentials such as ammunition and some food. With all their supply lines cut, the men were expected to feed themselves on whatever foraging parties could scrounge from Georgia's farms. Scrounge they did, stripping the countryside and engendering a lasting hatred across the state. Unencumbered by heavy wagon trains, Sherman's columns moved swiftly, 10 to 15 miles a day, and by veering around possible centers of resistance, they avoided any destructive battles.

On reaching Savannah, Sherman turned his army northward and embarked on a second campaign into the Carolinas that was in fact longer, more grueling, and more destructive than the famous march to the sea. One motive for the second march was to wreck South Carolina, which was loathed by the Federals as the original hotbed of secession. Sherman's primary purpose, however, was to catch and neutralize the last important Confederate army aside from Lee's, a force led by Sherman's old adversary Joseph Johnston. Sherman ultimately did just that, fighting the next-to-last big battle of the War at Bentonville, North Carolina.

At the start of his march to the sea, Sherman sends a last message from Atlanta before ordering the telegraph wires cut, severing all communications with the North. Wrapped around the pole are lengths of railroad track that were heated and twisted to render them useless.

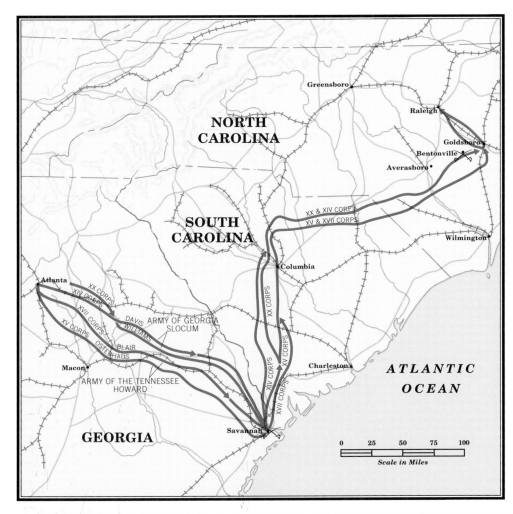

Leaving Atlanta, Sherman had his four corps march in separate but generally parallel columns in order to confuse the Confederates, cover a larger area for foraging, and gain speed. The two northern corps were under the command of Gen. Henry W. Slocum and together were soon designated the Army of Georgia. The other two corps on the right were from the old Army of the Tennessee under Oliver Howard. The two armies marched southeast across the virtually undefended Georgia countryside, leaving in their wake a 50-mile-wide swath of wrecked railroads, smoldering depots, and farms stripped bare. The only significant fighting encountered before reaching Savannah involved the Union cavalry, which skirmished repeatedly with Confederate troopers led by the skillful and persistent Joseph Wheeler. Turning north from Savannah, Sherman's four corps proceeded by various routes through South Carolina, took Columbia, and then marched into North Carolina. Leaving the now-isolated coastal cities to be mopped up by other Federal forces, Sherman headed for the vicinity of Goldsboro, tracking a Confederate army patched together from half a dozen small forces and led, after February 23, by General Johnston. The Confederate commander turned on his pursuers at Bentonville but, finding his force overmatched, retreated again, keeping out of Sherman's reach until the two generals met on April 17 near the town of Durham to arrange a surrender.

Federal troops pause on the march to tear up track, burn a depot, round up cattle, and, in the distance, destroy a bridge.

General William Hazen's Federals rush head-long at the breastworks of Fort McAllister, south of Savannah, despite exploding mines and other obstacles, including abatis and a deep ditch. Sherman was so delighted by the attack that he sent a jubilant message to Gen. Henry W. Slocum *(left)*, who faced the city's main defenses: "Take a good big drink, a long breath, and yell like the devil."

Torched to keep it out of enemy hands, the Confederate ram *Savannah* explodes shortly before dawn on December 21, at the same time William Hardee's Confederate army completed its escape from Savannah.

General Sherman's troops had slogged within four miles of Savannah on December 11 only to find the main approaches to the city barred by a line of fortifications manned by Gen. William Hardee's force of 10,000 defenders. Deciding against a frontal assault, Sherman resolved instead to capture Fort McAllister to the south and open up the Ogeechee River to Union navy gunboats and supply ships. It was quickly accomplished: William Hazen's division of Howard's south wing took the citadel in only a quarter of an hour on December 13. Not long thereafter, General Hardee, fearing that his outnumbered army would be bottled up, ordered a pontoon bridge strung across the Savannah River. On the night of December 20-21, the Confederates slipped away across the bridge to the north, allowing Sherman's force to enter the city of Savannah without opposition.

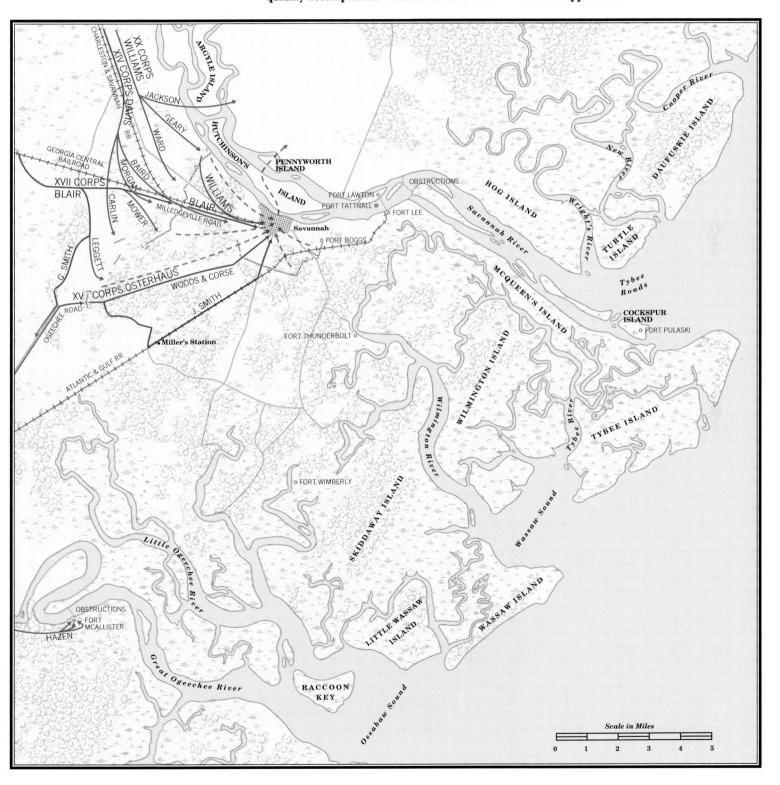

Slashing ahead, Federals under Gen. Joseph Mower sweep around the far left of the Confederate line during the third day of fighting at Bentonville, threatening to turn Johnston's flank. But the Rebels soon stopped Mower, and he was recalled by Sherman, who, expecting Johnston to retreat anyway, did not want to bring on a bloody general engagement.

General Sherman, on the left, argues a point with General Grant, President Lincoln, and Admiral David Porter during a meeting to discuss strategy aboard the *River Queen,* anchored on the James River near Grant's headquarters at Petersburg, Virginia. During the March 1865 session, Lincoln outlined the generous surrender terms he intended to offer the Confederates.

With Sherman's army strung out in two separate columns, Johnston decided to hit Slocum's wing with a last-ditch attack near Bentonville. Wade Hampton's cavalry slowed Slocum's advance units on March 18. The next day, Johnston threw his entire force at the surprised Federals, his veteran commanders—Bate, D. H. Hill, Stewart, Bragg, Hardee—sweeping back William Carlin's and James Morgan's divisions as they turned the Union left and pounded through gaps until darkness and Federal artillery slowed the assaults. But that night, reinforcements from Howard's wing marched for Bentonville, arriving on the 20th and forcing Johnston to pull back and entrench. Neither side attacked that day and an assault by Mower's Federals on the 21st was stalled. But Johnston, now heavily outnumbered, decided to withdraw, finally surrendering one month later near Durham.

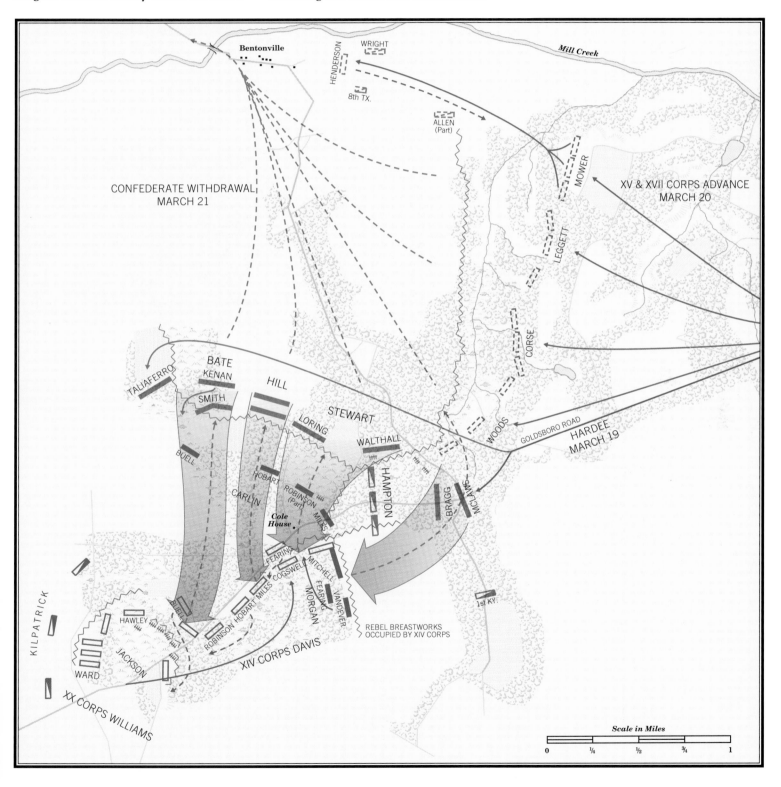

Neither the Union nor the Confederacy was prepared to wage a war at sea. When the conflict erupted in 1861, the U.S. Navy possessed only a limited peacetime fleet, and the Confederate Navy was little more than a figure of speech. In the frantic days that followed Fort Sumter, the opposing sides scrambled to acquire vessels of any kind—revenue cutters, wooden-hulled steam cruisers, and a variety of other stopgap craft—to build up their fleets.

Soon the makeshift navies were sparring in a battle over commerce crucial to the Confederate states. In one of its first strategic decisions, the Lincoln administration declared a blockade of much of the Southern coastline, concentrating on major ports: Wilmington, Charleston, and Savannah on the Atlantic coast; and Mobile, New Orleans, and Galveston on the Gulf. The object was to bottle up Confederate exports and prevent vital European imports from reaching the South. In response, Southern shipowners and British entrepreneurs established extensive blockade-running operations.

While maintaining the blockade, the Federal forces tightened their grip on the Southern coast by staging amphibious landings, targeting major ports that were connected by railroads or navigable rivers to the Confederate interior. Although the Union, with its greater manpower and naval resources, had the advantage in executing combined army-navy operations, the Confederacy employed this strategy as well when attempting to reclaim coastal enclaves that had been seized by the Federals.

By 1862, newly commissioned warships were introduced to break or defend the blockade—among them, the War's first two ironclads, the C.S.S. *Virginia* and the U.S.S. *Monitor.* Those two vessels met in March 1862 at Hampton Roads, Virginia, in the first battle ever between two ironclad warships.

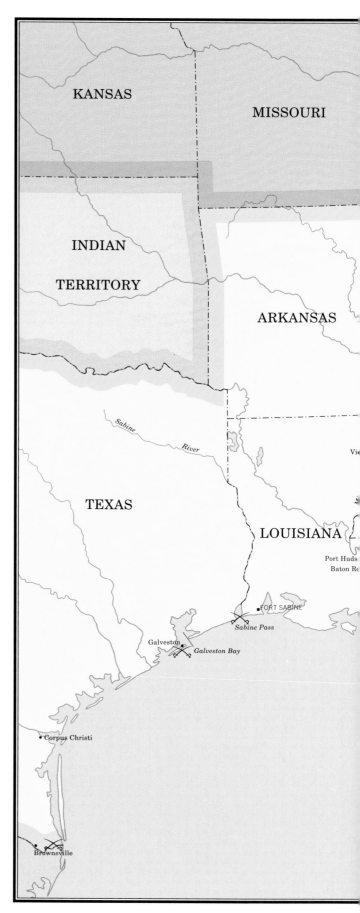

ILLINOIS

INDIANA

KENTUCKY

TENNESSEE

Nashville

MISSISSIPPI

ALABAMA

Atlanta

GEORGIA

Mobile

Pensacola

FORT PICKENS

FORT GAINES

FORT MORGAN

New Orleans

Ship Island

Mobile Bay

FORT JACKSON

FORT ST. PHILIP

GULF OF MEXICO

VIRGINIA

James River

Richmond

FORT MONROE

Hampton Roads

Roanoke River

Chesapeake Bay

Albemarle Sound

Roanoke Island

Plymouth

NORTH CAROLINA

Raleigh

Washington

Cape Fear River

New Bern

Pamlico Sound

Hatteras Inlet

Morehead City

Beaufort

FORT MACON

SOUTH CAROLINA

Pee Dee River

Wilmington

FORT FISHER

Cape Fear

Santee River

Savannah River

Charleston

FORT SUMTER

ATLANTIC

Alabama River

Savannah

Port Royal Entrance

FORT PULASKI

FORT MCALLISTER

OCEAN

Jacksonville

Olustee

FORT MARION

St. Augustine

FLORIDA

BAHAMA

ISLANDS

Scale in Miles

0   100   200   300   400

ATLANTIC COAST

NORTH CAROLINA

SOUTH CAROLINA

ATLANTIC OCEAN

Greensboro

Weldon

Winton

Elizabeth City

ALBEMARLE SOUND

Raleigh

Hamilton

Plymouth
APRIL 18-20, 1864

Roanoke Island

Washington

Goldsboro

Whitehall

Kinston

FORT ANDERSON

FORT CLARK

PAMLICO SOUND

FORT HATTERAS

New Bern
MARCH 14, 1862

FORT THOMPSON

Morehead City

Beaufort

FORT MACON
APRIL 26, 1862

Columbia

Wilmington

FORT FISHER JAN. 15, 1865

FORT JOHNSON
FORT CASWELL

Charleston

FORT MOULTRIE

FORT RIPLEY

FORT SUMTER

FORT WALKER

FORT BEAUREGARD
Port Royal Entrance

Savannah

FORT PULASKI

FORT THUNDERBOLT

| 0 | 25 | 50 | 75 | 100 |

Scale in Miles

To strengthen the blockade and gain footholds for incursions into the South, the Federal government early in the War ordered a series of amphibious assaults on strategic areas of the 3,000-mile Confederate coastline. The principal targets for these joint army-navy expeditions were key Southern ports, including Wilmington, Charleston, and Savannah. Each was to serve as a base to support the Union blockade. In addition, the sounds and waterways of coastal North Carolina were earmarked for seizure to enable the Federals to push inland and sever the vital rail link between the South Atlantic states and Virginia, where the bulk of the Confederate armies in the East were stationed. This strategy forced the Confederates to commit to the defense of coastal forts thousands of troops that might have been used for offensive operations.

As Union troops wade ashore at Cape Hatteras, North Carolina, on August 28, 1861, a U.S. Navy flotilla bombards the Confederate Forts Hatteras and Clark. This first Federal combined operation resulted in the capture of the forts, along with 670 prisoners, 1,000 small arms, and 35 cannon.

Federal troops guard the waterfront earthworks of South Carolina's Fort Walker, which was later renamed Fort Welles for Lincoln's secretary of the navy. The guns were left behind by fleeing Confederates after Union forces overwhelmed the garrison on November 7, 1861. With the simultaneous seizure of Forts Walker and Beauregard, the Federals gained control of Port Royal Sound, a spacious anchorage midway between the cities of Charleston and Savannah.

The southeast corner of Fort Pulaski at the mouth of the Savannah River stands riddled with craters after the Federal bombardment of April 10 and 11, 1862. The Confederate stronghold, once thought to be impregnable, succumbed in just 30 hours, and with its capture, the Union army succeeded in sealing off the crucial harbor of Savannah.

The former U.S. Navy frigate *Merrimack* emerges as a Confederate ironclad after nine months of renovation. Scuttled by retreating Federals when they evacuated Norfolk's Gosport Navy Yard in April 1861, the *Merrimack* proved salvageable. The Confederates raised the charred hull and improvised a giant ram, which they rechristened the C.S.S. *Virginia*.

The *Monitor* and the *Virginia* exchange shots at close range during their duel at Hampton Roads on March 9, 1862. The frigate *Minnesota,* which the *Monitor* was ordered to protect, sits grounded at the right. In the distance lie the wrecks of the *Congress* and the *Cumberland,* which had succumbed to the *Virginia* the day before.

In order to attack the Union fleet at Hampton Roads, Capt. Franklin Buchanan sailed the unwieldy *Virginia* up the Elizabeth River on the morning of March 8, 1862. There he engaged and sank the 30-gun *Cumberland* and crippled and set fire to the 50-gun *Congress*. The next day the *Virginia* met the Union *Monitor*. After the Confederate behemoth opened fire at 8:06 a.m., the two ships exchanged shells, which exploded harmlessly against thick iron. At about noon, a shell struck the forward view-ing slit of the *Monitor's* pilothouse and blinded its captain, John Worden, causing the Federal ironclad to withdraw. Although the duel ended in a draw, even the Southerners agreed that the *Monitor*, by preventing the destruction of the Union's wooden ships at Hampton Roads, had earned a strategic victory. When the Confederates evacuated Norfolk two months later, they destroyed the *Virginia* because it could not maneuver up the shallow James and was not seaworthy enough to sail to a new coastal base.

Flag officer Franklin Buchanan commanded the *Virginia* in its debut at Hampton Roads until he was wounded by a sharpshooter.

Lieutenant John Worden, known for aggressiveness and expert seamanship, was captain of the *Monitor*.

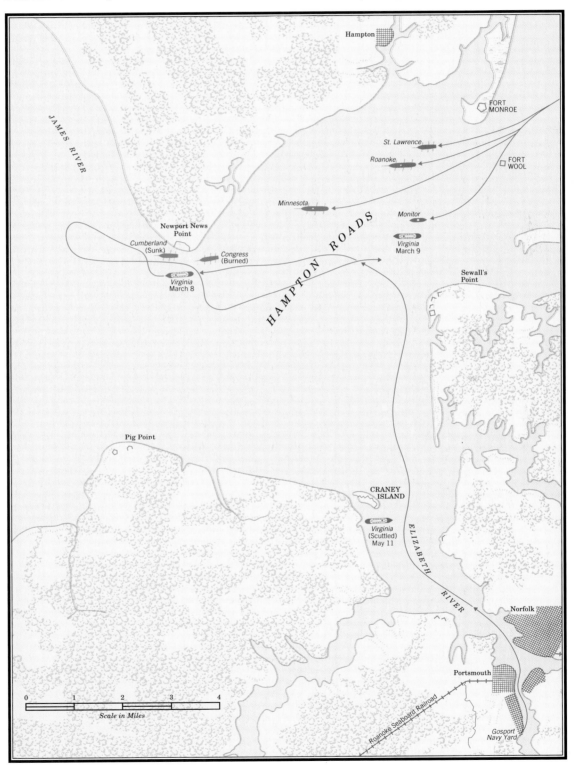

Confederate troops, probably those of Company I, Palmetto Battery, Charleston Light Artillery, train their gun for practice at one of the numerous defensive batteries protecting Charleston, South Carolina. These emplacements—along with Forts Sumter and Moultrie, as well as other harbor and river defenses—made Charleston the most formidable coastal city in the Confederacy.

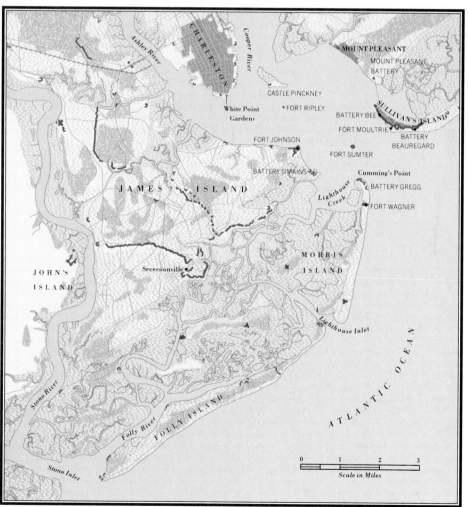

Charleston, birthplace of secession, was a hotly contested prize. Union forces tried and failed to conquer the city three times. On June 16, 1862, troops under Gen. Henry Benham were unable to take a small fort at Secessionville. The U.S. Navy tried next, on April 7, 1863, with a flotilla of ironclads and wooden steamers under Rear Adm. Samuel F. Du Pont. But the deadly ring of forts and batteries, anchored by Fort Sumter in mid-harbor, turned the Federal armada back with ease. The final and most serious attempt was a combined land and sea operation under Adm. John Dahlgren and Gen. Quincy Adams Gillmore between July and September of 1863. Gillmore ordered attacks across Lighthouse Inlet and landed a force on the beach at the south end of Morris Island on July 10. The next day, Gen. George Strong charged the outer defenses of Fort Wagner but failed to take the strongpoint. Aided by Dahlgren's ironclads, the Federals bombarded both Wagner and the mighty Fort Sumter for more than a month. By early September, Gillmore was ready to launch a final assault on Wagner but learned that the Rebels had abandoned both Wagner and Battery Gregg. The next night, Dahlgren tried to take Sumter with his ironclads but was turned back, and the situation lapsed into a stalemate.

The bodies of Federal soldiers lie in the ditch on the south side of Fort Wagner after the unsuccessful assault on July 18, 1863. Spearheaded by the 54th Massachusetts Colored Infantry, the attack cost the Federals 1,511 casualties; Confederate losses numbered only 174 men.

Flanked by his staff, Gen. Quincy Adams Gillmore, commander of Federal land forces at Charleston, pores over a large map at his headquarters on Morris Island. His strategy was to move up the length of the island, overwhelm Fort Wagner and Battery Gregg, and, from there, bombard Fort Sumter into submission.

"Chicora"
C. S. Gunboat

A sentry on a rampart *(above)* keeps watch at the Laurens Street Battery in Charleston. On the horizon are Fort Sumter in the center and Sullivan's Island at left; in the harbor the Confederate ram *Palmetto State* steams toward Castle Pinckney. In the photograph at left, another ironclad, the C.S.S. *Chicora,* guards Charleston Harbor. On January 31, 1863, the two rams attacked the Federal blockading fleet, capturing one ship and temporarily forcing the others to withdraw to offshore positions. On the night of September 6, 1863, the two ironclads successfully evacuated the garrisons of Fort Wagner and Battery Gregg. The fiercely defended city held out until February 17, 1865, when the Rebels evacuated their positions under threat from Sherman's army, marching north from Georgia.

The Union gunners of Battery Hays on Morris Island train their 4.2-inch 30-pounder Parrott rifles at Fort Wagner on the north end of Morris Island. After two Federal assaults against Fort Wagner had failed, Gillmore settled down to siege operations.

Inside the flooded and burned-out ruins of Fort Sumter, Confederate soldiers huddle around campfires on a chill dawn in December 1864.

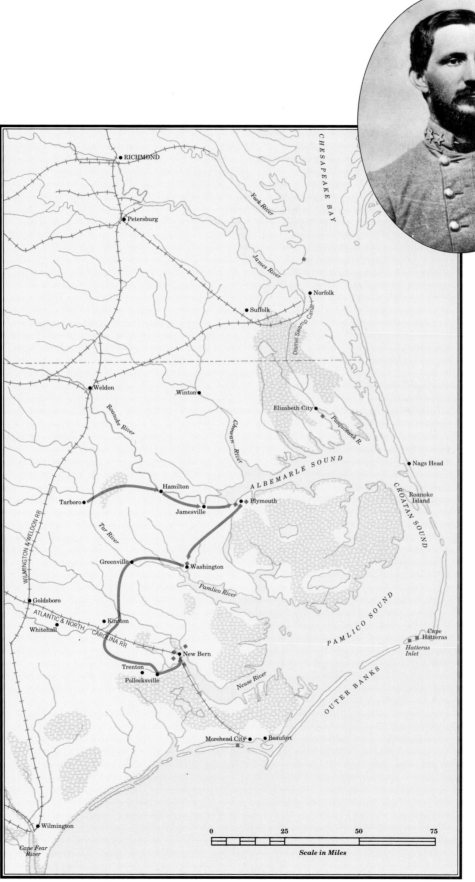

Robert Hoke, a 26-year-old North Carolinian, led the land attack on Plymouth at the mouth of the Roanoke River. For this first substantial defeat of the Federals in North Carolina, Hoke was promoted to major general.

In the spring of 1864, Brig. Gen. Robert Hoke laid out a strategy to retake Plymouth, a North Carolina coastal port in Yankee hands, through a combined land- and water-borne assault. A strategic supply depot at the mouth of the Roanoke River *(left),* Plymouth was strongly fortified, with a garrison of 2,834 men commanded by Brig. Gen. Henry Walton Wessels. Two gunboats, the *Southfield* and the *Miami,* guarded the harbor. Hoke's plan called for his infantry to invest the garrison by land while the formidable new ironclad ram C.S.S. *Albemarle,* docked 30 miles up the Roanoke at Hamilton, arrived to take care of the town's river defenses. Hoke's three brigades under Ransom, Mercer, and Terry attacked from the southwest at 4:00 p.m. on the 17th. By nightfall of the next day, they had captured a key strongpoint, Fort Wessels. But the *Albemarle* was delayed by mechanical problems and did not arrive until the 19th; it soon sunk the *Southfield* and drove off the *Miami.* On the morning of the 20th, Ransom's troops—redeployed —attacked from the east, charging through a cow pasture to overwhelm several companies of the 101st Pennsylvania at Fort Comfort; Conaby Redoubt soon fell as well. By 10:00 a.m., Hoke's men had surrounded the town and forced Wessel to surrender. Hoke quickly marched south to assail the Federals who occupied nearby Washington, only to find the defenders gone and the town a shambles of burned and looted buildings. Outraged, Hoke determined to drive the Union troops from their last major bastion in North Carolina: New Bern. His forces reached the town and were enjoying initial successes when Gen. P. G. T. Beauregard ordered Hoke to Virginia to reinforce the beleaguered Confederates at Petersburg. Hoke's men departed North Carolina, leaving the towns of Plymouth and Washington virtually undefended. Plymouth again fell to the Federals on October 31 and Washington soon after.

The *Albemarle* rams the *Southfield* and buries its 18-foot submerged beak deep in the Federal gunboat. After extricating itself from the *Southfield*, the ram went after the *Miami (background)*. The two vessels fought at such close range that a shell fired from the *Miami* rebounded off the *Albemarle* and landed back on the *Miami*'s deck, where it killed the ship's captain, Cmdr. Charles W. Flusser. The U.S. Navy gunboat then turned tail and fled downriver.

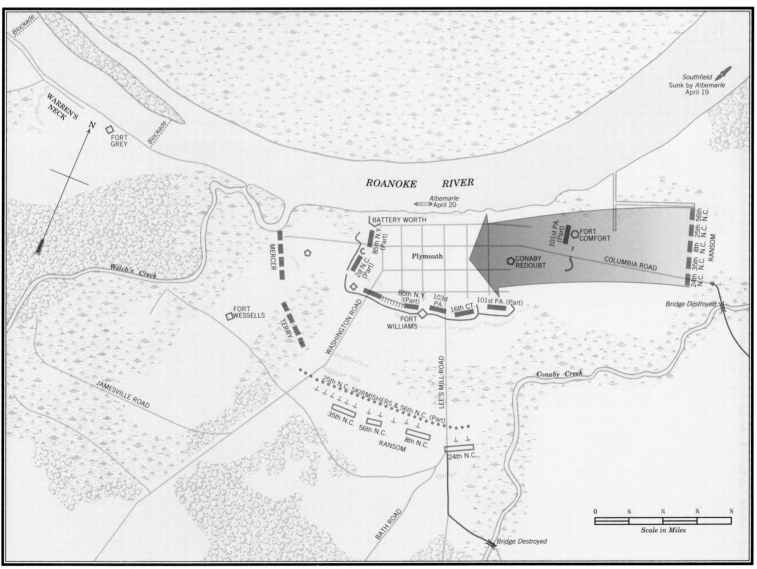

MOBILE BAY

David Glasgow Farragut, leader of the assault on Mobile Bay, poses in his rear admiral's uniform *(left)*. Below, his fleet trades fire with Fort Morgan and three Confederate gunboats led by the ironclad *Tennessee*. In the Federal van, the monitor *Tecumseh* founders after striking a mine. When warned by the *Brooklyn* that the *Tecumseh* had been sunk by a mine (a "torpedo"), Farragut issued the legendary order, "Damn the torpedoes! Full speed ahead!"

By the summer of 1864, the Federals had taken all but two of their principal objectives in the coastal war, Fort Fisher and Mobile Bay. Possession of Mobile Bay would provide a sheltered harbor for the U.S. Navy's West Gulf Blockading Squadron and clear the way for a large-scale land assault on Mobile itself, 30 miles up the bay. With the cooperation of Gen. Gordon Granger's XIII Corps, Admiral Farragut started out with 4 monitors and 14 wooden ships on August 5, 1864, on a mission to destroy the ironclad *Tennessee* and three gunboats under the command of Adm. Franklin Buchanan. The Federal fleet passed, with little loss, through the Confederate forts that guarded the bay to confront the *Tennessee*. Buchanan's Confederate ram took on the entire Federal flotilla, challenging 157 guns with 6. The Rebels held their own until a Federal round crippled the mechanism that opened and shut the gunports. The final blow came soon after, when the *Chickasaw* smashed the *Tennessee*'s exposed rudder chain and the ram could no longer be steered. After the *Tennessee*'s defeat, Farragut's fleet forced the surrender of Forts Gaines and Morgan; tiny Fort Powell had already been evacuated. Although the Union would not take the city of Mobile until the following April, Farragut's victory had the immediate effect of closing the entire Gulf Coast east of the Mississippi to Confederate shipping and blockade-runners.

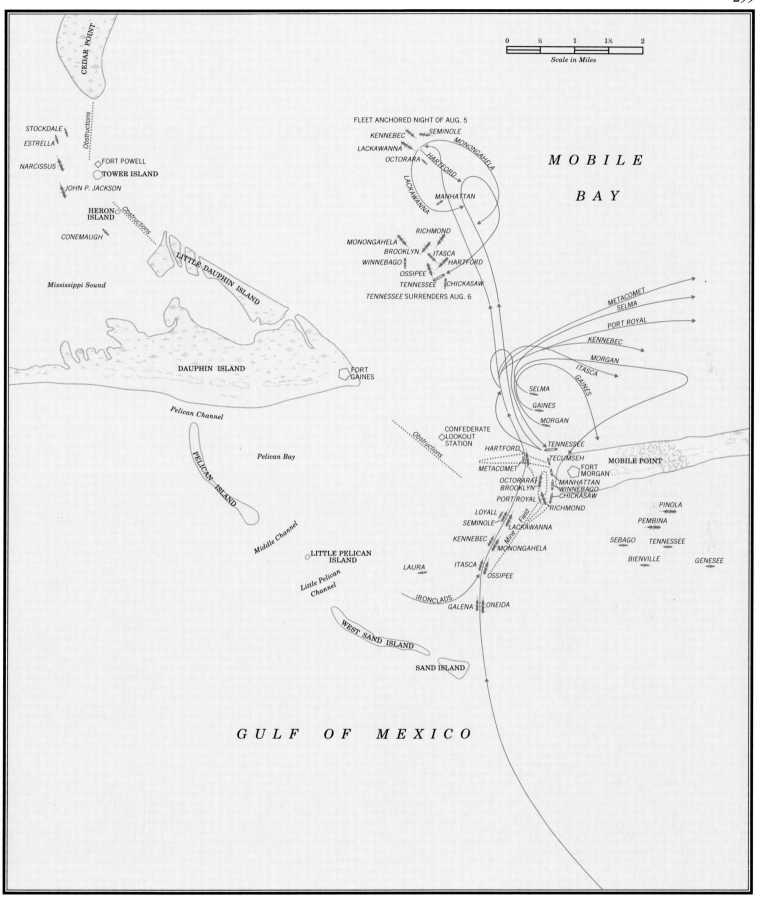

0   ½   1   1½   2
Scale in Miles

FLEET ANCHORED NIGHT OF AUG. 5

KENNEBEC   SEMINOLE
LACKAWANNA   MONONGAHELA
OCTORARA   HARTFORD

LACKAWANNA
MANHATTAN

M O B I L E

B A Y

CEDAR POINT

STOCKDALE
ESTRELLA
NARCISSUS

Obstructions

◇FORT POWELL
◯TOWER ISLAND

JOHN P. JACKSON

HERON
ISLAND   Obstructions

CONEMAUGH

LITTLE DAUPHIN ISLAND

Mississippi Sound

RICHMOND
MONONGAHELA
BROOKLYN   ITASCA
WINNEBAGO   HARTFORD
OSSIPEE
TENNESSEE   CHICKASAW
TENNESSEE SURRENDERS AUG. 6

DAUPHIN ISLAND

FORT
GAINES

Pelican Channel

Pelican Bay

METACOMET
SELMA
PORT ROYAL
KENNEBEC
MORGAN
ITASCA
GAINES

SELMA
GAINES
MORGAN

PELICAN ISLAND

CONFEDERATE
◇LOOKOUT
STATION

Obstructions

TENNESSEE
HARTFORD   TECUMSEH
METACOMET   FORT   MOBILE POINT
OCTORARA   ◉MORGAN
BROOKLYN   MANHATTAN
PORT ROYAL   WINNEBAGO
CHICKASAW
LOYALL   RICHMOND
SEMINOLE   Mine Field
LACKAWANNA
KENNEBEC
MONONGAHELA

PINOLA
PEMBINA
SEBAGO   TENNESSEE
BIENVILLE   GENESEE

Middle Channel

LITTLE PELICAN
ISLAND

*Little Pelican
Channel*

LAURA
ITASCA   OSSIPEE

IRONCLADS
GALENA   ONEIDA

WEST SAND ISLAND

SAND ISLAND

G U L F   O F   M E X I C O

A view from the inside of Fort Fisher shows some of the stronghold's 169 artillery pieces. Separating the gun platforms are thick, moundlike earthen traverses, which protected the gun platforms from enfilading fire.

U.S. Navy sailors and marines *(right)* break through the palisades protecting the northeast salient of Fort Fisher—only to be cut down by a fusillade from Confederate infantrymen on the traverse.

Commanding the entrance to the Cape Fear River and the port of Wilmington, North Carolina, Fort Fisher was—in the words of its commander, Col. William Lamb— "the last gateway between the Confederate States and the outside world." After an expedition led by Benjamin Butler on Christmas Eve 1864 failed to subdue the fort, U. S. Grant ordered Gen. Alfred Terry to organize another operation to take the stronghold by assault or siege. Terry's 8,000 troops, joined by the North Atlantic Blockading Squadron, arrived off Fort Fisher on January 12, 1865, and landed on the beach north of the fort. After the Union ships bombarded the stronghold, Terry launched a full-scale assault on the 15th. While Gen. Adelbert Ames led a division against the west side of the fort's land face, a contingent of sailors and marines under Lieut. Cmdr. K. R. Breese simultaneously charged the fort at the angle where the land and sea faces met. Breese's sailors and marines were soon repulsed, but Ames' men met with success. At 3:25 p.m., Curtis' brigade, followed by Pennypacker's and Bell's, charged the western salient, scaled the parapet, and captured the gun emplacements in hand-to-hand combat. All three of these brigade commanders were wounded in the fighting, Bell mortally. Colonel Lamb, the fort's commander, was also severely wounded. The coastal war ended at 10:00 p.m. with the surrender of the 400 surviving Confederate defenders at Battery Buchanan.

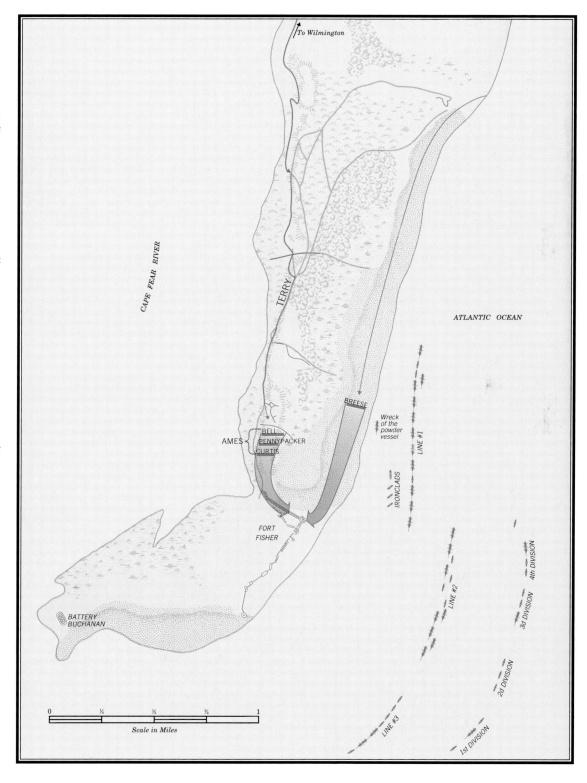

FAR WEST

The struggle for control of the trans-Mississippi West was fought by armies far distant from the attention and management of their respective governments. Always sideshows, the Confederate and Union forces contended for a region of great potential wealth to their respective nations. The fighting in the Far West also had a character all its own. Episodic, often chaotic, it stretched over vast reaches of territory, armies trudging hundreds of miles across deserts or through swamps to engage the enemy, and it was sometimes so implacable as to appall even veterans of Gettysburg or Spotsylvania.

The largest campaigns were fought for three strategic areas. One was the border state of Missouri, key to control of the central plains and the upper Mississippi. Split between Union and Southern sympathizers, the state endured a series of internecine battles *(map, right)* in the first two years of the War and again near the War's end.

The second area was the Southwest's huge New Mexico Territory. The Confederates viewed the New Mexico and Southern California territories as their due as part of the Western lands of the old Union. Texans in particular viewed the region as vital to the security of their state. A daring thrust for New Mexico by Texas troops in 1862 brought on several vicious little battles—and some astounding long-distance marching.

The third scene of major fighting was northwest Louisiana, thought by Lincoln's government to be the best route for an invasion of cotton-rich east Texas. The Union was also deeply concerned about the threat of French ambitions in Mexico. Union forces would first clear the Rebels from Louisiana and build up for an advance into Texas. In 1864 the Federals staged a powerful expedition up Louisiana's Red River; it was foiled by a brave Confederate defense—and by mismanagement on the part of the Federals.

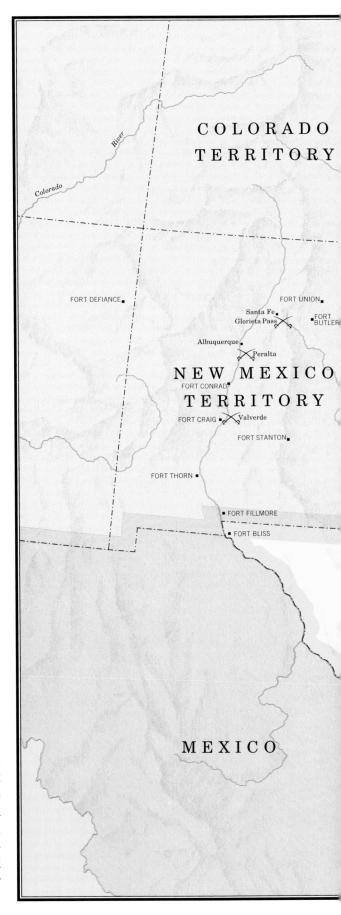

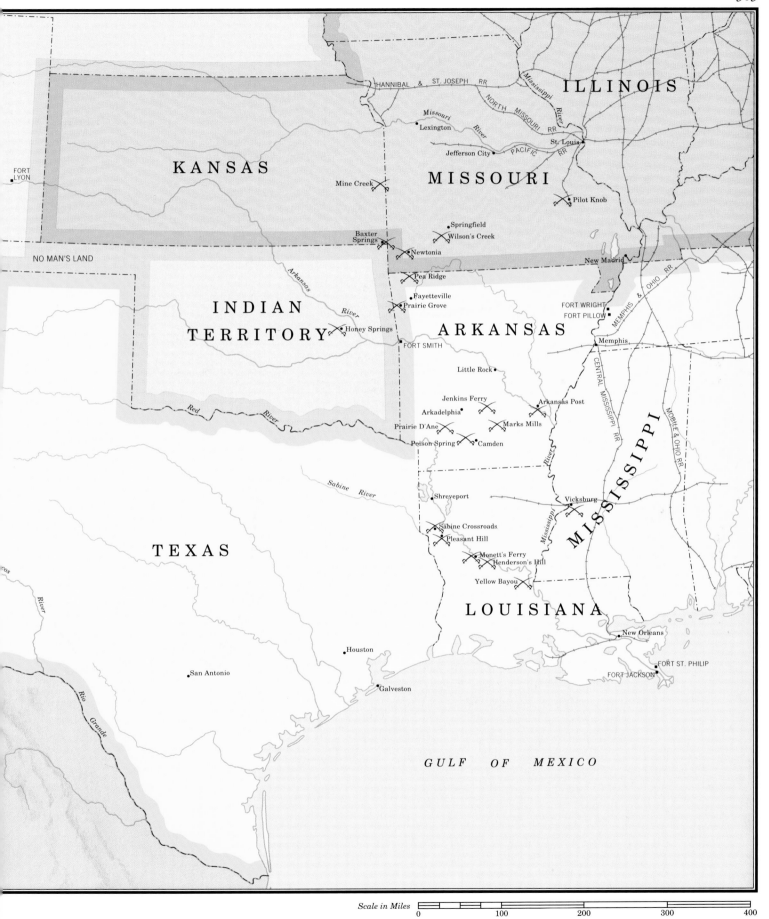

ILLINOIS

HANNIBAL & ST. JOSEPH RR

Mississippi River

NORTH MISSOURI RR

Missouri River

•Lexington

FORT LYON•

KANSAS

•Jefferson City

PACIFIC RR

St. Louis•

MISSOURI

Mine Creek

Pilot Knob

•Springfield
Wilson's Creek

Baxter Springs
•Newtonia

New Madrid

NO MAN'S LAND

Pea Ridge

Arkansas River

•Fayetteville
Prairie Grove

FORT WRIGHT
FORT PILLOW

MEMPHIS & OHIO RR

INDIAN

TERRITORY

Honey Springs

•FORT SMITH

ARKANSAS

Memphis•

Little Rock•

Jenkins Ferry

Red River

Arkadelphia•

Arkansas Post

CENTRAL MISSISSIPPI RR

MOBILE & OHIO RR

Prairie D'Ane

Marks Mills

Poison Spring •Camden

MISSISSIPPI

Sabine River

•Shreveport

Vicksburg

Mississippi River

TEXAS

Sabine Crossroads
Pleasant Hill

Monett's Ferry
Henderson's Hill

Yellow Bayou

LOUISIANA

Rio Grande

•Houston

New Orleans

•San Antonio

FORT ST. PHILIP
FORT JACKSON

•Galveston

GULF OF MEXICO

Scale in Miles

0   100   200   300   400

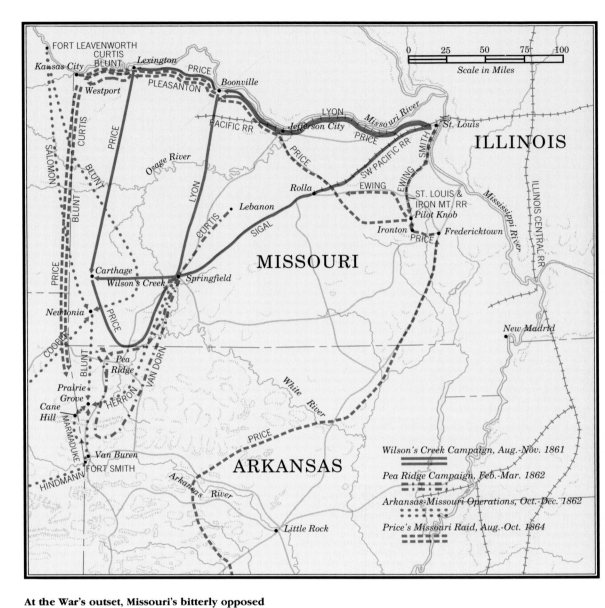

Wilson's Creek Campaign, Aug.-Nov. 1861

Pea Ridge Campaign, Feb.-Mar. 1862

Arkansas-Missouri Operations, Oct.-Dec. 1862

Price's Missouri Raid, Aug.-Oct. 1864

At the War's outset, Missouri's bitterly opposed factions formed armies to decide which side the state would be on. The Union initially gained the upper hand, securing St. Louis and expelling Governor Claiborne Fox Jackson and his Southern-leaning allies from the capital at Jefferson City. Soon a Federal force led by Gen. Nathaniel Lyon moved to counter a Confederate advance of Missouri, Arkansas, and Louisiana volunteers under Governor Jackson, Sterling "Pap" Price, and Ben McCulloch. Lyon planned to defeat his opponents before they could combine forces. He first attacked McCulloch's encampment at Wilson's Creek, south of Springfield. Combining his forces, Price defeated Lyon there on August 9 and, later in 1861, took Lexington. In response, the Federals in early 1862 sent an army under Samuel Curtis into southern Missouri, where Price's army had wintered. Price withdrew before Curtis but the new Confederate commander, Gen. Earl Van Dorn, rushed up reinforcements and attacked. The two-day Battle of Pea Ridge (opposite) ended in disaster for the Rebels, and although sporadic fighting continued, Missouri remained in Federal hands.

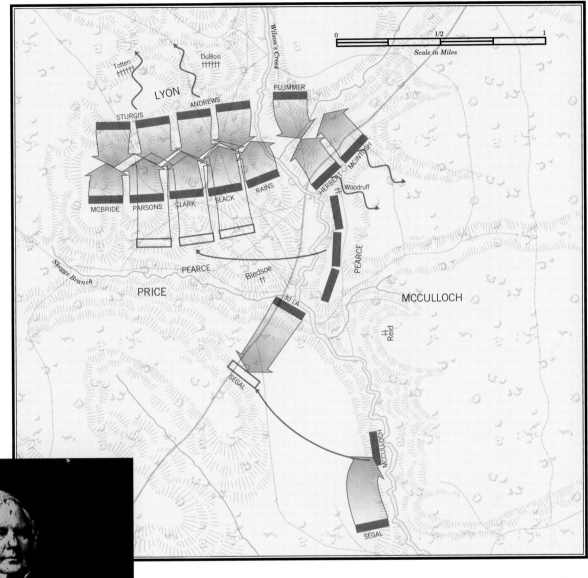

Courtly, silver-haired Pap Price, leader of Missouri's Confederates, was a prewar governor of the state and a U.S. congressman who had gained military experience leading a volunteer unit that served in the Mexican War. Like many of Missouri's pro-Southerners, Price had migrated west from Virginia with his family in 1831.

Boldly chasing the Confederates into southern Missouri in July 1861, General Lyon suddenly found himself in a perilous position, his army having dwindled to only 6,000 men as many 90-day volunteers decamped for home. The Confederates meanwhile had consolidated General Price's cavalry with Governor Jackson's 7,000 infantry, and they had been reinforced by 4,500 troops from Arkansas led by a tough Texan named Ben McCulloch. Outnumbered, Lyon decided his best hope was a bold attack. Sending a column under Franz Sigel around the right flank of the Confederate camp at Wilson's Creek on the night of August 9, Lyon attacked at dawn the next day with his main force of 3,600, hitting the enemy position on a rise soon known as Bloody Hill. Lyon's troops rolled the surprised Confederates off the hill and soon Sigel's artillery began blasting at the enemy rear. But the Confederates reacted swiftly. Price's men fought savagely for Bloody Hill, and McCulloch's infantry routed Sigel's troops. Soon Lyon, trying to rally his troops, was shot from his horse. Leaderless, the Federals fell back to Springfield and beyond.

Albert Pike *(far left)*, a 300-pound Boston-born scholar and Arkansas planter who knew several Indian languages, was the Confederate representative to the tribes of the Indian Territory—today's Oklahoma—and recruited a force of Cherokees who fought beside the troops of Ben McCulloch *(left)* as part of Van Dorn's army at Pea Ridge. McCulloch, a veteran of the Texas war for independence, had been a Texas Ranger and a Mexican War scout.

His arm in a sling, General Price *(left foreground)* rallies his men as Federals, in the distance, make a final advance at Pea Ridge.

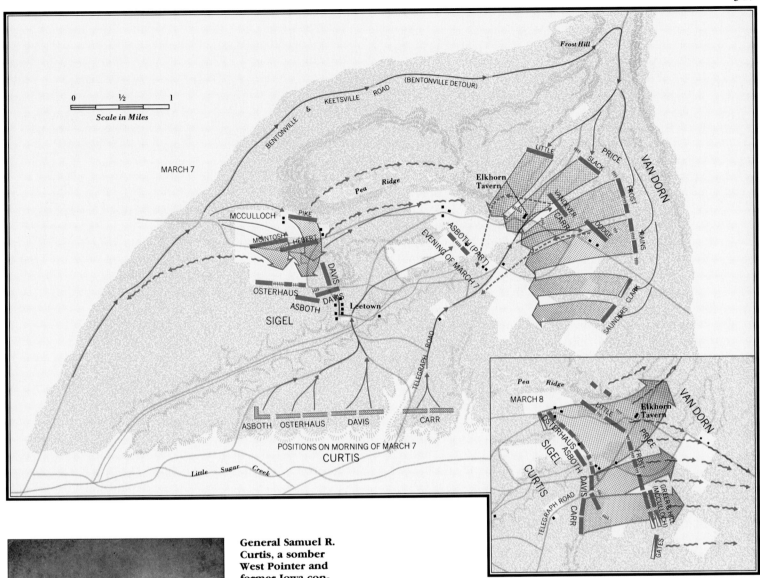

MARCH 7

Scale in Miles
0   ½   1

Pea   Ridge

BENTONVILLE & KEETSVILLE ROAD (BENTONVILLE DETOUR)

Frost Hill

LITTLE   PRICE   SLACK

VAN DORN

Elkhorn
Tavern

VANDIVER   FROST

CLARK   CARR   DODGE

RAINS

MCCULLOCH   PIKE

MCINTOSH   HEBERT

OSTERHAUS   DAVIS

ASBOTH   DAVIS   Leetown

SIGEL

ASBOTH (PART)

EVENING OF MARCH 7

SAUNDERS   CLARK

TELEGRAPH ROAD

ASBOTH   OSTERHAUS   DAVIS   CARR

POSITIONS ON MORNING OF MARCH 7
CURTIS

Little   Sugar   Creek

Pea   Ridge

MARCH 8

LITTLE   Elkhorn
Tavern

VAN DORN

OSTERHAUS   PRICE   FROST

SIGEL   ASBOTH   DAVIS

CURTIS   TELEGRAPH ROAD   CARR

GREER & HILL (McCULLOCH)

GATES

**General Samuel R.
Curtis,** a somber
West Pointer and
former Iowa con-
gressman, had
maneuvered the
Confederates back
into Arkansas be-
fore Van Dorn
made his abortive
thrust that ended
at Pea Ridge. The
overall Union
strategy called for
Curtis to deal with
Van Dorn and
Price in Missouri
while Ulysses S.
Grant attacked the
Confederates in
Tennessee.

On March 6, 1862, Van Dorn found Curtis' Federals
deployed atop Pea Ridge, a bluff overlooking the
main road to the north. Rejecting a frontal attack,
Van Dorn started his command on a night flanking
march up Bentonville Detour, a secondary road. But
the march was slow, and by morning, only Price's
troops were behind the Federals, and they had been
detected by Union cavalry at the junction of the Detour and Telegraph Road. McCulloch was late in
launching his secondary attack to drive off Federal
reserves. Curtis sent Col. Eugene Carr's division to
hold off Price, then moved units under Peter Osterhaus, Alexander Asboth, and Jefferson Davis to meet
McCulloch. McCulloch attacked first with Albert
Pike's Indian troops, driving back Osterhaus. But
Davis counterattacked from the east, and when Mc-
Culloch was killed, the Rebels abandoned the field.
To the east, Price and Van Dorn fared better, driving
Carr back onto the slopes; but by evening, the Con-
federates were low on ammunition. Early on the
8th, Curtis merged his forces and attacked *(inset
map)*. Price's troops made a stand on a ridge near
Elkhorn Tavern, but a strong Union charge sent the
Confederates reeling down Telegraph Road, many
not stopping until they were deep into Arkansas.

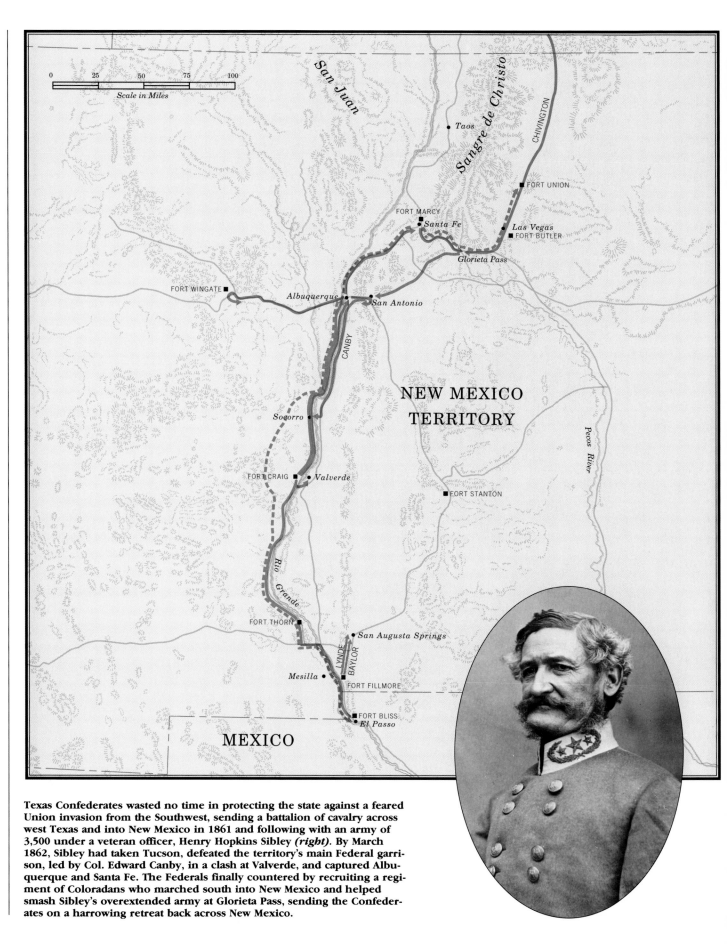

Texas Confederates wasted no time in protecting the state against a feared Union invasion from the Southwest, sending a battalion of cavalry across west Texas and into New Mexico in 1861 and following with an army of 3,500 under a veteran officer, Henry Hopkins Sibley *(right)*. By March 1862, Sibley had taken Tucson, defeated the territory's main Federal garrison, led by Col. Edward Canby, in a clash at Valverde, and captured Albuquerque and Santa Fe. The Federals finally countered by recruiting a regiment of Coloradans who marched south into New Mexico and helped smash Sibley's overextended army at Glorieta Pass, sending the Confederates on a harrowing retreat back across New Mexico.

Colonel Edward R. S. Canby, senior Union officer in New Mexico, led the garrison of Fort Craig in the February 20 attack at Valverde on Sibley's Texans as they thrust north along the Rio Grande past the Federal outpost. But the Federals, mostly untrained volunteers, were beaten after a sharp fight and were forced to retreat into the fort.

Having taken Santa Fe, Sibley's Confederates, under the field command of Col. William Scurry, boldly headed northeast to attack the remaining Federal strongpoint at Fort Union. But unknown to Scurry, 900 Colorado volunteers led by Col. John Slough, along with most of Fort Union's garrison, were headed south. On March 26, the two forces collided at Glorieta Pass. On the first day, the Federal van, under Maj. John Chivington, smashed into a detachment of Texans at Apache Canyon, a defile at the western end of the pass, forcing the Confederates back. On March 27, both commanding officers brought up the main bodies of their troops, Scurry moving to Johnson's Ranch, Slough to a ranch owned by a Polish immigrant named Kozlowski. The next day, both forces advanced through the pass—except that Slough detached Chivington with seven companies to take a circuitous route across the mountains to the Confederate rear. The battle at Pigeon's Ranch was a repeat of the first day, both sides hammering at each other until Slough pulled back. But the Federal defeat became a victory when word came that Chivington's men had destroyed Scurry's wagon train at Johnson's Ranch. Without ammunition or supplies, the Confederates retreated to Santa Fe, then fled through Albuquerque into Texas, shattering hopes of conquering the Southwest.

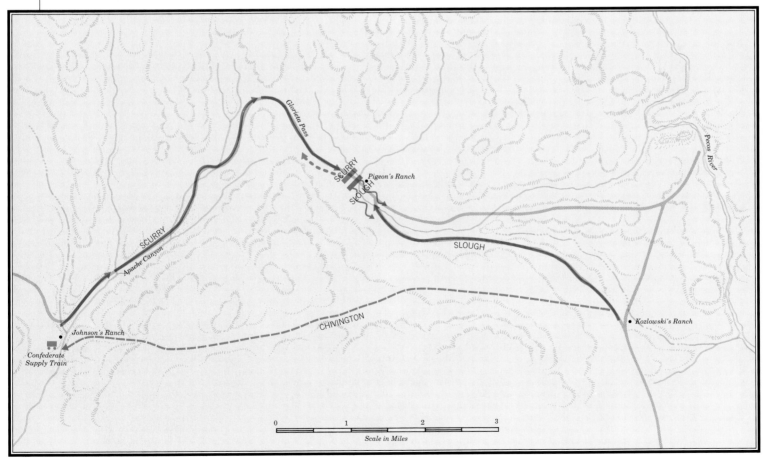

Glorieta Pass

Pecos River

SCURRY

SLOUGH

Pigeon's Ranch

SCURRY

Apache Canyon

SLOUGH

CHIVINGTON

Johnson's Ranch

Kozlowski's Ranch

Confederate Supply Train

0   1   2   3

Scale in Miles

Union troops of Gen. Joseph Mower's division of Andrew Smith's corps storm Fort De Russy near the mouth of the Red River.

The powerful ironclad U.S.S. *Neosho* with its big rotating turret glides warily past an exposed mud flat in the upper Red River.

Ordered to cross Louisiana to Shreveport and seize western Louisiana as a staging area for an invasion of east Texas, Gen. Nathaniel Banks in March 1864 assembled an army of about 30,000. Backed by Adm. David Porter's fleet, Banks launched an advance up the Red River. The Federals began well, brushing aside Confederate cavalry at Yellow Bayou and Mansura. They then took Fort De Russy on March 14, the infantry aided by shelling from Porter's fleet. The way open, Porter and two corps led by Gen. Andrew J. Smith, a veteran of the Army of the Tennessee, moved up the Red to Alexandria and met the rest of Banks' army, which had marched via the Bayou Teche. From Alexandria the combined force advanced in early April to Natchitoches, only four days from Shreveport. There Banks decided to move his army by what seemed the fastest route, an old coach road south of the river. It was a dreadful error: The road was muddy and tortuous and took Banks away from Porter's support. Ahead waited Confederate Gen. Richard Taylor, who at last felt he had enough troops to stand and fight. The result was three encounters starting with a Federal rout at Sabine Crossroads and ending in the Battle of Pleasant Hill *(page 312)*. Stiffening Confederate opposition, failure to link up with a stalled advance from south Arkansas, and the need for Banks to dispatch parts of his force to Sherman's advance on Atlanta, shattered the Union campaign.

Major General Nathaniel P. Banks, who had been soundly thrashed early in the war by Stonewall Jackson in the Shenandoah Valley, later restored some luster to his reputation by taking Port Hudson on the Mississippi and by efficiently running the Union occupation of New Orleans. He argued against the campaign up the Red River, perceiving its difficulties, but was forced to proceed by Halleck in Washington.

CONFEDERATE ATTACK

Beginning the major Red River battles, General Taylor's Confederates surprised and routed Banks' vanguard at Sabine Crossroads on April 8, then hit the Federals again at Pleasant Grove. Banks retreated another 14 miles to Pleasant Hill to regroup, bringing up Gen. Andrew Smith's two veteran corps and forming a line across open land that was anchored on both left and right by tree-clad hills. Taylor immediately pursued and, at 5:00 p.m. on April 9, ordered an attack, sending Thomas Churchill's division of Missouri and Arkansas infantry smashing ahead at the Union left while John Walker's Texas division assaulted the Federal center and Hamilton Bee's cavalry attempted to turn Banks' right. Churchill's troops quickly overwhelmed Col. Lewis Benedict's forward brigade, then charged ahead toward the center of the main Federal line and at the corps of General Smith, hidden on a wooded rise.

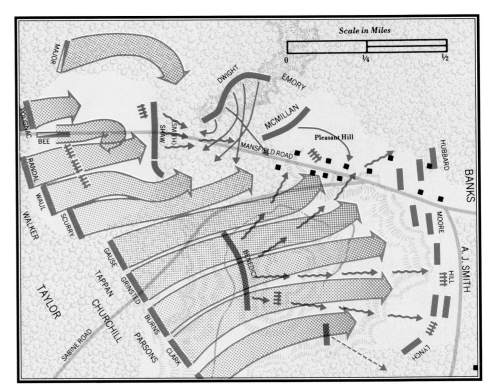

FEDERAL COUNTERATTACK

The tide of the battle swiftly turned as Smith's veterans charged out of the woods. Pivoting on James McMillan's brigade, the Federals smashed back Churchill's flank, sending some of his troops fleeing to the rear and driving others into Walker's regiments in the Confederate center. With his attack now hopelessly confused and with casualties piling up—the Confederates had lost 2,600 men in two days—Taylor ordered a general withdrawal. The battle was clearly a victory for the Federals, but the nervous Banks that night ordered an ignominious retreat all the way back down the stagecoach road to the river at Grand Ecore, there to rejoin Porter's gunboats. Porter for his part was determined to extricate his fleet before it was trapped by low waters and shot to pieces by Confederates on the high riverbanks. The two leaders soon abandoned the campaign, retreating down the river and barely saving Porter's boats by getting them over the Alexandria rapids (opposite).

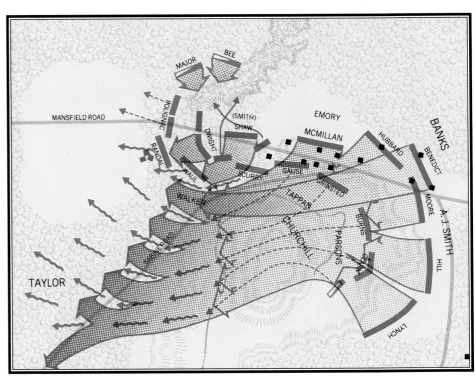

Lieutenant Colonel Joseph Bailey, a brilliant XX Corps engineer, devised an intricate system of dams *(below)* that backed up the Red River, raising its water level and allowing Porter's ships to escape by running the rock-strewn rapids at Alexandria.

As a section of Colonel Bailey's main dam gives way, the gunboat *Lexington* races through the churning break under a full head of steam. By May 13 all of Porter's remaining ships were through the gap and steaming for the Mississippi; by May 20, Banks' retreating army was safe from Confederate pursuit beyond the wide Atchafalaya River. The disastrous campaign had cost the Union more than 8,000 men in all, plus 9 ships and 57 guns.

314

ACKNOWLEDGMENTS

The editors wish to thank the following individuals and institutions for their valuable assistance in the preparation of this volume:

Virginia: Annandale—Homer Babcock. Petersburg—Chris Calkins, Petersburg National Battlefield.

123: From *The Gettysburg Campaign: A Study in Command*, by Edwin B. Coddington, Charles Scribner's Sons, New York, 1968—Library of Congress No. 3538, plate 44. 124: Kean Archives, Philadelphia; map by William L. Hezlep, overlay by Time-Life Books—Library of Congress No. USZC4 1530. 125: Map by William L. Hezlep, overlay by Time-Life Books; Museum of the Confederacy, Richmond, Va., copied by Larry Sherer—Library of Congress. 126, 127: Painting by Rufus Zogbaum, courtesy Minnesota Historical Society, St. Paul, and the State Capitol Building, photographed by Gary Mortenson—painting by Peter F. Rothermel, State Museum of Pennsylvania/Pennsylvania Historical and Museum Commission, photographed by Henry Groskinsky. 128: Map by R. R. Donnelley & Sons Co., Cartographic Services, overlay by Time-Life Books—painting by Edwin Forbes, Library of Congress. 129: Courtesy Don Troiani Collection—sketch by Alfred R. Waud, Library of Congress; Valentine Museum, Richmond, Va. 130: Map by Walter W. Roberts. 131: Map by William L. Hezlep, overlay by Time-Life Books; Library of Congress No. BH834 78—painting by W. G. Browne, courtesy Southern Historical Collection, Manuscripts Department, Wilson Library, University of North Carolina/Chapel Hill, copied by Fred Stipe. 132, 133: Library of Congress No. USZC4 977, inset Kean Archives, Philadelphia. 134: Library of Congress, Nos. B811 700A and B811 700B. 135: Painting by Paul Louvier, West Point Museum Collections, U.S. Military Academy, photographed by Henry Groskinsky—map by R. R. Donnelley & Sons Co., Cartographic Services. 136: Table by Time-Life Books; USAMHI, copied by A. Pierce Bounds. 137: Map by William L. Hezlep. 138: Library of Congress; Valentine Museum, Cook Collection No. 3078, Richmond, Va.—drawing by Edwin Forbes, Library of Congress. 139: Painting by Julian Scott, courtesy Robert A. McNeil, photographed by Sharon Deveaux. 140: Map by William L. Hezlep. 141: USAMHI, photographed by A. Pierce Bounds; Library of Congress—drawing by Alfred R. Waud, Library of Congress. 142: Drawing by Edwin Forbes, Library of Congress—USAMHI, copied by A. Pierce Bounds. 143: USAMHI, copied by A. Pierce Bounds—map by R. R. Donnelley & Sons Co., Cartographic Services. 144: USAMHI, copied by A. Pierce Bounds; courtesy Nick Picerno—Library of Congress No. B8184 5037. 145: Valentine Museum, Richmond, Va.—map by Walter W. Roberts. 146: Valentine Museum, Richmond, Va.—map by Walter W. Roberts. 147: Painting by Thure de Thulstrup, Seventh Regiment Fund, Inc., photographed by Al Freni—sketch by Alfred R. Waud, Library of Congress. 148: Library of Congress No. B8171 746—Library of Congress No. B8171 729. 149: The Kunhardt Collection—map by R. R. Donnelley & Sons Co., Cartographic Services. 150: Map by William L. Hezlep. 151: Chicago Historical Society Negative No. ICHi-07869—Frank and Marie-T. Wood Print Collections, Alexandria, Va. 152: Mass./MOLLUS/USAMHI, copied by A. Pierce Bounds. 153: Map by R. R. Donnelley & Sons Co., Cartographic Services. 154: Map by R. R. Donnelley & Sons Co., Cartographic Services, overlay by Time-Life Books. 155: Painting by Benjamin West Clinedinst, Jackson Memorial Hall, Virginia Military Institute, Lexington, Va., photographed by Michael Latil; National Archives Negative No. 111-B-6144—Valentine Museum, Cook Collection No. 2740, Richmond, Va. 156, 157: Painting by Jean-Adolphe Beauce, Museum of the Confederacy, Richmond, Va., photographed by Katherine Wetzel; Valentine Museum, Cook Collection, Richmond, Va.—Library of Congress No. B8172 1820; Washington and Lee University, the University Library

Special Collections, Michael Miley Collection, Lexington, Va. 158: From *Deeds of Valor* (Vol. 1), edited by W. F. Beyer and O. F. Keydel, the Perrien-Keydel Co., Detroit, 1906; Library of Congress No. BH82 3803—Library of Congress No. B817 7803. 159: Map by William L. Hezlep. 160: Frank and Marie-T. Wood Print Collections, Alexandria, Va.; Library of Congress No. B8184 10191—drawing by James E. Taylor, courtesy Western Reserve Historical Society, Cleveland, photographed by Michael McCormick. 161: Map by Walter W. Roberts. 162: From *Battles and Leaders of the Civil War* (Vol. 1), the Century Co., New York, 1884-1887—Department of Cultural Resources, North Carolina Department of Cultural Resources, Division of Archives and History, Museum of History, Raleigh; table by Time-Life Books. 163-164: Maps by Walter W. Roberts and William L. Hezlep. 165: Sketches by James E. Taylor, Western Reserve Historical Society, Cleveland, photographed by Michael McCormick (2); painting by Julian Scott, Vermont State House, Montpelier, photographed by Henry Groskinsky. 166: National Archives Negative No. 111-B-5176. 167: Map by Peter McGinn—Library of Congress No. B8184 10467. 168, 169: Painting by John Ross Key, Museum of the Confederacy, Richmond, Va., photographed by Katherine Wetzel; Museum of the Confederacy, Richmond, Va.—USAMHI, photographed by A. Pierce Bounds; map by R. R. Donnelley & Sons Co., Cartographic Services, overlay by Time-Life Books; USAMHI, copied by A. Pierce Bounds. 170, 171: Painting by Edward Lamson Henry, Addison Gallery of American Art, Phillips Academy, Andover, Mass., photographed by Henry Groskinsky—Mass./MOLLUS/USAMHI, copied by A. Pierce Bounds; map by R. R. Donnelley & Sons Co., Cartographic Services, overlay by Time-Life Books. 172: Painting by André Castaigne, 1892, West Point Museum Collections, U.S. Military Academy, photographed by Henry Groskinsky—Frank and Marie-T. Wood Print Collections, Alexandria, Va. 173: Map by William L. Hezlep. 174: Frank and Marie-T. Wood Print Collections, Alexandria, Va.—painting by Tom Lovell, © the Greenwich Workshop, Inc., Conn. 175: Map by Walter W. Roberts. 176: Map by William L. Hezlep. 177: State Historical Society of Wisconsin; USAMHI, photographed by A. Pierce Bounds—Frank and Marie-T. Wood Print Collections, Alexandria, Va. 178: Frank and Marie-T. Wood Print Collections, Alexandria, Va.—Civil War Library and Museum, Philadelphia. 179: Painting by Sidney King, National Park Service, Petersburg National Battlefield, photographed by Katherine Wetzel—map by William L. Hezlep, overlay by Time-Life Books. 180: Valentine Museum, Richmond, Va.; National Archives Negative No. 111-B-2735—Library of Congress. 181: Map by Walter W. Roberts. 182: Map by William L. Hezlep—© the Detroit Institute of Arts, gift of Dexter M. Ferry, Jr. 183: Painting by William L. Sheppard, Virginia Historical Society, Richmond, Va.; USAMHI, photographed by A. Pierce Bounds—Frank and Marie-T. Wood Print Collections, Alexandria, Va. 184, 185: Gift of Willis M. Rose, 1947-87-18, courtesy Cooper-Hewitt National Museum of Design, Smithsonian Institution/Art Resource, New York, photographed by Ken Pelka; Library of Congress No. B8171 7172—map by William L. Hezlep. 186, 187: Map by William L. Hezlep; Civil War Library and Museum, Philadelphia; USAMHI, photographed by A. Pierce Bounds; courtesy Bill Turner—Frank and Marie-T. Wood Print Collections, Alexandria, Va. 188: Frank and Marie-T. Wood Print Collections, Alexandria, Va.—map by William L. Hezlep. 189: Painting by Tom Lovell, © National Geographic Society—Frank and Marie-T. Wood Print Collections, Alex-

andria, Va. 192, 193: Maps by R. R. Donnelley & Sons Co., Cartographic Services. 194: USAMHI, copied by A. Pierce Bounds—U.S. Naval Academy, Beverly R. Robinson Collection. 195: R. R. Donnelley & Sons Co., Cartographic Services. 196: Map by William W. Roberts, overlay by Time-Life Books. 197: National Archives Negative No. 111-BA1172; table by Time-Life Books—Frank and Marie-T. Wood Print Collections, Alexandria, Va. 198, 199: Courtesy Chris Nelson; H. H. Bennett Studio Foundation—map by William W. Roberts, courtesy by Time-Life Books, courtesy the Seventh Regiment Fund, Inc., photographed by Al Freni; courtesy Herb Peck, Jr. 200: Library of Congress No. B8172 2173K; Library of Congress No. B816 2844 Al—map by Walter W. Roberts. 201: Frank and Marie-T. Wood Print Collections, Alexandria, Va.—Chicago Historical Society Negative No. ICHi-08002. 202: Map by Walter W. Roberts—Frank and Marie-T. Wood Print Collections, Alexandria, Va. 203: Library of Congress No. B818 100426—courtesy the Mariners' Museum, Newport News, Va. 204: Map by William W. Roberts, overlay by Time-Life Books. 205: Library of Congress; Frank and Marie-T. Wood Print Collections, Alexandria, Va.—Library of Congress No. B8184 1685. 206: USAMHI, copied by A. Pierce Bounds. 207: Map by R. R. Donnelley & Sons Co., Cartographic Services. 208: Courtesy Brian Pohanka—Library of Congress—USAMHI, copied by A. Pierce Bounds. 209: Portrait Library of Congress. Map by William L. Hezlep, overlay by Time-Life Books. 210: Valentine Museum, Richmond, Va.; Library of Congress No. US 262 14973 13246—table by Time-Life Books. 211: Portrait USAMHI, copied by A. Pierce Bounds. Map by William L. Hezlep. 212: From *Photographic History of the Civil War* (Vol. 10), edited by Francis Trevalyan Miller, the Review of Reviews Co., New York, 1912—map by William L. Hezlep. 213: From *Battles and Leaders of the Civil War* (Vol. 3), the Century Co., New York, 1884-1887 (2). 214: Atwater Kent Museum—map by William L. Hezlep. 215: Library of Congress—from *Battles and Leaders of the Civil War* (Vol. 3), the Century Co., New York, 1884-1887. 216, 217: USAMHI, copied by A. Pierce Bounds; map by R. R. Donnelley & Sons Co., Cartographic Services. 218: From *Battles and Leaders of the Civil War* (Vol. 2), the Century Co., New York, 1884-1887 (2). 219: Map by William W. Roberts, overlay by Time-Life Books. 220, 221: Chicago Historical Society Negative No. ICHi-12748; Frank and Marie-T. Wood Print Collections, Alexandria, Va.—Illinois State Historical Society; map by R. R. Donnelley & Sons Co., Cartographic Services, overlay by Time-Life Books. 222: Painting by Tom Lovell, © the Greenwich Workshop, Inc., Conn.—Frank and Marie-T. Wood Print Collections, Alexandria, Va. 223: Map by William L. Hezlep; Chicago Historical Society Negative No. ICHi-10503—USAMHI, copied by Robert Walch. 224: Map by R. R. Donnelley & Sons Co., Cartographic Services, overlay by Time-Life Books—from *Photographic History of the Civil War* (Vol. 10), edited by Francis Trevalyan Miller, the Review of Reviews Co., New York, 1912; Library of Congress No. BH82 4100. 225: Map by Walter W. Roberts—Frank and Marie-T. Wood Print Collections, Alexandria, Va. 226: USAMHI, copied by Robert Walch—painting by Thure de Thulstrup, courtesy Seventh Regiment Fund, Inc., photographed by Al Freni. 227: Map by Walter W. Roberts. 228, 229: Chicago Historical Society Negative No. ICHi-08022; from *Battles and Leaders of the Civil War* (Vol. 3), the Century Co., New York, 1884-1887—photograph courtesy the Kennedy Galleries, New York. 230: Map by R. R. Donnelley & Sons Co., Cartographic Services, overlay by Time-

Life Books. 231: Courtesy the Historic New Orleans Collection (Acc. No. 1979.130)—USAMHI, copied by A. Pierce Bounds. 233: Maps by R. R. Donnelley & Sons Co., Cartographic Services. 234: Portrait courtesy Seward R. Osborne. Map by R. R. Donnelley & Sons Co., Cartographic Services, overlay by Time-Life Books. 235: Table by Time-Life Books; painting by Nichole Marschall, Tennessee State Museum, Nashville, photographed by Bill LaFevor. 236: Pastel drawing by Sadie Waters, Tennessee State Museum, Nashville, photographed by Bill LaFevor; map by Walter W. Roberts. 237: From *The Mountain Campaigns in Georgia*, by Joseph M. Brown, Matthews, Northrup & Co., Buffalo, N.Y., 1890; painting by Alfred R. Waud, Library of Congress. 238, 239: Map by R. R. Donnelley & Sons Co., Cartographic Services, overlay by Time-Life Books; sketch by Walton Taber, Tennessee State Museum, Nashville, photographed by Bill LaFevor. 240: Valentine Museum, Richmond, Va.; USAMHI, copied by A. Pierce Bounds—sketch by Frank Vizetelly, Houghton Library, Harvard University. 241: Map by R. R. Donnelley & Sons Co., Cartographic Services, overlay by Time-Life Books—from *Battles and Leaders of the Civil War* (Vol. 3), the Century Co., New York, 1884-1887. 242, 243: Library of Congress; map by R. R. Donnelley & Sons Co., Cartographic Services, overlay by Time-Life Books—painting by James Walker, U.S. Army Center for Military History, Washington, D.C., photographed by Larry Sherer. 244, 245: Minnesota Historical Society, St. Paul—U.S. Army Center for Military History, photographed by Larry Sherer; map by R. R. Donnelley & Sons Co., Cartographic Services, overlay by Time-Life Books. 246: USAMHI, copied by A. Pierce Bounds—Library of Congress. 247: Courtesy Seventh Regiment Fund, Inc., photographed by Al Freni—Western Reserve Historical Society, Cleveland. 249: Map by Walter W. Roberts. 250: Library of Congress—Confederate Memorial Association, Washington, D.C., photographed by Larry Sherer; table by Time-Life Books. 251: Library of Congress—drawing by Alfred R. Waud, Library of Congress. 252: Library of Congress—from *Battles and Leaders of the Civil War* (Vol. 4), the Century Co., New York, 1884-1887. 253: Map by R. R. Donnelley & Sons Co., Cartographic Services, overlay by Time-Life Books. 254: Library of Congress (2). 255: Map by R. R. Donnelley & Sons Co., Cartographic Services, overlay by Time-Life Books. 256: From *Battles and Leaders of the Civil War* (Vol. 4), the Century Co., New York, 1884-1887—painting by Thure de Thulstrup, courtesy Seventh Regiment Fund, Inc., photographed by Al Freni. 257: Map by William W. Roberts. 258: USAMHI, copied by A. Pierce Bounds—painting by Thure de Thulstrup, courtesy Seventh Regiment Fund, Inc., photographed by Al Freni. 259: Map by R. R. Donnelley & Sons Co., Cartographic Services. 260: Valentine Museum, Richmond, Va.—map by R. R. Donnelley & Sons Co., Cartographic Services, overlay by Time-Life Books. 261: Special Collections (Orlando Poe Collection), West Point Library, U.S. Military Academy, copied by Henry Groskinsky—drawing by Alfred R. Waud, American Heritage Picture Collection. 262: From *Battles and Leaders of the Civil War* (Vol. 4), the Century Co., New York, 1884-1887—map by Walter W. Roberts. 263: Map by Walter W. Roberts—USAMHI, copied by A. Pierce Bounds. 264, 265: The Atlanta Cyclorama, City of Atlanta, Ga., photographed by Larry Sherer. 266, 267: Library of Congress No. B8172 3719; from *Photographic History of the Civil War* (Vol. 10), edited by Francis Trevalyan Miller, the Review of Reviews Co., New York, 1912—Chicago Historical Society; map by R. R. Donnelley & Sons Co., Cartographic Services, overlay by Time-Life Books—Frank and Marie-T. Wood Print Collections, Alexandria, Va. 268: Frank and Marie-T. Wood Print Collections, Alexandria, Va.—Special Collections (Orlando Poe Collection), West Point Library, U.S. Military Academy, copied by Henry Groskinsky. 269: Map by Walter W. Roberts. 270: Chicago Historical Society Negative No. ICHi-10739. 271: Map by R. R. Donnelley & Sons Co., Cartographic Services. 272: Map by William L. Hezlep, overlay by Time-Life Books—sketch by Alfred R. Waud, Library of Congress. 273: From *Civil War Times Illustrated* (Vol. 8, No. 1), April 1969, Historical Times, Inc.—Mass./MOLLUS/USAMHI, copied by A. Pierce Bounds. 274: USAMHI, copied by A. Pierce Bounds—Tennessee State Museum, Nashville, photographed by Bill LaFevor. 275: Map by William L. Hezlep, overlay by Time-Life Books. 276: USAMHI, copied by A. Pierce Bounds—Frank and Marie-T. Wood Print Collections, Alexandria, Va. 277: Map by Walter W. Roberts. 278, 279: Library of Congress (2); painting by Howard Pyle, courtesy Minnesota Historical Society, St. Paul, photographed by Gary Mortensen. 280: From *Battles and Leaders of the Civil War* (Vol. 4), the Century Co., New York, 1884-1887. 281: Map by R. R. Donnelley & Sons Co., Cartographic Services—Library of Congress. 282: USAMHI, copied by A. Pierce Bounds—Frank and Marie-T. Wood Print Collections, Alexandria, Va. (2). 283: Map by R. R. Donnelley & Sons Co., Cartographic Services, overlay by Time-Life Books. 284: Frank and Marie-T. Wood Print Collections, Alexandria, Va.—painting by George Peter Alexander Healy, the White House Collection. 285: Map by R. R. Donnelley & Sons Co., Cartographic Services, overlay by Time-Life Books. 286, 287: Map by R. R. Donnelley & Sons Co., Cartographic Services. 288: Map by R. R. Donnelley & Sons Co., Cartographic Services—painting by Alfred R. Waud, courtesy Franklin D. Roosevelt Library, Hyde Park, N.Y. 289: Library of Congress No. B8184 10175—courtesy The New-York Historical Society, New York. 290: The Chrysler Museum, Norfolk, Va.—courtesy Jay P. Altmayer, photographed by Larry Cantrell. 291: Library of Congress—the Mariners' Museum, Newport News, Va.; map by R. R. Donnelley & Sons Co., Cartographic Services. 292: USAMHI, copied by A. Pierce Bounds—map by Walter W. Roberts. 293: Houghton Library, Harvard University—USAMHI, copied by Robert Walch. 294, 295: Painting by Conrad Wise Chapman, Museum of the Confederacy, Richmond, Va., photographed by Larry Sherer—Old Court House Museum, Vicksburg, Miss. 295: South Carolina Historical Society—painting by Conrad Wise Chapman, Museum of the Confederacy, Richmond, Va., photographed by Larry Sherer. 296: Map by Walter W. Roberts; Valentine Museum, Richmond, Va. 297: From *Battles and Leaders of the Civil War* (Vol. 4), the Century Co., New York, 1884-1887—map by R. R. Donnelley & Sons Co., Cartographic Services. 298: National Archives No. 111-B-5889—The New-York Historical Society, New York. 299: Map by R. R. Donnelley & Sons Co., Cartographic Services. 300: USAMHI, copied by A. Pierce Bounds—courtesy Beverly R. Robinson Collection, U.S. Naval Academy. 301-303: Maps by R. R. Donnelley & Sons Co., Cartographic Services. 304: Map by R. R. Donnelley & Sons Co., Cartographic Services, overlay by Time-Life Books. 305: Map by R. R. Donnelley & Sons Co., Cartographic Services, overlay by Time-Life Books—Valentine Museum, Cook Collection 2869, Richmond, Va. 306: Courtesy Dr. Thomas P. Sweeney; Library of Congress—painting by Sgt. Hunt P. Wilson, Museum of the Confederacy, Richmond, Va., photographed by Katherine Wetzel. 307: Maps by Walter W. Roberts (2)—courtesy Dr. William J. Schultz. 308: Map by R. R. Donnelley & Sons Co., Cartographic Services, overlay by Time-Life Books—Library of Congress No. B8172 1976. 309: Library of Congress No. B8172 6574—map by William L. Hezlep, overlay by Time-Life Books. 310: Frank and Marie-T. Wood Print Collections, Alexandria, Va.—Paul De Haan. 311: Courtesy Chris Nelson; map by William L. Hezlep, overlay by Time-Life Books. 312: Maps by Walter W. Roberts. 313: Michael W. Waskul—M. and M. Karolik Collection of American Water Colors and Drawings, 1800-1875, Museum of Fine Arts, Boston.

BIBLIOGRAPHY

BOOKS

Barrett, John G., *Sherman's March through the Carolinas.* Chapel Hill, N.C.: University of North Carolina Press, 1983.

Bigelow, John, Jr., *The Campaign of Chancellorsville.* New Haven, Conn.: Yale University Press, 1910.

Boatner, Mark Mayo, III, *The Civil War Dictionary.* New York: David McKay, 1959.

Borcke, Heros Von, and Justus Scheibert, *The Great Cavalry Battle of Brandy Station.* Winston-Salem, N.C.: Palaemon Press, 1976.

Bowman, John S. (Ed.), *The Civil War Almanac.* New York: World Almanac Publications, 1983.

Castel, Albert, *General Sterling Price and the Civil War in the West.* Baton Rouge, La.: Louisiana State University Press, 1968.

Catton, Bruce:
Grant Moves South. Boston: Little, Brown, 1960.
Never Call Retreat. New York: Pocket Books, 1965.

Chambers, Lenoir, *Stonewall Jackson: The Legend and the Man* (Vol. 1). New York: William Morrow, 1959.

Coddington, Edwin B., *The Gettysburg Campaign.* New York: Charles Scribner's Sons, 1968.

Connelly, Thomas Lawrence:
Army of the Heartland. Baton Rouge, La.: Louisiana State University Press, 1982.
Autumn of Glory. Baton Rouge, La.: Louisiana State University Press, 1971.

Cozzens, Peter, *The Battle of Stones River: No Better Place to Die.* Chicago: University of Illinois Press, 1990.

Crownover, Sims, *The Battle of Franklin.* Franklin, Tenn.: Tennessee Historical Society, 1955.

Dabney, R. L., *Life and Campaigns of Lieut.-Gen. Thomas J. Jackson.* New York: Blelock, 1866.

Daly, R. W., *How the Merrimac Won.* New York: Thomas Y. Crowell, 1957.

Davis, Burke, *Sherman's March.* New York: Random House, 1980.

Davis, George B., Leslie J. Perry, and Joseph W. Kirkley, *The Official Military Atlas of the Civil War.* New York: Fairfax Press, 1978.

Davis, William C. (Ed.), *The Image of War, 1861-1865* (Vols. 1-6). Garden City, N.Y.: Doubleday, 1981.

Downey, Fairfax:
Clash of Cavalry: The Battle of Brandy Station, June 9,

1863. New York: David McKay, 1959.

Storming of the Gateway: Chattanooga, 1863. New York: David McKay, 1960.

The Editors of *Life, Great Battles of the Civil War.* New York: Time Inc., 1961.

The Editors of Time-Life Books, The Civil War series. Alexandria, Va.: Time-Life Books, 1983-1987.

Esposito, Vincent J. (Ed.), *The West Point Atlas of American Wars* (Vol. 1). New York: Frederick A. Praeger, 1967.

Fisher, Leroy H. (Ed.), *Civil War Battles in the West.* Manhattan, Kan.: Sunflower University Press, 1981.

Frank Leslie's The American Soldier in the Civil War: A Pictorial History. New York: Stanley-Bradley Publishing Co., 1895.

Frassanito, William A.:

Antietam: The Photographic Legacy of America's Bloodiest Day. New York: Charles Scribner's Sons, 1978.

Gettysburg: A Journey in Time. New York: Charles Scribner's Sons, 1975.

Freeman, Douglas Southall, *Lee's Lieutenants:*

Vol. 1, *Manassas to Malvern Hill.* New York: Charles Scribner's Sons, 1942.

Vol. 2, *Cedar Mountain to Chancellorsville.* New York: Charles Scribner's Sons, 1943.

Vol. 3, *Gettysburg to Appomattox.* New York: Charles Scribner's Sons, 1944.

Gibbons, Tony, *Warships and Naval Battles of the Civil War.* New York: Gallery Books, 1989.

Glatthaar, Joseph T., *The March to the Sea and Beyond.* New York: New York University Press, 1985.

Gragg, Rod, *Confederate Goliath: The Battle of Fort Fisher.* New York: Harper Collins, 1991.

Henderson, G. F. R., *Stonewall Jackson and the American Civil War* (Vol. 1). New York: Longmans, Green, 1909.

Horn, Stanley F., *The Army of Tennessee.* Norman, Okla.: University of Oklahoma Press, 1952.

Johnson, Robert Underwood, and Clarence Claugh Buel (Eds.), *Battles and Leaders of the Civil War.* 4 vols. New York: The Century Co., 1884-1887.

Lanier, Robert S. (Ed.), *The Photographic History of the Civil War* (Vol. 10). New York: The Review of Reviews Co., 1912.

McDonough, James Lee:

Chattanooga: A Death Grip on the Confederacy. Knoxville, Tenn.: University of Tennessee Press, 1984.

Shiloh: In Hell before Night. Knoxville, Tenn.: University of Tennessee Press, 1980.

Stones River: Bloody Winter in Tennessee. Knoxville, Tenn.: University of Tennessee Press, 1980.

McDonough, James Lee, and Thomas L. Connelly, *Five Tragic Hours: The Battle of Franklin.* Knoxville, Tenn.: University of Tennessee Press, 1983.

McWhiney, Grady, *Braxton Bragg and Confederate Defeat: Field Command* (Vol. 1). New York: Columbia University Press, 1969.

Pfanz, Harry W., *Gettysburg: The Second Day.* Chapel Hill, N.C.: University of North Carolina Press, 1987.

Scaife, William R., *The Campaign for Atlanta.* Atlanta: William R. Scaife, 1985.

Scott, Robert Garth, *Into the Wilderness with the Army of the Potomac.* Bloomington, Ind.: Indiana University Press, 1985.

Sears, Stephen W., *Landscape Turned Red: The Battle of Antietam.* New Haven, Conn.: Ticknor & Fields, 1983.

Stackpole, Edward J., *Chancellorsville: Lee's Greatest Battle.* Harrisburg, Penn.: Stackpole, 1958.

Symonds, Craig L., *Battlefield Atlas of the Civil War.* Baltimore: Nautical and Aviation Publishing Company of America, 1988.

Tanner, Robert G., *Stonewall in the Valley.* Garden City, N.Y.: Doubleday, 1976.

Tucker, Glenn, *Chickamauga: Bloody Battle in the West.* Dayton, Ohio: Press of Morningside Bookshop, 1976.

The War of the Rebellion: A Compilation of the Official Records of the Union and Confederate Armies. Series 1, 2, 3. Washington, D.C.: Government Printing Office, 1889.

Winters, John D., *The Civil War in Louisiana.* Baton Rouge, La.: Louisiana State University Press, 1979.

Wise, Jennings Cropper, *The Long Arm of Lee.* New York: Oxford University Press, 1959.

Zimmermann, Richard J., *Unit Organizations of the American Civil War.* Cambridge, Ontario, Canada: Rafm, 1982.

PERIODICALS

Ballard, Michael, "A Good Time to Pray: The 1864 Siege of Plymouth." *Civil War Times Illustrated,* April 1986.

Castel, Albert, "Victory at Corinth." *Civil War Times Illustrated,* October 1978.

OTHER PUBLICATIONS

National Geographic Society, "Battlefields of the Civil War." Map.

National Park Service:

"Chancellorsville: Part of the Master Plan." Map.

"Gettysburg, First Day, Second Day, Third Day." Maps.

"Troop Movement Map 1: Second Battle of Manassas, August 28, 1862: 5:00 p.m. to 7:00 p.m." Manassas National Battlefield Park, Va. October 1985. Map.

INDEX

Numerals in italics indicate an illustration of the subject mentioned.

A

Adams, John: *274*
Albemarle (ram): *296, 297*
Alexander, E. Porter: 10, 15, 21, 106, *107*
Ames, Adelbert: 301
Anderson, George B.: 80, *83*
Anderson, George T.: 80, 120, 122, 124
Anderson, James P.: 208, 269
Anderson, Richard: 64, 98, 101, 109, 143, *145,* 150, 186
Andrews, John W.: 94
Antietam Campaign: 68-85; *maps* 69, 71, 73, 74, 75, 76, 80, 85
Antietam/Sharpsburg, Battle of: 9, 16, 21, 72-85; *maps* 73, 75, 76, 80, 85; order of battle, 72
Appomattox: 184-189; *maps* 184-185, 188, 191
Archer, James J.: 59, 90, 106
Armistead, Lewis: 49, 131, 132
Asboth, Alexander: 307
Ashby, Turner: 34, 36, 38, *39, 41*
Atlanta, Battle of: 262-265; *maps* 262, 263
Atlanta Campaign: 19, 248-269; *maps* 249, 255, 257, 259, 260, 262, 263, 269; order of battle, 250
Atlantic coast amphibious operations: 288-289; *map* 288
Averell, William W.: 161
Avery, Isaac E.: 128, 129

B

Bailey, Joseph: *313*
Baird, Absalom: 234, 236, 245
Banks, Nathaniel P.: 13, 34, 36, 37, 38, 39, *41,* 56, 57, 59, 230, 231, *311,* 312, 313
Barksdale, William: 125
Barlow, Francis: 9-10, 146, 150
Bartow, Francis S.: 28, *29,* 30, *31*
Bate, William B.: 255, 260, 262, 275, 285
Battery Buchanan: 301
Battery Gregg: 292, 293
Battery Hays: *295*
Battery Robinett: *220,* 221
Beatty, John: 13
Beatty, Samuel: 213, 214
Beauregard, Pierre Gustave Toutant: 24, 25, 26, *27,* 28, 33, *166,* 169, 171, 172, 173, 191, 200, 202, *205,* 206, 296
Bee, Barnard E.: *28,* 30
Bee, Hamilton: 312

Bell, Louis: 301
Benedict, Lewis: 312
Benham, Henry: 292
Benning, Henry L.: 120, 122
Bentonville, Battle of: 280, 281, 284-285; *map* 285
Bermuda Hundred: action at, 167, 168-169; *map* 169
Berry, Thomas: 234
Blair, Francis P.: 269
Blenker, Louis: *32, 42, 45*
Bowen, John S.: 198, *224,* 225
Brady, Mathew: 19
Bragg, Braxton: *16,* 17, 191, 195, 197, 198, 199, 200, 202, *206,* 207, 208, 211, 213, 214, 232, 234, 235, 236, 237, 238, 243, 245, 246, 285
Branch, Lawrence O'Brien: 59
Brandy Station, Battle of: 112; *map* 112
Brannan, John: 234, 236, 238, 241, 242, 243
Brawner, John: 61
Breckinridge, John C.: 150, 153, 154, *155,* 161, 200, 201, 213, 214, 215, 238
Breese, K. R.: 301
Brockenbrough, John M.: 89, 115
Brooklyn (frigate): 298

Brown, John C.: *266, 267,* 275
Buchanan, Franklin: *291*
Buckland, Ralph P.: 197
Buckner, Simon B.: 208, 234
Buell, Don Carlos: 13, 16, *45,* 191, 195, 200, 203, *205,* 206, 207, 208, 211
Buford, John: 112, 115
Bull Run Campaign, Second: 56-65; *maps* 57, 59, 61, 62, 64, 65
Bull Run/Manassas, First: 7, 20, 24-33; *maps* 25, 26, 28, 30, 33; order of battle, 27
Bull Run/Manassas, Second: 13, 15, 21, 60-67; *maps* 61, 62, 64, 67; order of battle, 60
Burks, Jesse S.: 36
Burnside, Ambrose E.: 16, 19, 21, 26, 28, 29, 69, 73, 85, *86,* 87, 89, 90, 94, 96, 98, 135, 140, 143, 146, 171, 174, 178
Burnt Chimneys, skirmish at: 46
Butler, Benjamin F.: 13, 167, 168, *169,* 219, 301
Butterfield, Daniel: 96, 253

C

Caldwell, John C.: 80, 96, 124
Cameron, James: 7

Cameron, Simon: 7
Canby, Edward R. S.: 308, *309*
Carlin, William P.: 285
Carr, Eugene: 307
Carroll, Samuel S.: 128
Casey, Silas: *45,* 48
Cedar Creek, Battle of: 152, 153, 162-165; *maps* 163, 164; order of battle, 162
Cedar Mountain, Battle of, 57, 58-59; *map* 59
Chalmers, James R.: 198, 202
Chamberlain, Joshua: 15, *122, 123*
Champion's Hill, Battle of: 216, 224-225; *map* 225
Chancellorsville, Battle of: 15, 16, 21, 98-109; *maps* 99, 101, 106, 109; order of battle, 100
Chantilly, action at: 9, 69
Chapman, William: *65*
Charleston: naval operations at, 292-295; *map* 292
Chattanooga Campaign: 17, 191, 232-247; *maps* 233, 234, 236, 238, 241, 243, 245
Cheatham, Benjamin F.: 205, *208,* 209, 213, 257, 263, 271, *272,* 275, 276
Chestnut, Mary Boykin: 191
Chickamauga, Battle of: 17, 191, 232, 234-243; *maps* 234, 236, 238, 241, 243; order of battle, 235
Chickasaw Bluffs, Battle of: 217
Chicora (ironclad): *294*
Chivington, John: 309
Churchill, Thomas: 312
Clayton, Henry: 267
Cleburne, Patrick R.: 205, 211, 213, *236,* 237, 238, 245, 246, 255, 260, 262, 263, 269, *272,* 275
Cobb, Thomas R. R.: 94, *95*
Coburn, John: 260
Cold Harbor, Battle of: 19, 134, 150-151; *map* 150
Collis, Charles: 93
Colvill, William: *126*
Conasauga River: 253
Congress (frigate): *290,* 291
Cooke, Philip St. G.: 53, 94
Corinth, Battle of: 57, 220-221; *map* 221
Couch, Darius N.: 48, 89, 98, 107
Cox, Jacob D.: 70, 71, 85, 252, 253, 275
Crater, Battle of the: 174-175; *map* 175
Crawford, Samuel: 58, 59, 126
Crittenden, Thomas L.: 205, 208, 213, 215, 232, 234, 238
Crocker, Marcellus: 225
Crook, George: *160,* 161, 163, 165
Croxton, John: 235
Crutchfield, Stapleton: 186
Cumberland (frigate): *290,* 291
Cummings, Arthur: 30
Curtis, Newton M.: 301

Curtis, Samuel R.: 304, *307*
Custer, George A.: *160,* 164, 165, 180, 188

D
Dahlgren, John: 292
Davies, Henry E.: 184
Davis, Jefferson: 10, 14, 16, 17, 20, 25, 191
Davis, Jefferson C.: 211, 241, 243, 257, 269, 307
Devin, Thomas C.: 188
Dodge, Grenville: 262
Doles, George: 145
Doubleday, Abner: 61, 74, 75, 90
Drewry's Bluff: 46, 168
Duffié, Alfred: 112
Duncan, Johnson K.: *218*
Du Pont, Samuel F.: 292
Dwight, William: 230

E
Early, Jubal A.: 33, 89, 90, 98, 108, 109, 115, 140, 143, 146, 152, 153, *157,* 158, 159, 160, 161, 162, 163, 164, 176
Eastern Theater: *maps* 22, 23
Elliott, Samuel: 7, 8
Emery, William H.: 161
Essex (gunboat): *194*
Evans, Nathan G.: 26, *28,* 30
Ewell, Richard: 34, 37, 38, *39, 40,* 41, 42, 43, 52, 61, 110, 115, 118, 128, 135, 137, 138, 141, 143, 145, 149, 186, *187*
Ezra Church, Battle of: 259, 266-267; *map* 267

F
Fair Oaks/Seven Pines: 46, 48-49; *maps* 48, 49
Farragut, David Glasgow: 191, 216, 217, 218, 219, 298
Far West: *See* Transmississippi West
Ferrero, Edward: 85, 174
Fishers Hill, Battle of: 153, 163
Five Forks, Battle of: 180; *map* 181
Flusser, Charles W.: 297
Foote, Andrew H.: 194
Forrest, Nathan Bedford: 17, 217, 234, *235,* 238, 271, 272, 273, 275
Forsyth, James W.: *160*
Fort Beauregard: 289
Fort Clark: 288
Fort Comfort: 296
Fort Craig: 309
Fort Darling: *168-169*
Fort De Russy: 310, 311
Fort Desperate: *231*
Fort Donelson: 17, 190, 194, 195
Fort Fisher: *300*
Fort Fisher, Battle of: 300-301; *map* 301
Fort Gregg: 182
Fort Harrison: 176, *177*
Fort Hatteras: 288
Fort Henry: 17, 190, *194,* 195

Fort Jackson: *218,* 219
Fort McAllister: *282,* 283
Fort Mahone: 182, *183*
Fort Monroe: 45, 46
Fort Morgan: *298*
Fort Moultrie: 292
Fort Pemberton: 223
Fort Pulaski: *289*
Fort St. Philip: *218,* 219
Fort Stedman, Battle of: *178, 179;* map 179
Fort Stevens: 153, *158*
Fort Sumter: 286, 292, 293, *294, 295*
Fort Union: *309*
Fort Wagner: 292, *293,* 295
Fort Walker: *289*
Fort Welles: 289
Fort Wessels: 296
Foster, Henry C.: 229
Franklin, Battle of: 271, 274-275; *map* 275
Franklin, William B.: 30, *44,* 50, 69, 71, 89, 90
Fredericksburg, Battle of: 16, 19, 21, 86-97; *maps* 88, 91, 94, 96; order of battle, 89
Fremantle, Arthur: 16
Frémont, John C.: 34, 37, 42, *43*
French, Samuel: 257, 275
French, William H.: 79, 80, 83, 94
Front Royal, Battle of: 34; *map* 38
Fulkerson, Samuel V.: 36
Fuller, John W.: 262

G
Gaines' Mill, Battle of: 50, 52-53; *map* 52
Galena (gunboat): 55
Galveston, Texas: 286
Gardner, Franklin: 230, 231
Garland, Samuel: 70, 71
Garnett, Richard B.: 36, 59, 131
Getty, George W.: 137
Gettysburg, Battle of: 16; *maps* 111, 114, 119, 120, 122, 124, 125, 128, 130, 131; order of battle, 113
Gettysburg Campaign: 110-134; *maps* 111, 112, 114, 119, 120, 122, 124, 125, 128, 130, 131
Gibbon, John: 10, 61, 67, 71, 74, *74,* 90, 109, 131, 182
Gibson, Randall L.: 198, *199*
Gillmore, Quincy Adams: 292, *293,* 295
Gist, States Rights: 234
Glenn, Eliza: 241
Glorietta Pass, Battle of: 308, 309; *map* 309
Goldsboro, North Carolina: 281
Gordon, George H.: 80, 81
Gordon, John B.: *146,* 159, 161, 163, 164, 178, 179, 188
Gordonsville, VA: 56, 57, 59
Graham, Charles K.: 125
Granger, Gordon: *247*
Grant, Julia: 166
Grant, Lewis: 165

Grant, Ulysses S.: 17, *18-19,* 21, 134, *135,* 136, 140, *142,* 143, 146, *148,* 150, 152, 153, 157, 159, 160, 161, 166, 167, 168, 171, 174, 176, 180, 182, 184, 188, *189,* 190, 191, *194,* 197, 198, 200, 202, 205, 206, 216, 217, 221, 222, *223,* 224, 225, 226, 229, 232, 245, *247,* 248, *284,* 301, 307
Greene, George S.: 76, 79, 128
Gregg, David: 112
Gregg, John: 224
Gregg, Maxcy: 62, *90*
Griffin, Charles: 30, 96, *136,* 137
Grover, Cuvier: 62, 230

H
Halleck, Henry W.: 16, 195, 205, 311
Hamblin, Joseph E.: 186
Hampton, Wade: 25, 28, 112, 285
Hampton Roads: naval action at, 286, 290-291; *map* 291
Hancock, Winfield Scott: 94, *107,* 131, 135, 137, 140, 143, 146, 147, 148, 171, 173, 177
Hardee, William J.: 197, 202, 205, *210,* 211, 213, 248, 260, 262, 263, 269, 270, 272, 282, 283, 285
Harriet Lane (gunboat): *218*
Harrison, Benjamin H.: 260
Hartranft, John F.: 178, 179
Hatch, John: 61, 62, 70, 71
Haupt, Herman: *108*
Hayes, Rutherford B.: *70*
Hays, Alexander: 15, 131
Hays, Harry Thompson: 128, *129*
Hazen, William P.: *212,* 213, 282, 283
Hazlett, Charles: 122
Heintzelman, Samuel P.: 26, *44,* 57
Henry, Edward: 171
Heth, Henry: 106, *115,* 117, 131, 137
Hickenlooper, Andrew: 198, 199
Hildebrand, Jesse: 197
Hill, Ambrose Powell: 52, 57, 59, 62, 73, *85,* 90, 101, 110, 115, 118, 125, 131, 135, 137, 140, 143, 148, 150, 177, 182, *183*
Hill, Daniel Harvey: *48,* 49, 50, 52, 54, 69, 71, 74, 76, 83, 89, 236, 285
Hill, Sylvester: *276*
Hindman, Thomas: 241, 243, 253
Howe, Albion: 108
Hoke, Robert: *296*
Holmes, Oliver Wendell, Jr.: 16
Holmes, Theophilus: 25
Homer, Winslow: 182
Hood, John Bell: 19, 52, 53, 62, 64, 74, 76, 118, *120,* 124, 234, *240,* 248, 253, 255, 259, 260, 262, 263, 267, 268, 269, *270,* 271, 272, 273, 275, 276, 280
Hooker, Joseph: 16, 21, 49, 62, 71, 73, 74, 76, *98,* 100, 101, 106, 107, 109, 110, 112, 244, 245, 253, 255, 260, *261*
Hotchkiss, Jedediah: 34, 100
Hovey, Alvin: 225
Howard, Oliver O.: 31, 33, 96, 98, 101,

102, 107, 115, 253, 255, *266,* 267, 269, 281, 283, 285
Huger, Benjamin: 54
Humphreys, Andrew A.: 96
Hunter, David: 153, 154, *156*
Hurlbut, Stephen: 198, 200, 201

J

Jackson, Battle of: 216, 224
Jackson, Claiborne Fox: 304, 305
Jackson, James S.: 208
Jackson, John K.: 198, 202
Jackson, Thomas J. ("Stonewall"): 9, *11,* 20, 28, 30, 31, 33, *34,* 36, *37,* 38, *39, 40-41,* 42, 50, 52, 56, 57, 58, 59, 60, 61, 62, 63, 64, 66, 67, 69, 71, 73, 74, 79, 86, 89, 90, 97, 98, *100,* 101, 103, 104, 106, 110, 157, 311
Jenkins, Micah: 48, 49
Johnson, Bradley: 38, *53*
Johnson, Bushrod: 234, *240,* 241, 243
Johnson, Edward: 37, 137, 146
Johnson, Richard W.: 211, 236, 245
Johnston, Albert Sidney: 190-191, 195, *197,* 200
Johnston, Joseph E.: 18-19, 20, 24, 25, *31, 46,* 50, 166, 184, 191, 224, 226, 248, *250,* 251, 252, 253, 255, 256, 257, 259, 263, 280, 281, 284, 285
Joinville, Prince de: 45
Jones, David R.: 64, 74
Jones, John Marshall: 128, *138*
Jonesboro, Battle of: 259, 268-269; *map* 269
Joyce, John: 252
Judah, Henry: 253

K

Kautz, August: 173
Kearny, Philip: 48, 62, *63,* 67
Keifer, J. Warren: 186
Kemper, James: 64, 131
Kenly, John: 38
Kennesaw Mountain, Battle of: 248, 256-257; *map* 257
Kentucky-Tennessee Campaign (1862): 206-215; *maps* 207, 211, 214
Kernstown, Battle of: 34; *map* 36
Kershaw, Joseph P.: 96, 124, 151, 161, 162, 163, *187,* 241, 243
Keyes, Erasmus D.: 28
Kilpatrick, Hugh Judson: 112
Kimball, Nathan: 36, 94, 95, 275
King, Rufus: 61, 62
Kirby Smith, Edmund: 31, 33, 206, 207

L

Lamb, William: 301
Landrum, John J.: 226
Lane, James H.: 90
Laurens Street battery: *294*
Law, Evander: 60, 120, 122, 241
Lawler, Michael K.: 226
Lawton, Alexander R.: 62, 74
Ledlie, James: 174

Lee, Custis: 19
Lee, Robert E.: *12-13,* 14-15, 16, 18, 19, 20, 21, 25, 42, *50,* 52, 54, 56, 57, 61, *65,* 67, 68, 69, 71, 72, 73, 80, 85, 86, 89, 98, *100,* 101, 104, 106, 107, 109, 110, 112, *113,* 118, 128, 131, *133,* 134, 135, 140, 141, 143, 148, 150, 152, 153, 154, 157, 161, 163, 166, 167, 171, 179, 180, 181, 184, 186, 188, *189,* 191, 229, 248, 280
Lee, Stephen D.: 64, 79, 81, 267, 269, 271, 272, 275, 276, *278*
Lee, William Henry Fitzhugh: 112, *180,* 188
Lee's Mill, skirmish at: 46
Leggett, Mortimer D.: 262
Lexington (gunboat): *203, 313*
Liddell, St. John: 234, 238
Lincoln, Abraham: 10, 11, 13, *14,* 15, 21, 24, 42, 44, 56, 68, 86, 98, 134, 191, 216, 232, *284,* 286, 302
Logan, John A.: 225, *256,* 257, 263, 266, 267, 269
Longstreet, James: 10, 15, 52, 56, 57, 60, 61, 62, 64, *65,* 67, 69, 71, 73, 80, 85, 87, 89, 94, 98, 110, 118, 120, 124, 127, 135, 140, 143, 145, 188, 236, 237, 238, 240, 241, 242, 243
Lookout Mountain-Missionary Ridge: 191, 232, 244-247; *map* 245
Loring, William W.: 223, 225, 257, 260, 275
Louisville, Kentucky: 206, 207, 208
Lusk, William: 13
Lyman, Theodore: 17
Lyon, Nathaniel: 304, 305
Lytle, William: *240*

M

McArthur, John: 276, *278*
McCall, George A.: *45*
McClellan, George B.: 8, *14,* 15-16, 18, 19, 20, 34, 44, *45,* 46, 50, 54, 56, 57, 68, 69, 71, 73, 80, 85, 86
McClernand, John: 197, 198, 200, 202, 217, *224,* 225, 226
McCook, Alexander M.: 208, 211, 213, 234, 238
McCown, John: 211
McCulloch, Ben: 304, 305, *306,* 307
McDowell, Battle of: 34; *map* 37
McDowell, Irvin: 7, *24,* 25, 26, 28, 33, 42, *44,* 45, 56, 57, 64
McGinnis, George: 225
Mackenzie, Ranald Slidell: 19, *180*
McLaws, Lafayette: 69, 71, 80, 98, 109, 118, 122, 124, *125*
McLean, Wilmer: 189
McMillan, James: 312
McPherson, James B.: 223, 224, 226, 248, 251, 253, 255, 259, 260, 262, *263*
McRae, William: 76
Magruder, John: 50, 54
Mahaska (gunboat): *55*
Mahone, William: 49, 174

Malvern Hill, Battle of: 50, 54-55; *map* 54
Manassas, First Battle of: *See* Bull Run/ Manassas, First
Manassas, Second Battle of: *See* Bull Run/ Manassas, Second
Maney, George: 208, 257, 260, 262
Manigault, Arthur: 263, 264
Mansfield, Joseph: 73, 76, 77
Mathews, Alfred: 212, 213
Meade, George G.: 16, 21, 71, 74, 90, 93, 98, 107, 110, *118,* 120, 131, 132, 134, 135, 136, *148,* 174
Mechanicsville, action at: 50, 52
Mendell, George: 171
Mendenhall, John: 214, 215
Mercer, John T.: 296
Merrimack (frigate): 290
Merritt, Wesley: 19, *160,* 161, 164, 180, 186, 188
Mersy, August: 265
Miami (gunboat): 296, *297*
Middletown, Battle of: *map* 39
Miles, Nelson A.: 19, *96*
Miller, John: 215
Milliken's Bend: 217
Milroy, Robert H.: 34, 37, 66
Minnesota (frigate): *290*
Missionary Ridge, Battle of: *See* Lookout Mountain-Missionary Ridge
Mississippi River Campaign: 216-231; *maps* 217, 219, 223, 224, 225, 227, 230
Missouri/Arkansas Campaign: 302, 304-307; *map* 304
Mobile Bay, naval action at: 298-299; *map* 299
Monitor (ironclad): 286, *290,* 291
Monocacy, Battle of: 153, 158-159; *map* 159
Moor, Augustus: 154
Morgan, George: 207
Morgan, James: 285
Mosby, John S.: *156*
Mott, Gershom: 145
Mower, Joseph: *284,* 285, 310
Murfreesboro, Battle of: *See* Stones River/ Murfreesboro
Myers, Frank: 9

N

Naglee, Henry M.: 49
Nashville, Battle of: 276-279; *map* 277
Naval coastal operations: 286-301; *maps* 286-287, 288, 291, 292, 294, 296, 299, 301
Negley, James S.: 211, 213, *214,* 236, 238
Nelson, William: 200
Neosho (ironclad): *310*
New Hope Church, Battle of: 248, 254-255; *map* 255
New Madrid, Battle of: 57
New Market, Battle of: 153, 154-155; *map* 154
New Mexico Campaign: 302, 308-309; *map* 309

New Orleans Campaign: 218-219; *map* 219
Newton, John: 109, 257, 260
North Atlantic Blockading Squadron: 301

O

Oates, William: 14, *123*
Opdycke, Emerson: 273, 275
Ord, Edward: 176, *177,* 188
Osterhaus, Peter J.: 225, 307

P

Paine, Halbert E.: 230
Palmer, John M.: 211, 212, 213, 214
Palmer, Oliver H.: 94
Palmetto State (ram): *294*
Parke, John: 178, 182, 183
Patton, John M.: 42
Peachtree Creek, Battle of: 260-261; *map,* 260
Pea Ridge, Battle of: 304, 306-307; *map* 307
Pemberton, John C.: 224, 225, *226,* 229
Pender, William Dorsey: 59, 106, 115, 131
Peninsula Campaign: 20, 44-55; *maps* 46-47, 48, 49, 51, 52, 54
Pennypacker, Galusha: 301
Perryville, Battle of: 13, 16, 191, 206, 207, 208-209; *map* 209
Petersburg Campaign: 166-184; *maps* 167, 169, 171, 173, 175, 176, 179, 181, 182
Pettigrew, James Johnston: *131*
Pickett, George E.: 49, *131,* 132, 180
Pierce, Franklin: 10
Pike, Albert: *306,* 307
Pleasant Grove, Battle of: 312
Pleasant Hill, Battle of: 311, 312-313; *maps* 312
Pleasants, Henry: 174
Pleasonton, Alfred: 112
Plymouth, Battle of: 296-297; *map* 297
Polk, Leonidas: 197, 198, 202, 208, *210,* 211, 213, 238, 248, 251, 257, 260
Pope, John: 56, *57,* 59, 61, 62, 64, 66, 67, 69
Porter, Andrew: 26, 28, *44*
Porter, David D.: *218,* 219, 222, *223,* 224, *284,* 311, 312, 313
Porter, Fitz-John: *45,* 50, 52, 57, 62
Port Hudson, siege of: 216, 230-231, 311; *map* 230
Port Republic, Battle of: 34; *map* 42
Potter, Robert B.: *84*
Prentiss, Benjamin M.: 197, 198, *199, 200*
Preston, William: 241
Price, Sterling: 221, 304, *305, 306*

R

Ramseur, Stephen D.: 159, 161, *162,* 164, 165
Ransom, Robert: 97, *169,* 296
Reams' Station, Battle of: 176, *177*
Red River Campaign: 302, 310-313; *map*

311
Reno, Jesse L.: 67, 71
Resaca, Battle of: 248, 252-253; *map* 253
Reynolds, John: 67, 89, 98, 107, *115, 116-117*
Reynolds, Joseph J.: 241
Richardson, Israel: 49, 80, *83*
Ricketts, James B.: 30, 60, 74, 159, 160
Ricketts, R. Bruce: 129
River Queen: 284
Roberts, William P.: 15
Robertson, Jerome B.: 120, 122
Robinson, John C.: 93
Rodes, Robert E.: 80, 101, *102,* 115, 146, 159, *160,* 161
Rodman, Isaac P.: 85
Rogers, William P.: *220,* 221
Ronald, Charles A.: 59
Rosecrans, William S.: 16, 17, 191, 206, 207, *211,* 213, 214, 221, 232, 234, 238, 241, 242, 245
Rosser, Thomas L.: 9
Rousseau, Lovell H.: 213
Ruger, William: 275
Ruggles, Daniel: 195, *200,* 205
Russell, David A.: 13

S

Sabine Crossroads, Battle of: 311, 312
Savage's Station, Battle of: 50
Savannah, Siege of: 282-283; *map* 283
Savannah (ram): *282*
Sayler's Creek, Battle of: 184, 186-187; *map* 186
Schofield, John M.: 248, 253, 257, 259, 271, 272, *273,* 275, 276
Schurz, Carl: 67, 128
Scott, Julian: 6, 139
Scott, Winfield: 11, 24, 190
Scurry, William: 309
Sedgwick, John: 48, 80, 81, 98, 108, 109, 134, 135, 137, 138, 139, 140, *143*
Semmes, Paul J.: 124
Seven Days' Battles: 14, 16, 18, 20-21, 50-55; *map* 51; order of battle, 50
Seven Pines, Battle of: *See* Fair Oaks/Seven Pines
Seymour, Truman: 186
Sharpsburg, Battle of: *See* Antietam/ Sharpsburg
Shenandoah Valley Campaign (1862): 11-13, 20, 34-43; *maps* 35, 36, 37, 38, 39, 41, 42
Shenandoah Valley Campaign (1864): 152-

165; *maps* 153, 154, 159, 161, 163, 164
Sheridan, Philip H.: 148, 152, 153, *160,* 161, 162, 163, 164, *165,* 180, 182, 184, 188, 208, 211, 213, 236, 241, 243, 245, 247
Sherman, William T.: 17-19, 28, 30, 190, 191, 195, 197, *198,* 200, 202, 205, 217, 223, 224, 226, 245, 246, 248, *250,* 251, 252, 253, 254, 255, 256, 257, *258,* 259, 261, 263, 266, 267, 269, 270, 271, *280,* 281, 282, 283, *284,* 285, 294, 311
Sherman's March: 270, 280-285; *maps* 281, 283, 285
Shields, James: 34, 36, *42*
Shiloh, Battle of: 191, 194-205; *maps* 195, 196, 198, 200, 202, 204; order of battle, 197
Sibley, Henry Hopkins: *308,* 309
Sickles, Daniel E.: 98, 101, 106, 120, *124,* 125
Sigel, Franz: 13, 56, 57, 64, 153, 154, *155,* 156, 305
Slocum, Henry W.: 98, 106, 281, *282,* 285
Slough, John: 309
Smith, Andrew J.: 276, 279, 310, 311, 312
Smith, Giles A.: 226, 262
Smith, William F.: *44, 50,* 89, 150, 166, 172, 173, 176
Southfield (gunboat): 296, *297*
South Mountain, Battle of: 68, 69-71; *map* 71
Spotsylvania, Battle of: 19, 134, 143, 144-149; *maps* 145, 146, 149
Spring Hill, Battle of: 271, 272-273; *map* 272
Stahel, Julius: 154
Stainrook, Henry J.: 76
Stanley, David: 271, 272, 275
Starke, William E.: 75
Starkweather, John C.: 208
Steedman, I. G. W.: 230
Steedman, James: 238, 242, 243, 276
Steuart, George H.: 39, 128
Stevens, Isaac Ingalls: 7, *8, 9*
Stevenson, Carter L.: 207, 225, 245, 253, 263, 264, 269
Stewart, Alexander P.: 253, 255, 260, 267, 271, 275, *276,* 285
Stiles, Robert: 15
Stones River/Murfreesboro, Battle of: 16, 191, 206, 210-215; *maps* 211, 213, 214; order of battle, 210

Strong, George: 292
Stuart, David: 198
Stuart, James Ewell Brown "Jeb": 89, *106,* 109, 110, 112, 148
Sturgis, Samuel D.: 85, 96
Sumner, Edwin V.: 9, 69, 80, 89
Sykes, George: 67, 96

T

Taliaferro, William B.: 59, 61, 90
Taylor, James E.: 165
Taylor, Richard: 41, 42, 311, 312
Tecumseh (monitor): *298*
Tennessee Campaign (1864): 19, 270-279; *maps* 271, 272, 275, 277
Tennessee (ram): *298*
Terrill, William Rufus: *208*
Terry, Adrian: 296
Terry, Alfred: 301
Thoburn, Joseph: 154, 163
Thomas, George: 232, 234, 238, 241, *242,* 243, 245, *247,* 248, 257, 259, 260, 271, 272, 273, 276
Todd, William: 7
Toombs, Robert: 84, 85
Transmississippi West Theater: 302-313; *maps* 302-303, 304, 305, 307, 308, 309, 311, 312
Trego, William: 53
Trimble, Isaac: 42, 131
Tyler (gunboat): *203*
Tyler, Robert O.: 36
Tyndale, Hector: 76

U

Upton, Emory: 19, *144,* 145

V

Valverde, Battle of: 308, 309
Van Cleve, Horatio: 211, 213, 236
Van Dorn, Earl: 217, *220,* 221, 304, 306, 307
Vaughan, Alfred: 257
Vicksburg Campaign: 17, 222-229; *maps* 223, 224, 225, 227
Vincent, Strong: 120, 122
Virginia (ram): 286, *290,* 291

W

Wadsworth, James: 137, 141
Wagner, George: 272, 273, 274, 275
Wainwright, Charles: 135
Walker, John G.: 69, 80, 81, 312
Walker, Reuben Lindsay: 89, 188

Walker, William H. T.: 234, 238, 253, 260, *262*
Wallace, Lew: 153, *158,* 159, 200
Wallace, William H. L.: 197, 198
Walthall, Edward C.: *266, 267,* 275
Ward, John H. H.: 120
Ward, William: 253, 260
Warren, Gouverneur K.: 64, 120, 135, *138,* 143, 145, 171, 180
Watkins, Sam: 17
Webb, Alexander: 13
Weed, Stephen H.: 122
Weisiger, David: 174
Weitzel, Godfrey: 230
Wessels, Henry Walton: 296
Western Theater: *maps* 192, 193
Wharton, Gabriel C.: 161
Wheat, Chatham Roberdeau: 38
Wheaton, Frank: 186, *187*
Wheeler, Joseph: *252,* 281
White Oak Swamp, action at: *50*
White's Ford: *68*
Whiting, William H. C.: 48, 52
Wilcox, Cadmus: 126
Wilder, John T.: *234,* 241
Wilderness, Battle of: 19, 134, 137-143; *maps* 137, 140, 143
Wilderness Campaign: 21, 134-151; *maps* 135, 137, 140, 143, 145, 146, 149, 150; order of battle, 136
Willcox, Orlando B.: 85, 89
Williams, Alpheus S.: 11, 253
Williams, Jesse M.: 128
Williamsburg, Battle of: 46
Wilson, James: 19, 171, 273, 276
Wilson's Creek, Battle of: 304-305; *map* 305
Winchester, Battle of (1862): 34; *map* 41
Winchester, Battle of (1864): 153, 160-161; *map* 161
Winder, Charles: 41, *59*
Wise, Henry A.: 173, *187*
Withers, Jones M.: 213
Wofford, William T.: 125
Wood, Sterling A. M.: 205
Wood, Thomas: 213, 236, 241, 245, 275, 276
Worden, John: *291*
Wright, Horatio G.: 137, 145, 146, 161, 171, 182, 186, 188
Wyndham, Sir Percy: 112

Y

Yellow Tavern, Battle of: 148